D0123016

3 0600 00261 8528

PRE-TEXT / TEXT / CONTEXT

PRE-TEXT

TEXT

CONTEXT

Essays on Nineteenth-Century

French Literature

Edited by

Robert L. Mitchell

OHIO STATE UNIVERSITY PRESS : COLUMBUS

Library of Congress Cataloging in Publication Data

Main entry under title:

Pre-text, text, context.

　　Includes index.
　　1. French literature—19th century—History and
criticism—Addresses, essays, lectures. I. Mitchell,
Robert L., 1944–
PQ282.P87　　　　　840′.9　　　　　　　80-11801
ISBN 0-8142-0305-1

CONTENTS

Preface

The nineteenth century in France is a nightmare for literary historians. Their thirst for categorization is more easily quenched by prior centuries, which seem to be unified by cohesive preoccupations and goals: Renaissance, Classical Age or *le grand siècle,* and Enlightenment or Age of Ideas, for example, become appropriate appellations. But the protean nineteenth century—to which no such handy tag has been, or can be, appended—is beyond all else distinguished by extreme heterogeneity and eclecticism. It is a period of chaotic social and political instability, of scientific and industrial revolution. In literature it is, fundamentally, a time not of solidarity but of unprecedented individualism, when sparks of genius fly at the periphery of this social flux. Collective social consciousness yields to isolated probings into the uncharted recesses of the human mind and soul, and revolt against standardized (even valorized) literary practice—e.g., the slow undermining of the "accepted" literary lexicon and of the qualities of unity, clarity, and reason; the overhauling of the traditional system of prosody—proliferates.

If such divergence obfuscates potential coherence in nineteenth-century French literature, it can itself be recognized as the "organizing" element of this literary epoch. It is precisely this paradox that the present volume of essays intends to reflect. The studies to follow are not unified, as orthodoxy might dictate, by a common approach or theme or author, nor are they presented as festschrift or anniversary celebration. Rather, they are marked, as was the century that is their context, by divergence and variety, not harmony and consistency. Thematically, they examine such varied topics as pygmalionism, allegory, mirage, self-consciousness, plagiarism, madness, feminism, the grotesque, and dance. Critical approach further reflects a collective heterogeneity, as the volume includes discussions that are, in turn, thematic, intertextual, historical, stylistic, psychocritical, sociological, and semiotic. Furthermore, these essays consider virtually all the important writers of a prolific nineteenth-century France, with the exception of some of the romantic poets, Corbière, Laforgue, and Zola.

Eclecticism is also reflected in the basic conception of the volume, which approaches the process of writing from three discrete directions: *before* (pre-text), *during* (text), and *around* (context). The essays in part 1 are essentially thematic studies that illuminate three provocative and vital areas of nineteenth-century thought—the fantastic and the grotesque (Nash, Knapp, McLendon), madness (Lowe, McKenna), and feminism (Miller, Mercken-Spaas, Moss). These themes are presented as "pre-text" in the sense that they inform either authorial motivation or the orientation of a given text prior to the actual scriptural activity. Part 2 includes essays that approach the process of writing from the perspective of the text itself. These studies—basically stylistic in nature—examine texts by Stendhal (Sonnenfeld, Wahl) and Baudelaire (Peschel, Wing, Chambers), a novelist and a poet who were perhaps the two staunchest defenders and living embodiments of individual genius, which so characterized the century. Also included in this part of the volume are studies of three *poètes maudits* who were models of aesthetic individualism: Rimbaud (Porter), Mallarmé (La Charité), and Lautréamont (Nesselroth). Part 3 ("Context") is concerned with elements—spatial, temporal, and linguistic—that surround the literary text. The first three essays (Festa-McCormick, Franklin, Lewis) consider the relationship between texts written outside of France (specifically, in England, Italy, Germany, and Canada) and the French literary tradition. Next, the problem of "anteriority" is confronted: focus on nineteenth-century texts or reactions as they relate to texts of the seventeenth (Albanese) and eighteenth (McDonald) centuries helps to elucidate the temporal (historical) contexts of the former. Finally, the literary text in relation to the more general problem of language as a system of verbal signs forms the context for discussions of Flaubert (Prince) and Jarry (Issacharoff) that conclude the volume.

In his "Epigraphe pour un livre condamné," Baudelaire admonished the reader to discard his copy of *Les Fleurs du mal,* which would be meaningless reading unless he has "learned his rhetoric from Satan." Unlike that reader, the reader of the present volume—*dix-neuviémiste* or not—needs no such specialized training or inflexible orientation to appreciate, or find meaning in, its contents. And, whereas Baudelaire's ultimatum reflects a narrow field of vision, this book offers a global view of the richness and diversity that pervaded the literature of the past century in France.

Editor's Note

Scholarly interest in nineteenth-century French literature on this side of the Atlantic has grown tremendously during the past decade. Evidence of this are the journal *Nineteenth-Century French Studies*—founded and edited by Professor T. H. Goetz (State University College, Fredonia, N.Y.)—which first appeared in 1972; and an annual colloquium on nineteenth-century French studies, which has been held since 1975 on various American college and university campuses and which has attracted a broad range, and a growing number, of scholars of all ages and critical persuasions specializing in French literature (and related areas) of the nineteenth century. It was my pleasure to organize and host the third of these annual colloquia at the Ohio State University in October of 1977: the great majority of the essays in the present volume are expanded or revised versions of papers presented at that conference. It is my hope that all of the essays to follow reflect the quality and diversity of research that is being done today in this field and are a collective reminder that nineteenth-century French studies are alive and well and living in prosperity.

PART ONE : PRE-TEXT

Transfiguring Disfiguration in *L'Homme qui rit*: A Study of Hugo's Use of the Grotesque

SUZANNE NASH

The most coherently developed study of the function of the grotesque in Hugo's work has been presented by Anne Ubersfeld in *Le Roi et le bouffon*.[1] She relies for her analysis of dialogue in Hugo's theater on Mikhail Bakhtin's concept of dialogism as he elaborates it in his books on Dostoevsky and Rabelais.[2] The brilliance and ingenuity of Ubersfeld's textual analysis are undeniable, and her application of Bakhtin's theories to Hugo's work is, in my view, entirely justified; but it seems to me that her conclusions regarding Hugolian discourse generally invite close scrutiny. Ubersfeld seems to read both Bakhtin and Hugo through the decentering prism of Derrida and Lacan, causing her to depart dramatically from Bakhtin's vision of the grotesque as a fundamentally vivifying and revolutionary form to reach the conclusion that Hugo's theater enacts the absolute breakdown of communication. For her it is a stage of empty words ("la vaine parole"), where history is affirmed as a locus of derision.

Ubersfeld's conclusions clearly place her on the side of the moderns as opposed to the ancients in the current critical controversy that has begun to affect Hugo studies in a very fundamental way. Hers is a powerful deconstructive reading of Hugo's work that seeks to demonstrate how the formal organization of dramatic tirades subverts Hugo's professed humanitarian and liberal ideology, which, on the level of theme, places God, history, and progress at the center of its discourse. This essay will examine certain of Ubersfeld's theoretical presuppositions and propose a reading of *L'Homme qui rit* that suggests both the applicability of Bakhtin's mechanism of dialogism and a vision consonant with Bakhtin's belief in the restorative value of art and the revolutionary power of language to effect historic change.

For Bakhtin it is the degree to which the historial dialectic operates as a principle of organization within a text that determines the text's social or moral value as a liberating historical force. The only way a writer can participate in history is to prevent his own text from being absorbed into the canon of officialdom, by adopting a discourse at odds with the official one, a "grotesque" discourse in which dialogism or the simultaneous presence of two conflicting codes is a structural principle.[3] This potentially revolutionary discourse was realized most fully in medieval and Renaissance carnival forms, which found expression in the subculture of the marketplace, "a second World and a second life" outside of officialdom.[4] Carnival festivities, occurring at breaking points in the cycle of nature, are characterized by the "inside out" and the "upside down," which Ubersfeld calls the X of the Bakhtinian system. They provide a dialogistic experience in which language constantly doubles back on itself and in which participants are both actors and spectators. The parodistic and specular nature of carnivalesque language creates a three-dimensional drama rather than a linear, monologistic instrument of repression. The laughter this Renaissance grotesque releases is both gay and mocking, but above all unifying, participative, and regenerative. The buffoon who stands somewhere between art and life and who entertains the king by mocking him is the grotesque figure par excellence.

By the late eighteenth century, according to Bakhtin, the grotesque in literature developed a very different expression, although it still represented a rebellion against literary and political officialdom: "The carnival spirit was transposed into a subjective, idealistic philosophy," "marked by a vivid sense of isolation." The revolutionary drama occurs not in the marketplace but within the "interior infinite" of the individual, at odds with an atomized, class-structured society. The mask in romantic grotesque is no longer an outward sign of play and metamorphosis, but rather functions to hide the drama taking place in a "subjective, lyrical, or even mystical sphere." The laughter this form of the grotesque releases is ironic rather than jubilant. But despite the grotesque's connotations of alienation,[5] Bakhtin insists upon its fundamentally restorative value whenever it appears: "Actually the grotesque, including the Romantic form, discloses the potentiality of an entirely different world, of another order, another way of life. It leads men out of the confines . . . of the indisputable and stable. Born of folk humor, it always represents . . . the return of Saturn's golden age to earth—the living possibility of its return. . . . The existing world suddenly becomes alien . . . precisely because there is the potentiality of a friendly world. . . . The world is destroyed so that it may be regenerated and renewed. While dying it gives birth."[6] Bakhtin's language here takes on the messianic tone of Hugo's own utopian proclamations concerning the revolutionary power of language. In fact, Bakhtin was a great admirer of Hugo as reader of Renaissance literature, asserting that Hugo expressed "the most profound and full appreciation of Rabelais" of any writer in the nineteenth century.[7]

Hugo began to elaborate a concept of the grotesque in the preface to *Cromwell* in 1827, where he claimed that the grotesque must be included in modern art if it is to reflect the dual nature of man who is both body and soul. In fact, without the presence of the grotesque, the sublime, as a reflection of providential order, would not be conceivable even as an absent idea. The marxist Bakhtin objected to Hugo's introduction of this metaphysical level into the grotesque[8] and did not seem to consider the possibility that Hugo's concept of divinity was very close to Bakhtin's own ideal of a generative world body. He was mistaken in imagining that Hugo's grotesque functions as a mere contrast to the sublime, since in Hugo's work all grotesque figures are themselves dialogistic, containing the sublime within them. Providential order was conceived by Hugo in socialist utopian terms; and bodily disfiguration, such as we see it in Quasimodo or Gwynplaine, both victims of corrupt civilization, reflects the degree to which society is out of kilter with that generative power. In other words, the grotesque points to the generative power within the material bodily world that, if not perverted by society, will provide the force that will bring about the realization of the utopian condition.

Hugo goes on in the preface to trace the history of the grotesque in Western art; and, as Ubersfeld notes, his references correspond almost work for work to those that Bakhtin singles out in his examples of the grotesque in ancient, medieval, and Renaissance literature. That Hugo should include a history of the grotesque in his own elaboration of the concept would seem proof of his faith in dialogue as regenerative communication as Bakhtin also understood it: "The ideal of mother geniuses . . . induced the Romantics to seek the seed of the future in the past and to appreciate the past from the point of view of the future which it had fertilized and generated."[9] Like Bakhtin, Hugo identifies the grotesque with "le peuple" throughout the preface, thus insisting upon its revolutionary context from the beginning of his career. Avatars of the buffoon figure crucially linked to the people—Quasimodo, Triboulet, Don César, Gwynplaine—are a constant in Hugo's work, and their development reflects his own evolving attitude toward the themes of history and revolutionary change.

Ubersfeld seems clearly authorized, then, to apply Bakhtin's theory of dialogism as a measure for her own evaluation of the function of the grotesque in *Le Roi s'amuse,* which for her serves as a model for Hugo's theater generally. It is a play of the conjunction of two laughters—the king's and the fool's—neither of which is funny; in fact, she points out, there is a total absence of the comical in this play whose title suggests comedy. If anything, laughter kills. The main character, Triboulet, is a grotesque inversion of the conventional tragic configuration: king/father. Despite the hideous death of his child, brought about ironically by his own efforts to kill the king, Triboulet is not ennobled through suffering but figuratively castrated, and he remains throughout a scandalous travesty of the noble father. The same distortion of the tragic code that exists on the level of character is true for language in this play. Triboulet speaks in the place of a king, who, in turn, disguises himself throughout the play as if he were a carnival figure speaking in the vulgar idiom of the people. Thus neither character can function as a constitutive consciousness because neither is a unified self. No matter what Triboulet talks about (revolution, love, justice, suffering), no matter what self he seeks to enunciate (the people, father, king), he is always perceived as the fool; and his message, within the play, falls on deaf ears. Thus the principle of dialogism, the presence of two simultaneous codes of which one does not belong to the enunciating subject, controls and disseminates every tirade. According to Ubersfeld, the king and the fool both fall into a locus of derision and remain there, with history, unrecuperated: "L'inversion grotesque demeure au stade de la destruction. Elle ne débouche pas sur la renaissance, elle ne repasse pas de la mort à la vie. Ainsi, comme il y a une place en creux de l'Histoire, il y a une place en creux du rire."[10] For Ubersfeld, Hugolian discourse is entirely drained of its restorative value and leaves only a theater of rupture, eccentricity, and parody: "Ce qui règne dans le drame hugolien, c'est la permanence de ce que Bakhtine appelle l'excentrique et les mésalliances . . . dialogue où il y a a confrontation plutôt que communication et échange."[11]

Although Ubersfeld's analysis of the breakdown of communication on stage in Le Roi s'amuse seems valid, one may well question her right to conclude that Hugolian discourse generally is nonconstitutive. How is it that we, as recipients of that discourse, can perceive and lament the breakdown we observe within the texts themselves, unless we have a very different relationship to authorial voice from that of recipients to speakers figured within the fictional space?

What is more, Ubersfeld's strong new reading of Hugo, clearly informed by Derridean theory on the nature of language, raises a number of questions for anyone coming to Hugo from a more traditional, historically based critical stance. Most important, one may ask whether Ubersfeld's presuppositions as to the cause of the breakdown of communication within Hugo's work are justified. The fundamental characteristic causing the emptiness of Hugolian discourse, according to Ubersfeld, is the decenteredness of the enunciating subject. The "je" who speaks is not only mistaken for someone he is not, but he is fractured on the inside himself: "Si le sujet hugolien . . . ne parle à rien ou à personne, c'est que son discours n'est pas parlé par un vrai sujet. C'est toujours le discours . . . de celui qui n'est pas ce qu'il est. . . . Le dialogisme grotesque interdit au sujet de se faire le sujet de sa propre parole."[12] Thus a "vrai sujet" means for Ubersfeld a unified subject. But to privilege unity in Hugo's thought is to ignore an important aspect of his concept of the grotesque as he describes it in the preface to Cromwell, where dualism is understood within a Christian context. It is not, as it is for Lacan or Freud, a sign of loss of self, but rather the authentic spiritual condition of all men, a condition necessary if one is to participate meaningfully in history. Christianity teaches man, he says in the preface, "qu'il est double comme sa destinée, . . . qu'il est le point d'intersection, l'anneau commun des deux chaînes d'êtres qui embrassent la création . . . la première, partant de la pierre pour arriver à l'homme, la seconde, partant de l'homme pour finir à Dieu" (3:47; my italics). In saying that human consciousness is a "point d'intersection," Hugo proposes the X of the grotesque as a mediating figure, not a figure of radical discontinuity.[13] Doubleness is conceived not as alienation but as a means of transfiguration.

Further, is it fair to use *Le Roi s'amuse* as a model for all of Hugo's plays written in the 1830s? Triboulet cannot be recuperated on a moral or spiritual level because he never accepts this truth of his condition; Ruy Blas, on the other hand, does and is able to influence the queen in such a way as to help her rise to her historic destiny as sovereign rather than remain an isolated, lyrical subject. Ubersfeld states that the drama of Hugo's theater is to reconstitute the "je pulvérisé," but that is the drama of his most deluded protagonists. In fact, loss of the lyrical, individual self is an important step in the Hugolian quest toward finding mankind in oneself. Ubersfeld seems, on the contrary, to be privileging that individualized self when she says: "Ce n'est pas le sujet seul qui est touché, mais tout ce qui dans la définition des actants touche au statut de l'individu."[14] *L'Homme qui rit* (The Man Who Laughs/Mankind Laughing) is a novel whose ambivalent title reflects this important development from atomized individual to Everyman necessary for prophetic language. At the end of *L'Homme qui rit* Gwynplaine will in fact hand his historic destiny over to his bastard double, Lord David Dirry-Moir, whose marketplace pseudonym is a constellation of names, Tom-Jim-Jack, which means Everyman.

Although Ubersfeld explicitly states that she is speaking only for Hugo's theater, it seems unlikely that Hugo's views on language would be different in his lyrical or narrative works.[15] One may well ask, however, if there has been a change in the writer of *Le Roi s'amuse* by the late 1860s, when he claimed in notes for his project that he intended to write a trilogy whose works (*L'Homme qui rit*, *La Monarchie*, and *Quatre-Vingt Treize*) would symbolize the great achievements of the revolution—hope, freedom, and progress, respectively. This is the same writer who said in a note in 1868: "Si l'on demande à l'auteur de ce livre pourquoi il a écrit *L'Homme qui rit*, il répondra que, philosophe, il a voulu affirmer l'âme et la conscience, qu'historien, il a voulu révéler des faits monarchiques peu connus et renseigner la démocratie, et que, poète, il a voulu faire un drame" (14:388).

The ironic echoings between *L'Homme qui rit* and *Le Roi s'amuse* would suggest that there exists a generative dialogue poeticized within Hugo's work. We know from the prefaces, the one to *Ruy Blas* in particular, that Hugo liked to present, as part of his mythic scheme, his individual works as chapters in a larger narrative reflecting the trajectory of historic change and of the development of his own consciousness. The powerfully active and syntactically open title of the later novel, *The Man Who Laughs*, comments ironically on the reflexive purposelessness of the formulation *The King Amuses Himself*. It is by order of the king ("jussu regis") that Gwynplaine is abducted and disfigured in order not to be recognized as the legitimate heir to a rebellious nobleman who refused to accept a restoration monarchy after the fall of Cromwell's Republic. Thus the later work admits much more revolutionary ferment than the earlier one, which takes place in France under the reign of Francis I. The particular form of disfiguration chosen for the child, a gaping smile surgically carved into his face, makes him an ideal buffoon for the people's amusement in the marketplace world of folk culture. When Gwynplaine's aristocratic identity is restored, he delivers a speech to the House of Lords announcing the Revolution that will, as we know, wipe the smile off the king's face. But because the nobles can see only the grinning mask, they pay no attention to Gwynplaine's message and almost laugh their own heads off listening. The mask that the king had carved into Gwynplaine's face is, as he tells us, the symbolic face of the people who laugh to forget their suffering.

Thus a mirror image emerges as well as an important transformation. Gwynplaine is both the dramatically idiosyncratic individual, disfigured freak of the carnival show, and a figure for mankind, which includes both the people laughing to forget and the lords, laughing to suppress or deny the suffering presence demanding affirmation, a presence which, as we know, will have the last laugh in *Quatre-Vingt Treize*. The relationships of Gwynplaine as buffoon to these two audiences (the people and the lords) and of the audiences to each other suggest that this is indeed a novel of hope, as Hugo asserted in his notes, and that the man who laughs is an enunciating subject who constitutes himself as the powerfully determining symbolic subject of his own discourse.

I shall turn now to the two key scenes in which Gwynplaine's appearance is received by a laughing audience.

Hugo's protagonist comes of age under the sign of the Bakhtinian X. Gwynplaine and a blind baby named Dea are adopted by a traveling mountebank, a skeptic with a tender heart who always says the opposite from what he means. He calls himself Ursus and has named his tame wolf Homo, for example, thus: "Homo n'était pas le premier loup venu" or "et Homo était un vrai loup." Throughout this section we are obliged to read the narrative *à l'envers,* so to speak. The little family of social rejects forms an idyllic world of its own as it rolls around England in its circus wagon, "The Green Box": "Dans cette baraque, il y avait la liberté, la bonne conscience, le courage, le dévouement, l'innocence, le bonheur, l'amour" (14:203). Out of their lyrical isolation, Ursus conceives of an "interlude" to entertain the marketplace public, a simple allegorical drama that he calls "Chaos vaincu."[16] In it Gwynplaine, who is Man, struggles against Chaos, figured by Ursus and Homo. Just as Man is about to be defeated, Dea appears, bathed in ethereal light and singing Spanish verses that claim the redemptive power of song. Man responds to her summons in a voice "plus profonde et . . . plus douce encore, voix navrée et ravie, d'une gravité tendre et farouche" (14:199). The narrator informs us that "C'était le chant humain répondant au chant sidéral." At the moment of salvation, however, as Gwynplaine's face is drenched in light to reveal "le monstre épanoui," the crowd bursts into gales of laughter: "Dire la commotion de la foule est impossible. Un soleil de rire surgissant, tel était l'effet" (14:199). The laughter is not cruel, but rather a kind of effulgence that attests to the triumph of light over darkness depicted on stage. The audience identifies with Gwynplaine without realizing it: "On sentait qu'elle aimait son monstre. Le savait-elle monstre? Oui, puisqu'elle le touchait. Non, puisqu'elle l'acceptait"; and, through the sight of the grotesque coupling, they experience his transformation from monster to divinity: "Dea adorait l'ange, pendant que le peuple contemplait le monstre et subissait, fasciné lui aussi, mais en sens inverse, cet immense rire prométhéen." Hugo underscores the potentially cataclysmic nature of this communal hilarity in terms that recall Bakhtin's insistence on the utopian nature of the grotesque quoted earlier ("Born of folk humor, it always represents . . . the return of Saturn's golden age to earth. . . . The existing world suddenly becomes alien . . . precisely because there is the potentiality of a friendly world"): "Toute cette nuit et tout ce jour mêlés se résolvaient dans l'esprit du spectateur en un clair-obscur où apparaissaient des perspectives infinies. Comment la divinité adhère à l'ébauche . . . comment le défiguré se transfigure, comment l'informe devient paradisiaque, tous ces mystères entrevus compliquaient d'une émotion presque cosmique la convulsion d'hilarité soulevée par Gwynplaine" (14:200).

But, although the official churches are drained of their faithful, who prefer to attend the performance at the Green Box, Ursus's lyrical text does not produce revolutionary action. In fact, the play functions as an opiate, helping the people forget their suffering. Whatever their laughter may imply about the communal body of mankind, the audience and the actors perceive themselves as separate from each other after the play is over. Gwynplaine, Dea, Ursus, and Homo are immured in their private happiness and the audience is convinced of its superiority over the actors: "le dernier calfat . . . se considérait comme incommensurablement supérieur à cet amateur de 'la canaille'" (14:201).

Nevertheless, the daily transformation of the Green Box from *locus amoenus* to theater opening onto the world inevitably brings with it a rift in the idyllic fabric of the players' existence. That rift, the loss of innocence, is, as always for Hugo, the opening onto another, superior level of awareness. As Gwynplaine watches the laughing audience day after day, he begins to see beyond the mask of laughter into their suffering interior: "Il était ravi d'être muré, mais de temps en temps, il levait la tête par-dessus le mur. Que voyait-il autour de lui? . . . une promiscuité de ruines. Chaque soir toutes les fatalités sociales venaient faire cercle autour de sa félicité . . . il lui venait des idées . . . il sentait des velléités de secourir le monde . . . il perdait le sentiment de la proportion jusqu'à se dire: 'Que pourait-on *faire* pour ce pauvre peuple?'" (14:203–4; my italics).[17]

The opportunity to act comes when Gwynplaine discovers his identity as lord of England. The room where he will deliver his speech in the House of Lords, with its elaborately hierarchical and ritualized seating arrangements, is a translation into political reality of the ironic inscriptions enumerating the rights of the nobility that covered the walls of Ursus's carnival wagon. Thus we recognize in another locus of immurement and delusion a possible stage for a theater of revolution.

The sign of the X continues to inform Hugo's text. Gwynplaine's sudden ascent to the very top of the social hierarchy represents a temporary moral fall in terms of his perception of his relationship to his fellow man. He now sees himself on top of an illusory mountain, in control of others, a unified self like the "right" kind of sovereign who will be the epic spokesman for God and humanity. Hugo uses theater imagery to describe this phase of self-delusion: "Il se représentait une entrée splendide à la chambre des lords. Il arrivait gonflé de choses nouvelles . . . il leur montrerait la vérité" (14:285). It is here that he most resembles Triboulet, the buffoon "gonflé d'illusions."

As I see it, Gwynplaine's speech can be divided into three major movements according to the changes in the speaker's perception of himself in relation to his audience, changes that can be charted according to his use of the three pronouns of tragic discourse (here I am adopting Ubersfeld's model): the *je* of the enunciating subject (Gwynplaine), the *vous* of the addressee (the lords), and the *il* who is the subject of the discourse (the people).

The illusion of being in control, of being a unified self, is translated in the first few moments of his speech by the fleeting control he is able to exert over the grin carved into his own face: "Par une concentration de volonté égale à celle qu'il faudrait pour dompter un tigre, il avait réussi à ramener pour un moment au sérieux le fatal rictus de son visage" (14:347). Yet it is this unified face that the narrator describes as "un masque sur un fond de fumée." This first movement is structured according to an almost perfectly balanced *je-vous* opposition, an ironic inversion of the relationship of dominance the nobility exerts over the people that Gwynplaine has come to denounce. "Mylords, *j'ai à vous* parler. . . . *Je suis* celui qui vient des profondeurs . . . *vous êtes* les grands et les riches. . . . *Moi, je* ne suis qu'une voix. . . . *Vous m'en-*tendrez. . . . *Je puis vous dire ce que vous pesez*" (my italics). During this phase the narrator compares Gwynplaine to Michael and his audience to the dragon: "On est, pour ainsi dire, debout sur une cime d'âmes. On a sous son talon un tressaillement d'entrailles humaines" (14:348). Thus Gwynplaine has moved from one form of isolation to another—from withdrawal into the personal happiness of the circus wagon-idyll to a stance of superiority and dominance in the House of Lords. In both cases the stage from which he speaks is cut off from his audience, and they are, in a sense, justified in perceiving him as monstrous alterity. As long as Gwynplaine can control his face, the lords listen respectfully, but a relationship of antagonism has been established ("L'auditoire hait l'orateur," 14:350), and at the first sign of weakness, rebellion breaks out. This weakness occurs, significantly, when Gwynplaine evokes that lyrical *je* of the circus wagon that he abandoned in becoming a public figure.

Infuriated by the laughter he provides, Gwynplaine pursues his denunciation of the monarchy's repressive control of the people, this time suppressing the first person pronoun almost entirely from his rhetoric and moving from the past tense of his own history to the present tense of society's dilemma. Instead of the *je-vous* opposition, he focuses on the relationship of the *vous* to the *il*, on the ties that bind nobles to people. Rather than "Je puis vous dire ce que vous pesez," he says, "Dieu vous pèse . . . vous êtes des hommes comme les autres," and he seeks to describe the specific social ills that beset the people. The reaction of his audience to this part of his speech is even more intensely derisive than before.

At this point Gwynplaine recognizes the absolute breakdown in communication that has occurred between himself and his audience and lapses into a kind of soliloquy in which his own consciousness becomes the theater of convergence that he had imagined his message would create. His speech is now powerfully revolutionary, a discourse of prophecy spoken in the future tense: "While dying it gives birth" (Bakhtin).[18] The future is there in the room, personified by a very young lord, not laughing, but staring gravely at Gwynplaine in the midst of the hilarity: "Un des pairs mineurs . . . se leva debout sur son banc, ne riant pas, grave comme il sied à un futur législateur, et, sans dire un mot, regarda Gwynplaine avec son frais visage de douze ans en haussant les épaules" (14:353).

Both *je* and *vous* merge with the *il* of that otherness they would seek to understand: "Ah, je suis un des leurs. Je suis aussi un des vôtres, ô vous les pauvres. . . . O mes frères d'en bas, je leur dirai votre dénûment" (14:352). He addresses the reified people of his opening remarks as if they were now there, living presences in the room—in the place of the lords: "Qu'est-ce que c'est que *ces gens* qui sont à genoux? Qu'est-ce que *vous* faites là? Levez-vous, *vous êtes des hommes*" (my italics). The laughter that greets this phase of the speech is different from the derisive laughter of the first two movements. Since the lords are no longer the recipients of the speech, they are left in a state of ambivalence from which they cannot transform Gwynplaine into the ineffectual subject of their interpretation. The laughter is no longer triumphant but jubilant, the kind of participative laughter we heard in the marketplace: "On bondissait, on criait *bis,* on se roulait. On battait du pied. On s'empoignait au rabat. La majesté du lieu, la pourpre des robes, la pudeur des hermines, l'in-folio des perruques, n'y faisait rien. Les lords riaient, les évêques riaient, les juges riaient. Le banc des vieillards se déridait, le banc des enfants se tordait" (14:354). With the internalization of the dialogue as a structuring principle of his own discourse and the multiplication of himself into the world's body, Gwynplaine as the man who laughs or mankind laughing takes on a symbolic plenitude he never before possessed. He now speaks of himself in the third person, as the cosmic laughter of transfiguration announcing the oncoming apocalypse: "C'est la fin qui commence, c'est la rouge aurore de la catastrophe, et voilà ce qu'il y a dans ce rire, dont vous riez . . . tout ce que vous voyez, c'est moi. Vous avez des fêtes, c'est mon rire. Vous avez des joies publiques, c'est mon rire. Vous avez des naissances de princes, c'est mon rire. Vous avez au-dessus de vous le tonnerre, c'est mon rire" (14:354). Instead of representation by language, there occurs, as Bakhtin proposes, experience in language. The laughter of his speech is echoed in the wild laughter that rings throughout the hall, causing an absolute collapse of the ceremony that characterized the opening of the session. The "rire" as subject of Gwynplaine's discourse begins to constitute the action: "On ne savait plus où l'on allait, ni ce qu'on faisait. Il fallut lever la séance" (14:355). The House of Lords dissolves in front of our eyes; a space riddled with cracks, it collapses and disappears: "Les assemblées ont . . . toutes sortes de portes dérobées par où elles se vident comme un vase par des fêlures" (14:355). Gwynplaine thinks the truth without realizing it when he says to himself: "Ce qui était triomphe à la Green Box était chute et catastrophe à la chambre des lords." As Gwynplaine leaves the closed space of the House of Lords, he hears his bastard double, Lord David Dirry-Moir/Tom-Jim-Jack, pick up the challenge that Gwynplaine has hurled: "je fais de sa cause ma cause . . . et de vos ricanements ma colère" (14:358).

Thus Hugo sees Gwynplaine as a figure for the grotesque fulfilling a historic function much as Bakhtin describes it: "The cyclical character is superseded by the sense of historic time. The grotesque images . . . become the means for the artistic and ideological expression of a mighty awareness of history and historic change."[19] The figure of disfiguration becomes, in this novel at least, a prophetic and transfiguring agent, opening the way to a more promising future.

1. Anne Ubersfeld, *Le Roi et le bouffon: Etude sur le théâtre de Hugo de 1830 à 1839* (Paris: José Corti, 1974).

2. Mikhail Bakhtin, *Poétique de Dostoievski,* introduction by J. Kristeva (Paris: Seuil, 1970), and idem, *Rabelais and His World* (Cambridge: M.I.T. Press, 1965).

3. Julia Kristeva, *Semeiotikè* (Paris: Seuil, 1969), p. 144.

4. Bakhtin, *Rabelais,* p. 6. The following is a summary from Bakhtin's introduction to *Rabelais and His World.*

5. Wolfgang Kayser, in *The Grotesque in Art and Literature* (Bloomington: Indiana University Press, 1965), interprets the grotesque as a fundamentally alienating form. Bakhtin disagrees with this view, stating: "The author sees the Romantic age through the prism of his own time and therefore offers a somewhat distorted interpretation" (*Rabelais,* p. 46).

6. Bakhtin, *Rabelais,* p. 48. Most of Hugo's novels begin under the sign of life emerging out of death. In *L'Homme qui rit* the first human voice Gwynplaine hears after he has been abandoned in a wasteland landscape is that of a baby's cry. He finds the baby, Dea, under the snow, still attached to her dead mother's breast, the last drop of milk having turned to ice. His own coming into being is described syntactically as emergence from oblivion: "Il venait d'être—oublié—par eux" (*Œuvres complètes,* ed. Jean Massin, 18 vols. [Paris: Club français du livre, 1967–70], 14:60; all references to Hugo's work will be from this edition).

7. Bakhtin, *Rabelais,* p. 125.

8. "Victor Hugo has a true awareness of these moments of crisis in history, but his theoretic expression of it is false. To a certain extent it is metaphysical" (ibid., p. 127).

9. Ibid., pp. 123–24.

10. Ubersfeld, p. 517.

11. Ibid., p. 469.

12. Ibid., p. 539.

13. Guy Robert has pointed out that Hugo was fascinated by the hieroglyphic significance of the alphabet. In 1839 he listed in a travel notebook a symbolic value for each letter. Among others, there were: "H, c'est la façade de l'édifice avec ses deux tours. . . . X, ce sont les épées croisées, c'est le combat; qui sera vainqueur? . . . aussi les hermétiques ont-ils pris X pour le signe du destin . . . Z, c'est l'éclair, c'est Dieu" (cited by Robert in *"Chaos vaincu": Quelques remarques sur l'œuvre de Victor Hugo* [Besançon: Annales littéraires de l'Université de Besançon, 1976], p. 172).

14. Ubersfeld, p. 491.

15. See ibid., p. 535: "L'analyse que nous venons de tenter peut être étendue à l'ensemble de la dramaturgie hugolienne qui serait alors comprise comme dramaturgie de la vaine parole."

16. Lucien Döllenbach proposes that this play within the narrative functions as a specular "mise en abyme" that inevitably mediates our reading of the novel as a whole (*Le Récit spéculaire, essai sur la mise en abyme* [Paris: Seuil, 1977], pp. 79–80).

17. This move from private spiritual communion to public forum is an essential step in Hugo's redemptive scheme: "Il y a des êtres qui . . . ayant l'azur du ciel, disent: c'est assez! songeurs absorbés dans le prodige, puisant dans l'idolâtrie de la nature l'indifférence du bien et du mal, contemplateurs du cosmos radieusement distraits de l'homme, qui ne comprennent pas qu'on s'occupe de la faim de ceux-ci, de la soif de ceux-là . . . esprits paisibles et terribles, impitoyablement satisfaits. Chose étrange, l'infini leur suffit. Ce grand besoin de l'homme, le fini, qui admet l'embrassement, ils l'ignorent. Le fini, qui admet le progrès, ce travail sublime, ils n'y songent pas" (*Les Misérables,* 11:851–52).

18. In his "Présentation" to *L'Homme qui rit,* Pierre Albouy has aptly described the last part of Gwynplaine's speech as "la béance ouverte vers l'avenir" (14:26).

19. Bakhtin, *Rabelais,* p. 25.

La Fée aux miettes:
An Alchemical *Hieros Gamos*

BETTINA L. KNAPP

For Charles Nodier the dream world had incised itself into his life and had acted upon all aspects of it.[1] It enabled him to communicate with other species, the dead, and past civilizations as well as to anticipate future events. In his short story *La Fée aux miettes* (1832), the dream became the transformer of reality into illusion, the *rite de passage* into a world where an alchemical drama was enacted. Under the guise of specific individuals and events, it is the collective domain that is at issue in *La Fée aux miettes:* two cosmic principles, the universal male and female forces as they participate, symbolically, in a *hieros gamos,* the alchemical formula for the sacred marriage of sun and moon.

La Fée aux miettes opens as the carpenter Michel, interned in the Glasgow "lunatic" asylum, narrates the events of his life. Orphaned at an early age, he is brought up by his uncle, a carpenter, at Granville in Normandy. A solitary lad, he makes friends with a tiny old lady whom the children of the district call the Fée aux Miettes (Crumb Fairy) because she lives on the crumbs given her. She claims to be a descendant of Belkiss (another name for the Queen of Sheba), and her goal in life is to settle in Greenock, where she owns a house. Michel gives her enough money to pay for her trip. After his uncle's departure for the sea, Michel's life-style changes. The money he earns as a carpenter he gives away to the needy. He becomes destitute; but miraculously, he finds seven louis his uncle has sewn into the buttons of his jacket and these save him from starvation. Out of gratitude he goes on a pilgrimage to Mont-Saint-Michel. On his way he saves someone (whom he later discovers is the Crumb Fairy) from sinking into quicksand. They become engaged. Since she has lost all of her possessions he gives her his louis. He then hears that his uncle, who is now considered insane, claims to be the superintendent of Princess Belkiss's palace. Michel goes in search of him and leaves on the ship *The Queen of Sheba;* but the ship sinks. Once again Michel saves the Crumb Fairy, who has followed him secretly. In return she gives him a diamond-studded medallion with a portrait of the Queen of Sheba, who, she asserts, is really herself when young and beautiful. Michel eventually lands on the Scottish coast and meets the charming Folly Girlfree. Since no rooms are available at the inn, he must share one with the bailiff. That night he has a nightmare and in the morning is found with the bailiff's wallet in one hand, a dagger in the other, and the dead bailiff beside him. He is arrested. His lawyer pleads insanity, but Michel is found guilty and sentenced to death. A letter arrives: Michel must choose between the portrait on the medallion and the diamond frame. He chooses the portrait and the judge receives the frame. However, unless a girl consents to marry him, Michel must die. Folly offers herself, but Michel refuses because he is already affianced and wants to keep his vow to the Crumb Fairy. He prefers to die, Michel maintains, rather than break his engagement. Then the Crumb Fairy arrives and releases him from his vow. Michel is found innocent, and the bailiff is found very much alive.

The story now switches to Greenock. Michel and the Crumb Fairy are living together in blissful contentment: by day she is a wizened old woman and by night she comes to him as the beautiful Belkiss. Their union is complete. Only one cloud emerges on the horizon: unless her husband finds the mandrake, the miraculous plant that will return her youth to her, the Crumb Fairy will die within a year. Michel leaves in search of the mandrake and finds it at an herbalist's shop in Glasgow. It is at this point that he is interned in the lunatic asylum. In an epilogue Michel returns to Belkiss, and they live happily ever after.

It is within the framework of insanity that Nodier broaches the cosmic problem of the *hieros gamos,* or marriage of sun and moon. In conventional alchemical practice the sun is considered the male principle and represents spirit, order, and illumination, the purest and highest thinking processes known to man. The moon, on the other hand, is viewed as feminine, fickle, dark, enigmatic, and therefore frequently dangerous. In *La Fée aux miettes,* interestingly enough, the situation is reversed. The sun becomes the feminine force, a composite of two anima figures: the ancient and wizened Crumb Fairy, who represents wisdom in its most active form; and the passive Belkiss, who emerges at night and represents passion. They are the regulators of Michel's life.

Michel is the moon figure, the "lunatic" (from the French *lune*) who not only incorporates certain aspects of the feminine personality (purity, tenderness, gentleness) but also is under its dominion. He functions only as a reflection, not an instigator, of the two anima figures and has no identity of his own; he is what psychologists term a "medium" personality, that is, he is influenced by outside events, by feelings and sensations generated by others. Physically he is male, psychologically he is female. As a composite of male and female characteristics, he may be referred to as androgynous, one of the most archaic, archetypal images known—a being that existed, according to Platonic and Kabbalistic belief, before the two sexes came into being.

Androgynism is also found in the symbol of the mandrake, the plant that

Michel cultivates in the lunatic asylum and that is mentioned at the beginning and end of *La Fée aux miettes*.[2] The mandrake, an age-old plant, is associated with both poisonous and healing properties. Theophrastus saw it as half man and half woman because its roots resembled human form and it was self-reproductive. It was also likened to the human being because it was said to scream when uprooted from the ground. The metaphysician Eliphas Lévi was convinced that the first men on earth to walk were "giant mandrakes." Joan of Arc, it was said, traveled with a mandrake hidden under her breast, and it was this plant that gave her the power to foretell the future and to command armies. The mandrake image in *La Fée aux miettes* symbolizes what alchemists would call the philosopher's stone—the elixir of life or the *élan vital*. The philosopher's stone was supposed to bring about the spiritual recreation of man; psychologically, a rebirth within the psyche. To achieve such a goal, the alchemists had to transform the imperfect (imbalanced) into the perfect (harmonious)—a reblending of nature, a reforming of matter, a reshuffling of inner contents. The mandrake, as the philosopher's stone, belongs to the world of absolutes; it is, therefore, inimical to life, the very antithesis of its energetic process that is based on opposition and acausality. To conceive of the reality of the mandrake or the philosopher's stone is an attempt to shy away from the workaday world, to escape into an Eden-like atmosphere, or to regress into an infantile state.

The mandrake, given narcotic values—by Hippocrates among others—was capable of prolonging Michel's beautiful fantasy world. Hence it was fitting that he should cultivate the plant in the lunatic asylum, the implications here being that only in the protected atmosphere of the asylum, where people live out their illusions, can the mandrake—the symbol of utopia and perfection—flourish.

As an androgyne, Michel, serving to illustrate an inability to identify completely with either sex, is an in-between. He is the antithesis of the masculine hero type (Roland, Bayard, David) and resembles more fully the effeminate romantic figures (René, Adolphe, Obermann) peopling the literary scene in nineteenth-century Europe. Michel's lack of sexual identity is apparent in the moon-and-sun imagery, which is the heart of the tale. In archaic times these astral bodies were personified, and each took on the personality traits and sexual configuration of gods and goddesses.

Before the moon came to be identified with women (after the advent of patriarchal societies, such as that of Egypt), the sun was female and was known to the ancient Sabbaean worshippers in Yemen as the goddess Shams. She was the all-powerful force that regulated cosmic activity. With the advent of patriarchal civilizations, however, the woman yielded her power to the man and became associated with the moon, whereas male qualities were attributed to the sun. Psychologically, such a change in religious power mirrored a concomitant trend within the human psyche: while the male figures were in the ascendancy and becoming identified with the sun (the most powerful force on earth), female forms were relegated to what was considered a lesser sphere, the moon. But the female element was still a potent force. Counting, for example, was based on the rhythmic life of the moon. This astral body also stood for love and fertility. It caused rain, storms, floods, and tidal waves, and therefore influenced nature's growth power. Moon goddesses of antiquity (Ishtar, Hathor, Artemis) were regulators of life on earth and were instrumental in the continuation of the great death-rebirth cycles by playing the prime role in the dismemberment mysteries (Zagreus, Pentheus, Orpheus, Osiris).

Neither political, economic, social, nor psychological conditions remain fixed. Just as flux exists in the universe, so it is present in all phases of life; in the sexual sphere the power struggle between the male and female principles pursued its course throughout the ages. At one period in time, one force dominates while the other struggles for recognition; at another, the reverse is true. In nineteenth-century France the rigid patriarchal system was giving way to matriarchal forces. This change of emphasis is translated in Nodier's tale in the sun and moon imagery (and in the protagonists with which each of these astral bodies is identified).

The moon has been endowed with many characteristics. Said to be responsible for outer disturbances (e.g., storms and tidal waves), it also supposedly includes chaos within the mind, arousing turmoil, generating overactivity, and causing many people to go insane.[3] It is the moon that radiates an eerie light in darkness, that dulls illumination, thus becoming the instigator of vision. The ancient moon goddesses Cybele and Hecate were named Antea, defined as "the sender of nocturnal visions." Museos, the Muse-Man, Hecate's son, was also called "the son of the moon."[4] The moon has also inspired magic, understanding, ecstasy, and intuitive insights—those forces emanating from the darkest and most archaic regions within man.

In alchemy, silver is associated with the moon. Although a pure and high metal within the hierarchy of metals and chemicals, it is neither as dazzling nor as perfect as gold (associated with the sun) and thus illuminates only partially. Fantasy, fear, and the dream are born in such penumbra. It is here too, in the silvery aspects of the moon, that intuitive forces reside within man: that which shines at night in darkness. Hence the moon is identified with poets. It is subdued and enigmatic and arouses the ineffable and intangible entity—the creative element in man.

Michel is such a "moon man." He is not a thinking power and functions solely in the realm of feeling and intuition. Fantasies and strange ideas are forever aroused within him and always in opposition to the orderly, logical, and rational domain lauded by society. Nodier describes him as having compassion and love, both physically and spiritually and in terms of the moon. Michel is "pale," his eyes have the "transparency" and liquid "gaze" of a person from whom the fire of "an astral body" had been "eclipsed" (p. 181); his world is bathed in darkness; it is ambiguous, lost in the illusions of the imaginary world. Like the moon, Michel stands solitary in the vast expanse of blackness surrounding him.

To become a moon man requires a long period of gestation. According to alchemical tradition—and Nodier believed in this concept—a *rite de passage* has to be endured before a higher spiritual state of consciousness can come into being. Unlike the eighteenth-century rationalists, who believed reason to be the supreme form of consciousness, Nodier, in accord with the alchemists, was convinced that the realm of logic alone could not lead to greater knowledge. Higher consciousness was to be found in "obscure movements," in the variety of impulses buried in man's being, in his intuitions. It is no wonder that the Gnostics associated the moon with the divine Sophia, who symbolized "the fallible aspects of God."[5] In ancient days moon people were considered the spokesmen of the gods, the possessors of some divine power. One listened to their statements and prognostications with awe and fear. Moon-thinking, it was believed, opened new insights and fresh orientations.

Michel is capable of divining and understanding more deeply than the so-called rational person: "Les lunatiques . . . occuperaient selon moi le degré le plus élevé de l'échelle qui sépare notre planète de son satellite" (p. 176). It is from this superior vantage point that moon people are able to communicate with supreme intelligences, those that remain incomprehensible and unknown to the normal human being: "il est absurde d'en conclure que leurs idées manquent de sens et de lucidité, parce qu'elles appartiennent à un ordre de sensations et raisonnements qui est tout à fait inaccessible à notre éducation et à nos habitudes" (p. 179). The insane are free from the constrictive time-space limitations imposed upon the ordinary individual and are therefore capable of embedding their thoughts into cosmic spheres of influence, thereby gaining greater wisdom from their peregrinations: "et qui empêche que cet état indéfinissable de l'esprit, que l'ignorance appelle folie, ne le conduise à son tour à la suprême sagesse par quelque route contenue qui n'est pas encore marquée dans la carte grossière de vos sciences imparfaites?" (p. 310).

A price must be paid for divining cosmic secrets. The collective sphere in which the lunatic lives divests him of all identity. Solitude and an inability to communicate with others result. Michel, for example, could not fall in love with a flesh-and-blood woman. He lived exclusively in a world of fantasy; as he himself confessed, his entire life was filled with dreams and caprices from the moment he became involved with the Crumb Fairy.

Michel, the moon man, functioned relatively well in the everyday world as a carpenter. It was his attitude toward women that was out of the ordinary. His mother having died shortly after his birth, he had been deprived of maternal warmth and had never learned to relate to the female principle. Hence he could never consider the woman as an individual and friend but saw her instead as a transpersonal, mythological, or spiritual creature to whom he could turn for solace and comfort. In this respect Michel was a true lunatic; under the influence of the moon he lived in a perpetual dream, acquiring insights and perceptions in this vast and, according to Nodier, superior world. The profound knowledge he acquired, however, was not compatible with conventional social order. Michel was attuned only to the cosmic field—to transcendental values— to the All.

The sun principle is incarnated in the Crumb Fairy and Belkiss, or Michel's unconscious inner attitude toward women. The ancient Crumb Fairy is a supraterrestrial, spiritual power. She stands for what Michel had lacked in his life: the positive mother figure, the wise, understanding, gentle, loving, and tender being. "Mon affection pour toi," she says to Michel, "est plus vive que l'affection d'une mère, mais elle en a la chasteté" (p. 280). Due to the Crumb Fairy, Michel experiences love and security. Since he was twelve years old, she had inspired feelings "de vénération tendre et de soumission presque religieuse qui tendait à un autre ordre d'idées et de sentiments" (p. 193). She was Michel's "guardian angel" during his school years and helped him and his friends with their studies. She is a miracle worker, in other words, the helping mother type; and this role she plays throughout his life, or at least as long as he needs her: "J'ai eu le bonheur de te servir quelquefois de mon expérience et de mes con- seils, et tu n'es pas encore arrivé au point de t'en passer toujours" (p. 200). No matter how kind or solicitous a mother may be, such a helping attitude, if pro- longed for too long, becomes destructive. It prevents growth, which results from a confrontation with the realities of the world. Examples of possessive mothers have existed since antiquity: Cybele and Attis, Ishtar and Tammuz —each of these young men died after an unsuccessful attempt to win indepen- dence from his overwhelming mother-influence.

A price must be paid for everything in life—even for kindness. The Crumb Fairy extracts her pound of flesh: the golden louis to return to her home in Greenock; a second gift in gold when she claims to have been divested of all she owned; a choice she forces on Michel during his trial (the portrait of Belkiss on the medallion or the diamond frame). These tests are all part of the initiation ritual required of Michel to become a moon man. He passes the tests, which means, in psychological terms, that he will remain under the dominion of the Crumb Fairy, that is, his relationship with her must lead to a condition of stasis. Michel's withdrawal from the existential world and submission to the dictates of the Crumb Fairy represent a regression into an archaic and infantile realm: the serenity and security of a paradisiac state. The Crumb Fairy undermined the very foundations of Michel's personality, or he permitted such a disintegration of his ego because of his own fallibility. The ego, defined as the center of consciousness, stands as a mediating force between the inner and outer worlds. Its function is to adapt to both. In Michel's case the ego had lost its power and gradually found itself incapable of acting outside of the fantasy world. Why should he battle out his existence on an external level when all was taken care of so beautifully in his inner domain?

The loss of his ego made him helpless and childlike; thus, he had to be forever cared for and guided. It is significant that, at the end of the story, the Crumb Fairy's home is compared to a doll's house. He lives protected and content in all ways: "Le bonheur, c'est de n'avoir rien à se reprocher" (p. 290). Conflicts are gone, as are feelings of guilt, rebellion, and chaos—all of those irritating, frustrating, yet growth-provoking qualities. Michel will never ascend to superior knowledge (either spiritual or terrestrial) because he is caught in a vise: he is prisoner of his inner domain, not master of it. A world in which the dynamic qualities of opposition and energy—those life-giving forces—are absent is a dead one.

Belkiss (the beautiful, sparkling, and youthful side of the Crumb Fairy, the Queen of Sheba) is also a symbolic representation of an archaic sun figure. She appears only after Michel passes the first stage of the initiation process: from son-mother motif to son-lover. In Arab legends, many of which Nodier had read, Sheba is known under the name Nilqis or Balqis (Balkis). Sheba came from the sun-drenched land of Yemen and followed the oldest religion known to man: the Sabbaean cult that adored the supreme cosmic force—the sun. Michel describes the "divine Belkiss" in terms of the solar disk and calls her "la Princesse du Midi." For Michel she is pure sunlight. When Michel's passion is aroused, Belkiss is transformed into fire: "Je sentis que la chaleur de son baiser versait des torrents de flammes dans mes veines . . . ma vue se voila d'un nuage de sang et de feu" (p. 234). When she appeared to Michel at night, she was radiant light, a celestial illumination around whom "tous les flambeaux s'allumèrent à la fois" (p. 306); a diamond, "souveraine de tous les royaumes inconnus de l'Orient et du Midi, héritière de l'anneau, du sceptre et de la couronne de Salomon" (p. 239). Since Belkiss is transformed into a fire figure, she radiates sparks as powerful as the solar conflagration and becomes a dangerous force. Like Circe she has the power to entice, hypnotize, mesmerize, and eventually destroy. Michel will become the passive instrument, victimized by her sway. Men who have difficulty relating to women on certain levels frequently succumb to them; Venus, for example, destroyed those who did not fall under her dominion. Michel rejected the flesh-and-blood woman, the charming Folly Girlfree, and became progressively engulfed in Belkiss's image, eventually drowning in it. Like the novitiate who loses himself in prayer, the mystic in contemplation, and the artist in his creative endeavor, so Michel, suggested Nodier, became united with his sublime collective figure— Belkiss, or the Queen of Sheba, who took on the traits of the Virgin Mary—the woman in front of whose image he knelt, whose "mysterious voice" spoke to his soul. Like Dante's Beatrice, Belkiss was Michel's spiritual bride, as Mary became the bride of God and the Queen of Heaven.

By day Michel conversed with the wise Crumb Fairy; his nights were devoted to Belkiss. His existence revolved around these formidable powers— the eternal feminine as symbolized in the solar principle. The *hieros gamos* between Michel and the dual anima figures brought about a symbolic union between sun and moon; hence Michel may be looked upon as a "heavenly lover," the "bridegroom of the soul."

The third force, earth (or matter), which would have solidified the union between the solar and lunar principles, is missing. Michel rejected the terrestrial sphere in the form of Folly Girlfree. Although he liked her and found her kind and gentle, she did not "live in the same region" that he did, he told her. His bond with her could never have been "sacred." Moreover, his heart could know "no love for any earthly creature."[6] Even though the *hieros gamos* between sun and moon as personified by the protagonists occurred, only a duality emerged. The third force, manifestation, which would have given balance to the union, had been rejected.[7] The *hieros gamos* as experienced in *La Fée aux miettes* is therefore one-sided. It describes a cosmic union that could never, by its very limitations, lead to spiritual regeneration. Because the earth principle is lacking, a conflict of opposites, generating the growth process, has been dissipated. Michel's rejection of the existential domain led to vegetation and incarceration in the insane asylum. No rebirth was possible under such circumstances, only a prolonged condition of stasis.

What is of utmost interest in *La Fée aux miettes* is the exigency felt by Nodier to unify what was divided in the *hieros gamos*. That an androgynous figure such as Michel pervaded the literary scene answered a need among the people—to rectify an imbalance on the contemporary social structure—to reshuffle the system. The society that both Nodier and his protagonist rejected was based on rigid patriarchal tradition, a system in which reason, logic, and rational attitudes prevailed: characteristics personified by the masculine sun principle. The world of feeling, tenderness, understanding, and Eros had been neglected: qualities embodied in the female moon principle. For sensitive people such as Nodier and the German and French romantics, the dichotomy between these two ways of life grew until it became a gaping wound. The soul, or anima, got lost amid the stiff, unbending clarity of consciousness. *La Fée aux miettes* delineated in symbolic terms the necessity of rehabilitating certain aspects of the female principle—those long-neglected characteristics of warmth, tenderness, and compassion.

1. For further information on Nodier, see Pierre-Georges Castex, *Le Conte fantastique en France* (Paris: Corti, 1952); Alexandre Dumas, *Mes Mémoires,* vol. 5 (Paris: Seghers, 1970);

Hubert Juin, *Charles Nodier* (Paris: Seghers, 1970); Michel Salomon, *Nodier et le groupe romantique* (Paris: Perrin, 1908); Auguste Viatte, *Les Sources occultes du romantisme*, vol. 2 (Paris: Champion, 1969). All references to *La Fée aux miettes* will be given in the text and will be to the following edition: Charles Nodier, *Contes* (Paris: Garnier, 1961).

2. Gustave Le Rouge, in his *Mandragore Magique*, wrote that according to Laurens Catelan (1568–1647), this root was "virile sperm." Rabbinic tradition claimed that the mandrake grew in the garden of Eden at the foot of the tree of knowledge. Shakespeare speaks of this plant in *Anthony and Cleopatra:* "Give me to drink mandragora." That the plant shrieked when touched is referred to in *Romeo and Juliet:* "And shrieks like mandrake torn out of earth, that living mortals, hearing them, run mad." Machiavelli's *The Mandragora* tells of the plant's erotic powers that aroused men to sexual delights.

3. C. G. Jung, *The Structure and Dynamics of the Psyche* (Princeton: Princeton University Press, 1969), p. 456.

4. Ester Harding, *Woman's Mysteries* (New York: G. P. Putnam's, 1979), p. 109.

5. Hans Jonas, *The Gnostic Religion* (Boston: Beacon Press, 1967), p. 176.

6. As there are three forces in the universe (God, nature, man) in alchemical tradition, which are manifested in three chemicals (sulfur, salt, mercury), so man is divided into spirit, body, and soul. Michel's relationships could also have consisted of a triumvirate, each an analogy of the other, had the third force been acceptable to him.

7. Erich Neumann, *Depth Psychology and a New Ethic* (New York: G. P. Putnam's, 1969), p. 30.

The Grotesque in Jean Lorrain's New Byzantium: *Le Vice errant*

WILL L. McLENDON

It is a well documented if not generally well known fact that the word *grotesque* has evolved far beyond its etymology during the past two hundred years.[1] Originally, in the decorative arts, it was conventional to apply the noun *grottesques* to ornamentation derived from frescoes and other embellishments that had been discovered in Rome in the grottoes or ruins of Titus's palace during the late fifteenth century; and the term was originally spelled with two *t*'s. These bizarre ornaments, both the ancient Roman ones and their myriad imitations, were characteristically composed of divers motifs that, when super-imposed, grafted on one another, or otherwise confused, struck the viewer as being illogical, amusing, absurd, or even distressing. In these decorative curiosa, referred to during the Renaissance as "artists' dreams," one often found, for example, a human figure, or part of it, evolving from some lower animal form which, in turn, appeared to be springing from a tree branch. The whole was frequently ensconced in wreaths of flowers, fruits, musical instruments, and birds. A surprisingly modern consciousness of the evolution of the term *grotesque* from such pictorial beginnings to its present-day banality is everywhere expressed in writings of the romantic period,[2] so that the meanings attached to it today are scarcely novel or recent. For nearly two centuries now the noun *grotesque* has been losing ground in Western languages to the adjective, which is universally applied to anything that strikes us as absurd or incongruous. And so it is no abuse of the term to apply it to the fin-de-siècle lucubrations of Jean Lorrain, a novelist who reveled in paradox, whether in highly improbable dramatic concoctions or the most outrageous stylistic effects. Furthermore, in *Le Vice errant* Lorrain regularly labels "Byzantine" his and his hero's efforts to graft beauty on ugliness, to surround the resulting improbable and monstrous hybrids with garlands of flowers springing from the luxuriance of an idealized Mediterranean setting.

One of the constants in this novel is the unrelenting juxtaposition of extremes on every conceivable level: structural, narrative, sociological, aesthetic, and so forth. To begin with the most general, we observe the extremes of romantic frenzy coupled with that sterile contemplation so typical of the

. decadent attitude. Indeed, it is the curious mixing of the static and the active that sets *Le Vice errant* and its hero apart from Lorrain's earlier efforts in the novel, *Monsieur de Bougrelon* and *Monsieur de Phocas,* [3] and distinguishes it as well from several of its principal models, such as *A rebours* and *Le Culte du moi.* By taste and temperament Lorrain was much more inclined to follow a Barbey d'Aurevilly or an Elémir Bourges, and thus he strove instinctively, if not intellectually, to reconcile diametrically opposed principles (stasis/motion). He paid lip service to the concept of the beauty of inertia so assiduously advocated by Huysmans, Gustave Moreau, and the young Barrès, but in his deepest and most visceral reactions Lorrain always recognized the undeniable attraction of violent action so dear to romantic souls such as his mentor, Barbey d'Aurevilly.[4]

If one can indeed speak of Lorrain's efforts in the realm of the grotesque as having a Byzantine quality, this latter term must be taken only in the loosest historical and aesthetic sense. It is deemed appropriate in this study primarily because Lorrain himself uses it frequently in *Le Vice errant* and elsewhere, and secondly because it generally connotes, among many other things, a multiplicity of disparate influences and an interplay of different realms that lead to a fusion of extremes that some would dub crude, farfetched, or even monstrous. The crossroads of contradictory influences during the *belle époque,* a veritable New Byzantium, a hotbed of cross-pollination producing the most extraordinary flora and fauna, were, to Lorrain's way of thinking, to be found on the French Riviera. This land of juxtapositions par excellence was Lorrain's place of semiretirement and self-imposed exile from the turn of the century until his death in 1906. However, in this New Byzantium the aggressors and barbarian hordes—those idle rich and fortune seekers who flocked to Cannes, Nice, and Monte Carlo—were no longer the Turks, Arabs, or Huns, but Russian aristocrats whose opulence and wastefulness knew no bounds, British lords endowed with distinction even in perversity, overstuffed and puppetlike German nobles, and the American counterparts of all the foregoing, the "filthy" rich robber barons and their progeny. The list could be continued by mentioning astute if destitute Italians and calculating Balkan adventurers; many others would be required to complete the enumeration of demographic elements in the invading hordes. Thus constituted, Lorrain's Riviera adds up to a heteroclite society reminiscent of the Byzantine Empire, a macrocosm faithfully mirrored in the microcosm of the villa and entourage of Prince Wladimir Noronsoff, hero of *Le Vice errant.*

Coming after the nauseous whiffs from the sewers of Octave Mirbeau's *Le Jardin des supplices,* after the *delectatio morbosa* of the subjects popularized by such as Oscar Wilde, Maurice Barrès, Albert Samain, and Maurice Maeterlinck, Jean Lorrain was indeed somewhat foolhardy to attempt to "up the bid," so to speak, in these chambers of horror and depravity. But he was not born and reared a Norman for nothing, as his friend and literary executor Georges Normandy was fond of saying.[5] Whatever the traits—virtues or vices—supposedly typical of Normans may be, Jean Lorrain was unquestionably endowed with a great measure of daring and bravado. And so, early in his novelistic endeavors, he grasped the necessity of avoiding the pitfalls of an exaggerated exoticism, whether historical or geographical, that might fail to arouse the jaded sensibilities of his reading public. Mirbeau's China, the Judaea depicted in Wilde's *Salomé,* even Flaubert's Carthage invite the reader to project into settings that are so far removed from him in manners and time as to appear to be almost pure fantasy. The reader's system of values and that extolled by the text have little or no common ground; the gaps of time and space are too great to be adequately bridged by the efforts of sluggish imaginations.

In *Le Vice errant,* however, as indeed in one of its principal models, *Le Crépuscule des dieux* (1884) by Elémir Bourges, stress is at once placed on certain aspects of the contemporary European world that, although they may be unfamiliar to the reader, nevertheless appear to be easy to admit of in various systems of values known to him and his society. Jean Lorrain, perhaps far better than most of his contemporaries in the French novel, was in tune with his reading public, thanks to his journalistic experience and the phenomenal success of his "Pall-Mall Semaine" in the Parisian newspaper *Le Journal.*[6] As a reporter on the arts and a gossip columnist on all matters concerning high society—from which he was not entirely excluded, despite his ever-worsening reputation—Lorrain had learned to characterize the passing parade in brilliant but often biting and ludicrous terms. Perhaps the most important lesson of this apprenticeship for the mature novelist had been his recognition that through his eyes and pen his readers had delighted in living cosmopolitan and contemporary adventures, by proxy as it were.

When we consider *Le Vice errant* in the perspective of Lorrain's two best-known novels, *Monsieur de Bougrelon* and *Monsieur de Phocas,* it is at once obvious that he has a predilection for a central male protagonist whose habits and actions impress the reader as being grotesque. It is equally clear that a decided spirit of deep-seated rancor pervades *Le Vice errant,* and further that its complex architecture, the intensity of its lighting, and the variety of its themes take it far beyond the scope of the other two works. Yet *Le Vice errant* departs from them even more fundamentally by virtue of the great emphasis the author places on realistic geographical setting through the description of places, interior furnishings, and objects of many kinds. The Amsterdam and Paris settings of the two previous novels are perfunctory, resembling at times simple stage props. But in the palpable Mediterranean surroundings of *Le Vice errant,* the intrinsic beauty of places and the contrived beauty of artistic objects constitute an objective reality that ensures the desired contrast with the hero's deformed physique and personality. Realities such as these provide the conditions needed to root this novel firmly in a soil from which the outrageous excesses dreamed up by Lorrain and his hero, Noronsoff, can spring. The setting, which is natural, is analogous then to the garlands we earlier spoke of in connection with the extravagant convolutions of grotesque decorative motifs: it sets off, it enhances that which appears to be most contrary to it, most unnatural.

This important geographic, even urban, dimension equates with a new dimension in social structures that the ailing and beleaguered Lorrain discovered on the Riviera after turning his back on a Paris he had dubbed "la ville empoisonnée." Prince Noronsoff, who constantly pushes one step further into extravagant conduct than did his literary elders, Des Esseintes (*A rebours*) and Charles d'Este (*Le Crépuscule des dieux*), rules like an enthroned monarch over his corner of this Mediterranean paradise. The word is not too strong: from his throne, a *chaise percée* strategically located in the baths of his villa, because he suffers from unrelenting intestinal disorders, Prince Noronsoff presides over a kind of *cloaca maxima,* that is to say over a stream of courtiers drawn from the heights and depths of Riviera society as Jean Lorrain conceived it in the cynicism and despair of his last years. This "Coin de Byzance," as the subtitle of the novel designates it,[7] is none other than Nice and its surrounding area, a land of aching beauty both geographically and ethnically, but raped and polluted, as previously noted, by demonic groups of "invaders" who form the cast of an apocalyptic spectacle that serves as the field or backdrop for the *mise en abyme* of Prince Noronsoff's decline and fall. Such a setting is indeed fitting for what Lorrain calls "l'agonie d'une race"[8]—that of the Noronsoffs—and it reflects on every hand the disintegration of Byzantium.

The grotesque character of this novel derives in large part from the ostentation and extravagance of the Russian colony on the Riviera whose fairest flower, Lorrain ironically states, is Wladimir Noronsoff. This detailed and highly unflattering study of a sick specimen delves into the background of neuroses that appear to be the result not only of a dissipated life but also of a weighty family heritage. The Noronsoff clan, since the Middle Ages, has been cursed with barbaric and criminal offspring; an evil spell cast by a vengeful gypsy many centuries past has periodically returned to plague members of the illustrious Russian family. And to all these woes Lorrain rather prophetically has added the influence of a certain Russian culture that seemed to him already to have spent itself and was indeed destined, as we know, to go into eclipse only a few years later. As though such an assortment of adverse factors were not enough, Lorrain adds to them for good (one might say grotesque) measure a Slavic temperament sullied with ennui and chronic, almost Baudelairean, spleen; the stigma of such a temperament transcends all notions of class distinction.

This central Russian focus is achieved through juxtaposition of other ethnic groups, such as the Anglo-Saxon colony, whose mania and mores pale in comparison. The wealthy Lord Feredith, one of the principal English figures in this international pageant, is more bent on rehabilitating a disgraced poet and fellow countryman, Algernon Filde, than he is on displaying his wealth. Living on the fringes of these authentic aristocratic groups there is a bevy of other creatures whose titles are somewhat doubtful and whose wealth has long since disappeared. Some are Polish, like Countess Schoboleska. Lorrain has obviously modeled her after the intriguing Italian opera diva, La Belcredi, in *Le Crépuscule des dieux*. Both these intrepid heroines are excellent examples of the femme fatale, since they have but one goal in mind: to cajole their "masters" by lending their considerable talents to their masters' every whim and thereby to triumph over the weak and dissolute male in the end. The ranks of this borderline aristocracy include other members such as the Hungarian adventuress called La Mariska. She distinguishes herself by standing up to Noronsoff and forcing him to a draw in their social jousts. Then there is "Doctor" Ytroff, of unknown origin, a veritable charlatan who ministers to the sick prince and other wealthy patients with the help of cheap amulets and old wives' recipes. All the foregoing creatures have in common their intelligence, cunning, and extraordinary although disturbing beauty.

In a totally different social sphere the Byzantine palette of colors is intensified through the introduction of a cosmopolitan array of artists engaged to distract Noronsoff and dispell his boredom: dancers, actors, poets, singers of art songs, acrobats, jugglers, and so on. Representing a kind of Diaghilev *Ballet russe* before its time—*Le Vice errant* was first published in 1902—they add spice to stimulate the prince's benumbed palate. All these artists and performers seek to obtain the favor of the wealthy and the powerful, and they market their talents with considerable spirit and success. By far the most brilliant member of this category is Algernon Filde, an English poet of real genius who is in disrepute in London because of his homosexuality.[9] Filde demonstrates his many-faceted genius by conceiving and organizing exquisite artistic pageants, thereby assuring himself the patronage of the Riviera's richest and most ambitious social climbers. At the opposite end of the artistic spectrum we encounter such pathetic creatures as the "human serpent," a kind of circus performer who puts on a show during one of Noronsoff's parties.

By the very uncertainty of their social position, this conglomeration of performing artists amounts to a transition between the aristocratic groups previously mentioned and the common people of Nice, who appear only in the background but manage, nevertheless, to heighten the color in many a passage of this novel. The latter group is composed mainly of idlers, passersby, and what are so aptly called "rubbernecks." Like the supernumeraries in a Cecil B. de Mille extravaganza, they are always to be seen when Noronsoff takes an outing and are always ready to ogle and to be astounded. Further still down the ladder comes the category of shady and suspicious characters, and the list is quite a long one: urchins, beggars, gigolos, swindlers, bullies, panderers, prostitutes, usurers, pilferers, brothel keepers, and so on. Lorrain refers to them with undisguised admiration and affection as "la racaille" or "la tourbe." They too actually make their way into Noronsoff's stronghold perched high up on Mont Boron overlooking the Baie des Anges, seeking the crumbs of his legendary prodigality. Although these creatures generally remain in the background, theirs is a collective presence that occasionally threatens the precarious balance of forces by asserting itself as a mass, by intruding into the limelight, as in the near mutiny that breaks out during the abortive "Festival of Adonis" that Noronsoff's courtiers had organized in an attempt to bolster the prince's declining status as a party giver.

Sailors on shore leave in the port of Nice might be expected to belong to the category of *racaille*; in this novel, however, they depart from the stereotype and assume a major role as the characters Marius Robanol and Pierre Etchegarry. These two prototypes of the southern Frenchman, a Marseillais and a Basque, are the only "natives" who attain any measure of preeminence in the New Byzantium: "Fanfarons, communicatifs et hâbleurs, une joie dans leur œil luisant, la joie du matelot en bordée et du commerçant roublard en affaires, ils vont souriant aux servantes, l'air de pirates bons enfants. Tannés par les embruns, le teint cuit et robustes, ils ont gardé dans leurs prunelles le bleu profond de la Méditerranée et le gris changeant de l'océan; ils sentent le goudron, la liberté et le large" (p. 184). They are in every sense magnetic personalities, since they incarnate the charms of the land from which they spring. And Prince Wladimir loses no time in falling under their spell. They are not mercenary like all the others who frequent the prince's retreat. The favors that befall them are accepted as providential; as for admiration, they are quite accustomed to that. Above all, their freedom of movement remains intact throughout the entire time of their favor at Noronsoff's court. This fact alone would suffice to distinguish the two sailors from all the other favorites, including Countess Schoboleska, who invariably compromise themselves in this respect. This total freedom allows Marius and Pierre to disappear from the scene once the caprice that imposed them on the court has come to an end. These two healthy and seductive specimens incarnate the fundamental charm of the south, as Lorrain experienced it. Thanks to them and their robust natures, Noronsoff finally sees the ignominious character of all the others who contribute to his corruption through flattery, encouraging him in his bid for pleasure at any price. Such a formula would make a proper definition of Jean Lorrain's conception of vice.

Incongruousness, that essential element of all that is grotesque, reigns supreme in both detail and concept throughout this Mediterranean mosaic. The color and pungency of sulphur blend with the scent of mimosa and heliotrope.

This novel is indeed a turn-of-the-century Satyricon, as Philippe Jullian has so aptly termed all of Lorrain's work and career.[10] And Lorrain himself underscores the analogies between the puppets in his novel and those who flit across the stage of Petronius's famous narrative. In the banquets given by our Russian Trimalcion, exquisite truffle pâtés must share the table with an enormous and disturbing pastry construction from which a man emerges during the course of the festivities—stark naked. This for the benefit of guests who think they have already seen everything. Victor Hugo himself would have been obliged to give his approval to so faithful a realization of the principles extolled in his preface to *Cromwell*. On every hand in Lorrain's novel the ugly and the beautiful travel side by side and sleep in the same bed.

Following the example first set by Huysmans, whom he admired and knew quite well for some ten years,[11] Lorrain was bent on weaving important artistic elements into the fabric of his novel. He was not, however, to be satisfied with the awkward insertion of rather dry and static dissertations such as we find in many a page of *A rebours*. The artistic elements, Lorrain felt, must be associated as intimately as possible with the plot and action of the novel. This conviction and Lorrain's determination to write an eventful narrative constitute unquestionable superiorities over the Huysmans novel, which was a "long shot," as its author conceded, given the novelistic tradition up to that point and the almost universal desire of readers to be entertained as well as to be instructed.[12] Lest it be supposed that Lorrain's approach at incorporating art as a major structural and dramatic element in the novel was original, we must note that he appears to have drawn many of his ideas and techniques from Elémir Bourges. As early as 1884 Bourges had assigned to music, and specifically to Wagnerian music drama, a major role in the fabric and intrigue of his *Crépuscule des dieux*.

The most obvious analogous feature in *Le Vice errant* is eighteenth-century French painting, for Lorrain chose to have Prince Noronsoff embark on a foolhardy project destined to bring to life, quite literally, certain famous paintings by Fragonard: *L'Heureuse Illusion, L'Escarpolette,* and *Le Verrou.* And this recourse to art, which is the culmination of a series of frantic efforts to bolster Noronsoff's worsening reputation as a barbarous *débauché,* succeeds in producing some of the most grotesque scenes in the entire novel. The plan is to dazzle the most snobbish members of the international set with an evening of gastronomic and visual delights such as they have never known. Wladimir would offer them living reconstitutions of the three famous Fragonard paintings, reputed to be in the hands of an eccentric American collector whose villa, in nearby Grasse, is off limits to all the winter visitors on the Riviera, however exalted their fortunes and social standing. This event, then, promises to be a much-awaited revenge on the unapproachable collector, who has become the bête noire of all and sundry.

As a means of heightening suspense in the narrative this unusual plan succeeds, despite the fact that the event itself proves to be a dismal failure. Valiant efforts by the prince's majordomo and several art specialists hired in Nice and Paris to mastermind the living reproductions of the Fragonard canvases do not result in the expected triumph. The chic public Wladimir has invited fails to materialize to witness a spectacle much more suggestive of art nouveau than the eighteenth-century aesthetic. To play the role of what Lorrain calls "les hommes jolis, pétulants et maniérés de Fragonard" the stage directors and specialists have chosen women in male costume, a solution regularly adopted in turn-of-the-century theatrical productions from Rostand to Richard Strauss.

This example of the *travesti* is symptomatic of a more general tendency in fin-de-siècle art, whether it be called *décadent* or art nouveau: namely that the ruling aesthetic principle seems obstinately bent on effeminizing the man and virilizing the woman. Traditional male traits, so sorely lacking in Noronsoff, are to be found abundantly in La Schoboleska, a most domineering woman who finally triumphs over the prince. But Lorrain, with a typically ironic twist, manages to have this strong woman's apparent material victory directed toward ensuring the future welfare of her less-than-aggressive sons, two Adonis-like youths who have already been compromised by the prince and his court. This reversal of male and female roles is in itself incongruous enough to qualify as grotesque. It is, of course, hardly novel with Jean Lorrain, who, to some degree, was only following a trend very much in favor around 1880–90,[13] the reasons for which are too numerous and too complex to examine here. The grotesque confusion of both moral and physical attributes of the sexes is frequently represented in the person of an ephebus whose appearance and manners invite doubt. One need only call to mind Saint Sébastien as represented by D'Annunzio, Debussy, and the boyish, flat-chested Ida Rubenstein; or the androgynous creatures invented by Joséphin ("Sâr") Péladan for the edification of his Rosicrucian adepts;[14] or the pale, listless heroes (heroines?) of certain pictures by Gustave Moreau. Other periods of French history show this confusion of the sexes following quite a different pattern. In the graphic arts of the *grand siècle* and even in interior furnishings of the régence and Louis XV styles a more robust and sanguine grotesque rears its head. Certain pieces of furniture executed by the master cabinetmaker Nicolas Heurtaut (1720–?), for example, are intricately carved and embellished with torsos of bearded old men sporting opulent breasts worthy of a young nursemaid.

This type of grotesque, which depends on reversal and confusion of male and female attributes, is magnificently exemplified on the level of the temperament by Noronsoff's own mother. The despotic old princess has learned to live with all manner of insult and injury coming from her raving and pleasure-mad son; like a man she can "take it on the chin." The princess even endures disgrace and exile so long as La Schoboleska dominates Wladimir and rules over his demonic pursuits. Despite her advanced years and apparent calm, the old princess has a will as hard as steel and an inner passion worthy of her Italian forebears, the Borgias. She proves to be an adversary to reckon with, one who calculates like a chess player, knowing full well that with patience everything will come her way—everything, including death, which she had not reckoned on. Having finally recovered her powers over a Wladimir driven quite mad by pain and pleasure, she ends up becoming his victim.

During the closing pages of this abrasive novel the demented hero's outburst of rage against the tyrannical domination of his mother strongly suggests fictional sublimation on the author's part. This grotesque scene may well be read as the sensational confession of a man who, all his life, was chained to his mother, Mme Duval-Lorrain,[15] whom he "kills" in this supposed and transposed description of one aspect of his personal drama. With an emotional intensity rare in his work, Jean Lorrain has dared to suggest the frustration and hatred that had so long been hidden under one of his most constant and successful masks, that of the loving and dutiful son. It is a mask he appears never to have taken off in real life, despite his frequent and notorious excursions off the beaten path of respectability.

The power of the final scenes in *Le Vice errant* derives from the unexpected resolution of forces that are so diametrically opposed and so incongruous that their juxtaposition fully deserves the label "grotesque." How can the reader suspect that a hero so consistently unattractive as Noronsoff has been will suddenly manage to touch his deeper emotions and engender compassion? Throughout the novel this Nero-like personage has exemplified depraved sentiments, eliciting ridicule and disgust from all quarters. How then has Lorrain managed the about-face in reader and narrator response? I believe it is by his decision to "force the dose" of grotesque ingredients to such a point that the intense spasms of the dying Noronsoff miraculously transform him by allowing him to attain truly heroic levels as the martyr of vice. He accedes to saintliness in much the same way a Jean Genet does, according to Sartre. Such an about-face might suggest transformation of the grotesque into the sublime; such, however, is not the case.

The final section of the novel, composed of several distinct scenes, builds to a paroxysmal climax in which release and resolution are heavily dependent on grotesque and even slapstick comedy effects. Noronsoff's last desperate acts are comparable to a last gasp, the ultimate spasm: "Dans un hoquet suprême il crachait enfin la vieille âme de Byzance trop longtemps attardée en lui" (p. 363). The extraordinary tragic intensity of these moments, particularly the imprecations hurled at his mother, is heightened or attenuated, depending on one's tastes and point of view, by the surprising detail of the mortal blow sustained by Wladimir in a public marketplace at the hands of a fishwife, a femme fatale if ever there was one. She reacts violently to Noronsoff in defense of her boyfriend, a handsome fisherman whom Noronsoff has pursued all the way to home base. The consummate grotesqueness of this scene, in which the prince flounders to the pavement after having been slapped with a fish of the same name, ends *en queue de poisson,* as the French expression would have it:

> C'était la première fois que Wladimir se risquait en pareil milieu. Il ne savait pas à qui il avait affaire; il ne voyait que son Tito. Il allait droit à lui et d'un ton de reproche: "Perchè sei partito hieri? Forse nonsei contento di me, non sono stato sufficentemente genoroso?"
>
> Une formidable gifle était toute la réponse, une gifle pesante et gluante qui étourdissait le prince et l'aplatissait, cassé en deux comme un fantoche, au milieu des merlans, des langoustes, des raies et des calamares de l'étal. La marchande de marée, empoignant une sole par la queue, en avait giflé le misérable. La poupée macabre et fardée qu'était Wladimir s'éffondrait sur le coup, le Russe s'abattait tout de son long sur les dalles parmi les écailles et les vidanges, salué des huées de tout le marché. [P. 362]

So humiliating and comical an end does not, however, detract measurably from Noronsoff's demoniacal grandeur: quite to the contrary. Henceforth nothing can degrade one who is no longer degradable. Lorrain would like for him to elicit, if not admiration, at least the pity due to truly extravagant souls, those who have left the beaten paths (*extravagare*) and ventured far into the unknown. A dedicatory foreword included in the early editions of *Le Vice errant,* but later suppressed, eloquently expresses the compassion that Lorrain had felt in approaching the subject matter of this novel:

> A l'hypocrisie et à la lâcheté humaines, à la férocité des honnêtes gens et à l'honnêteté des parvenus, aux défenseurs patentés de la vertu, aux souteneurs mariés, à tous ceux à qui la prostitution et la morale font des rentes, aux redresseurs de torts et aux épouseurs des filles, aux escarpes enrichis et aux matrones à qui la quarantaine a refait une virginité, aux détracteurs farouches des vices dont ils ont vécu, je dédie ces pages de tristesse et de luxure, la grande luxure dont ils ignorent la détresse affreuse et l'incurable ennui, convaincu et flatté d'avance des cris indignés que soulèvera chez eux la chronique navrante d'une effroyable usure d'âme.
>
> Aux grands hommes de mon époque j'offre ce livre de pitié.

And so it becomes apparent that paradox presided over the genesis of this novel as well as over its realization. The true materials of the Byzantine grotesque are elements that strike us at first glance as being incompatible and irreconcilable; and Lorrain has exploited them according to a formula that suggests that his basic principle of composition is generation by shock. The Riviera, the New Byzantium according to him, is an Edenic setting that is particularly favorable, not only to plants that have been brought from the four corners of the earth, but also to the development of monsters of Noronsoff's ilk. It is the ideal theater, the chosen ground for all manner of predatory creatures and, in a word, the dung heap most favorable to the development of the "fairest" flowers of neurosis and corruption.

1. Most informative of recent studies in the grotesque are Wolfgang Kayser, *The Grotesque in Art and Literature,* trans. Ulrich Weisstein (Bloomington: Indiana University Press, 1963); and Frances K. Barasch, *The Grotesque, a Study in Meanings* (The Hague: Mouton, 1971).

2. See this term in the *Encyclopédie des gens du monde* (Paris: Treuttel et Würz, 1840).

3. Published respectively in 1897 and 1901. The Byzantine origin of the latter title is obvious, since Phocas was a well-known ruler of the empire.

4. See particularly Lorrain's "Barbey d'Aurevilly" in his *Du temps que les bêtes parlaient* (Paris: Courrier français, 1911), pp. 181–97; and the novel *Monsieur de Bougrelon,* whose hero was inspired by Barbey's eccentric attitudes and manners.

5. Georges Normandy, *Jean Lorrain: Son enfance, sa vie, son œuvre* (Paris: Bibliothèque Générale d'Edition, 1907); idem, *Jean Lorrain intime* (Paris: Albin Michel, 1928).

6. Many of these articles were published posthumously in book form under the title *La Ville empoisonnée* (Paris: Jean Crès, 1936).

7. The designation disappeared in later editions of the novel.

8. Jean Lorrain, *Le Vice errant* (Paris: Ollendorff, 1902), p. 118. Subsequent references to this novel are indicated in parentheses in the text.

9. Lorrain was both dismayed and intrigued by Oscar Wilde's recent fall and frequently alluded to him in his journal, in chronicles, and in the novels. A major character in *Monsieur de Phocas,* Claudius Ethal (note the overtones of "lethal" and "ether," to which Lorrain was addicted), is a rather obvious hybrid suggesting both Wilde and the painter Whistler.

10. Philippe Jullian, *Le Satiricon 1900* (Paris: Fayard, 1974).

11. Huysmans clearly abandoned Lorrain toward the end of his life, as evidenced by his policy of nonintervention in the quarrel and litigation between Jeanne Jacquemin and Lorrain. See Jacques Lethève, "L'Amitié de Huysmans et de Jean Lorrain," *Mercure de France* 331 (1957): 71–89; also Gabriel Langé, "J.-K. Huysmans et Jean Lorrain," *Bulletin de la Société J.-K. Huysmans* 21 (1949): 37–38.

12. Emile Zola, though confused and deeply hurt by the "betrayal" implicit in the publication of *A rebours,* pretended to find something amusing in its meager intrigue and wrote to Huysmans about his concern lest the jewel-studded tortoise soil the Persian carpet. See Zola's letter to Huysmans reproduced in Huysmans, *Lettres inédites à Emile Zola,* edited and annotated by Pierre Lambert (Geneva: Droz, 1953), p. 106 n.

13. Many novels of the variety labeled *mœurs parisiennes* had already set the tone. Prime examples are Rachilde, *Monsieur Vénus,* preface by Maurice Barrès (Paris: Félix Brossier, 1889); Paul Bonnetain, *Charlot s'amuse* (Brussels: Kistemæckers, 1886); Dubut de Laforest, *Le Gaga* (Paris: Dentu, 1886); and idem, *L'Homme de joie* (Paris: Dentu, 1889).

14. See Joséphin Péladan's "Ethopée" entitled *La Décadence latine,* particularly the novels *Le Vice suprême, Istar, L'Androgyne,* and *Le Panthée.*

15. Jean Lorrain is, of course, a pseudonym for Paul Duval. So totally did he become the personage of his mask that his mother and lifelong companion added the pseudonym to her own name and used it until her death, at the age of ninety-three, in 1926.

The *Roman tragique* and the Discourse of Nervalian Madness

CATHERINE LOWE

Perhaps the most stunning and certainly the most engaging aspect of Gérard de Nerval's writings is the ubiquity of the first person narrator. Although this narrative strategy has frequently been as much an excuse as a trap for those readers who would insist that "l'étude de l'œuvre sera constamment mariée à la connaissance approfondie de la biographie,"[1] it is no less symptomatic of Nerval's personal rhetoric. However, if the interdependence of "la vie" and "l'œuvre" is confirmed by certain incontrovertible biographical data, the force of any conclusions to be drawn should be directed less toward the assumption that the texts at hand are only thinly veiled attempts at autobiography than toward the establishment of a henceforth undeniable relationship between events in the life of Gérard Labrunie and the literary creations of Gérard de Nerval. Rather than a superposition of biography and autobiography, there is a causal relationship to be discerned between fact and fiction:

> la crise de 1841 marque une étape importante de l'"organisation" de son œuvre. Toutes sortes de documents indiquent qu'à travers son expérience du rêve et du désordre mental de nombreux thèmes se fixent, de nombreuses pensées et réflexions se cristallisent, qui entreront dans ces écrits à venir.[2]

> Il entre désormais dans une période de sa vie où internements et hospitalisations se succéderont à un rythme serré, où le désordre de l'esprit, en dépit de nombreuses et longues rémissions, le submergera de plus en plus. Il est caractéristique que ce soit celle de ses chefs-d'œuvre.
>   En effet, les crises de 1851–1853 paraissent coïncider avec une étonnante recrudescence de l'inspiration et du travail de Nerval.[3]

That an intimate relationship exists for Nerval between madness and literary creation cannot be contested. Yet the nature and degree of the coincidence itself is not of concern here, nor will there be offered any description of, or explanation for, the "mental disorder" itself, since, even if a reader were able to present some reasonable speculation, it would, at best, remain necessarily suspect. The factual lacuna is, however, compensated for by Nerval himself, who, on several occasions, makes explicit the exact dimensions of a textual coincidence of madness and artistic creation. Moreover, if he announces at the end of his

preface to *Les Filles du feu* his intention to recount the *story* of his madness
—"Quelque jour j'écrirai l'histoire de cette 'descente aux enfers' "[4]—it is with
the aim of its *definition* that he includes the *Roman tragique* in this same
preface.[5] It is, therefore, in terms of this textual definition that I shall speak of
Nervalian madness and attempt to determine precisely of what it consists.[6]

The preface to *Les Filles du feu* is a short dedicatory piece entitled "A
Alexandre Dumas." It was written in reply to some rather injudicious remarks
made by Dumas in his introduction of *El Desdichado* to the readers of *Le
Mousquetaire* on the occasion of its original publication in 1853. In a sentence
that Nerval omitted from his citation of this introduction in his own preface,
Dumas insinuated that the extreme to which the poet's imagination had taken
him was that of madness: "Alors notre pauvre Gérard, pour les hommes de
science, est malade et a besoin de traitement, tandis que pour nous, il est tout
simplement plus conteur, plus rêveur, plus spirituel, plus gai ou plus triste que
jamais" (p. 1264). Nerval countered vehemently with the assertion that, quite
to the contrary, an author's identification with a fictional character, the gesture
upon which Dumas had founded his claim of madness, was a hazard of the
profession to which some writers, more than others, occasionally fell prey:

> Je vais essayer de vous expliquer, mon cher Dumas, le phénomène dont vous avez
> parlé plus haut. Il est, vous le savez, certains conteurs qui ne peuvent inventer sans
> *s'identifier aux personnages de leur imagination.* . . .
>   Hé bien, comprenez-vous que l'entraînement d'un récit puisse produire un effet
> semblable; que l'on arrive pour ainsi dire à *s'incarner dans le héros de son imagina-
> tion,* si bien que sa vie devienne la vôtre et qu'on brûle des flammes factices de ses
> ambitions et de ses amours! C'est pourtant ce qui m'est arrivé en entreprenant
> l'histoire d'un personnage qui a figuré, je crois bien, vers l'époque de Louis XV,
> sous le pseudonyme de Brisacier. . . .   Ce qui n'eût été qu'un jeu pour vous, maître
> . . . était devenu pour moi une obsession, un vertige. [P. 150; italics mine.]

Thus the *Roman tragique,* which Nerval then offers Dumas and his readers, is
both an example and a product of his obsession, a gesture of madness that takes
its own definition as its object. Within this epistolary fragment, not only will
the narrator, Brisacier, further repeat this significant gesture as he assumes the
various roles he plays on the theatrical stage, but the entire narrative premise of
the "livre infaisable"[7] will be predicated upon his identification with Le Destin,
the fictional hero of Scarron's *Roman comique.* To the extent, then, that
Brisacier incarnates what was for Dumas and "les hommes de science" the
symptomatic gesture of this madness of identification, the *Roman tragique*
formulates a *mise en abyme* of the gesture itself and, more than merely defining
it, discloses, through its narrative of the consequences of Brisacier's imper-
sonations, exactly what the player's stake is in this game of role-playing.

The *Roman tragique* posits an ostensibly rigorous opposition between daily
existence in the world, epitomized by the innkeeper, and role-playing on the
theatrical stage, exemplified by Brisacier. Each of these two worlds implicates

its own "signifying convention," a linguistic ethic to be observed for the purpose of effective communication within that world. Discourse in the non-theatrical world is founded upon the assumption of inherent truthfulness and thus presumes, without ever questioning this tenet, an absolute correspondence between words and their meaning. It can be said, therefore, that what would be valorized by this sort of discourse is denotation as it informs syntactical meaning. The theatrical world, on the other hand, exists only within the limits of the successful illusion of a representation, perceived not as a re-presentation but rather as an original presentation, the very precondition of which *appears* to require a willing suspension of precisely this referential constraint. Hence, in the instance of the theatrical metaphor, it would necessarily be according to the categories of connotation and paradigmatic meaning that its language is to be understood. Pursuing this analogy, the difference between the ethic of the innkeeper's world and that of the stage is like that between a grammatical logic of univocal meaning and a rhetorical logic that is not simply equivocal, but entirely other.[8] Yet this is a difference that, nonetheless, does not preclude the coexistence of both discourses within the same circumscribed space; and difficulties will arise relative to the way in which the innkeepers and the actors are willing to abandon temporarily their respective linguistic convention in order to participate in that of their hosts. When the professional actor, for example, gives little evidence of distinguishing between being-in-the-world and being-on-stage, this delicate balance between nature and art is imminently imperiled, if not altogether destroyed. For the impersonator himself, whether the performance is voluntary or not, there are complications inhabiting the imbrication of these two worlds far more consequential than may be immediately evident from this simple questioning of territorial jurisdiction, since it is not so much their boundaries as the very distinctions they delimit that are ultimately blurred.

Like the metaphorical masks of the roles he assumes onstage, Brisacier has the misfortune of wearing a real mask offstage, in a world where masks and role-playing have no place in the linguistic convention: "Ma bonne mine défigurée d'un vaste emplâtre, n'a servi qu'à me perdre plus surement" (p. 152). Assuming that a face provides the authentic means by which to verify the identity of the person to whom it belongs, the person's name—considered as his identity—relates to this face in a way analogous to that in which proper meaning or a signified relates to its signifier.[9] Thus, when truthfulness is a cognitive function of the adequate relationship between the word and the thing to which it refers, as it is in the offstage world, the fact that Brisacier's face has been obfuscated by a plaster mask makes utterly impossible the authentification of any adequation between the face and the proper name. Furthermore, insofar as the mask is a substitute for the original face, it is inauthentic, or improper. It then surreptitiously introduces into this linguistic ethic, founded on grammatical logic, the possibility of that rhetorical dimension of fictionality proper to the theatrical world. But if doing so implicitly calls into question the uncomplicated logic that is its premise and that appears to exclude fiction from participation in its convention, discourse itself is not perceptibly disrupted.

The mask indeed conceals the propriety of what is proper and allows the free substitution of what is improper in its place. It does so under the aegis of the assumed propriety of the relationship between the (masked) face and the name. In other words, the a priori correspondence between signifier and signified upon which the convention itself is predicated validates as authentic and adequate to each other any terms that may come to occupy the places of this correspondence. Although it can be supposed that Brisacier is perfectly cognizant of who he is, and though he would only need to identify himself as "Brisacier" in order to concretize the equation between this proper name and his masked face, it is rather La Rancune who (mis)names him: "L'hôte, séduit par les discours de La Rancune, a bien voulu se contenter de tenir en gage le propre fils du grand khan de Crimée envoyé ici pour faire ses études, et avantageusement connu dans toute l'Europe chrétienne sous le pseudonyme de Brisacier" (p. 152). La Rancune has no difficulty whatever convincing the innkeeper that Brisacier is "le propre fils du grand khan de Crimée" since, at that moment, he participates in a semiotic ethic whose established logical and semantic norm is what has been described as the absolute and unambiguous adequation between the signifier and its signified. In fact, the question of his putative identity is not even raised by the innkeeper precisely because he has no reason to believe this to be anything other than truthful discourse. The damage perpetrated by the mask is considerable indeed, for in the absence of a reliable mode of verification, the mask obscures any means of self-authentification and assures infinite possibilities of assumed or imposed identities, none of which would be proper, but any of which could be so construed. Only the other actors, presumably aware of Brisacier's proper identity, could, with some degree of reliability, adjudicate the problem of the face behind the mask. But they will abandon Brisacier, leaving him with the innkeeper for whom he is just another face (mask).

La Rancune's glibness and the ease with which he establishes as verifiably authentic the fiction of Brisacier's identity would be remarkably significant were it not for the fact that, because he wears a plaster mask, Brisacier has himself abetted this deliberate creation of an illusion. Precisely because the mask has radically severed the correspondence of his face and his proper name, the name is displaced—it is, in fact, *mis*placed—in such a way that La Rancune can assert unequivocally that Brisacier is "le propre fils du grand khan," while he at times only assumes the pseudonym of "Brisacier" in order to mask his authentic identity. The mask's elimination of even the possibility of ambiguity colludes with and reinforces the implicit claim that the alleged identity is the proper one.

If from Brisacier's perspective the situation is equally unambiguous, it is a result of the privileged knowledge he holds regarding the validity of La Rancune's pronouncement. But because he is behind rather than in front of the mask, the consequences of his privilege are ultimately as effacing as the mask itself. Henceforth, he can only affirm his proper name—Brisacier—to state implicitly its impropriety, since it is recognized by the innkeeper only as a pseudonym; whereas assenting to the identity affirmed by La Rancune implies acknowledging the propriety of what is improper. Brisacier is unable to denounce La Rancune's rhetoric as a verbal fiction by asserting what *he* knows to be his proper identity, since, even if Brisacier were speaking the language of truth, the innkeeper would not comprehend it as such, but as an obvious falsehood instead. Whatever linguistic strategy he might employ, Brisacier would remain powerless to realign the signifiers and signifieds of that discourse by which he has been "nominally" figured. Brisacier has been literally defaced by his face, by the mask that obscures his face; and he has been figuratively disfigured by the figure of himself, by the (fictive) "fils du grand khan" who sometimes seeks anonymity in the figure of "Brisacier." While "Brisacier" may be both proper and improper, depending upon which side of the mask one is on, Brisacier himself exists only in that space *between* the proper and the improper wherein the criterion of truth, as a means of distinguishing between them, has been divested of its validity. The success of La Rancune's deceit results from the fact that, on the one hand, the necessity of any means of authentification has been eliminated, since the truth value of his identification of Brisacier remains unquestioned, whereas on the other hand, the very possibility of proclaiming any distinction between proper and improper has been so complicated that it has become impossible.

In contrast to the offstage world where the play of illusion is not only unanticipated but also clearly illegal, it is only *within* the limits of the game of illusion that the theater manages to sustain itself as valid representation. Furthermore, the actor can only rightfully exercise his role as a professional deceiver once he is onstage. In the innkeeper's world a rose is not a rose by any other name, but onstage anything can be a rose. The exigencies of the theater are such that, if the apparent nonfictionality of the illusion is to be assured, an actor must temporarily forfeit his personal identity and his proper name when he identifies himself with the characters he plays. However, the rules of the game likewise guarantee him the recovery of his proper identity once the play has ended. The possibility of illusion was introduced into a structure of adequate reference only through the mediation of the plaster mask. Yet on-stage, where this play of illusion—which is founded upon a displacement of the original terms of the correspondence between signifier and signified—is an integral part of the semiotic ethic, where it is, in fact, the fundamental premise of the linguistic convention, the role the actor plays, the character with which he identifies, simply functions as if it were a mask, rendering a real mask absolutely inessential.

It should be evident then that, contrary to the initial evaluation of a difference between the two linguistic ethics, role-playing on the theatrical stage involves exactly the same substitutive structure as role-playing in the innkeeper's world; they differ only with respect to the nature of the mask they require: one is implicit and the other explicit. But if the convention of the theater demands nothing less than the renunciation of that unwavering belief in adequate reference defining the world of innkeepers, the mode of reference postulated by the theatrical stage is no less dependent upon that referential constraint it pretends to ignore. It simply admits that the association between signifier and signified that it wishes to establish, instead of being authentic and adequate, is an illusion, and that it is purposefully deceitful as well. Furthermore, according to Brisacier, if the allegory that is being played out on the stage is to be comprehended by the audience, the fictionality of the play must be ignored so that it may be considered not as a play but rather as a literal signified, facilitating, as it were, the augmentation of the play's rhetorical coefficient:

> Et quelle pitié c'était alors de voir un père aussi lâche qu'Agamemnon disputer au prêtre Calchas l'honneur de livrer plus vite au couteau la pauvre Iphigénie en larmes! J'entrais comme la foudre au milieu de cette action forcée et cruelle; je rendais l'espérance aux mères et le courage aux pauvres filles, sacrifiées toujours à un devoir, à un Dieu, à la vengence d'un peuple, à l'honneur ou au profit d'une famille! . . . car on comprenait bien partout que c'était là l'histoire éternelle des mariages humains. Toujours le père livrera sa fille par ambition et toujours la mère la vendra avec avidité. [P. 153]

Reading the rhetoric of the play literally concomitantly guarantees that the staging of the event will not be taken for what it is—a representation—but for what it pretends to be—an original presentation. Theatrical representation is, therefore, predicated upon a willing and unquestioning belief in the authenticity of what is, in fact, a tropological deceit, a rhetorical mode that inexorably names and exhibits its own fictionality. Yet this is not the simple admission of an ambiguity that disrupts the referential correspondence; it is rather a matter of displaced reference quite similar to the free substitution of proper names facilitated by the plaster mask.

The fiction of the play can only come into being once it has apparently invalidated as authentic that correspondence between an original signifier and the signified upon which it is founded and according to which it is sustained. The validity of the adequation between the masked Brisacier and "le propre fils du grand khan" was never challenged by the innkeeper; nor is the question of the absolute fictionality of theatrical representation ever entertained by the audience. Both on- and offstage, the rhetoric of the mask and the success of the illusion presuppose the same deletion of that term of reference likely to denounce the illusion for what it is: a pure verbal fiction. In each instance, if the discourse is to function as it has been intended, the actor must mystify and the audience must remain mystified. But if, here, mystification is accomplished through the willing and acknowledged complicity of the audience, there, in the innkeeper's world, it is the apparent ignorance of unwitting complicity that creates and promulgates the mystification. From the point of view of the impersonator himself, the logic of the mask makes evident the fact that, without the support of an exterior context that clearly defines whether this mask of rhetoric is to be read literally or figuratively, it becomes impossible for the actor himself to impose his preference on the audience.

It might well seem that La Rancune bears allegiance only to the theatrical convention, regardless of its appropriateness. Brisacier, however, avows himself to be absolutely scrupulous in preserving the separation between the two domains, attesting to a sincere respect for the different modes of each linguistic convention. So fervently does he believe in the illusion as he plays his roles that he avers himself to be "un comédien qui a de la religion" (p. 152). The possibility of sustaining this separation and of remaining true to this religion without concurrently compromising his own self-identity should present no difficulty whatever, since Brisacier's willingness to comply with the respective codes seems evident. That he may find himself in a situation of noncompliance with the offstage world is less his own fault than that of the mask and La Rancune's seductive discourse. However, when the *comédien* is confronted with the task not of self-representation but of representing an act of violence, it is this religion itself that is finally to be compromised; for violence is simply that one event that can never be innocently represented. It derives from the nature of the event that either it accuses the artifice of its representation and corrupts the theatrical metaphor of original presentation, if it is "represented"; or, if it is indeed the presentation of an act of "real" violence, it violates the fundamental theatrical convention of representation. Violence is the one event with respect to which it becomes impossible to fictionalize successfully, for the purposes of the theater, a figurative representation into a literal illusion.

If Brisacier's initial confrontation with violence in the *Roman tragique* occurs within the confines of the offstage ethic, it necessarily engages a juxtaposition and comparison with onstage violence, since it is with the implicit intention of making clear the distinction between those two different worlds that Brisacier attempts to explain why "une épée de comédie" is ineffectual as an instrument of suicide:

l'aubergiste inquiet a soupçonné une partie de la triste vérité, et m'est venu dire tout net que j'étais *un prince de contrebande*. A ces mots, j'ai voulu sauter sur mon épée, mais La Rancune l'avait enlevée, prétextant qu'il fallait m'empêcher de m'en percer le cœur sous les yeux de l'ingrate qui m'avait trahi! Cette dernière supposition était inutile, ô La Rancune! on ne se perce pas le cœur avec une épée de comédie, on n'imite pas le cuisinier Vatel, on n'essaie pas de parodier les héros de roman, quand on est un héros de tragédie: et je prends tous nos camarades à témoin qu'un tel trépas est impossible à mettre en scène un peu noblement. [P. 152; Nerval's italics]

La Rancune, who does not respect the propriety or the impropriety of illusion within each separate convention, has removed Brisacier's sword, fearing he will use it to commit suicide. But, as Brisacier attempts to explain, it is impossible to make use of the elements of the theater outside the limits of that theater: "on ne se perce pas le cœur avec une épée de comédie." What derives from the onstage world cannot invade the offstage world and expect to enjoy the same status as signifier as it did previously. Like the actors themselves, what is proper to the theater cannot anticipate maintaining its onstage properties in a situation where it is out of place. Indeed the appropriate functioning of the sword, the property of which is to support or to sustain the illusion of the theatrical metaphor, inasmuch as it is a theatrical prop, is contingent upon the relevant propriety or impropriety of its use. "Une épée de comédie" is, therefore, highly improper in the innkeeper's world, which does not admit even the illusion it is intended to sustain. In fact, its very impropriety divests it of its property as a prop: offstage it cannot even pretend to represent a sword. Current with the loss of its status as a signifier onstage is the loss of its metaphorical cutting edge; it is as if it were nothing more than an improper (s)word in an inappropriately rhetorical discourse.

In addition, Brisacier makes quite explicit the fact that even within the realm of illusion, each separate mode poses its own limitations. Although it can be admitted that the novel, because of the mediation of its representational aspect through writing, always denounces its blatantly fictional mode, the theatrical illusion of visual, unmediated representation is designated as that of either comedy or tragedy according to the way in which the illusion respects its own status as illusion. If both comedy and tragedy are founded on a similar theatrical metaphor, tragedy depends upon a temporary belief in the veracity of the illusion it creates, whereas comedy constantly points to its theatrical dimension, bringing into play—within the play itself—the *écart* between the illusion and its denunciation as pure fiction. Comedy constantly and overtly subverts the very illusion upon which it depends for its duration.

It is, consequently, due to this particular aspect of comedy that Brisacier's sword—in fact, any sword used on the theatrical stage—can always only be "une épée de comédie." Since a sword is that precise instrument by means of which an act of violence is effected, like the violence itself, any attempt at its representation according to the theatrical ethic will always violate that code within which it is inscribed. The sword can be either real or the prop of the illusion onstage; as either one or the other, it is forever condemned to denounce the fictionality of the tragic representation, yet its capacity to render present the *écart* between fiction and nonfiction is ideally suited to comedy. A tragic sword is, in fact, an anomaly within the play of the theater. Unlike the mask, which is inherent to the illusion of the stage, the sword is inimical to it, belonging rather to the world of the innkeepers. Yet like the mask, its improper presence in the other ethic causes that ethic to malfunction; but whereas the mask camouflages as truth the illusion that has been smuggled into the innkeeper's discourse, the sword brandishes the fictionality of the metaphorical masks of the theater.

Thus, when the violent event, or its instrument, must be represented on-stage, the inherent premises of that convention necessarily intervene in the production of the illusion; but they do so not at all in the way adequate reference managed to diminish the figurative power of the misplaced theatrical signifier. Brisacier is confronted with a choice according to which he must either profane the tragic illusion with an event that points to itself as illusion; or he must present the event, in which case the violence would have to be real rather than staged and would express a profanation of a comparable, if different, sort. Whichever solution he may choose, it is obvious that the illusion upon which the theatrical convention is founded would be violated by his representation:

> Oh! tenez mes amis! J'ai eu un moment l'idée d'être vrai, d'être grand, de me faire immortel enfin, sur votre théâtre de planches et de toiles, et dans votre comédie d'oripeaux! Au lieu de répondre à l'insulte par une insulte, qui m'a valu le *châtiment* dont je souffre encore, au lieu de provoquer tout un public vulgaire à se ruer sur les planches et à m'assommer lâchement . . . , j'ai eu un moment l'idée, l'idée sublime, et digne de César lui-même, l'idée que cette fois nul n'aurait osé mettre au-dessous de celle du grand Racine, l'idée auguste enfin de brûler le théâtre et le public, et vous tous! et de l'emporter seule à travers les flammes, échevelée, à demi-nue, selon son rôle, ou du moins selon le récit classique de Burrhus. Et soyez sûrs alors que rien n'aurait pu me la ravir, depuis cet instant jusqu'à l'échafaud! et de là dans l'éternité!
>
> O remords de mes nuits fiévreuses et de mes jours mouillés de larmes! Quoi! j'ai pu le faire et ne l'ai pas voulu? Quoi! vous m'insultez encore, vous qui devez la vie à ma pitié plus qu'à ma crainte! Les brûler tous, je l'aurais fait! jugez-en: Le théâtre de P*** n'a qu'une seule sortie; le nôtre donnait bien sur une petite rue de derrière, mais le foyer où vous vous teniez tous est de l'autre côté de la scène. [Pp. 155–56; Nerval's italics]

In this instance the nature of the violent event envisaged by Brisacier is not simply representational; rather, he imagines an actual presentation of violence onstage. Like La Rancune's false biography of Brisacier, the introduction of a claim for authenticity—"J'ai eu un moment l'idée d'être vrai"—involves a similar crossing of purposes, as truth is exemplary of the notion of adequate reference and, therefore, clearly derives from the offstage world. And since Brisacier's religious devotion to the tragic illusion would insist that violence onstage not assert its blatantly fictive nature, any violence would have to be played as real violence, which is to say that it could not be played. Consequently, the real fire he would introduce into the play could never be delimited by the space of the theater, because it is the property of another world and not a theatrical prop: it would be neither contained nor controlled by the theater and its semiotic ethic.

To represent violence tragically it would be necessary to create a hyperbole of violence that would ultimately destroy the text of the illusion (the play) as well as the semiotic ethic within which it is inscribed (the theater). If violence is to be recognized as such within the ethic of the theater, it would involve nothing less than the complete and irrevocable destruction of it and its illusion. Yet this annihilation of the theater would blur the distinction between the two worlds; in fact, one would explode into the other. Hence, burning down the theater would also imply either that Brisacier never abandon his role or, conversely, that he never again accept a theatrical role. But even this statement of alternatives is inaccurate, since after the conflagration the distinction between on- and off-stage would be not simply unnecessary but highly inappropriate, as there would no longer be two worlds. The difference Brisacier recognizes between theater and nontheater affords that exterior context according to which he determines not only the propriety or the impropriety of the play of illusion, but also the way in which his or another's discourse will be perceived. Once the means for formulating this distinction is destroyed, it would be impossible for him to decide whether or not he was playing a role, since there would be no way of differentiating between actors and innkeepers. He would lose his identity both as an actor onstage and as Brisacier offstage. Whereas the mask he wears offstage allows him to remain readable, albeit incorrectly so, to the innkeeper, the vicissitudes of the metaphorical masks he voluntarily assumes onstage— unless he accepts to compromise his "religion"—would ultimately make him radically unreadable to himself.

Clearly, violence derives from a logic that is not that of illusion; and its appearance onstage in either form, real or represented, would undermine the play of illusion and subvert the linguistic convention of the theater. Similarly, in the world where only literal meaning is admitted, the fictive discourse of the actor, whose logic is equally foreign to the innkeeper's ethic, caused that convention to misfire and to make a dubious truth out of an obvious falsehood, convincing the innkeeper of its authenticity precisely because he had no reason to relinquish willingly his belief in its truthful mode. Whereas the demise of offstage discourse was evident only to those aware of its inauthenticity, the theatrical illusion risks an infinitely more visible defeat when it is confronted with the task of representing violence. The choice is between feigning the violent event, in which case it manifests its inauthenticity, and its performance as real, rather than represented, violence, which explodes the illusion and destroys the theater.

The two semiotic ethics are not at all dissimilar, for, despite appearances, no essential difference can be articulated between the on- and offstage worlds, either with respect to the way in which each representational logic has determined how discourses are to be understood, or regarding the ultimate aim of these discourses to mystify their audience. Nor do the innkeeper and the actors differ significantly in their functions, since, in either world, they occupy the same places of audience and performer. Signification in each world depends upon the establishement of a fundamental correspondence between signifier and signified; it is the ethic itself that determines how this correspondence is to be understood: as authentic and adequate, or as illusory and deceitful. There is, however, harbored within each performance, a potential, not for differentiation, but for destruction, for the destruction of that apparent difference upon the recognition of which the proper understanding of the discourse is contingent. According to the terms of the narrative itself, in the innkeeper's world, discourse, which was thought to have been truthful, was but a convincing performance: it persuaded its audience that what was really fiction was actually fact. Such discourse can thus be said to have exhibited the seductive function of rhetorical language. On the other hand, onstage discourse immediately affirmed its deceit, implicitly manifesting what had been deleted for its effective performance. It avowed itself to be tropological language and asked to be understood as such.

Brisacier's relationship to the language of both the on- and offstage worlds is much like that of a verbal sign to its corresponding discourse; he was, in essence, a signifier to be read either literally or figuratively as determined by the appropriate convention. Furthermore, whether he was Brisacier-"le propre fils du grand khan" or Brisacier-Achille, he was always prefigured by and within the discourse he would subsequently appropriate.[10] Brisacier's role-playing involved what can be termed his self-animation in a language that had already predisposed a place for him, a gesture curiously analogous to the rhetorical figure of personification. Each time that he assumed the person of his role—and correspondingly the first person pronoun of that discourse—he made of himself "une espèce d'être réel et physique, doué de sentiment et de vie, enfin ce qu'on appelle une personne," and this was accomplished "par simple façon de parler, ou par une fiction toute verbale."[11] Yet, if Brisacier did occupy that place "grâce à quoi le discours peut survenir,"[12] it rendered him painfully aware of the fact that untroubled existence there was impossible, as he risked either miscomprehension or self-annihilation. That he found himself in this privileged, but no less intolerable, situation was, therefore, a direct result of his complete identification with the fictional role he was playing, be it "le propre fils du grand khan" through the mediation of the mask, or Achille through the convention of the theater itself. Rather than finally having been able to make sense of his situation and to choose between one world and the other, he was obligated to exist according to both modes of signification—and not alternately, one after the other, but simultaneously, because each mode was always present in the other. Hence, to the extent that the analogy between Brisacier and a signifier is valid, it can be said that he personifies the aporia between persuasion and trope, the two aspects of rhetorical language that have described as well the discursive logics of the two conventions. He thus brilliantly dramatizes the contradiction inherent in and named by the rhetoric of person-(i)fic(a)tion, which attempts to create in language the figure of the person necessitated by a fiction it then wishes to conceal. For example, either Brisacier personified his role through the persuasive rhetoric of illusion, which subsequently could not know its own illusory nature; or he manifested rhetoric's fundamentally tropological character and revealed the person-fiction, the pure fiction of the person. The figure of Brisacier demonstrates that both aspects of discourse were present in each world; their recognition was simply a matter of the degree to which their presence had been admitted. However, the actual conditions of their misalliance were only disclosed when, through Brisacier, each ethic was asked to comprehend the presence of that aspect of its discourse upon the exclusion of which its existence was founded. To Brisacier, who was aware of their cohabitation, seductive rhetoric and tropological language immediately revealed the fact that they were mutually dependent and mutually destructive, and that they circumscribed the very impossibility of the dimension they created. According to the *Roman tragique,* then, rhetorical language, their impossible copresence, was both where it was averred to be and where it seemed not to be, where it was concealed by an ethic that rejected the possibility of its existence. Rhetorical language figuratively armed and disarmed that discourse whereby it was uttered. Its logic neither respected nor even recognized that of its vehicle, and the play of its figures could not be controlled, as they always exceeded the limits of their inscription and threatened imminent destruction to the discourse itself and to its comprehension.

Yet, at the same time as he created the figure of the person, Brisacier refused to be content merely with his awareness of the linguistic deceit and to remain within the bounds of that language which had figured him: "j'ai eu un moment l'idée d'être vrai"; "comment me dépêtrer de l'infernal réseau d'intrigues où les récits de La Rancune viennent de m'engager?" (p. 157). Brisacier's desire for authenticity incited him to attempt to go beyond his awareness of both the fallacy inherent in language as it pretends to describe a reality and the fiction it is capable of creating through its staged representations. But although his religious devotion to role-playing made it impossible for him to *play* the role, his desire to *be* a person was equally impracticable, for he was condemned to play according to the rules of the game of language, which itself constantly confounded his very status. If the problem that first confronted Brisacier was that of the difference between being someone one is not and believing in the temporary authenticity of that belief, the paradox is that finally it was just that state of belief in the being which led him to demystify the belief. Because of his own status as a "figurer of figures," he learned of the impossibility of being authentically in his inherently rhetorical language. And if he ultimately accepted the pretense of the role he was playing, he did discover that he was only its locus, a place marked by the rhetorical masks he wore.

Although the *Roman tragique* may well wager the lucidity of Nervalian madness in its own self-definition, it finally warns against the desire to go beyond an awareness of the deceit of language, which was its privileged discovery. Furthermore, Brisacier himself explicitly defines madness as a belief in the authenticity of the illusion: "ma folie est de me *croire* un Romain" (p. 156; italics mine).[13] And since it is precisely that symptomatic gesture of role-playing which has left the impersonator figured by, and inexorably trapped within, the play of rhetorical forces, Nervalian madness has asserted its knowledge that real madness, in fact, lies in that desire to go beyond one's awareness of an impossible choice, whereas sanity, Dumas's perhaps, does not even recognize that there is a choice. The impersonator's dizzying obsession, like Rimbaud's, is that of attempting, nonetheless, to trap within this recalcitrant and inadequate language the impossibility of its truth: "Ce fut d'abord une étude. J'écrivais des silences, des nuits, je notais l'inexprimable. Je fixais des vertiges."[14]

1. Jean Richer, *Nerval: Expérience et création,* 2d ed. (Paris: Hachette, 1970), p. 11.

2. Raymond Jean, *Nerval par lui-même* (Paris: Seuil, 1964), pp. 37–39.

3. Ibid., p. 43.

4. Gérard de Nerval, *Œuvres I,* ed. Albert Béquin and Jean Richer (Paris: Gallimard, 1974), p. 158. All page references to Nerval's works are to this edition.

5. Léon Cellier: "Il enrobe le tout [the various fragments composing "A Alexandre Dumas"] de variations à la fois humoristiques et profondes où, sans avoir l'air d'y toucher, il définit sa folie" ("Préface" in Gérard de Nerval, *Les Filles du feu, Les Chimères* [Paris: Garnier-Flammarion, 1965], p. 13). The *Roman tragique* had originally appeared in the 10 March 1844 issue of *L'Artiste* and was reprinted in the same periodical in March 1879. The three versions reproduce essentially the same text, offering only a few variants (Nerval, p. 1264). Aristide Marie has published a manuscript fragment that precedes the letter known as the *Roman tragique,* situating Brisacier and indicating Nerval's own intention to write an epistolary novel that would be a sequel to the *Roman comique* (*Gérard de Nerval: Le poète et l'homme* [Paris: Hachette, 1955], pp. 110–11).

6. The present essay has been abstracted from a longer study dealing with Nervalian rhetoric. Because of the limitations it has imposed upon itself in its present form, it is but an outline, a suggestion of a direction for an eventual elaboration. It is for this reason that certain more theoretical aspects of the analysis have been sketched out or briefly intimated rather than pursued to their logical conclusions. See Catherine Lowe, "The Person and the Fiction: The Figure of Nervalian Rhetoric" (Ph.D. diss., Yale University, 1978).

7. P. 151: "je n'ai à vous offrir que ce que vous appelez si justement des théories impossibles, *un livre infaisable,* dont voici le premier chapitre" (Nerval's italics).

8. The distinction between grammatical and rhetorical logic has been examined by Paul De Man in "Semiology and Rhetoric," *Diacritics* 3 (Fall 1973): 27–33.

9. Although the analogy face/name // signifier/signified has been determined as the one appropriate to this discussion, there are other possible variations, equally valid and equally justifiable, such as name/face // signifier/signified. The analogy could be expanded to include the notion of referent as well, which might engender other variations on the model of referent/sign (signifier/ signified).

10. Emile Benveniste, "La Nature des pronoms," in *Problèmes de linguistique générale* (Paris: Gallimard, 1966), pp. 251–57.

11. Pierre Fontanier, *Figures du discours,* ed. Nicolas Ruwet (Paris: Flammarion, 1968), p. 111. It should also be noted that in order for language to be appropriated by a narrating subject, what must take place is an animation—a personification—of an inanimate linguistic element, a personal pronoun.

12. Jean-Louis Galay, "Esquisses pour une théorie figurale du discours," in *Poétique* 20 (1974): 399.

13. Cf. Nietzsche: "Wahn eben Glauben an die Wahrheit ist" (*Das Philosophenbuch*, trans. A. Marietti [Paris: Aubier-Flammarion, 1969], p. 204).

14. "Délires II" in Arthur Rimbaud, *Œuvres,* ed. S. Bernard (Paris: Garnier, 1960), p. 228.

Baudelaire and Nietzsche:
Squaring the Circle of Madness

ANDREW J. McKENNA

In the notes he was accumulating for *The Will to Power,* Nietzsche describes the modern artist as an "intermediary species" between the madman and the criminal: "restrained from *crime* by weakness of will and social timidity, and not yet ripe for the *madhouse,* but reaching out inquisitively toward both spheres with his antennae."[1] When Nietzsche declared himself to be God, he completed a pantheon of madmen—Hölderlin, Nerval, van Gogh—whose works are ranked among the most profound, provocative, and forward-looking of the nineteenth century. The twentieth century has its illustrious madmen as well, but it is fair to say that it will be best remembered for its great criminals. The importance of Baudelaire is precisely his intermediary status in this respect. He was on the one hand haunted by the prospect of his own madness. After a visit with the painter Meryon, who was suffering intermittently from insanity, he wrote to Poulet-Malassis, "Après qu'il m'a quitté, je me suis demandé comment il se faisait que moi, qui ai toujours eu dans l'esprit et dans les nerfs, tout ce qu'il fallait pour devenir fou, je ne le fusse pas devenu."[2] It is on the other hand his fascination with crime, with palpable evil, that drew him in part to the writings of Poe, and that prompted in him the atrocious suggestion of a "Belle conspiration à organiser pour l'extermination de la Race Juive"[3] At another point in his intimate journals he prophesied the conditions in which such a crime would be possible: "Mais ce n'est pas particulièrement par des institutions politiques que se manifestera la ruine universelle, ou le progrès universel; car peu m'importe le nom. Ai-je besoin de dire que le peu qui restera de politique se débattra péniblement dans les étreintes de l'animalité générale, et que les gouvernements seront forcés, pour se maintenir et pour créer un fantôme d'ordre, de recourir à des moyens qui feraient frissonner notre huma-nité actuelle, pourtant si endurcie?" (p. 1263). Toward the end of this passage, which begins "Le monde va finir . . . , " Baudelaire states that he feels in himself at times "le ridicule d'un prophète." But given the accuracy of his prophecy, it would seem that Baudelaire, somewhat mad, somewhat criminal, is just the sort of artist who should command our attention at present, for the sake of both sanity and survival. The example of Nietzsche will serve to inform our reflections, to the extent that his madness fulfills a destiny that Baudelaire feared for himself.

Baudelaire, then, was not mad, but, by his own reckoning, he should have been. Certain entries in his intimate journals seem to prolong this conjecture— "Mes ancêtres, idiots ou maniaques, dans des appartements solennels, tous victimes de terribles passions" (p. 1259)—and still others testify more concretely to conditions of its possiblity. There is above all the famous passage on his "sensation du gouffre":

> Au moral comme au physique, j'ai toujours eu la sensation du gouffre, non seulement du gouffre du sommeil, mais du gouffre de l'action, du rêve, du souvenir, du désir, du regret, du remords, du beau, du nombre, etc.
> J'ai cultivé mon hystérie avec jouissance et terreur. Maintenant j'ai toujours le vertige, et aujourd'hui 23 janvier 1862, j'ai subi un singulier avertissement, j'ai senti passer sur moi *le vent de l'aile de l'imbécillité*. [P. 1265]

The notions of "jouissance," "terreur," and "vertige" suggest elements of a scenario familiar to Greek tragedy. In *The Bacchae* of Euripides a hysterical orgy—lead by women inspired by Dionysus—leads to the dismemberment of the king and the establishment of the cult of the god.[4] These elements recur in Baudelaire's writings with an insistence that suggests that Baudelaire is talking the same language as Euripides because he is in fact dealing with the same experience.

It is of course to imbecility, and not to any violent immolation, that Baudelaire finally did succumb. It will remain for a later portion of this essay to suggest in what way the two fates are the same. Suffice it for the moment to point out that Baudelaire prophesied his own abjection repeatedly. We see it in the fate of the rebellious monk in "Le Châtiment de l'orgueil" (1850): "Sale, inutile et laid comme une chose usée, / Il faisait des enfants la joie et la risée." It is prefigured again in the fate of Edgar Poe, with whom Baudelaire identified so strongly: "Lamentable tragédie que la vie d'Edgar Poe! Sa mort, dénouement horrible dont l'horreur est accrue par la trivialité."[5] We find it again in "L'Ecole païenne," in which he draws a caricature of his own aesthetic program and its consequences. In this text he speaks in the name of "la religion et la philosophie" to declaim against "la destinée des insensés qui ne voient dans la nature que des rhythmes et des formes":

> Mais combien ils seront châtiés! Tout enfant dont l'esprit poétique sera surexcité, dont le spectacle, excitant des mœurs actives et laborieuses ne frappera pas incessamment les yeux, qui entendra sans cesse parler de gloire et de volupté, dont les sens seront journellement caressés, irrités, effrayés, allumés et satisfaits par des objets d'art, deviendra le plus malheureux des hommes et rendra les autres malheureux. A douze ans, il retroussera les jupes de sa nourrice, et si la puissance dans le crime ou dans l'art ne l'élève pas au-dessus des fortunes vulgaires, à trente ans il crèvera à l'hôpital. Son âme, sans cesse irritée et inassouvie, s'en va à travers le monde, le monde occupé et laborieux; elle s'en va, dis-je, comme une prostituée, criant:

Plastique! plastique! La plastique, cet affreux mot me donne la chair de poule, la plastique l'a empoisonné, et cependant il ne veut vivre que par ce poison. Il a banni la raison de son cœur, et par un juste châtiment, la raison refuse de rentrer en lui. [P. 627]

By his reference to the poet "à douze ans" we are reminded, as he noted in *Fusées,* that he loved his mother "pour son élégance. J'étais donc un dandy précoce" (p. 1259). By his reference to the poet "à trente ans"—Baudelaire is thirty at this time of writing—he anticipates his own foreshortened destiny by but fifteen years, when he would die at forty-six of syphilis, having entirely lost his creative faculties. The "comédie dangereuse" that Baudelaire deplores in "L'Ecole païenne" (p. 628) is one that he will play out in his own life.

In Baudelaire's description we recognize as well a caricature of what Nietzsche exalts in the preface to *The Birth of Tragedy* as "the purely esthetic interpretation and justification of the world," which he contrasts, as if in refutation of Baudelaire, to the "unconditional will of Christianity to recognize *only* moral values."[6] Nietzsche was fond of describing Christianity as "folie circulaire,"[7] a nineteenth-century term for manic-depressive insanity: alternating cycles of self-exaltation and self-deprecation, which he saw reflected in the Christian dialectic of repentance and redemption. It is just such an oscillation, heavily laden with religious imagery, that Baudelaire thematized in *Les Fleurs du mal* as "Spleen et idéal," and that he claimed to have experienced in his own life since childhood:

Tout enfant, j'ai senti dans mon cœur deux sentiments contradictoires, l'horreur de la vie et l'extase de la vie.
C'est bien le fait d'un paresseux nerveux. [P. 1296]

For Nietzsche such a fact is owed to the peculiar hysteria of the modern artist: "As one may today consider 'genius' as a form of neurosis, so perhaps also the artistic power of suggestion—and indeed our *artists* are painfully like hysterical females!!! But that is an objection to 'today,' not to 'artists.'"[8] For his own time Baudelaire offers the most thorough interrogation of aesthetic experience and of the "sentiments contradictoires" that arise from it. And he articulates a "Morale," as he calls it in *Le Poëme du haschisch,* that Nietzsche's own madness cannot fail to confirm.

The complementary notions of madness and tragedy pervade the significance of *Les Paradis artificiels* as a whole, as we note from its "Dédicace." The first sentence is ironically Cartesian, that is, anti-Cartesian, in its evocation of dreams: "Le bon sens dit que les choses de la terre n'existent que bien peu et que la vraie réalité n'est que dans les rêves" (p. 345). Interweaving the themes of "volupté" and spirituality with the evocation of a woman, the text translates these themes into the specific language of tragedy. "Voluptés artificielles" are transformed into "des jouissances nouvelles et subtiles [tirées] même de la douleur, de la catastrophe et de la fatalité" (p. 346). The "bon sens" and "rêves" of the first sentence culminate in the last in the nightmare of madness: "et tu devineras la gratitude d'un autre Oreste dont tu as souvent surveillé les cauchemars, et de qui tu dissipais, d'une main légère et maternelle, le sommeil épouvantable" (p. 346). This tragic motif recalls the end of "Le Voyage," which portrays the entreaty of "Nos Pylades" to the mad Orestes: "'Pour refraîchir ton cœur nage vers ton Electre!'" (p. 126). Limiting ourselves mostly to a consideration of *Le Poëme du haschisch,* we will observe the relation of madness and tragedy emerging in a classically Greek pattern.

The "Dédicace" performs the kind of thematic inversion, or demonization, that we witness in the first section of *Les Fleurs du mal* as we move from "Idéal" to "Spleen," that is, for instance, from "ce beau diadème éblouissant et clair" of "Bénédiction" (p. 9) to the "Puits de Vérité, clair et noir" of "L'Irrémédiable" (p. 76). We recognize this inversion again in the "expansion des choses infinies" of "Correspondances" (p. 11) which is transformed seventy-five poems later into "Obsession" (p. 71). The "vivants piliers" of nature, with their "confuses paroles" and their "longs échos qui de loin se confondent," become the "échos de vos *De Profondis,*" "un langage connu" against which the poet seeks "le vide, le noir et le nu." The poet's despair here is echoed again in the "bonds" and "tumultes" of the ocean:

> ce rire amer
> De l'homme vaincu, plein de sanglots et d'insultes,
> Je l'entends dans le rire énorme de la mer.

We find this laughter again in "L'Héautontimorouménos" (p. 74):

> —Un de ces grands abandonnés
> Au rire éternel condamnés,
> Et qui ne peuvent plus sourire!

It is laughter that will serve as an emblem for the "Morale" of hashish, just as it is laughter that marks its first stage.

There is at first an aconceptual giddiness, which Baudelaire describes as "des ébauches de comique" and which already evokes the spectre of madness: "Le démon vous a envahi; il est inutile de regimber contre cette hilarité, douloureuse comme un chatouillement. De temps en temps vous riez de vous-même, de votre niaiserie et de votre folie, et vos camarades, si vous en avez, rient également de votre état et du leur; mais, comme ils sont sans malice, vous êtes sans rancune" (p. 357). The paragraph that follows elaborates on the relation between laughter and madness, articulating a progression from "ce malaise dans la joie, cette insécurité, cette indécision de la maladie" to "cette folâtrerie et ces éclats de rire," which appear "comme une véritable folie, au moins comme une niaiserie de maniaque." To this the text contrasts the unintoxicated "témoin prudent" whose "sagesse" and "bon sens" are experienced ironically as a kind of "démence": "Les rôles sont intervertis. Son sang-froid vous pousse aux dernières limites de l'ironie. N'est-ce pas une situation mystérieusement comique que celle d'un homme qui jouit d'une gaieté incompréhensible pour qui ne s'est pas placé dans le même milieu que lui? Le fou prend le sage en pitié, et dès lors l'idée de sa supériorité commence à poindre à l'horizon de son intellect. Bientôt elle grandira, grossira et éclatera comme un météore" (pp. 357–58). Baudelaire's language exercises tight control over the progression from "insécurité" to "supériorité," from the burst of laughter to the burst of a meteor. Laughter is the sign of a madness that consists of the idea of superiority to others.

In this notion we find a résumé of Baudelaire's reflections on laughter in *De l'essence du rire,* which is devoted to elucidating just such a "situation mystérieusement comique" as we have in the first stage of hashish, and which examines the moral experience of hashish under the heading of the comic: "Signe de supériorité relativement aux bêtes, je comprends sous cette dénomination les parias nombreux de l'intelligence, le rire est signe d'infériorité relativement aux sages, qui par l'innocence contemplative de leur esprit se rapprochent de l'enfance" (p. 982). The notion of intelligence here, which is repeated four times in the vicinity of this passage, points to the very human nature of this idea of superiority. In *Le Poëme du haschisch* Baudelaire plays on this word in order to evoke a dialectic of self and other: "J'ai été témoin d'une scène de ce genre qui a été poussée fort loin, et dont le grotesque n'était intelligible que pour ceux qui connaissaient, au moins par l'observation sur autrui, les effets de la substance et la différence énorme de diapason qu'elle crée entre deux intelligences supposées égales" (p. 358). Laughter is the sign of an implicit rivalry of human intelligence, in which an imbalance between subjects is presumed, in which a reciprocity or equality is denied. The horizontal plan of human relationships inclines vertically with the self claiming superiority to others.

In *De l'essence du rire* Baudelaire illustrates this imbalance, together with the contradiction it reflects, in the very establishment of the theory of superiority by physiologists: "Le rire, disent-ils, vient de la supériorité. Je ne serais pas étonné que devant cette découverte le physiologiste se fut mis à rire en pensant à sa propre supériorité. Aussi, il fallait dire: le rire vient de l'idée de sa propre supériorité. Idée satanique s'il en fut jamais! Orgueil et aberration!" (p. 980). Laughter here is the sign of pride—"orgueil"—in the classical (i.e., Greek) sense of the word: hubris. Laughter is the sign of a hybrid situation in which, in the manner of Oedipus, the accusation rebounds to the guilt of the accuser. In this situation, as in Sophocles' play, hubris is not the function of a temperament but of a relation, which Sophocles stages progressively as Oedipus versus Creon, Oedipus versus Tiresias, and finally Oedipus versus Oedipus.[9] Laughter for Baudelaire is the sign of a pretention, a presumption, a kind of usurpation in a dialectic of self and other. It reflects an imbalance that is active and violent rather than static or natural. We are placed in a duel, a situation of horizontal doubles that is arbitrarily verticalized into a hierarchy of superior and inferior, like that of "bourreau" and "victime." It is precisely in terms of hubris that we can best understand Baudelaire's later remark that laughter is "profondément humain," "essentiellement humain," "essentiellement contradictoire" (p. 982). The essence of this contradiction is perceived in its excess, madness, as Baudelaire establishes with only seeming abruptness: "Orgeuil et aberration! Or, il est notoire que tous les fous des hôpitaux ont l'idée de leur propre supériorité développée outre mesure. Je ne connais guère de fous d'humilité. Remarquez que le rire est une des expressions les plus fréquentes et les plus nombreuses de la folie" (p. 980). Baudelaire's comments here confirm the logic of his earlier remark "que le rire est généralement l'apanage des fous, et qu'il implique toujours plus ou moins d'ignorance ou de faiblesse" (p. 977).

The evidence that Baudelaire adduces for laughter as "faiblesse," as "débilité" is itself primarily physiological. Laughter manifests itself as a "convulsion nerveuse, un spasme involontaire comparable à l'éternument, et causé par la vue du malheur d'autrui" (p. 980). Here, as elsewhere, what constantly reasserts itself in Baudelaire's text is the narrator's role of observer-witness who perceives the symmetry, the reciprocity of weaknesses: "Ce malheur est presque toujours une faiblesse d'esprit. Est-il phénomène plus déplorable que la faiblesse se réjouissant de la faiblesse?" (p. 980). There will be more to say of this role, Baudelaire's most ingenious imposture, when the dialectic of self and other is more fully revealed.

The symmetry manifest in the intellectual pride of the physiologist is evidenced again in the decidedly everyday example that Baudelaire offers of an "infirmité dans l'ordre physique." It is the example of the man who loses his balance and falls: "Pour prendre un des exemples les plus vulgaires de la vie, qu'y a-t-il de si réjouissant dans le spectacle d'un homme qui tombe sur la glace ou sur le pavé, qui trébuche au bout d'un trottoir, pour que la face de son frère en Jésus-Christ se contracte d'une façon désordonnée, pour que les muscles de son visage se mettent à jouer subitement comme une horloge à midi ou un joujou à ressorts? Ce pauvre diable s'est au moins défiguré, peut-être s'est-il fracturé un membre essentiel" (pp. 980–81). The reciprocal loss of control is communicated to the reader by the use of the words "face" and "visage" for the laughter and "défiguré" for the man who falls. The irony of their equality is communicated by the designation of the victim as a "pauvre diable" and of the laugher as "son frère en Jésus-Christ." Baudelaire has already stated that "le comique est un élément damnable et d'origine diabolique" (p. 978). Here, as with "le fou" and "le sage" in Le Poëme du haschisch, and as with the physiologist in this essay, "les rôles sont intervertis." Like the laughter of Melmoth he will describe in the following paragraph, the situation here is of a "double nature contradictoire."

The spectacle to which we are made a witness in this example is precisely of the kind that Baudelaire evokes in *Le Poëme du haschisch:* "Cependant se développe cet état mystérieux et temporaire de l'esprit où la profondeur de la vie, hérissée de ses problèmes multiples, se révèle tout entière dans le spectacle, si naturel et si trivial qu'il soit, qu'on a sous les yeux,—où le premier objet venu devient symbole parlant" (pp. 375–76). In this altogether trivial and natural spectacle—"un des exemples les plus vulgaires de la vie"—what is symbolized as "la profondeur de la vie" is nothing less than the fall of man through pride, through hubris, which takes the form of an imbalance, an "outre mesure," a "façon désordonnée" equal to the imbalance it mocks. Thus Baudelaire's theological imagination, his "intelligence de l'allégorie," is on occasion ("temporaire") informed by his daily natural experience, as this tragic fall is trivially reenacted on the sidewalks of Paris. Earlier in the essay we read that "le rire humain est intimement lié à l'accident d'une chute ancienne, d'une dégradation physique et morale" (p. 978). In this spectacle the "dégradation physique" is the "symbole parlant" of a "dégradation morale." The laughter that erupts in this situation is itself most telling "symbole parlant": "Cependant, le rire est parti, irrésistible et subit. Il est certain que si l'on veut creuser cette situation, on trouvera au fond de la pensée du rieur un certain orgueil inconscient. C'est là le point de départ: *moi,* je ne tombe pas; *moi,* je marche droit; *moi,* mon pied est ferme et assuré. Ce n'est pas *moi* qui commettrais la sottise de ne pas voir un trottoir interrompu ou un pavé qui barre le chemin" (p. 981). To "la profondeur de la vie" corresponds the "fond de la pensée du rieur," in which we witness again "la faiblesse se réjouissant de la faiblesse." Again we are confronted with hubris in the classical sense, in the sense in which we see Oedipus presuming to walk straight toward the criminal even as he stumbles in a circle back to himself: Oedipus the King whose own downfall is traced back to the symbolic crossroads, where he triumphed over the obstacle that barred his way. The symbolism is the same because the meaning is the same.

What Baudelaire discusses under the heading of the comic is something that we identify as quintessentially tragic in Sophocles' play. The difference between the two modes derives less from the gravity of the matter—parricide versus slapstick—than from the manner in which it is perceived. The horror of Oedipus's crime marks him as different, as utterly, abhorrently other. What is revealed in slapstick is the reciprocity, the equality in violence or in weakness. In like fashion, the perception of the comic in Baudelaire's presentation is owing to the perspective of the narrator, a spectator-witness exterior to the rivalry of consciences to whose eye the symmetry of weakness is apparent. This exteriority is for Baudelaire the necessary condition of art, as we read at the conclusion of his essay:

je ferai remarquer . . . que, pour qu'il y ait comique, c'est-à-dire émanation, explosion, dégagement de comique, il faut qu'il y ait deux êtres en présence;—que c'est spécialement dans le rieur, dans le spectateur, que gît le comique;—que cependant, relativement à cette loi d'igorance, il faut faire une exception pour les hommes qui ont fait métier de développer en eux le sentiment du comique et de le tirer d'eux-mêmes pour le divertissement de leurs semblables, lequel phénomène rentre dans la classe de tous les phénomènes artistiques qui dénotent dans l'être humain l'existence d'une dualité permanente, la puissance d'être à la fois soi et un autre. [P. 993]

It is this alterity to self that explains that "Ce n'est point l'homme qui tombe qui rit de sa propre chute, à moins qu'il ne soit un philosophe, un homme qui ait acquis, par habitude, la force de se dédoubler rapidement et d'assister comme spectateur désintéressé aux phénomènes de son *moi*" (p. 982). That Baudelaire is such a rare case is evidenced in the strategically philosophical pose he adopts throughout his essay on laughter: "Ceci est donc purement un article de philosophe et d'artiste" (p. 974). It is from this posture, or imposture, that Baudelaire can analyze his own hubris in *Le Poëme du haschisch:* "J'assiste à son raisonnement comme au jeu d'un mécanisme sous une vitre transparente" (p. 381). Finally, it is owing to this perspective that the apotheosis of "L'Homme-Dieu" will resolve on a mysteriously comic note, which resembles in its logic the pantomime of the English Pierrot as it is described in *De l'essence du rire*.

What shows through in the description of the English Pierrot is that the matter of tragedy and the matter of comedy are the same. The "signe distinctif" of this kind of comic is "la violence" (p. 988), and the scenario that is described conforms to the substance of tragedy: "insouciance et neutralité, et partant accomplissement de toutes les fantaisies gourmandes et rapaces, au détriment, tantôt de Harlequin, tantôt de Cassandre ou de Léandre" (p. 989). What we have in this "singulière pièce" is an orgy, a sabbath of desire, which inspires laughter by its hyperbole, its vertiginous excess: "c'était le vertige de l'hyperbole" (p. 989). Baudelaire's text hints at a tragic potential with the further demonstration of Pierrot's amorous pursuits: "C'était vraiment une ivresse de rire, quelque chose de terrible et d'irrésistible" (p. 989). This spectacle of desire inspires something like terror and will culminate in sacrifice. Little matter the nature of the transgression, there must needs be a victim, transformed into an animal: "Pour je ne sais quel méfait, Pierrot devait être finalement guillotineé. . . . Après avoir lutté et beuglé comme un bœuf qui flaire l'abattoir, Pierrot subissait enfin son destin" (p. 989). There follows a mock resurrection, when the torso steals back its head and stuffs it into its pocket: "Mais voilà que, subitement, le torse raccourci, mû par la monomanie irrésistible du vol, se dressait, escamotait victorieusement sa propre tête comme un jambon ou une bouteille de vin, et, bien plus avisé que le grand saint Denis, la fourrait dans sa poche!" (pp. 989–90). Pierrot's excesses emulate the "triomphante orgie spirituelle" of hashish (p. 381) right down to the same vocabulary. For Pierrot's final gesture offers a caricature of the "victorieuse monomanie" (p. 383) of "L'Homme-Dieu," who at the moment of his apotheosis shows himself as impervious to irony as Pierrot is to death: "Quel est le philosophe français qui, pour railler les doctrines allemandes modernes, disait: 'Je suis un dieu qui ai mal dîné?' Cette ironie ne mordrait pas sur un esprit enlevé par le haschisch; il répondrait tranquillement: 'Il est possible que j'aie mal dîné, mais je suis un Dieu'" (pp. 382–83). The "monomanie" of the thief who snatches "victorieusement" his own decapitated head offers a rigorous parody of the same logic: "You cut off my head. Good, I'll steal that too." One suspects that it is to the sort of irony enjoyed by the narrator of *Le Poëme du haschisch,* and exercised at the expense of "L'Homme-Dieu," that Baudelaire owes his own fragile sanity.

Baudelaire's choice of words for Pierrot and for "L'Homme-Dieu" is the same because their situation is the same, just as Baudelaire's vocabulary is religious because, whatever his belief, it alone is capable of translating his moral experience intelligibly. The reference to Saint Denis, however fleeting and comical, is significant in this respect. It evokes the sacred in the form of martyrdom, sacrifice, in conformity with the violent scenario of tragedy that recurs so insistently in Baudelaire's writings: desire carried to vertiginous excess, which leads to terror and sacrifice. What Pierrot represents in comic hyperbole is the same scenario that Baudelaire conjures up from the music of Wagner: "Aux titillations sataniques d'un vague amour succèdent bientôt des entraînements, des éblouissements, des cris de victoire, des gémissements de gratitude, et puis des hurlements de férocité, des reproches de victimes et des hosanna impies de sacrificateurs, comme si la barbarie devait toujours prendre sa place dans le drame de l'amour, et la jouissance charnelle conduire, par une logique satanique inéluctable, aux délices du crime" (p. 1224). The continuity between the essay on Wagner and *Le Poëme du haschisch* is apparent when Baudelaire evokes Wagner's music as the expression of "l'excès dans le désir et dans l'énergie, l'ambition indomptable, immodérée, d'une âme sensible qui s'est trompée de voie" (p. 1225). It is this excess that is explored in "l'homme sensible moderne" (p. 375) of *Le Poëme du haschisch,* whose "goût de l'infini" is "un goût qui se trompe souvent de route" (p. 348).

The route that is followed always describes the same familiar, tragic arc. At the peak of this experience, all of reality is subjugated to the individual's intelligence: "Tous les objets environnants sont autant de suggestions qui agitent en lui un monde de pensées, toutes plus colorées, plus vivantes, plus subtiles que jamais, et revêtues d'un vernis magique. . . . '—toutes ces choses ont été créées *pour moi, pour moi, pour moi*! Pour moi, l'humanité a travaillé, a été martyrisée, immolée,—pour servir de pâture, de pabulum, à mon implacable appétit d'émotion, de connaissance et de beauté!'" (p. 382). Here again divinity is acknowledged in the wake of sacrifice—"martyrisée, immolée." It is only afterward, in the "terrible lendemain" of hashish, that the poet will acknowledge himself as the victim as well, comparing hashish "à une arme toujours sanglante et toujours aiguisée" (p. 385): "Mais le lendemain! le terrible lendemain! tous les organes relâchés, fatigués, les nerfs détendus, les titillantes envies de pleurer, l'impossibilité de s'appliquer à un travail suivi, vous enseignent cruellement que vous avez joué un jeu défendu. La hideuse nature, dépouillée de son illumination de la veille, ressemble aux mélancoliques débris d'une fête" (p. 383). The notion of "fête," an "orgie" that culminates in sacrifice, is continuous with Baudelaire's evocation of Wagner, whose music he identifies with a "crise solennelle de l'art" at the beginning of his essay (p. 1209), with a "grande crise morale ou physique" at the end (p. 1236). The crisis is, properly speaking, a sacrificial crisis of a distinctly modern kind, in which the "*moi*" is both executioner and victim, immolated to a divinity that forever eludes him. The divinity is always only a "projection," to use Baudelaire's word, of his own pride, of his own deluded "will to power": "Je saute, j'abrège. Personne ne s'étonnera qu'une pensée finale jaillisse du cerveau de rêveur: '*Je suis devenu Dieu!*' qu'un cri sauvage, ardent, s'élance de sa poitrine avec une énergie telle, une telle puissance de projection, que, si les volontés et les croyances d'un homme ivre avaient une vertu efficace, ce cri culbuterait les anges disséminés dans les chemins du ciel: 'Je suis un Dieu!'" (p. 382). Baudelaire's sentence speaks for itself, and against Nietzsche, in a manner that grammarians call "conditional contrary to fact."

The distinct modernity of this sacrificial crisis reveals in its contradiction the profane individualism of Baudelaire's time and ours. The divinity who demands sacrifice and the sacrificial victim are one and the same, bound up, as Baudelaire's luminous figure announces, in a "cercle unique," a "cercle tragique" (p. 374): "Epouvantable mariage de l'homme avec lui-même!" (p. 372). The contradictory relations of inferiority and superiority that characterize the "situation comique" are internalized and united within a single individual, who exists in a state of permanent disequilibrium, revolving incessantly between grandeur and misery, from which the only release is perhaps the mad delusion of divinity.

It is this very circularity that is the prelude to "folie" for Baudelaire and that is revealed in the veritable manic-depression of Melmoth, "cet admirable emblème" (p. 383). His laughter, "rire terrible," is described in *De l'essence du rire* as the superlative incarnation of pride, "l'expression la plus haute de l'orgueil": "Et ce rire est l'explosion perpétuelle de sa colère et de sa souffrance. Il est, qu'on me comprenne bien, la résultante nécessaire de sa double nature contradictoire, qui est infiniment grande relativement à l'homme, infiniment vile et basse relativement au Vrai et au Juste absolus. Melmoth est une contradiction vivante" (p. 981). Baudelaire's language here is textually reminiscent of Pascal: "S'il se vante, je l'abaisse, s'il s'abaisse, je le vante; et le contredis toujours, jusqu'à ce qu'il comprenne qu'il est un monstre incompréhensible."[10] For Pascal the acknowledgment of his own monstrosity was to humble man to conversion—"Abêtissez-vous"[11]—if it did not lead him to madness: "Les hommes sont si nécessairement fous, que ce serait être fou, par un autre tour de folie, de n'être pas fou."[12] In *The Will to Power* Nietzsche concurs with Pascal, paraphrasing him to the effect that " '*Without the Christian faith*' " man will become for himself " '*un monstre et un chaos.*' "[13] Nietzsche's own destiny, foreshadowed in *The Birth of Tragedy,* suggests that he was consistent with the rigor of the Pascalian alternative.

It is this text of Nietzsche's that most clearly articulates the tragic scenario common to *Le Poëme du haschisch* and to the essays on Wagner and laughter as well. To Nietzsche's idea, stated in the preface to the 1886 edition, of Dionysiac madness as a "neurosis of *health*"[14] corresponds the experience of hashish, which makes the user "un homme malade de trop de vie, malade de joie" (p. 359). Dionysiac madness emanates from "joy, strength, overflowing health, overgreat fullness,"[15] a feeling that he "crowns" with the "holy laughter" of Zarathustra.[16] Nietzsche's own notion of laughter is diametrically opposed to Baudelaire's dialectical analysis. In *The Gay Science* laughter betokens "ultimate liberation and irresponsibility"; rather than the sign of any kind of mad delusion, it betokens a joyful wisdom that is the "gay science" itself. It is not, for all that, any less dialectical, as a sign of superiority to "the age of tragedy, the age of moralities and religions"[17] (that is, Nietzsche's age and Nietzsche's contemporaries).

In the body of his text, Nietzsche draws upon the "analogy of intoxication" to suggest the "nature of the Dionysian" (p. 36). At the peak of this experience, Dionysian man "feels himself a god, he himself now walks about enchanted, in ecstasy, like the gods he saw walking in his dreams. He is no longer an artist, he has become a work of art: in these paroxysms of intoxication the artistic power of all nature reveals itself to the highest gratification of the primordial unity. The noblest clay, the most costly marble, man, is here kneaded and cut, and to the sound of the chisel strokes of the Dionysian world artist rings out the cry of the Eleusinian mysteries: 'Do you prostrate yourselves, millions? do you sense your Maker, world?' "[18] The "paroxysms of intoxication" here recall Baudelaire's experience of Wagner's music, which he likens to the "vertigineuses conceptions de l'opium" (p. 1214), and which he describes in his prefatory letter to the composer in a manner highly evocative of Nietzsche's text: "Et la musique en même temps respirait quelquefois l'orgueil de la vie. Généralement ces profondes harmonies me paraissaient ressembler à ces excitants qui accélèrent le pouls de l'imagination. . . . Ce sera, si vous voulez, le cri suprême de l'âme montée à son paroxysme" (p. 1206). One readily understands Baudelaire's need, as he formulates it, to "transformer ma volupté en connaissance" (p. 1215). It is the need to distance himself intellectually from an experience, "une extase *faite de volupté et de connaissance*" (p. 1214), whose terrible consequences for his sanity were well known to him. It is the terror of the god rising within him, who is appeased only by the sacrifice of his mental equilibrium, who is revealed only upon the sacrifice of his human intelligence: "En effet," we read in *Le Poëme du haschisch,* "il est défendu à l'homme, sous peine de déchéance et de mort intellectuelle, de déranger les conditions primordiales de son existence et de rompre l'équilibre de ses facultés avec les milieux où elles sont destinées à se mouvoir, en un mot, de déranger son destin pour y substituer une fatalité d'un nouveau genre" (p. 383). Of Wagner's music Baudelaire writes, "Ma volupté avait été si forte et si terrible, que je ne pouvais pas m'empêcher d'y vouloir retourner sans cesse" (p. 1214). The terror that threatens his will is theophantic, properly theo-logical, and its transformation into "connaissance" is a veritable exorcism.

A "Morale" such as Baudelaire formulates is nowhere articulated in Nietzsche's writings, but the sense of a "terrible lendemain" emerges obscurely in his Wagnerio-Baudelairean evocation of the bacchanal. Speaking of "an extravagant sexual licentiousness,"[19] he goes on to suggest a devastating fall: "The horrible 'witches' brew' of sensuality and cruelty becomes ineffective; only the curious blending and duality of the emotions of the Dionysian revellers remind us—as medicines remind us of deadly poisons—of the phenomenon that pain begets joy, that ecstasy may wring sounds of agony from us. At the very climax of joy there sounds a cry of horror or a yearning lamentation for an irretrievable loss."[20] Nietzsche's own "terrible lendemain" of January 1889 will be decisive, definitive for his intelligence. In the dawning of his madness, when he signs his letters alternately "Dionysus" and "The Crucified," there is the belated intuition of the identity of sacrificial victim and divinity, the intuition that man is the victim of the claim to divinity. Baudelaire emerges from the experience of hubris closer to Pascal than to Nietzsche, who nonetheless prescribes in *The Will to Power* the moral and psychological advantage of his theological predecessors: "One does not get over a passion by representing it: rather, it is over *when* one is able to represent it."[21] Baudelaire owed his sanity to his comic vision as much as to anything else, but this could not restore his health, which he had fairly systematically ruined. His morose decline is perhaps more terrible to our profane eyes than Nietzsche's brilliant, fulgurating collapse. For by the "déchéance et mort intellectuelle" he suffered in his last months, he escaped the tragic only to succumb to the grotesque. This is how we finally see him, lying in imbecilic paralysis, muttering an oath that is symbolic of the satanism he both cultivated and mocked and that is just as symbolically uncompleted: "Cré Nom, (Nom de Nom de Sa)cré Nom."

    1. Friedrich Wilhelm Nietzsche, *The Will to Power,* trans. Walter Kaufmann and R. J. Hollingdale (New York: Vintage Books, 1968).

2. Charles Baudelaire, *Correspondance générale,* ed. Jacques Crépet, vol. 3 (Paris: Conard, 1948), p. 8.

3. Charles Baudelaire, *Œuvres complètes,* ed. Y.-G. Le Dantec (Paris: Gallimard, Bibliothèque de la Pléiade, 1961), p. 1300. Unless otherwise indicated, all subsequent references are to this edition.

4. For a lengthy analysis of this play in a way that reveals its significance for Baudelaire, consult René Girard, *La Violence et le sacré* (Paris: Grasset, 1970), especially chap. 5, "Dionysos."

5. Charles Baudelaire, "Edgar Poe, sa vie et ses œuvres," *Œuvres complètes* (Paris: Seuil, 1968), p. 337.

6. In *Basic Writings of Nietzsche,* trans. Walter Kaufmann (New York: Modern Library, 1968), p. 23.

7. This diagnosis is to be found in the concluding paragraphs of *Ecce Homo,* as well as in *The Will to Power* (no. 232) and *The Anti-Christ.*

8. *The Will to Power,* no. 812.

9. Consult Girard, chap. 3.

10. Pensée no. 420. See Blaise Pascal, *Pensées et opuscules,* ed. Leon Brunschvicg (Paris: Hachette, 1900), p. 516.

11. Ibid., no. 233.

12. Ibid., no. 414.

13. *The Will to Power,* no. 83.

14. In *Basic Writings,* p. 21.

15. Ibid.

16. Ibid, p. 26.

17. Friedrich Wilhelm Nietzsche, *The Gay Science,* trans. Walter Kaufmann (New York: Vintage Books, 1974), p. 74.

18. *Basic Writings,* pp. 37–38.

19. Ibid., p. 39.

20. Ibid., p. 40.

21. *The Will to Power,* no. 814.

Il m'est impossible—plutôt admettre
l'existence de Dieu—qu'elle désire être
possédée, qu'elle rêve de ça.

J. Laforgue, *Carnet*, 1884–1885

My choice of epigraph deliberately replicates Béatrice
Didier's in "Sexe, société et création: *Consuelo* et
La Comtesse de Rudolstadt," *Romantisme* 13–14 (1976).

"Tristes Triangles":
Le Lys dans la vallée and Its Intertext

NANCY K. MILLER

Apocrypha has it that Balzac, having been panned by Sainte-Beuve in the *Revue des deux mondes,* exclaimed to Jules Sandeau: "Il me le payera; je lui passerai ma plume au travers du corps. . . . Je referai *Volupté.*"[1] Whether or not Balzac articulated exactly those "machistic" desires, evidence exists that he was stimulated enough by Sainte-Beuve's "livre puritain"[2] for us to include it as an important page—at least on the level of (rivalrous) intentionality—in the intertext of *Le Lys dans la vallée.* Balzac's primary conscious objective in redoing *Volupté* appears to stem from his objection to the character of its heroine; more specifically, to the dosage of her femininity: "Mme de Couaën n'est pas assez femme et le danger n'existe pas."[3] The challenge, as it can be read here, was to rewrite what has been rather elegantly described as "l'aventure blanche de cet amour sans espoir,"[4] intensifying the excitement implicit in such a drama without, however, changing the outcome of the script; to rewrite, then, making his heroine more of a woman, but without changing the color of her destiny.

The creation of Mme de Mortsauf, the (white) flower announced in the novel's title, proves to have challenged the critics as much as it apparently challenged Balzac; the question for them was, curiously, despite (or perhaps because of) the ostensible intertext, posing itself in terms of origins, Was there a model (other than Mme de Couaën), and if so, who was she?[5] Although source hunting is a commonplace pursuit in traditional Balzacian scholarship, in the case of Mme de Mortsauf, the mystery to be solved (*cherchez la femme*) is complicated by a peculiarly insistent enigma: "de qui Mme de Mortsauf pouvait tenir le *goût du plaisir,* innocent ou non, que Balzac prête à son héroïne?"[6] The earliest textual model of feminization pointed to is Marguerite de Navarre's lady of Pamplona,[7] for whom, like Mme de Mortsauf, the double bind created by the conflicting demands of virtue and illicit desire is resolved by and in death. The intratextual commentary on that resolution in *L'Heptaméron* provides the following analysis: "Pensez . . . que voylà une saige femme, qui, pour se monstrer plus vertueuse par dehors qu'elle n'estoit au cueur, et pour dissimuler ung amour que la raison de nature voulloit qu'elle portast à ung si honneste seigneur, s'alla laisser morir, par faulte de se donner le plaisir qu'elle désoirait couvertement!"[8] The verdict is clear enough: having repressed her natural desire, the lady falls victim to nature's revenge. Her death, however, is only half the story; as she exits from this world, our "saige femme" tells all. The trajectory of the *nouvelle,* therefore, links death with an end to denegation; *telos* emerges as *topos:* the revelation of truth *in articulo mortis.* Thus, "L'heure est venue qu'il fault que toute dissimulation cesse, et que je confesse la verité que j'ay tant mis de peine à vous celler: c'est que, si vous m'avez porté grande affection, croyez que la myenne n'a été moindre . . . car, entendez . . . que Dieu et mon honneur ne m'ont jamais permis de la vous declarer . . . mais sachez que le *non* que si souvent je vous ay dict m'a faict tant de mal au prononcer, qu'il est cause de ma mort" (*H,* p. 218). Her denial, her "non," is italicized in the text and designates (by hypotyposis) the specifically linguistic forum of repression.

The lady of Pamplona, however, dies happy: "puis que Dieu m'a faict la grace de morir, premier que la viollance de mon amour ayt mis tache à ma conscience et renommée" (*H,* p. 218). The conviction of her victory is such— and this is the topical twist that interests us here—that it permits her to ask her lover (as secular confessor) to share the good news with her husband, "affin qu'il congoisse combien j'ay aymé Dieu et luy" (*H,* p. 218). This gesture of sublime confidence is Julie de Wolmar's too; with the latter, however, it is the husband who delivers the message to the lover, and in writing. In both cases, by putting a term to all future intercourse, death brings freedom of sexual expression, permits the enunciation of desire, for which—on balance—death seems a small enough price to pay: "Trop heureuse," Julie concludes, "d'acheter au prix de ma vie le droit de t'aimer toujours sans crime, et de te le *dire* encore une fois!"[9] Death reactivates a silenced discourse, giving the lie to a politics of neutrality, to what Mme de Mortsauf will call "ce bonheur négatif."[10]

But if Mme de Mortsauf's last words in the linearity of the novel, that is, in her farewell letter (also communicated to the beloved with the sanction of the husband) reflect (as do those of her predecessors) a measure of optimism about God's mercy and her own righteousness—"Dieu saura mieux que moi si j'ai pratiqué ses saintes lois selon leur esprit. J'ai sans doute chancelé souvent, mais je ne suis point tombée" (*LV,* p. 322)—those last words must be read in counterpoint to her own earlier vocal confession. Unlike Julie—who can write peacefully from her deathbed, "Je me suis longtemps fait illusion. Cette illusion me fut salutaire; elle se détruit au moment que je n'en ai plus besoin. Vous m'avez crue guérie, et j'ai cru l'être. Rendons grâces à celui qui fit durer cette erreur autant qu'elle était utile: qui sait si, me voyant si près de l'abîme, la tête ne m'eût pas tourné" (*NH,* p. 728), thus embracing death as the *garde-fou* that will prevent her from acting out, from acting on what she now knows to be true—Mme de Mortsauf, disillusioned and enlightened, yearns at death's door for a reprieve: "Tout a été mensonge dans ma vie, je les ai comptées depuis quelques jours, ces impostures. Est-il possible que je meure, moi qui n'ai pas vécu? moi qui ne suis jamais allée chercher quelqu'un dans une lande" (*LV*, p. 301). Whereas Julie feels that heaven can deprive her of nothing, since life has nothing left to offer—"Que me restait-il d'utile à tirer de la vie? En me l'ôtant, le ciel ne m'ôte plus rien de regrettable" (*NH*, p. 729)—Mme de Mortsauf wants her heaven on earth: "Une heure de lady Dudley vaut l'éternité" (*LV*, p. 513).

That last equation, however, does not appear in the final version of the novel. It was excised, we are told, to placate Balzac's superegoistic reader Mme de Berny. As Wurmser describes the operation in his *Comédie inhumaine:* "C'est plus que le modèle n'en pourra supporter et, docile, Balzac coupera la parole à Mme de Mortsauf, falsifiera le récit de son agonie."[11] Mme de Mortsauf is not completely silenced, but her bitterness at dying without having known sexual pleasure is attenuated by the deletions; the violence of her desire muted by a periphrastic retreat from the explicit; her feminization euphemized. For what is eliminated in the final version—one hundred or so lines available to the reader in the *choix de variantes* reprinted in the Garnier edition—is nothing less than the heroine's rejection of the underlying assumptions that support and justify the sublimation of female desire. A refutation of the *doxa* is accomplished (not so paradoxically) by the simple assertion of female sexuality (drive) as an operative reality. (I should mention here that even without the actual suppression of the "offensive" material, its potentially subversive content is undercut by the context of enunciation: namely, the act of enunciation itself is placed under the sign of madness. Thus, the abbot in attendance, horrified at Mme de Mortsauf's passionate outburst, exclaims: "Si toutefois elle est complice de ces mouvements de folie!" Félix reassures him: "Non, . . . ce n'est plus elle" [*LV*, p. 302], and she is given opium.)

To return to eu-feminization, following the periphrasis cited earlier—"chercher quelqu'un dans une lande"—Mme de Mortsauf in the unexpurgated edition asks, rhetorically: "A qui mon bonheur aurait-il nui?" (*LV*, p. 513). And she answers, reversing the nineteenth-century novelistic cliché that sexual mothers kill their children, or at least are bad for their health:[12] "Si vous aviez été moins soumis, Félix, je vivrais, je pourrais veiller au bonheur de mes enfants" (*LV*, p. 513). The reversal is radical (even if subsequently repressed) in terms of her own, which is to say Félix's, previous discourse and narrative. Thus before Félix set out for Paris, he had exclaimed: "je donnerais l'éternité pour un seul jour de bonheur, et vous!" "Et moi?" Mme de Mortsauf had then replied to such a sacrilegious trade-off, "Moi! . . . de quel *moi* parlez-vous? Je sens bien des moi en moi! Ces deux enfants . . . sont des *moi*" (*LV*, p. 219). In that (domestic) economy, to give herself over to love for "un seul jour de bonheur" would be to kill her children: "leur mort serait certaine" (*LV*,

p. 220). And she concludes, melodramatically: "Mariez-vous, et laissez-moi mourir!" (*LV*, p. 220).

In the "dedoxatized" variants, however, where another economy is at work, Mme de Mortsauf refutes this notion that a mother and a sexual woman cannot coexist in the same body; she refutes too the notion that spiritual love is superior to, and more complete than, sensual fulfillment: "Le ciel ne descend pas vers nous, ce sont nos sens qui nous conduisent au ciel. Nous ne nous sommes aimés qu'à demi. L'union des âmes ne précède pas l'amour heureux, elle en est la conséquence" (*LV*, p. 513). The potential for scandal in such a transvaluation is easily measured by contrasting this passage with Julie's "feminine" invitation to Saint-Preux: "Viens avouer, même au sein des plaisirs, que c'est de l'union des cœurs qu'ils tirent leur plus grand charme" (*NH*, p. 121); or with Julie's nostalgia for heavenly bliss: "Un feu pur et sacré brûlait nos cœurs; livrés aux erreurs des sens, nous ne sommes plus que des amants vulgaires" (*NH*, p. 76). Mme de Mortsauf's disinvestement of the platonic and the vertical, moreover, though a significant departure from the canon, is not presented as idiopathic dissent. In her "délire sensuel"[13] she diagnoses *all* women: "Toute femme est voilée et tout voile veut être levé; vous avez manqué de hardiesse, une hardiesse m'aurait fait vivre!" (*LV*, p. 513). These assertions, however, have a curious ring to them; they sound both false and familiar. Indeed, Mme de Mortsauf would seem to be mouthing standard, fictional *masculine* discourse, adopting the language of the "vil séducteur." It is in this sense (and in this sense only) that one might agree with M. Le Yaouanc when he claims: "Et l'on a peine à tenir pour *vraisemblables* les regrets, les cris sensuels,—contre lesquels Mme de Berny a protesté, mais surtout pour des raisons morales et esthétiques,— proférés par une femme à l'agonie, épuisée par la faim, torturée par la souf-france."[14] What is not "vraisemblable" is neither the content nor the context of her regret but its language, its intertext. For in making Mme de Mortsauf "more of a woman," Balzac attributes to his heroine the phallocratic discourse of an eighteenth-century roué. It is as though in tampering with the perfect model—Mme de Couaën, for example, who says nothing but whose silence is eloquent—Balzac, at a loss for a countermodel, puts a man in her place. Feminization spirals into virilization.

Mme de Mortsauf's revelation of desire and of the claims of the body is not entirely buried in the variants; it survives in the final edition, primarily in the tempered, less subversive written testament that is her deathbed letter. (This letter is less subversive because of its intertextual resonance: Mme de Mort-sauf's final words, like Julie's, are to be read through the reassuring grid of an older [Ovidian] rhetoric—the art of persuasion a posteriori. Mme de Mortsauf, "cette Didon chrétienne" [*LV*, p. 237], whose husband's name cannot save her, writes with consummate control, the pyre in sight.) The thematic parallels linking Henriette de Mortsauf's letter to Julie de Wolmar's have not been ignored by the critics. And we shall not rehearse them here except to signal an important dyssymmetry. Julie touches but briefly upon the past; she has already rewritten history, that is, the etiology of their passion, for Saint-Preux, in other letters.[15] Her farewell, therefore, is bearer of revelation only in its account of continuing desire. Thus, to the extent that Rousseau's fiction functions as intertext to Balzac's, the letter itself will serve us as an emblematic counter-point.

Mme de Mortsauf frames her final analysis within the parental strategy that had characterized her relationship with Félix. As she describes her status at the time of writing: "Heureusement la femme est morte, la mère seule a survécu" (*LV*, p. 316). This assertion, though confirmed in part by the preceptorial program set forth in the letter, remains open to scrutiny; for the reader will remember that when the letter literally is transmitted to Félix, Mme de Mortsauf says to her husband: "Il est maintenant mon fils d'adoption, voilà tout"; but having thus justified the establishment of a last will and testament for this honorary member of the family, she adds: "Je suis toujours femme" (*LV*, p. 310). The structure of the letter reflects the strain of the screen scenario, the family romance in which she and Félix negotiate their subtextual desires. How do you love me, she had asked in an earlier catechism: "Comme une mère?" To which Félix had replied: "Comme une mère secrètement désirée" (*LV*, p. 189). The letter, then, articulates the split in Mme de Mortsauf's self-concept— mother and woman—and the history of that split as it played itself out between Henriette and her "adopted" son: Félix, addressed in the beginning of the letter as "ami trop aimé" (*LV*, p. 315), and at the end, "cher enfant de mon cœur" (*LV*, p. 321)—problematic object of desire, illicit and legitimized.

Saint-Preux's status as addressee is less ambiguous: he remains "l'ami" throughout; a shift in intensity is marked, however, by the passage from the initial "vous" over whom Julie exercises control to the final "tu," the dangerous relation from whom death alone protects her. By their allocutionary strategies, then, the two letters stand in chiasmatic relation to each other: Julie's is metaphoric and overdetermined by the jubilation of desire sublimated (at last) in death: "Quand tu verras cette lettre, les vers rongeront le visage de ton amante" (*NH*, p. 731); Mme de Mortsauf's is metonymic and structured by the resignation of substitution: "N'ayant pu être à vous, je vous lègue mes pensées et mes devoirs!" (*LV*, p. 321).

Mme de Mortsauf writes as a mother in order to persuade Félix to replace her in that function: "Je mets . . . à profit les dernières heures de mon intelligence pour vous supplier . . . de remplacer auprès de mes enfants le cœur dont vous les aurez privés" (*LV*, p. 316). For this politics of guilt to work, Mme de Mortsauf must demonstrate Félix's responsibility: "Vous allez voir, cher, comment vous avez été la cause première de mes maux" (*LV*, p. 316). There follows her "novel," which as readers we receive as the deconstruction of the text we have just assimilated: Félix's fiction. In this sense we might go so far as to suggest that Félix's story is Mme de Mortsauf's intertext; or, as Peter Brooks comments in his elegant and illuminating Freudian reading of *Le Lys*, "Mme de Mortsauf's ultimate letter which, read only after her death, in fact presents another perspective on the whole story from its beginning, thus creating a true effect of palimpsest."[16]

CHAPTER 1: THE AWAKENING

Jusqu'à cette fête donnée au duc d'Angoulême, la seule à laquelle j'aie assisté [and during which Félix, having been mistaken for a child, responds with equal misprision, embracing Mme de Mortsauf, as he puts it, "comme un enfant qui se jette dans le sein de sa mère" (*LV*, p. 25)] le mariage m'avait laissée dans l'ignorance qui donne à l'âme des jeunes filles la beauté des anges. J'étais mère, il est vrai; mais l'amour ne m'avait point environnée de ses plaisirs permis. Comment suis-je restée ainsi? je n'en sais rien; Je ne sais pas davantage par quelles lois tout en moi fut changé dans un instant . . . vos baisers . . . ont dominé ma vie . . . j'éprouvais une sensation pour laquelle je ne sais le mot dans aucun language. . . . Je compris qu'il existait je ne sais quoi d'inconnu pour moi dans le monde. . . . Je ne me sentis plus mère qu'à demi. . . . Si vous avez oublié ces terribles baisers, moi, je n'ai jamais pu les effacer de mon souvenir: j'en meurs! . . . Ni le temps, ni ma ferme volonté n'ont pu dompter cette impérieuse volupté. [*LV*, pp. 316–18]

This description of passion at first kiss is not without echoes,[17] since it is a conventional concretization of love at first sight. Julie, for example, remembering her first kiss in the grove, underlines the same instantaneity and indelibility: "un instant, un seul instant embrasa [mes sens] d'un feu que rien ne put éteindre; et si ma volonté résistait encore, dès lors mon cœur fut corrompu" (*NH*, p. 321). And in her farewell letter, where the sensual is spiritualized after the fact: "Oui, j'eus beau vouloir étouffer le premier sentiment qui m'a fait vivre, il s'est concentré dans mon cœur" (*NH*, p. 728). For both heroines, passion is an irreversible narrative.

CHAPTER 2: COMBATTING PASSION

For Julie giving in to passion is to be a "bad" daughter; for Mme de Mortsauf, a "bad" mother. And for both, the encounter with the imperatives of sexuality threatens the fundamental equilibrium of the female self, setting in motion a life-and-death struggle. Thus, Julie, reviewing the past, recollects: "Je souhaitai d'être délivrée de la vie . . . mais la cruelle mort m'épargna pour me perdre. Je vous vis, je fus guérie, et je péris" (*NH*, p. 322). She succumbs where Mme de Mortsauf cannot. Although Julie survives this moment of weakness to make a voluntaristic sacrifice of her "bad" self in her marriage to M. de Wolmar, and as Mme de Wolmar—wife and mother—(re)lives at Clarens a struggle roughly parallel to Mme de Mortsauf's martyrdom at Clochegourde, the fact that she has experienced those feelings that are not permitted—to use Mme de Mortsauf's code—constitutes a fundamental discriminant of difference between the two texts. For although in tribute to Félix's "grandeur d'âme" (*LV,* p. 320) during her husband's nearly fatal illness, Henriette contemplates the total gift—"je souhaitais me donner à vous comme une récompense due à tant d'héroisme" (*LV,* p. 320) (a notion to be paired with Julie's famous "pity" for Saint-Preux)—she dismisses, in retrospect, this courtly notion as madness—"cette folie a été courte" (*LV,* p. 320)—and gives herself over to God instead. Félix is to enjoy her sexuality by synecdoche only; he is made a gift of her hair, the price of her resistance: "Il y eut un moment où la lutte fut si terrible que je pleurais pendant toutes les nuits: mes cheveux tombaient. Ceux-là vous les avez eus!" (*LV,* p. 320).[18]

CHAPTER 3: VIRTUE REWARDED?

The trial of Julie's virtue as Mme de Wolmar differs from that of Mme de Mortsauf in several important ways: as we have seen, Julie knows what she is resisting for having experienced it; moreover, Julie and Saint-Preux are partners in innocence, or rather, in sublimation; then too, Julie's second awakening (to "corrupt" desire for Saint-Preux), if we are to believe her account, is *à retardement* and short-lived. Finally, she is spared jealousy, for Saint-Preux is committed to total chastity: "Je n'ai plus rien d'un homme ordinaire" (*NH,* p. 666). Unlike Saint-Preux (and unlike Amaury), Félix believes in an invincible masculine condition: "Nous possédons une puissance qui ne saurait être abdiquée, sous peine de ne plus être hommes. . . . La nature ne peut donc pas être longtemps trompée" (*LV,* p. 249). And he gives in to that nature.

Mme de Mortsauf, for her part, not only does not know what she is missing, so to speak, but she only discovers the depth and violence of her own erotic desire when she learns that Félix has made love to another woman: "Votre amour si naturel pour cette Anglaise m'a révélée des secrets que j'ignorais moi-même" (*LV,* p. 320). In a strangely hysterical process, Mme de Mortsauf becomes sexualized vicariously through the pleasures experienced by Félix with Arabelle. The variants make clear the ideological implications of such an illumination: "Mon don de seconde vue m'a révélé ces plaisirs pour lesquels vous m'avez trahie, vous aviez raison de m'abandonner pour les goûter, c'est toute la vie, et je me suis trompée moi-même, car mes sacrifices ont été faits au monde et non à Dieu! Et l'on me console en me parlant de l'autre vie, mais y a-t-il une autre vie?" (*LV,* p. 513). But this wordly epiphany, this newly found understanding of her own erotic potential, has no place for expression; it takes her on a death trip. Instead of going to Paris and killing the other woman—"Je voulais aller à Paris, j'avais soif de meurtre, je souhaitais la mort de cette femme" (*LV,* p. 320)—she allows herself to die of hunger and thirst; instead of acting on her fantasmatic impulses, she passively acts out; as a self-inflicted punishment for not having given in, she gives up. And like the lady of Pamplona, that renunciation is written in the body.

In both cases the symptoms mime the aporia that generated them: the heroine of *L'Heptaméron,* we are told, suffers from an unabated fever and melancholia, "tellement que les extremitez du corps luy vindrent toutes froides, et au dedans brusloit incessamment" (*H,* p. 217); the heroine of *Le Lys,* as Brooks writes, "the representative of humidity and tenderness, is burning hot, and the water of the Indre . . . only increases her thirst."[19] Feverish and apathetic, hot and cold, the (body) language of the two patients is characterized by the oxymoron of their double bind. Thus, Mme de Mortsauf's physician explains: "Cette affection est produite par l'inertie d'un organe dont le jeu est aussi nécessaire à la vie que celui du cœur. Le chagrin a fait l'office du poignard" (*LV,* p. 288). Medicine cannot cure so fundamental a dysfunction. Upon Félix's reappearance, however, Mme de Mortsauf's appetence miraculously returns: "Ils croient que ma plus vive douleur est la soif," she explains to him, "j'avais soif de toi" (*LV,* p. 301). Her illness, then, which dates from the day she learned of Félix's affair with Lady Dudley, might be diagnosed more interestingly as a form of conversion hysteria,[20] specifically as anorexia nervosa, than as generally interpreted: cancer of the pylorus.[21] Mme de Mortsauf's autopunishment is a violence of privation, a refusal of sustenance engendered by the undeniable proof of her own sexuality.

But if what Henriette learns about herself "kills" her, ultimately it makes her want to live because it revises the scenario, abolishing the distinctions, the dichotomies upon which the logic of the novel (her text) is founded. On the one hand, as Mme de Mortsauf explains in her letter: "Je n'étais pas insensible," and as a result, "nos souffrances d'amour étaient bien cruellement égales" (*LV,* p. 320)—which is to say that desire's challenge to the body existed on both sides, female as well as male. (And here the counterpoint to *La Nouvelle Héloïse* is particularly pertinent: "Sans doute," Julie writes to Saint-Preux, "je sentais pour moi les craintes que je croyais sentir pour vous" [*NH,* p. 729]. In her [hysterically] "feminine" innocence, she had been blind by virtue of what we might call denegation by projection.) On the other hand, Mme de Mortsauf abolishes the difference, removes the *cordon sanitaire* separating Henriette, "l'épouse de l'âme," and Arabelle, "la maîtresse du corps" (*LV,* p. 232). At the end of her life Mme de Mortsauf asserts the identity of contraries: "Arabelle n'avait aucune supériorité sur moi. J'étais aussi une de ces filles de la race déchue que les hommes aiment tant" (*LV,* p. 320). To measure the reversal at work here, one has only to look back to the "official" narrative: "La marquise Dudley m'a sauvée. A elle les souillures, je ne les lui envie point. A moi le glorieux amour des anges!" (*LV,* p. 259).[22] In the end, then, Mme de Mortsauf asserts not only equality in infelicity between her and Félix, but equipollence between the pure and the impure. She would be a fallen angel. Indeed, in her "delirium," in the stage of her acting out that was not corrected for the final edition, Mme de Mortsauf made it quite clear that what she wanted was to be just like Arabelle: "Je veux être aimée, je ferai des folies comme Lady Dudley, j'apprendrai l'anglais pour bien dire: *my dee*" (*LV,* p. 302). Those are the last words of her outburst: she would learn another language, the other woman's maternal language, the better to name the object of desire; to name, and hence make hers, that feeling for which, as she says in her letter, "je ne sais de mot dans aucun langage" (*LV,* p. 317). Having at last given voice to her desire, she adds calmly: "Nous dînerons ensemble" (*LV,* p. 302).

EPILOGUE

Félix refuses this collapsing of polarities and imagines for himself castration, death, and the monastery—in that order. If Henriette were no different from Arabelle, then he was "comme tous les hommes" (*LV,* p. 303) and barred from the sublime. So at the end of his narrative, his love letter to yet another woman, he attempts to reinscribe ideal femininity and define its function: "Auprès des âmes souffrantes et malades, les femmes d'élite ont un rôle sublime à jouer, celui de la sœur de charité qui panse les blessures, celui de la mère qui pardonne à l'enfant" (*LV,* p. 329). His addressee rejects the (de)nomination: "Votre programme est inexécutable. . . . Vous ne connaissez donc pas les femmes?" (*LV,* p. 332). She thus condemns the necrophilic impulse of Félix's fantasy.

The epigraph to *La Nouvelle Héloïse* consists of two lines from Petrarch, translated by Rousseau himself: "Le monde la posséda sans la connaître, / Et moi, je l'ai connue, je reste ici-bas à la pleurer."[23] Félix, who before Henriette's death had wished she had been more like Dante's Francesca than Petrarch's Laura, concludes in mourning: "Seul je devais savoir en son entier la vie de cette grande femme inconnue, seul j'étais dans le secret de ses sentiments, seul j'avais parcouru son âme dans toute son étendue; ni sa mère, ni son père, ni son mari, ni ses enfants ne l'avaient connue" (*LV,* pp. 325–26). Both novels, then, are presented to the reader as acts of revelation, of the lifting of the veil: "Ceci est la vie humaine dans toute sa vérité" (*LV,* p. 326), Félix exclaims upon reading Mme de Mortsauf's parting words. And both novelists choose, as vehicles of that truth, deathbed confessions; specifically, articulations of female desire simultaneously hyperbolized and euphemized. The mourner's consolation is to have unlocked that private door; the artist's, to have created fictions of what was hidden.

But if the ending of *Le Lys* (in exposing as truth the "secret" that merely the fine line of denegation makes "la différence d'une folle et saige dame") not only rewrites the Renaissance tale and the Rousseauian fiction, but by evoking, to use Girard's terms, "la transcendance verticale," conforms in a wider perspective to the rules of closure proper to "vérité romanesque" (the inevitability, as he describes it, of "la banalité absolue de ce qui est essentiel dans la civilisation occidentale"),[24] then what transposition has Balzac wrought upon his intertext? And has he in fact redone (outdone) *Volupté*? I would suggest that Balzac's repenning can be deciphered in an intensity, in an ambivalent impulse (as attested to genetically by the variants) to deconstruct, as Peter Brooks reads it, "the intoxication of virtue" and "much of the Romantic structure of self,"[25] but perhaps more insistently to interrogate the geometry of desire, the ideology of representation that reposes upon the assumption that positive femininity (since Rousseau inseparable from the maternal function) and female sexual desire are incompatible in one and the same body. In this sense, both of the novel's triangles, the courtly love triangle (married woman, older husband, young lover) and its double (chaste woman, fallen woman, divided-heart lover), prove to be "cover" triangles: obviously fragile but no less persistent constructs dependent upon a cultural aporia, and a logic of contraries that might be transcended or superseded. This might be, were it not for the power of the matrix in which they are inscribed: a "doctored" theology in the service of the teleology of fiction; a ritualization of (male) textual desire.

Not surprisingly, Mme de Lafayette came up with another angle on the triangle. Her heroine does not have to die in order to reveal the truth of her desire; she survives her *aveu* to go on at a healthy distance from the court, far from what Girard diagnosed as "la contagion métaphysique."[26]

1. Charles Augustin Sainte-Beuve, *Portraits contemporains* (1882), 2: 256–57; as cited by Moïse Le Yaouanc in his introduction to *Le Lys dans la vallée* (Paris: Garnier, 1966), p. x.

2. Honoré de Balzac, *Lettres à l'étrangère* (Paris: Calmann-Lévy), 1: 186; as cited by Le Yaouanc, p. xi.

3. Ibid.

4. André Vial, "De *Volupté* à *L'Education Sentimentale:* Vie et avatars de thèmes romanesques," *Revue d'histoire littéraire de la France* 57 (1957): 194.

5. M. Le Yaouanc has the longest list of possible suspects (p. xxxv), but he is not alone in his speculations. See, for example, Jacques Borel's chapter (chap. 4) on Mme de Mortsauf in *Le Lys dans la vallée et les sources profondes de la création balzacienne* (Paris: Corti, 1961).

6. Nicole Mozet, preface to *Le Lys dans la vallée* (Paris: Garnier Flammarion, 1972), pp. 21–22; italics mine. The enigma of female sexuality constitutes a problem that of course is not restricted to Balzac's fiction. For a mapping of the territory in Zola, see Naomi Schor's brilliant article "Le Sourire du sphinx: Zola et l'énigme de la féminité," *Romantisme* 13–14 (1976): 183–95.

7. See Maurice Serval's "Autour d'un roman de Balzac: *Le Lys dans la vallée*," *Revue d'histoire littéraire de la France* 33 (October–December 1926): 574–76.

8. Marguerite de Navarre, *L'Heptaméron* (Paris: Garnier, 1967), p. 218; all future references to this work will appear, as *H* followed by the page number, in the text.

9. Jean-Jacques Rousseau, *La Nouvelle Héloïse* (Paris: Garnier, 1960), p. 731; italics mine. All future references to this work will appear, as *NH* followed by the page number, in the text.

10. Honoré de Balzac, *Le Lys dans la vallée*, p. 199. References to *Le Lys* are drawn from the Garnier edition (see note 1); all future references will appear as *LV* followed by the page number in the text itself.

11. André Wurmser, *La Comédie inhumaine* (Paris: Gallimard, 1964), p. 625. See too his remarks on Mme de Mortsauf's sexuality and the variants, pp. 624–25.

12. Schor, p. 189.

13. M. Le Yaouanc in his commentary on variants, p. 446.

14. Ibid., p. lxxiii; italics mine.

15. In particular, the famous letter 18 of part 3, Julie's first letter as Mme de Wolmar.

16. Peter Brooks, "Virtue-Tripping: Notes on *Le Lys dans la vallée*," *Yale French Studies* 50 (1974): 158–59.

17. Of two sorts: Le Yaouanc footnotes the obvious reference to Mme de Rênal p. 317; and Brooks describes the kisses as "a memory trace that she was never able to exorcise," an event that has "determined the rest of her life, all the counter-cathexes she has been obliged to form," pp. 157–58.

18. Perhaps the only use of hair that rivals this unromantic, *unheimlich* one is George Sand's in *Indiana* (where the hair fetishized belongs to a dead woman).

19. Brooks, p. 157.

20. Ibid., pp. 155–56: "Mme de Mortsauf's final illness is patterned as a conversion hysteria, that is, as a flight into illness in which the somatic symptoms are symbolic of the repressed."

21. Le Yaouanc, for example, concludes from the symptoms described (p. 251 n. 2, p. 288 n. 1, and elsewhere) that such is her illness. But his diagnosis is an interpretation and not a textual fact.

22. Brooks, p. 156, commenting on these lines in the context of his analysis of Mme de Mortsauf's conversion hysteria, points out: "But the terms of the denial make it textually inevitable that the repressed will take its revenge"—which it does.

23. Sonnet 294; see title pages of the Garnier edition.

24. René Girard, *Mensonge romantique et vérité romanesque* (Paris: Grasset, 1961), p. 306.

25. Brooks, p. 161.

26. Girard, p. 180.

Death and the Romantic Heroine: Chateaubriand and de Staël

GODELIEVE MERCKEN-SPAAS

Authors have always been fascinated by the theme of death. More than any other aesthetic, the romantic aesthetic has taken death as one of its paradigms. Two representations of death have attained the status of prototypes in the romantic novel: Richardson's *Clarissa* has become the classical example of female death, Goethe's *Werther* of male death. Whereas Clarissa induced many authors to "execute" their heroines, Werther inspired more imitations in actual life than in literature. Even after the appearance of *Werther,* death seems to strike the female character more readily than the male character.

Such narrative preference can only be accounted for by hypothesis. It may well be that the preference follows from social convention or circumstance; women may be particularly likely symbols of sensibility, suffering, and death. Pierre Fauchery writes ironically: "C'est dans la mort que la femme se 'réalise' pleinement."[1] Novelists may also have believed what present-day psychologists tend to assert, that women more than men have erotic associations with death. The preference for the death of the female character may also be dictated by the rhetorical convention according to which writing is a male enterprise. The code to which male and female authors adhere is one in which the speaker and seer are male, whereas the person spoken to or seen is female. Death would more naturally be inflicted upon the other (female) than upon the self (male). It is interesting to note in this perspective that Werther chooses a prompt and solitary death witnessed by nobody, whereas female death scenes in romantic novels are usually observed and described at length.

Such interpretations remain conjectural; only an analysis of numerous treatments of death can validate the hypotheses. It is therefore necessary to single out the narrative function of death, not as a reductive procedure, but as a way of tracing a pattern that may persist in an author's work, in a given historical period, or in an aesthetic mode. As an initial step toward a more general study, I shall investigate four cases of female deaths that occur in novels written between 1800 and 1807, some thirty years after *Werther.* They are Chateaubriand's *Atala* (1801) and *René* (1802), and Mme de Staël's *Delphine* (1802) and *Corinne* (1807).[2] The choice of these four texts is prompted by the belief that culturally close texts yield a well-defined selection in a comparative study of this nature. The four texts are composed by authors socially and intellectually alike, are separated by a very short time span, and offer the interesting symmetry of one male and one female author, each contriving two female deaths.

Each of the four novels is structured around the same narrative nucleus: love, prevented by obstacles, leads to the death of the heroine. The love/death paradigm is undoubtedly one of the most common romantic clichés, a rhetorical convention so widespread and potent that it seems unsuitable as an element of differentiation between authors. Yet, while having recourse to this cliché, each author may create a context for the cliché in which a specific imaginary vision of self and world is expressed. The cliché imposed upon the text then becomes the pretext for the metaphorical expression of the author's fictive self.

Two kinds of narrative variants will be singled out in the four texts. The first kind of variant is common to both authors and can be considered an aesthetic variation of romantic rhetoric; the second represents the distinctive features of an individual author's narrative universe. Even for a corpus limited to four novels, such an assumption may be made without danger as long as any conclusion based on it is considered hypothetical. Examination of further culturally close texts might indeed narrow down the category of distinctive features.

Let us first look at the variants that occur in the work of both authors; these variants link the heroines in crossed pairs. The central couples whose love forms the essence of the narratives are Atala-Chactas (*Atala*) and Amélie-René (*René*) for Chateaubriand, Delphine-Léonce (*Delphine*) and Corinne-Oswald (*Corinne*) for de Staël. Love is a fatal condition for all four couples, a kind of illness for which there is no cure. Love, a passion as absolute as its prohibition, becomes the obstacle to happiness. Self-destruction is then preferable to an existence tormented by the prohibition of what is both necessary and impossible. In order to escape such a destiny, two of the heroines, Amélie and Delphine, enter convents. This step is a symbolic death for Amélie but does not have such absolute power for the latter.[3] Delphine later commits suicide by poisoning herself, as does Chateaubriand's Atala. The identities of Amélie and Delphine are known at the outset of the novels but are renounced by their religious vows. Although they are both orphans, their parentage is not surrounded by enigma; the identities of Atala and Corinne, however, are shrouded in mystery and are not revealed until later in the novels.

Both Atala and Corinne have a stepparent, and both combine two cultures. Atala is the daughter of a white father and an Indian mother; Corinne has an English father and an Italian mother. The same two heroines are further distinguished from Amélie and Delphine by their long death scenes. In both *Atala* and *Corinne,* the deaths of the heroines are a focus on the narrative; the lovers are conscious of the imminent death, and the death scene is recorded at length. The deaths of the other two heroines, Amélie and Delphine, are rendered in an off-stage manner without the lovers' full consciousness of the approaching death.

Chateaubriand and Mme de Staël have made equal use of these narrative details. Each author has one suicide, one heroine who enters a convent, one with a mysterious identity, and one to whom a long death scene is devoted. These narrative characteristics—suicidal death, withdrawal from society, unknown identity, exoticism—taken from the cultural materials available to the authors, can be seen as stylistic variants of the romantic rhetoric. They are likely to recur in romantic texts independently of authorship; they are indicative of a period, not of an individual.

The distinctive narrative features, however, characterize a particular writing and are thus a means of differentiation between authors. Instead of linking authors of a given period, they link texts of an individual author. The distinctive features in this study reveal a fundamental difference between the visionary worlds of de Staël and Chateaubriand rather than showing a parallelism between them. Whereas the stylistic variants linked the fictive heroines of the four novels in crossed pairs, the distinctive narrative features link them in parallel pairs. For the analysis of these features, death is studied within three contexts: death and love, death and discourse, and death and eroticism.

Love in Chateaubriand's novels remains at an embryonic stage. In both *Atala* and *René* the lovers are separated at the outset of love, and death occurs when the lovers have not yet established a relationship. The obstacles preventing love and causing the separation—intrinsic to the love situation itself—are of an absolute nature and connot be overcome. Atala's love for Chactas is prevented by her mother's oath that she remain a virgin; Atala commits suicide when she feels she might give in to her love. Amélie's love for her brother is incestuous, hence forbidden in her eyes; her entering the convent is a symbolic death, which occurs before René himself has become conscious of the ambiguity of his feelings. Both women renounce love, or rather a promise of love, leaving their lovers to indulge in sensuous mourning.

In Mme de Staël's novels, death occurs when love is at its decline. In both *Delphine* and *Corinne* love has failed; the women go through years of separation and agony before they die, and in each case the lover has turned to another woman who is related to the abandoned heroine. The obstacles to love in de Staël are not of an absolute nature; there is not *one* barrier to love but a series of misunderstandings, difficulties, and moral conflicts that arise each time love seems possible. The main obstacle—social convention in *Delphine,* the wish of Oswald's father for his son to marry someone else in *Corinne*—may be overcome, but in each case a choice to the contrary is made.

In Chateaubriand's novels the women bring about the separation, but the narrative focuses on the suffering of the male characters. The situation is reversed in de Staël: the male characters cause the break, and the reader follows closely the distress of the heroines. For both authors, the deaths of the women are directly linked to love, but the deaths of the male characters are not love-related and, if mentioned at all, are only briefly described. Chactas and René are murdered by Indians, Léonce is executed for political reasons, Oswald's death is not mentioned, but he returns to his wife out of "duty and fondness [*attachement*]."

For both authors death frees the women, rather than the men, from a love that seems (Chateaubriand) or has proven (de Staël) impossible. For Chateaubriand the mourning of the male characters becomes an obstinate declaration of love, a denial of the illusory nature of love. The mourning in de Staël's texts is brief: the male characters are made to feel guilty for having been unable to overcome external obstacles to love. The novels close with the knowledge that, even if life went on, love would remain impossible. Where Chateaubriand creates a discourse of illusions, Madame de Staël creates a discourse of disillusion.

Upon dying all four heroines have recourse to verbal language. Unlike Julie in *La Nouvelle Héloïse* or Ellénore in *Adolphe,* whose final messages are written and read after their deaths, Atala, Amélie, Corinne, and Delphine communicate with their lovers at the moment of death. For Chateaubriand's heroines the final discourse is one of confession and separation. The male characters discover the passionate nature of the love of Atala and Amélie. The avowal of the heroines is not only a confession but also an imploring for love. "L'aveu," writes Michel Foucault, "est devenu, en Occident, une des techniques les plus hautement valorisées pour produire le vrai."[4] The confessional discourse of Chateaubriand's heroines is a love-creating device through which the heroines take vengeance for their own deaths. The pain caused by the discourse of love allows the women to contemplate the pain experienced by their lovers. They receive from them a last token of love that gives meaning to their deaths; the pain of dying is lessened by the narcissistic pleasure of the love injury inflicted upon the other. Atala and Amélie die after having instilled in their lovers by means of discourse the feelings that caused their own deaths.

If the confession of love is direct in the final discourse of Chateaubriand's heroines, it is displaced in the final discourse of de Staël's heroines. Delphine, having poisoned herself, accompanies Léonce to his execution and talks incessantly about the religious duty of the dying person. Corinne has a young girl read her last poetic composition, in which she takes leave of Rome, her beloved city. Corinne's procedure creates at the same time a distance and a mediation between the two lovers and allows her to observe Oswald in the audience while remaining unseen herself. Her love for Oswald is transferred to the city of Rome, for which she expresses a vivid passion. This displacement allows the hyperbolic tone of Corinne's poetic discourse.

In *Delphine* the discourse is not transferred to another person, but Delphine herself assumes the discourse of someone else, taking the role of the priest who would accompany the condemned Léonce to his place of execution. Here also a double displacement occurs, the first in the transfer of roles, the second in the fact that Delphine's feelings are displaced onto the religious level. In the final discourse of both novels, the object of love thus undergoes a substitution that reflects the one that occurred in the love relationship itself, where Delphine and Corinne were supplanted by cousin or stepsister. If Madame de Staël's female characters distantiate themselves from the lovers in the final discourse, they repeat verbally the actions of their lovers.

The final discourses of the heroines fulfill the function of a funeral rite for both authors; discourse exorcises death by adding a specular dimension to the act of dying. All four heroines contemplate at the moment of their death the suffering of their lovers and seek their approbation; Chateaubriand's heroines seek confirmation of sentiment, de Staël's heroines admiration of character. Atala's and Amélie's confessions seek reciprocation of love, Delphine's and Corinne's discourses admiration for the intellectual and moral qualities by which they have transcended love.

The final discourses of the heroines also reflect a fundamental difference between the two authors. Highly erotic in Chateaubriand, unerotic in de Staël, the discourses of the dying heroines sustain the specific quality of the love relationship in each author. The heroines of Chateaubriand experience love as a sexual longing, whereas the passion of the Staëlian woman has no sexual overtones.

The erotic desires that accompany the feelings of love in Chateaubriand's heroines awaken the sense of guilt that leads to their deaths. The obstacle to love is a sexual taboo for both heroines—oath of virginity for Atala, incest taboo for Amélie. Atala curses the virginity, which she says devours her life, and Amélie speaks of her "burning chastity": the malediction of virginity weighs upon both heroines. Because of the powerful erotic imagery in *Atala,* I shall give particular attention to this novel in this part of the study.

The imposed virginity is the price paid for Atala's life, which was endangered at birth, and for the sexual transgression of her mother—the premarital intercourse with Atala's father. Atala's passion for Chactas is as absolute as the mother's oath, since only death can preserve her virginity. Virginity also becomes a recurrent motif in Chactas's story of his love for Atala and her love for him. Chactas's vision of virginity is given to him by his mother, according to whom virgins are "des fleurs mystérieuses qu'on trouve dans les lieux solitaires" (p. 80). When he perceives Atala for the first time, he believes she is the virgin sent to prisoners of war to comfort them in their last moments. An ironic reversal occurs here: instead of being the virgin who comforts Chactas in his death, she dies a virgin, and her virginity will be carried as a burden by Chactas throughout his life. Chactas's final blindness suggests an emasculation, a forced virginity that prolongs the one imposed upon Atala. A symbolic and sensuous form of blinding occurred earlier at Atala's funeral when her long hair veiled Chactas's eyes.

Although suffering because of Atala's virginity, Chactas savors virginal eroticism. Having spent a chaste evening with Atala, he describes himself as "plus heureux que la nouvelle épouse qui sent pour la première fois son fruit tressaillir dans son sein" (p. 101). Virginity is linked to both maternity and death in Chactas's narrative. His image of virgins is given by a mother and passed on to mothers. He also relates how virgins of the Indian tribe pass the tomb of a dead child in the hope of becoming pregnant.

Chactas's blending of death, virginity, and motherhood is expressed in the imagery of female breasts. Breasts, or rather the "sein" referring to both breast and womb, are especially powerful in Chactas's erotic vision. He twice gives the picture of a mother burying her son and wetting the tomb with maternal milk. To the mothers of the Indian tribe he describes the situation of man: "L'homme sort de votre sein pour se suspendre à votre mamelle et à votre bouche" (p. 80). Breasts haunt Chactas's sensuous discourse. In a ritual game he notices and reports how the nipples of the breasts of two young girls come in contact. Upon meeting Atala he is struck by the small golden cross "sur son sein," and the final image of the dead Atala is also that of her breasts: "son sein surmonta quelque temps le sol noirci, comme un lis blanc s'élève du milieu d'une sombre argile" (p. 134).

Breasts are the focal point of various relationships: mother/child, woman/lover, and woman/woman; they also symbolize Chactas's sexual desires imprisoned in the fertility/sterility contradiction. The narrative ends with the report of the death of René's great grandchild, conceived, the mother tells the child, by a kiss of his father on her lips. This image of virginal eroticism contrasts with the macabre sterile union of Chactas and Atala. Chactas returns, after his wanderings, to Atala's tomb, unearths what he believes to be her remains and those of the priest buried beside her, places them under his pillow, and dreams of love and virtue. A gruesome virginal triangle it is, in which each person exemplifies a different kind of virginity: male chastity (priest), female virginity (Atala), symbolic male castration (Chactas). Virginal fertility and erotic sterility are dreams that exemplify sexual fantasy in Chateaubriand's novel. The *Atala-René* texts begin and close with two male relationships, those of foster father and foster son (Lopez/Chactas; Chactas/René), relationships that do not imply or require a sexual union and thus do not threaten virginity.

Virginity, an essential feature in Chateaubriand, is unimportant for the Staëlian woman. Virginity is not referred to in the Staëlian novels, where the passion of the heroines has no erotic overtones. Delphine is a widow, and the vows of chastity that she takes later are easily renounced; for Corinne, who has several male friends, virginity is not an issue. Highly eroticized in Chateaubriand, virginity, if at all present, is asexual in de Staël's novels. Neither Delphine nor Corinne suffers from sexual jealousy; both indulge in voyeuristic mourning by seeking to capture the moment when their lovers declare themselves to someone else. Love, then, is a specular system in which the rejected heroines become spectators of love and relate to the lovers in a displaced manner. In de Staël's novels, female desire is not expressed in erotic terms; the claims of the women upon the lovers are of an ethical and not a sexual nature. Although the rejection by the lovers arouses a longing for death in both women, death itself is not associated with Eros as it is by Chateaubriand.

Because the Staëlian couples indulge very little in physical expressions of fondness, distance between the characters is maintained. The various countries in which the characters travel in de Staël's novels increase this distance, whereas traveling in Chateaubriand's works has a centripetal force that abolishes distance and brings the characters of the two novels together. The fictional world of Chateaubriand thus closes in upon itself. The grieving lovers of the two texts meet, the older one becoming the foster father of the younger one. This creates a relationship that transcends time and space and allows individual grief and memory to be shared.

Whether the differences between the authors that have come to light through intertextual parallelism reflect a male-female dichotomy is difficult to assess. For both Chateaubriand and de Staël, sexuality is avoided. The avoidance consists in the characters' abstinence in Chateaubriand, in the absence of references in de Staël. The censorship thus resides with the characters in Chateaubriand, with the author in de Staël. In each author there is a distinct emphasis on the mourning of one sex, female for de Staël, male for Chateaubriand. The gender concurrence of author and character is, I believe, incidental. In both cases the preference for female death prevails.

For Chateaubriand female death has been shown to be a self-protective mechanism through which the male character remains in the stage of autoerotic mourning. For Mme de Staël female death is a last attempt to keep intact the stature of the female self narcissistically constructed throughout the novel. By choosing female death Chateaubriand and de Staël have adhered to romantic aesthetics; the contexts elaborated for this conventional cliché, however, reveal opposing imaginary visions. In their representation of the Eros/Thanatos paradigm, the authors have stressed different elements. Mme de Staël emphasizes the love relationship while systematically desexualizing it; Chateaubriand indulges in the narrative of death to which he assigns strong erotic connotations. The authors, then, differ radically in their treatment of Eros and Thanatos: where de Staël desexualizes Eros, Chateaubriand sexualizes Thanatos.[5]

1. Pierre Fauchery, *La Destinée féminine dans le roman européen du XVIIIe siècle* (Paris: Colin, 1972), p. 790.

2. Chateaubriand, *Atala, René* (Paris: Garnier Flammarion, 1964); Mme de Staël, *Delphine* (Paris: Garnier, n.d.) and *Corinne ou l'Italie* (Paris: Garnier, n.d.). Page references in the text are to this edition of *Atala*.

3. Although Amélie dies later in life of a contagious disease, the vow-taking is considered here as her death scene. The ceremony is described as a death scene by the narrator: Amélie is stretched out as if on a death bed, covered by a funeral shroud, while funeral prayers are said. No such connotations characterize Delphine's vow-taking.

4. Michel Foucault, *Histoire de la sexualité: La volonté de savoir* (Paris: Gallimard, 1976), p. 79.

5. On the desexualization of Eros and the sexualization of Thanatos, see Gilles Deleuze, *Présentation de Sacher Masoch* (Paris: Editions de Minuit, 1967).

Don Juan and His Fallen Angel:
Images of Women in the Literature of the 1830s

MARTHA N. MOSS

The decade between 1830 and 1840 produced a series of novels remarkably similar in theme, structure, and characterization. All of the novels, which include some of the best of the nineteenth century, are variations on the structure of the *Bildungsroman,* and all owe some debt to that earlier (1816) novel of cruel and inconstant youth, Constant's *Adolphe.* The parallels between the bored, weak, and vacillating Adolphe, seeking emotional and sexual fulfillment always at the expense of others, and the literary heroes of that fecund decade are manifold. Julien Sorel in 1830, Balzac's Gaston de Nueil and Félix de Vandenesse in 1832 and 1836, Amaury in the 1834 publication of *Volupté,* and Musset's Octave in 1836 all suffer the dilemma of young men soon to embark upon careers made meaningless by the end of the Napoleonic Wars. These dispirited and effete young heroes seek solace in society and society women for the disappointments of their professional lives, and from this search comes a second and parallel structure, which draws upon the myth of the archetypal seducer Don Juan and the fallen angel who attempts to save his soul. The struggle between the young seducer and the virtuous woman who resists his advances (the traditional Don Juan–Donna Elvire story) permeates all of these novels and sheds light in particular on the role women play in romantic literature.

The preoccupation with Don Juan in the novels of the 1830s, strangely enough, tells us more about the women he would seduce than it does about the legendary character himself. For one thing, the Don Juan figure that fascinated the romantics is quite different from the mythic rebel-son archetype of the seventeenth and eighteenth centuries. Indeed, the triumph of romanticism in the early decades of the nineteenth century brought with it a veritable metamorphosis of the Don Juan legend. Lost is the implacable seducer—the son who deliberately and blindly disobeys his father's wise counsel—and in his place is a far more complex character who merits at least a margin of our sympathy. There are certainly a variety of reasons for the change in the portrayal of Don Juan in romantic literature, but perhaps the most compelling of these is the weakening of the influence of the Catholic church after the French Revolution.

With the disappearance of sin as a powerful imaginative conception came an experimentation with the ingredients of the Don Juan legend as it had been conceived by earlier writers. Such experimentation had already deeply influenced the English romantics (I am of course thinking of Byron's *Don Juan* in particular), and the result was that by the 1830s in France the Don Juan figure was less dangerous quite simply because it was no longer surrounded by an atmosphere of sin and evil. The romantics added dimensions to the mythic Don Juan that, if only because there seem to be strata of his personality never before explored, render his characterization more intricate. He is still a seducer of women, obviously—restless seduction and Don Juanism are practically synonymous—but his motives are now more diverse. He is linked, for example, with the general malaise of romanticism; the romantic hero's disappointed dreams are not far different from Don Juan's repeated disappointments with women. The romanticized Don Juan's abandonment of women is merely an extension of his search for an ideal of womanhood that simply cannot be satisfied by any one person. If he yearns for the unattainable, it is because his dreams dazzle him and reality is too cruel a disappointment. If he is bored by too constant an association with a single woman, it is because all of romanticism's young heroes suffer from the terrible ennui that cursed their generation. Like Mérimée's Darcy of *La Double Méprise,* Julien Sorel, Gaston de Nueil, Amaury, and Octave all set out to seduce their victims because they simply have no better way to occupy their time. The initial conquest is later treated with equal dispassion: "N'ai-je manqué à rien de ce que je me dois à moi-même?" Julien asks himself. "Ai-je bien joué mon rôle?"[1] Amaury too speaks only in terms of his own ego when he describes "L'orgueil d'émouvoir ainsi deux êtres à la fois, de faire dépendre peut-être deux bonheurs de mon seul caprice."[2] Too, the women are attractive; as Adolphe says of Ellénore: "[elle] me parut une conquête digne de moi."[3]

But what of this worthy conquest? In the legend of Don Juan, after countless seductions, after the murder of the father of one of his victims, God sends to earth an angel in the form of a woman to convert the infamous seducer. The angel falls in love with Don Juan, but his love for her does not save him. Instead, the angel loses her divine inspiration and is finally abandoned by God. As George Sand describes the tragic conclusion of the Don Juan legend in *Lélia,* "il y eut au ciel un ange de moins, et dans l'enfer un démon de plus."[4]

Just as many of romanticism's young heroes are characterized in terms of an archetypal Don Juan, so too does the romantic heroine resemble in many respects Don Juan's fallen angel. Mme de Rênal in *Le Rouge et le noir,* Henriette de Mortsauf in *Le Lys dans la vallée,* Claire de Beauséant in *La Femme abandonnée,* Mme de Couaën in *Volupté,* and Musset's Brigitte of *La Confession d'un enfant du siècle* are all attracted to their restless seducers in part at least because they feel that their lovers must be saved from their own destructiveness. The penchant of "good" women for attractive men with reputations is a commonplace, and certainly the fallen angels of romantic literature suffer from that conceit. But the Don Juan aspects of the romantic hero also challenge the heroine's urge to possession. The fallen angel wishes to be the successful rival of her sisters, to be the one woman to possess the eternal seducer, to incorporate him in herself, and to satisfy his passion as no other woman can.

The parallels between these representative heroines of the novels of the 1830s are as numerous as the similarities between the weak and ambitious Don Juan figures who populate romantic literature. Like the fallen angel of the myth, these young heroines all suffer at the hands of the young men who would seduce them. They suffer in part at least because they are not free. They are either married or, like Musset's Brigitte, determined to remain free of romantic involvement. Obviously they do not submit easily to seduction despite the fact that they are married to men who are much older than they and either cruel or mad (and sometimes both, as is the case with M. de Mortsauf in *Le Lys dans la vallée*). Like Constant's Ellénore, Brigitte, Claire de Beauséant, and Henriette de Mortsauf all acknowledge a growing passion in their would-be seducers, and all manifest a desire to remain free of romantic entanglement. Scruples crumble, nevertheless, despite enormous guilt, and, predictably, all of the heroines fall in love with their young lovers. Structurally, then, the novels follow a similar line of action: an unattainable older woman is repeatedly besieged by a young and passionate lover, she is eventually seduced, he in turn becomes interested in other women, she regrets her submission and is eventually destroyed by it.

But the parallels between these fallen angels go far beyond their situation vis-à-vis the men they love and indeed tell us a great deal about the romantics' feminine ideal, for if not all of these women share every characteristic of their sisters, they are in so many respects similar that they provide patterns by which we may understand them all. Without exception they are women who are older than their lovers; they are "femmes de trente ans" who have experienced life and its vicissitudes if not love and passion. As a matter of fact, they are all utterly inexperienced in matters of physical love and, as a result, are as naïve as children. Félix de Vandenesse insists that he has never known anyone "de plus jeune fille qu'[Henriette],"[5] and Mme de Rênal is described in the same terms in *Le Rouge et le noir*. Her laughter reflects the gaiety of a young girl, and Julien insists several times that she is a woman of no more than twenty in demeanor and behavior.[6]

Despite their youthful appearance and naïveté, these devoted women exhibit a strong maternal instinct; and most are, in fact (with Brigitte offering the only exception), conscientious mothers passionately fond of their children. Most are introduced to the reader surrounded, in somewhat clichéd fashion, by either children or animals, and maternal passion indeed plays a dominant role in these novels of love and seduction. Both Henriette de Mortsauf and Mme de Couaën, for example, believe that their children will suffer for their inconstancy. They are, in fact, punished through their children, for Henriette's son nearly dies and Mme de Couaën loses her child by what she believes to be divine retribution. Mme de Rênal swears that she will give up Julien if her ill child is spared, and she is indeed freed from further torment by Julien's departure for Paris. Brigitte does not have children of her own, but she is a mother figure for the capricious Octave; she insists that God "m'a chargé de veiller sur toi comme une mère."[7]

This stability, this predictability (and one might well wish for even one moment's capriciousness in these devoted women) is accompanied by a certain wise intuition but no formal education. These angelic characters never compete intellectually with their lovers, and indeed their ignorance is stressed in order to enhance their femininity. Like Ellénore, who is described as possessing "un esprit ordinaire,"[8] Madame de Rênal has forgotten everything she learned as a child in a convent and has replaced that void with nothing ("et elle finit par ne rien savoir," as Stendhal reminds us).[9] Mme de Couaën has had no formal training, and the inherent intelligence of Henriette de Mortsauf and Brigitte is dismissed in favor of their simple and kind goodness. All of these ladies are wise by intuition, but none possesses the native ability or education to survive outside of the sphere of family and home.

Nevertheless, these romantic heroines must compete (and compete outside of their own spheres) for their seducer's love and attention. Like the restless Adolphe, whose boredom with Ellénore anticipates romanticism's ennui a decade later, Félix de Vandenesse, Julien Sorel, Octave, Gaston de Nueil, and Sainte-Beuve's Amaury are all tempted, as young Don Juans, by women radically different from their chaste mistresses. These tempting rivals are women as capricious as the romantic heroines are faithful, as sexually provocative as the angels are chaste, as independent and masculine as their counterparts are passive and feminine. They are represented by Lady Dudley in *Le Lys dans la vallée,* by Mathilde de la Mole in *Le Rouge et le noir,* and by Octave's first mistress and the redoubtable courtesan Marco in *La Confession d'un enfant du siècle.* Even the mysterious Mme R in *Volupté* incorporates the characteristics of these capricious rivals and represents in the novel an alternative to Mme de Couaën's angelic goodness.

The portrayal of these *femmes-démons* of romantic literature is nearly as consistent as the depiction of the fallen angels with whom they compete. Perhaps no novelist captures the cold cruelty of these provocative courtesans more effectively than does Musset with his portrait of the dreadful Marco in *La Confession.* In an initial episode of the novel, after an evening of dissipation, Marco seduces Octave only to explain later that her mother has just died that morning. Even if Lady Dudley hardly matches Marco in cold insensibility, she is described in surprisingly similar terms. Unlike the open, utterly transparent Henriette, Arabelle Dudley is said to possess "un masque impénétrable qu'elle met et qu'elle ôte flegmatiquement."[10] She is a woman of steel; her strength is such that she fears no man in combat, and her heart is unbreakable. At one point, near the conclusion of the novel, Félix insults her by recounting an incident that should strike her like a knife thrust to the heart, except that, as he explains, the weapon would shatter upon contact with so hard an object.

In contrast to Mme de Couaën's utter innocence and kind heart, Mme R is capricious, jealous, impenetrable, "un malicieux sphinx de bronze," as Amaury describes her.[11] Mathilde de la Mole functions in similar fashion as the antithesis of Mme de Rênal in *Le Rouge et le noir*. Not only is she utterly capricious and cold-hearted, she is also decidedly masculine. Unlike Mme de Rênal, whose voice is angelic, Mathilde's voice "n'a rien de féminin."[12] She shuns "la délicatesse féminine"; her vast intelligence should have been at the disposal of the opposite sex. She should have been a man, as Julien himself observes.[13]

Ironically, these cold-hearted women succeed in seducing the young men who have been guided to manhood by their faithful mistresses. The sacrifice of reputation, of health, of children, indeed, of life itself for the young Don Juans of romantic literature is fruitless. At the dénouement of each one of these fine novels, each angel has indeed fallen.

But the chaste and pure women of these tragic love stories share a final ironic triumph, for their young Don Juans realize, too late, the consequences of their brutal treatment and the value of what they have lost. Unlike their male counterparts and their female rivals, the fallen angels are never treated with irony. Stendhal is of course repeatedly ironic about Julien; he mockingly complains at one point that "Julien s'obstinait à jouer le rôle d'un don Juan," despite his lack of experience with women, for example.[14] But the angelic women of romantic literature are never subjected to ironic comment by their creators; rather, they are presented as ideals. They are open, transparent characters who know themselves and who function, as John Mitchell says of Mme de Rênal, as the "principal repository of the author's values."[15] They come as close to representing a vision of idealized womanhood as can be found in romantic literature.

But what are we to say of this romantic ideal that seeks to create a dichotomy between sensitivity and intelligence, between the pure and the sexual, the masculine and the feminine? The virtues ascribed to the feminine ideal are uniform and consistent in these representative romantic novels, for in all of them the women are valued only because of their sensitivity, their resignation, their very martyrdom. Even the heroines of the great adventure novels of the decade, women like Esmeralda of Hugo's *Notre Dame de Paris* and Pauline in Dumas's 1838 historical novel of the same name, exhibit similar tendencies toward resignation and passivity.[16] Félix de Vandenesse himself comments on the problem when he complains that he is the victim of two irreconcilable passions. "J'aimais un ange et un démon," he says, "deux femmes également belles, parées l'une de toutes les vertus que nous meurtrissons en haine de nos imperfections, l'autre de tous les vices que nous déifions par égoïsme."[17] It would seem that the split between the *femme-ange/femme-démon* is everywhere in this literature of the 1830s; and the whole woman, independent and educated, sensitive and creative, strong and tender, is but too rarely to be found.

There is of course one major novelist of the decade who stands utterly opposed to the depiction of feminine protagonists as fallen angels. George Sand's Lélia addresses the question directly in one of the most bitter monologues concerning male-female relations ever written—certainly there is nothing in the decade of the 1830s to rival its black despair and blanket condemnation of romanticism's Don Juans. Sand's criticism is in fact further intensified by the parallels between her novel of love's inconstancies and the psychological novels of the decade. Like romanticism's fallen angels, Lélia is ten years older than the young poet Sténio who would seduce her; like the inconstant heroes of the decade, Sténio is tempted and seduced by Lélia's sister and antithesis, Pulchérie, who incarnates sensual love and carnal enjoyment. But the parallels stop there, for Lélia is as different from the martyred romantic heroines of her generation as Sand could portray her. Lélia's austere and tormented asceticism has nothing in common with the affectionate sensibility of her sisters, and yet she understands, with the wisdom of an outsider, the forces that bind them to their faithless lovers. Society demands that a woman's existence be absorbed by the man she loves. Lélia's response is simply that she wants her own existence: "moi, je voulais exister."[18] To do so she feels that she must expose the endless cycle of seduction that characterizes male-female relations, for her time and for all time. She sees clearly that Don Juan has become a symbol, a divinity, in fact, and that "les hommes plaisent aux femmes en ressemblant à Don Juan."[19] How many women, she wonders, have been destroyed by their mindless admiration for this personification of vice, this hideous phantom adorned with poetry and grandeur? For women, she complains, imagine themselves to be the angels sent from heaven to save Don Juan. Tragically, like the fallen angel of the legend, they fail to convert the seducer and are lost with him. Lélia's ironic command, "faites-vous victimes, faites-vous esclaves, faites-vous femmes," illustrates the depth of her bitterness toward the fallen angels of romantic literature.[20]

The alternatives to the martyr's role that Sand proposes in *Lélia* relate principally to feminine awareness and education. She counsels against endless patience and resignation, for example, just as she warns against timidity and irresolution: "Oubliez don Juan, prouvez-lui que vous êtes aussi forte, aussi légère que lui."[21] Lélia's role as teacher and prophet at the conclusion of the novel provides Sand an opportunity to expose her views on female education but unhappily does little to enhance the value of the novel as literature.

Indiana suffers from something of the same problem, but it is far less a philosophical treatise than is *Lélia,* though it espouses the same radical view of women as whole and independent creatures. Musset's insistence that the novel is not a treatise against marriage but is rather a profound analysis of seduction, "de l'inconstant,"[22] is confirmed by Sand's letter to the poet in which she complains that her Raymon is only a miserable travesty of the great Don Juan figure Musset creates so effortlessly.[23] Raymon de Ramière is indeed a ruthlessly inconstant young man who finds a close brother in Merimée's Darcy of *La Double Méprise;* and Indiana, as his intended victim, seems initially to resemble the martyred Henriette de Mortsauf, Mme de Rênal, and Mme de Couaën. But she does indeed turn out to be a singularly different kind of woman. As Sand's Edmée de Mauprat would do in 1837, Indiana, at the dawn of the decade, insists on her autonomy to her tyrannical husband. "I know that I am the slave and you the master," she says. "Vous pouvez lier mon corps, garrotter mes mains, gouverner mes actions. Vous avez le droit du plus fort, et la société vous le confirme; mais sur ma volonté, monsieur, vous ne pouvez rien, Dieu seul peut la courber et la réduire."[24] Imagine such words from Henriette, who was incapable of addressing the mildest reproach to her despotic husband! Indiana in turn censures Raymon for his belief that men are the masters of the world: "je crois que vous n'en êtes que les tyrans."[25] And her ideas on the reciprocity of love are revolutionary for the decade. Raymon must be ready to sacrifice all—fortune, reputation, duty, career, principles, and family. "Tout" she says firmly, "parce que je mettrai le même dévouement dans la balance et que je la veux égale."[26] When Indiana finds in Sir Ralph the man who can both understand her and support her, she agrees to live with him as his wife, although the two of them never have children. It may be that Sand denied Indiana maternity in order to underscore her repudiation of the values embodied in the romantic heroines of the decade.

Sand indeed spoke while others remained silent. But her female characters are too few, her novels too uneven, her ideas too untested to have exercised much influence on that prolific decade's depiction of women in literature. Sand's condemnation of the Don Juan archetype and the fallen angel who abortively attempts his salvation fell on barren ground.

The limitations of the romantic view of women, with Sand as the exception, are illustrated by the narrow oppositions forced upon female characters in these novels of the 1830s. When we contrast the *femme-ange* and the *femme-démon,* we see that any "masculine" strength or aggressiveness, any inclination toward behavior independent of the domestic environs, makes women little more than prostitutes. Women must be either naïve or worldly, either tender or callous, either wife or whore, either maternal or manipulative, either angel or demon.

The repeated appearance of the Don Juan motif in romantic literature verifies this dualistic view of women, for the choice of the young hero of the decade of the 1830s was, with few exceptions, the prostitute who corrupted him or the angel who failed to save him.

1. Stendhal, *Le Rouge et le noir* (Paris: Garnier, 1961), p. 87.

2. Charles-Augustin Sainte-Beuve, *Volupté* (Paris: Garnier-Flammarion, 1969), p. 193.

3. Benjamin Constant, *Adolphe* (Paris: Garnier-Flammarion, 1965), p. 67.

4. George Sand, *Lélia*, 2 vols. (Paris: Calmann Levy, 1891), 2:99.

5. Honoré de Balzac, *Le Lys dans la vallée* (Paris: Seuil, 1966) 6:308.

6. Stendhal, p. 29.

7. Alfred de Musset, *La Confession d'un enfant du siècle* (Paris: Gallimard, 1973), p. 219.

8. Constant, p. 65. See also Han Verhoeff, *"Adolphe" et Constant, une étude psychocritique* (Paris: Klincksieck, 1976), pp. 45–53.

9. Stendhal, p. 36.

10. Balzac, p. 378.

11. Sainte-Beuve, p. 240.

12. Stendhal, p. 281.

13. Ibid., p. 488.

14. Ibid., p. 83.

15. John Mitchell, *Stendhal: "Le Rouge et le noir"* (London: Edward Arnold, 1973), p. 52.

16. Théophile Gautier's *Mademoiselle de Maupin* appeared during the decade of the 1830s, in 1835 to be exact (Paris: Garnier, 1966); and the heroine of that amusing novel of mistaken identity and transvesticism does present an alternative of sorts to the romantic heroine of the nineteenth century. The explicit condemnation of feminine timidity and resignation echoes George Sand, but essentially the novel has little in common with the psychological novels of the decade, which are structured upon the legend of Don Juan and his fallen angel. The novel's apology for sensual enjoyment sets it apart from those novels in which sensual and elicit love cause only torment and pain, and in any case the bisexuality of Mlle de Maupin creates a character utterly different from the romantic heroine who suffers only as a result of her passion for one inconstant man. "En vérité," says Mlle de Maupin, "ni l'un ni l'autre de ces deux sexes n'est le mien; je n'ai ni la soumission imbécile, ni la timidité, ni les petitesses de la femme; je n'ai pas les vices des hommes, leur dégoûtante crapule et leurs penchants brutaux: je suis d'un troisième sexe à part qui n'a pas encore de nom" (p. 352).

17. Balzac, p. 377.

18. Sand, *Lélia,* 2:122.

19. Ibid., p. 99.

20. Ibid., p. 104.

21. Ibid., p. 106.

22. George Sand, *Indiana* (Paris: Garnier, 1965), p. 86.

23. Ibid., p. 86.

24. Ibid., p. 225.

25. Ibid., p. 242.

26. Ibid., p. 136.

PART TWO : TEXT

Ruminations on Stendhal's Epigraphs

ALBERT SONNENFELD

An arid statistical survey would soon show that in *Armance* Stendhal inserts ten epigraphs with texts from Shakespeare and two only from Byron, whereas in *Le Rouge et le noir* he turns seven times to Byron's *Don Juan* and only four to Shakespeare; and that every time he puts the name of Schiller after an epigraph, Stendhal himself seems to be the author! I shall here avoid such magisterial precision in favor of a more properly Stendhalian (that is to say, playful) approach. Our author himself expressed a modest view of the function of the epigraph when he noted in May 1830:

> Je cherche des épigraphes le 25 mai 1830 en corrigeant la 9e feuille de Julien.
> L'épigraphe doit augmenter la sensation, l'émotion du lecteur, si émotion il peut y avoir et non plus présenter un jugement plus ou moins philosophique sur la situation.[1]

Should we accept the author's reticence? Why bother researching this old novelistic convention? But then why did Stendhal himself bother?

An epigraph in *Le Rouge et le noir,* one attributed by Stendhal to Malagrida, a Portuguese Jesuit, *and* to Talleyrand, gives an initial clue: "La parole a été donnée à l'homme pour cacher sa pensée." Now this sentence had already appeared in *Armance* (chap. 25). Thrice quoted, could these words in fact hide something as well? We know, of course, that Octave, in *Armance,* had a secret—his impotence, which is never mentioned in the text. Julien Sorel also has numerous secrets: his love for Napoleon, his atheism (he knows the part of Tartuffe by heart [p. 523]), his symbolic marriage to Mathilde (Cimarosa's opera *Il Matrimonio segreto* is mentioned several times), and another secret, one that is fictional, one his dreams have invented—the "secret" of his birth. Julien would give everything to have been the illegitimate son of a squire or of a man of noble blood, instead of the "offspring of a woodcutter" (M. de Rênal's disdainful words). Julien's story can (if we remember Freud's theory of the "family romance") easily be read as his quest for a secret, substitute father: the surgeon-major, Abbé Chélan, Abbé Pirard, Comte Altamira, the Marquis de la Mole, and even (and perhaps, above all) M. de Rênal, all are father figures, Julien's imaginary and secret fathers.[2] The secret surfaces only when dream has apparently (and for a brief moment) become reality: Julien has been named Lieutenant de la Vernaye; rumors concerning his "secret" noble origins circulate; his clandestine "wife" Mathilde is expecting his child (he is convinced it will be a boy), and Julien exults: "mon roman est fini, et à moi seul tout le mérite" (p. 637). But his "novel" is not complete—he will race off to attempt to kill Mme de Rênal; the novelist controls the novel; it is he who commands "the word," even when his characters are "speaking." What secrets are hidden in *his* words? Does he express himself to hide, instead of to reveal?

When an author chooses an epigraph, he provisionally becomes a reader; he instinctively satisfies the Baudelairean criterion for the modern poet, one who is simultaneously creator and critic, writer and reader. And when Stendhal notes, in 1830, that he is selecting epigraphs while correcting proofs, he is at that moment the interpreter of his own text. His choice of epigraphs constitutes an essential interpretative gesture. The words that disguise the thoughts, his words, yield to the words of another, which, in contrast, unveil and reveal, since a reader decodes while an author encodes. The author's mask falls at times, since the choice of an epigraph can give us, the readers of the author-as-reader, a subtle signal for possible interpretations of Stendhal's text. In choosing an epigraph Stendhal somehow seeks to appropriate some of our freedom as readers, interpreters, and critics by revealing himself as the reader of another's text, the text from which the epigraph was drawn.

The importance Stendhal attaches to reading is manifested by a network of associations in *Le Rouge et le noir*. If Stendhal is the reader of the epigraphs to be selected, Julien Sorel is equally avid as reader; he quotes rigorously selected passages from the *Mémorial de Sainte-Hélène,* from Rousseau's *Confessions* and *La Nouvelle Héloïse,* from *Tartuffe* (pp. 523, 539, 678). When we first encounter him, he is sitting on a roof reading that *Mémorial* which, in its Napoleonic gospel, has replaced the Bible, which Julien can quote without really having read: "Mon métier est de faire réciter des leçons et d'en réciter moi-même" (p. 347). Both Stendhal and Julien are thus inveterate quoters, but with this difference: whereas Julien has a dazzling memory and quotes without error, Stendhal offers us quotations quite often deliberately distorted or else invents a quotation or attribution in order to send out a purposely confused but nonetheless perceptible signal.

When Mme de Rênal sees Julien Sorel for the first time (chap. 6, "L'Ennui"), the famous meeting takes place under the sign of an equally famous epigraph: "Non so più, cosa son / Cosa facio," identified laconically as "Mozart (*Figaro*)." This reduced title, *Figaro,* also constitutes a quotation and serves to remind us that Julien, scaler of ladders, seeks to reach the summit of society while remaining free to criticize its foibles exactly like Figaro, who represents the now upwardly mobile people and its entrepreneurial energies and who allows himself the freedom to denounce the aristocracy that has earned its eminence by merely taking the trouble to be born. If Figaro is a prophet of the Revolution, Julien is perceived as the Danton of a future uprising by the monarchists in the Hôtel de la Mole. But let us not forget that the epigraph is taken from an aria sung by Cherubino in the first act of the opera, not from the play. In it he laments his inability to resist the call of love. Julien, in turn, cannot help but win the approval of the local girls, thanks to his "pretty face" ("la jolie figure" [p. 231]). Cherubino will know an impossible love for a married woman, the countess; Julien will love Mme de Rênal, a married woman and mother. But the true signal sent by the epigraph is more subtle still. Cherubino, whose name embodies his juvenile features, is the first page of Count Almaviva, but his part is always sung by a mezzo-soprano. In act 2 the mezzo-page is to replace Susanna at her nocturnal rendezvous with the count; to assume a female disguise in act 3, Barberina, trying to rescue Cherubino from the threat of exile in the army, puts him into a peasant woman's costume. In other words, the pattern is of a certain sexual ambivalence, which redirects our reader's eye toward other signals in the text. Thus, Julien is described with tears in his eyes ("les larmes aux yeux" [p. 230]), with a young girl's face ("cette figure de jeune fille, si pâle et si douce" [p. 237]), as weak in appearance ("faible en apparence"), and as a nineteen-year-old who looks more like seventeen (p. 239). Mme de Rênal at first thinks that Julien is a young girl in disguise ("une jeune fille déguisée"), with his young girl's blushing timidity ("son air timide d'une jeune fille qui rougit" [p. 240]); she is struck by his beauty ("son extrême beauté"), and the almost feminine cast of his features ("la forme presque féminine de ses traits" [p. 242]) makes her feel younger as she momentarily forgets the vulgar manners of M. de Rênal. Julien has no mother, and the sexual ambivalence signaled by the epigraph's associations indicates that at Verrières at least he is still at the androgynous Oedipal stage. Beaten repeatedly by his brothers and by his father, Julien fails in the world of men: he is seeking maternal love—he finds a "mother" in Mme de Rênal, who responds in kind when she seeks to escape adultery by transforming her passion into a desexualized love:

> Souvent au milieu du récit de quelque friponnerie savante . . . l'esprit de madame de Rênal s'égarait tout à coup jusqu'au délire. Julien avait besoin de la gronder, elle se permettait avec lui les mêmes gestes intimes qu'avec ses enfants. C'est qu'il y avait des jours où elle avait l'illusion de l'aimer comme son enfant. Sans cesse n'avait-elle pas à répondre à ses questions naïves sur mille choses simples qu'un enfant bien né n'ignore pas à quinze ans? Un instant après, elle l'admirait comme son maître. Son génie allait jusqu'à l'effrayer; elle croyait apercevoir plus nettement chaque jour le grand homme futur dans ce jeune abbé. Elle le voyait pape, elle le voyait premier ministre comme Richelieu.—Vivrai-je assez pour te voir dans ta gloire? disait-elle à Julien, la place est faite pour un grand homme; la monarchie, la religion en ont besoin. [Pp. 305–6]

Psychoanalysis has taught us that the archetypal family structure in psychically caused homosexuality is the matriarchy—we find the pattern in *Armance*, where Octave's mother and fiancée are in league against him; we also find it in the lives (and works) of Gide and Proust. It is that matriarchy that the mother-less Julien is seeking with Mme de Rênal—he seeks and finds that mother unconsciously, of course, but he will remain faithful to the image even at the apogee of his social triumph: when, thanks to the Marquis de la Mole, he has changed name and identity in becoming M. de la Vernaye (p. 637), when he has become Mathilde's fiancé and is about to become a father himself. He forces the marquis to look into his credentials and his past by writing to Mme de Rênal: Julien is thus himself responsible for his fall. And why? Because he was tired of heroism ("fatigué d'héroisme" [p. 663]), tired of the virile world of Mathilde with her dreams of swords, her Salomé-like obsessions that make her want to relive the decapitation of her ancestor Boniface. Julien shoots twice at Mme de Rênal, not to punish her, not through jealousy, but so that *he* can be punished and be forever united with his ideal Jocasta in death.

Another epigraph provides further signals. At the opening of the chapter describing their first night of love, we read:

> Amour en latin faict amor
> Or donc provient d'amour la mort,
> Et, par avant, soulcy qui mord,
> Deuil, plours, pieges, forfaix, remords.
>
> [P. 294]

For it is in prison, as Victor Brombert has demonstrated,[3] that Julien finds happiness of a sort (just like Fabrice in *La Chartreuse*): "Jamais il ne pensait à ses succès de Paris; il en était ennuyé" (p. 662). He wants to rid himself of Mathilde, of his father, of the whole virile world. As for his own as yet unborn son, he states his cruel but psychologically necessary plans to Mathilde herself: "Mettez votre enfant en nourrice à Verrières, madame de Rênal surveillera la nourrice" (p. 663). This "son" will obtain what Julien wanted, that mother he was deprived of, for Julien will proclaim his secret to the very tribunal that will condemn him to death: "Madame de Rênal avait été pour moi comme une mère" (p. 672). But the real psychic crime, his consummation of Oedipal desire, will not thus be admitted; Julien uses words to hide his thoughts, when he tells the jury he is Figaro, not Cherubino: "punir en moi et décourager à jamais cette classe de jeunes gens qui, nés dans une classe inférieure et en quelque sorte opprimés par la pauvreté, ont le bonheur de se procurer une bonne éducation, et l'audace de se mêler à ce que l'orgueil des gens riches appelle la société" (pp. 664–75). Julien and Mme de Rênal finish operatically, in ecstatic stichomythia: "Who could have thought it true!" ("Qui me l'eût dit!"); "never had they been so happy" ("jamais il n'auraient été si heureux" [p. 681]). And the novel ends with a sentence that in the perspective of the epigraph from Figaro strikes me as eminently equivocal: "trois jours après Julien, elle mourut en embrassant ses enfants" (p. 697).

One might be tempted to protest at thus being steered along a map of misreading, that this network of sexual ambivalence hardly depends on the epigraph. But the signals both sent and screened by "Non so più, cosa son / Cosa facio" have not yet been entirely decoded. Like his hero Julien, Stendhal knew all too well the *Confessions* of Rousseau and the story of Mme de Warens. And Henry Brulard (that is to say, Henri Beyle [Stendhal]) lived that story: "Ma mère, Madame Henriette Gagnon, était une femme charmante et j'étais amoureux de ma mère. . . . Je voulais couvrir ma mère de baisers et qu'il n'y eût pas de vêtements. Elle m'aimait à la passion et m'embrassait souvent, je lui rendais ses baisers avec un tel feu qu'elle était souvent obligée de s'en aller. J'abhorrais mon père quand il venait interrompre nos baisers."[4] Let us not forget that Julien Sorel had no mother (Henry Brulard lost his when he was seven). Julien found a mother in Mme de Rênal; he covered her with kisses and without clothes. But let us also not forget that the hated father, the father of Marie-Henri Beyle, bore the name of Chérubin-Joseph Beyle.

If the epigraph as covert signal from an author who is simultaneously critic, reader, and interpreter is what interests me most immediately, such a limited view by no means exhausts the richness of the epigraph's functions in *Armance*[5] and *Le Rouge et le noir,* moving toward its ultimate disppearance from *Lucien Leuwen* and *La Chartreuse de Parme.* The epigraph can be inserted as an *apparent* generative or motivating force in the text. Let us remember that Cherubino in Mozart's opera has to hide, first behind a chair, then under dresses in the armchair, to avoid meeting the count; Julien, hearing M. de Rênal about to enter his wife's room, has to slip under the sofa to avoid the jealous husband. Cherubino escapes through a window and falls in the flower beds, and Julien escapes from Mathilde's room the same way a few pages after letting the ladder (his means of access) fall into the flower beds near the wall (p. 538). In a chapter narrating the birth of Julien's love for Mme de Rênal (chap. 16), we find an epigraph from Byron's *Don Juan*: "He turned his lip to hers, and with his hand / Call'd back the tangles of her wandering hair" (p. 297); two hundred fifty pages later we notice that verses (from this same stanza) that Stendhal had read but did not quote contributed to his novel:

> "Come, come, 't is no time now for fooling there,"
> She whispered, in great wrath—"I must deposit
> This pretty gentleman within the closet."
>
> [Canto 1, stanza 170]

For at the sound of steps in the room adjacent to Mathilde's, she hides him in a mahogany armoire (p. 541). At another key moment, Julien, proud to have fulfilled his heroic task of taking Mme de Rênal's hand, now resolves to hold her hand in the very presence of her husband; the epigraph of the chapter in question, also drawn from *Don Juan,* shows the origins of his strategy:

> Yet Julia's very coldness still was kind,

And tremulously gentle her small hand
Withdrew itself from his, but left behind,
A little pressure, thrilling, and so bland
And slight, so very slight that in the mind
'Twas but a doubt.

[P. 275, canto 1, stanza 71]

An epigraph that seems to me to express one key way these quotations function is attributed to Ennius (p. 234): "Cunctando restituit rem" ("Delaying restitutes the thing"). Many of the epigraphs that activate the text—that is, that are incorporated or transformed within the body of the narrative—are, so to speak, textual time bombs: they explode into significance with some delay. For example, Fleury's remark, "Un curé vertueux et sans intrigue est une Providence pour le village" (chap. 3, p. 223), would seem most innocuous, were it not that two hundred pages later Abbé Pirard will tell Julien: "Il ne faut jamais dire le hasard, mon enfant, dites toujours la Providence" (p. 442). An epigraph attributed to Girodet—"Se sacrifier à ses passions, passe; mais à des passions qu'on n'a pas! O triste XIXe siècle!" (p. 610)—perfectly describes Julien's subsequent situation in prison and contains the text of his reflections in the penultimate chapter, eighty pages later: "L'influence de mes contemporains l'emporte, dit-il tout haut et avec un rire amer. Parlant seul avec moi-même, à deux pas de la mort, je suis encore hypocrite. O dix-neuvième siècle" (p. 690).

This time-fuse effect can also lead from the text to the epigraph. In describing the Hôtel de la Mole, Stendhal brings out its vacuity in the following formulation: "La moindre idée vive semblait une grossièreté. Malgré le bon ton, la politesse parfaite, l'envie d'être agréable, l'ennui se lisait sur tous les fronts" (p. 457). This will form an epigraph, attributed to Faublas, in the following chapter: "Une idée un peu vive y a l'air d'une grossièreté, tant on y est accoutumé aux mots sans relief. Malheur à qui invente en parlant" (p. 467). The effect of such an epigraph is structural, almost musical. Isolated in the midst of white space, the epigraph draws itself to our attention as a leitmotiv whose importance will be definitively revealed only in the total structure of the text. It therefore constitutes an ironic interface, a subliminal meaning dependent on the total text perceived simultaneously, not in linearity. Thus, the epigraph of the novel itself, "La vérité, l'âpre vérité," attributed to Danton, seems to steer us toward a realistic reading of *Le Rouge,* whereas what matters is the *name* Danton—he was decapitated in 1794, and his fate foreshadows Julien's. Three hundred pages later we find a chapter entitled "Serait-ce un Danton?", a question Mathilde answers: "Ce sera un Danton! . . . Eh bien! la révolution aurait recommencé. . . . Mon petit Julien brûlerait la cervelle au jacobin qui viendrait l'arrêter" (pp. 512–13). And one hundred fifty pages later, Count Altamira will explain to the prisoner Julien that the night before his death Danton said whimsically that the verb *guillotiner* could not, in the first person, be conjugated in the past tense. At the Rênals', as at the Hôtel de la Mole, the threat of the great Revolution hangs as a sword of Damocles. As a witness to one of Julien's terrible rages, Mme Derville is reminded that humiliation has shaped the personality of the dreaded Robespierre (p. 268); Mathilde's brother says of Julien: "Si la révolution recommence, il nous fera tous guillotiner" (p. 512).

The same effect of *cunctando restituit rem*—first a false or screened meaning before the unveiling of the true kernel—characterizes the epigraph of the first chapter: "Put thousands together / Less bad / But the cage less gay," which Stendhal attributes to Hobbes. The reader, deceived by the linearity of his first reading of the novel, here sees what strikes him as an evocation of the town of Verrières, whose mayor, M. de Rênal, spends time and money erecting walls: "plus on bâtit de murs, plus on acquiert de droits aux respects de ses voisins" (p. 219). Later the epigraph would seem to apply to the cell in the seminary at Besançon from which Julien has a splendid view of the two walls. But a more important meaning is made manifest only at the end of the novel, when we realize that the "cage" is the dungeon where our would-be Don Juan finds ineffable happiness with Mme de Rênal, the ideal mother and mistress.

"Ce siècle est fait pour tout confondre! Nous marchons vers le chaos" (p. 631). These words by the Marquis de la Mole reflect the pessimistic view of the nineteenth century reiterated by the vision of the novel. "Il n'y a plus de passions véritables au XIXe siècle: c'est pour cela que l'on s'ennuie tant en France" (p. 494), Altamira says. The la Moles are aristocrats, and Mathilde thinks only of her ancestor Boniface, decapitated in 1574; Julien remembers Napoleon, is nostalgic for the *grande armée* and for Rousseau, his spiritual brother. And Stendhal? He should be viewed not as a political thinker but as novelist and creator. He does not want to write a realistic novel, he does not want the truth, the bitter truth; what he strives for in *Le Rouge et le noir* (and ultimately achieves in *La Chartreuse*) is the lightness, the aleatory, the joyous energy of Montesquieu, of the Cimarosa of *Il Matrimonio segreto,* of the Mozart of *Figaro*; the carefree humor, the freedom of narrative techniques of Scarron's *Roman comique,* of Fielding's *Tom Jones,* of Diderot's *Jacques le fataliste.* He wants to write a novel that, taking as its point of departure the Berthet affair chronicled in the *Gazette,* will achieve freedom within the constraints of the historical givens. And Stendhal will use the epigraph to lighten the ponderous weight of the bitter historical truths of his *Chronique de 1830,* the subtitle of *Le Rouge.*

A few chapter titles from *Tom Jones* will sound the right note:

The hero of this great history appears with very bad omens. A little tale of so *low* a kind that some may not think it worth their notice. A word or two concerning a squire, and more relating to a gamekeeper and a schoolmaster. [Bk. 3, chap. 2]

A most dreadful chapter indeed; and which few readers ought to venture upon in an evening, especially when alone. [Bk. 7, chap. 14]

Obviously, in 1830, with the example of the laconic chapter titles of a Balzac as exemplary, Stendhal could not easily return to the playfulness of his beloved eighteenth century, especially when *Le Rouge* is subtitled *Chronique de 1830*. He turned instead to the freedom afforded by the epigraph, which serves as surrogate eighteenth-century Fieldingesque title describing the chapter it heads. For example, the last chapter of part 1 of *Le Rouge* has the Marquis de la Mole explaining to Abbé Pirard that he is involved in various legal plots and needs a discreet and competent secretary—that will be Julien, of course—to assist him in the judicial proceedings. The epigraph is supposedly taken from the *Edinburgh Review* (for which Stendhal served as correspondent): "Il n'y a plus qu'une seule noblesse, c'est le titre de *duc*; marquis est ridicule, au mot *duc* on tourne la tête" (p. 414). The epigraph as chapter title explains the motivation behind la Mole's machinations "pour faire accepter à la fois au roi et à la nation un certain ministère, qui, par reconnaissance, le ferait duc" (p. 414). The title *marquis* is used nine times in the course of the first three pages of the chapter to designate la Mole. The effect is to reduce the political plot to ironic social ambition. Another chapter, "Pensées d'une jeune fille," dramatizes the amorous Mathilde's distress, her insomnia, her remorse at having written those compromising notes to Julien, concluding with his plans to leave town. The epigraph, attributed to Musset, sums up the action of the chapter, which contains at various moments words taken directly from the epigraph:

Que de perplexités! Que de nuits passées sans sommeils! Grand Dieu! vais-je me rendre méprisable? Il me méprisera lui-même. Mais il s'éloigne. [Epigraph; p. 525]

Le jour de la bataille était presque celui des moindres *perplexités*. [P. 526; italics mine here and in the following quotations]

En ce temps-là . . . Mathilde *ne pouvait dormir*. [P. 527]

Quelle phrase eût-on pu leur donner à répéter pour amortir le coup de l'affreux *mépris*. [P. 527]

Il avait oublié de songer sérieusement à la convenance du *départ*. [p. 529]

The false seriousness of the epigraph makes the movement of the game of amorous stratagems so comic and unromantic that Julien says to himself, like a real eighteenth-century Marivaux lover: "Il paraît que ceci va être le roman par lettres" (p. 529); these words are uttered by the young hero who is so excessively aware of living a nineteenth-century novel of social mobility made possible by ambitious energy: "Au milieu de tant de périls il me reste MOI" (p. 528).

An epigraph supposedly by Schiller, that apostle of dynamic Sturm und Drang, introduces Julien's hesitations at Mathilde's order to him to climb to her room on a ladder in the moonlight. "Est-ce un complot?" is the chapter title (p.

531); and the epigraph: "Ah! que l'intervalle est cruel entre un grand projet conçu et son exécution! Que de vaines terreurs! que d'irrésolutions! Il s'agit de la vie. —Il s'agit de bien plus: de l'honneur!" (p. 531). The action of this chapter recounts precisely this painful interval, and Julien himself quotes the words of old Don Diègue in Corneille's *Le Cid,* "Mais il n'est qu'un honneur!" (p. 532), before hiding copies of Mathilde's letters in a volume of Voltaire in the la Mole library. One final example is another fictitious attribution to Schiller: "Et elle me l'avoue! Elle détaille jusqu'aux moindres circonstances! Son œil si beau fixé sur le mien peint l'amour qu'elle sentit pour un autre!" (p. 547). In this chapter, entitled "Moments cruels," Mathilde does precisely what the epigraph-as-chapter-title indicated to torment the jealous Julien. She tells him what she had felt for MM. de Croisenois and de Caylus (p. 548). And Stendhal intervenes (by what Victor Brombert called "the oblique road"),[6] like a real eighteenth-century playful narrator:

> le sujet de conversation auquel ils semblaient tous deux revenir . . . c'était le récit des sentiments qu'elle avait éprouvés pour d'autres. . . .
> On voit que Julien n'avait aucune expérience de la vie, qu'il n'avait pas même lu de romans; s'il eût été un peu moins gauche et qu'il eût dit avec quelque sang-froid à cette jeune fille. . . . Convenez que quoique je ne vaille pas tous ces messieurs, c'est pourtant moi que vous aimez. [P. 549]

It is no accident that in this essential function of the epigraph, the replacing of the whimsical chapter titles dear to a Fielding, Stendhal usually invented the epigraphs themselves, while playfully attributing them to the most serious writers of his own and preceding times.

With a political background in his *Chronique de 1830* that is so controversial that Stendhal was obliged to write a fictitious disclaimer informing the reader (and the censor) that his novel had been written in 1827 (three years before the events of July 1830 [p. 215]) and with a plot drawn from the *Gazette des Tribunaux* (the case of Anthoine Berthet, who was guillotined in February 1828), Stendhal must make a real effort to "lighten" his novel, to remove it at least partially from the realism that allowed the eminent *stendhalien* Henri Martineau to call *Le Rouge* "un roman de mœurs et un tableau politique en même temps qu'un roman psychologique" (p. 199). What Stendhal is seeking (and will only truly find in *La Chartreuse*) is the playful tonality and sparkle of Cimarosa, of Scarron, of Diderot: "Comment s'étaient-ils rencontrés? Par hasard, comme tout le monde. Comment s'appelaient-ils? Que vous importe? D'où venaient-ils? Du lieu le plus proche. Où allaient-ils? Est-ce que l'on sait où l'on va? Que disaient-ils? Le maître ne disait rien; et Jacques disait que son capitaine disait que tout ce qui nous arrive de bien et de mal ici-bas était écrit là-haut."[7] By these questions (and the frivolous answers) Diderot establishes a playful tone, that of a novel where metaphysical questions will be treated with the light touch. Stendhal will fully acquire this luminous freedom of the narratology of the Enlightenment only in *La Chartreuse*; in *Le Rouge,* he will use the epigraph to modulate the seriousness of his plot and his chronicle of 1830 into a playfulness worthy of his predecessors. Sometimes the text of the epigraph itself will have less importance than the purported name of the author in the ironic texture of the novel. Thus, the four epigraphs attributed to Barnave are there because their author was decapitated; another, in a joke at the expense of one of the great traditional sources of epigraphs, is attributed to *Mme* Goethe. At times, an epigraph of utter vacuity will bear the name of a famous author. "Que fait-il ici? s'y plairait-il? Penserait-il y plaire?" (p. 456) is supposedly by Ronsard; and "Hélas! pourquoi ces choses et non pas d'autres?" (p. 622) is by Beaumarchais.

The disparity between the epigraph and the content of a particular chapter similarly produces an ironic effect: "O rus quando ego te aspiciam?" ("O countryside, when shall I see you?") inaugurates a chapter detailing that the countryside is as filled with political intrigue and schemingly ambitious men as the metropolis. And the name of the "author" adds to the irony; the quotation is not from Virgil, as Stendhal pretends, but from Horace's *Satires* (2. 6. 60). We then remember that at the Rênals' Julien had memorized only the Bible, but that he had learned Horace subsequently and had thereby impressed the bishop of Besançon. Finally, he uses his knowledge of Horace to show off in the salon of the Hôtel de la Mole—and with all this Stendhal mistakes Virgil for Horace! Sometimes, too, the epigraph is a mere word game that lightens the realistic materials of the novel. Thus, the narration of Julien's first days in the capital at the house of la Mole follows an epigraph whose concluding figurative words, "Ma tête se perd," will finally assume an all too literal (and prophetic) meaning.

Stendhal's continuing struggle against his "triste 19e siècle" manifests itself most strikingly in the most famous epigraph of *Le Rouge et le noir*: "Un roman: c'est un miroir qu'on promène le long d'un chemin" (p. 286). Generations of critics have seen in this epigraph the signboard of Stendhalian realism. They conjecture that since the author of the lines is Stendhal himself and since the author of *Racine et Shakespeare* is an admirer of Hamlet's "mirror up to nature," he must be speaking of *his* novel and of his preoccupations as chronicler (Saint-Réal, the purported author, is a bit of Stendhalian whimsy, though the pun on the root of *réaliste/Réal* is amusing). But this invented epigraph reenters the text of the novel precisely at the moment where the author is most successful in appropriating the narrative voice of the eighteenth century—in a chapter narrating Mathilde's night at the Italian opera, hearing that sparkling piece of eighteenth-century froth, Cimarosa's *Il Matrimonio segreto*. She spends the whole night singing the cantilena from the opera, "Devo punirmi, / Se troppo amai" (p. 554). Then Stendhal picks up the epigraph he introduced two hundred fifty pages earlier, this time in the middle of a long parenthetical authorial intervention worthy of Diderot:

Eh, Monsieur, un roman est un miroir qui se promène sur une grande route.
Tantôt il reflète à vos yeux l'azur des cieux, tantôt la fange des bourbiers de la route.
Et l'homme qui porte le miroir dans sa hotte sera par vous accusé d'être immoral.
Accusez bien plutôt le grand chemin où est le bourbier, et plus encore l'inspecteur
des routes qui laisse l'eau croupir et le bourbier se former.

Maintenant qu'il est bien convenu que le caractère de Mathilde est impossible
dans notre siècle, non moins prudent que vertueux, je crains moins d'irriter en
continuant le récit des folies de cette aimable fille. [P. 555]

'The figurative meaning of the mirror is rendered comical by a reduction to the
literality of the highway inspector, but what really matters is that Stendhal is
here celebrating not realism, but his narrative triumph over realism.

We might now ask the arid statistical question once more. Why two epigraphs from Byron's *Don Juan* in *Armance* as against seven in *Le Rouge*?
Armance is a novel that is both a satirical depiction of Paris salons in 1827 and a
profoundly serious psychological study of psychic impotence. The latter is by
far the more important theme, especially because of Stendhal's own preoccupation with the subject. The author forces himself to use words to hide Octave's
affliction, which is in fact never mentioned. In *Le Rouge,* on the other hand,
Byron can assume greater importance because, like Stendhal in 1830, he wrote
with prodigious rapidity and could never resist irony when speaking of love;
Byron has the feeling for the couplet of an Augustan. In *Le Rouge* the epigraphs
from *Don Juan* are there to allow Stendhal to mock the love strategy of the
would-be seducer, Julien Sorel, who finds a mother in his mistress and who
will himself become the "mistress" of the virile Mathilde, whose extravagant
energies surpass his own. Julien does not succeed in living the Napoleonic
saga, but Mathilde makes him play the drama of Boniface de la Mole. Julien
will not be Don Juan, although he is certainly aware of his Byronic incarnation:
"Julien s'obstinant à jouer le rôle d'un Don Juan, lui qui de la vie n'avait eu de
maîtresse, il fut sot à mourir toute la journée" (p. 293).

In the courtroom Julien accuses himself of matricide, and in a grandiose
operatic aria he denounces society and makes the ladies in the audience cry. But
Stendhal has him race off to Verrières in an apparently implausible (and much
criticized) twist of plot, not to allow the author to finish his novel expeditiously,
but to allow Julien to finish his own. Lieutenant de la Vernaye now, Julien cries
out: "Mon roman est fini" (p. 637). He is wrong; his novel does not conclude
with this apogee. His novel must finish "novelistically": a wild horseback ride
to Verrières worthy of a Sturm und Drang narrative, two pistol shots in a
church. Yet these are pistol shots that are the very parody of heroic action,
because, like Uncle Vanya, Julien does not kill his victim even when shooting
at such close quarters (p. 642). In this miserable nineteenth century, it is
already too late for real actions, for heroism. The novel is set in an age of
intrigue, of money, of corruption, not of heroism. Stendhal no longer needs the

epigraph in his last chapters to communicate his irony: the entire novel floats in an ironic half-light, illuminated only by one authentic flame, the love that unites mother and son-and-lover: Mme de Malivert and Octave; Mme de Rênal and Julien; Henriette Gagnon and Henry Brulard–Henri Beyle–Stendhal. The last word should be Byron's:

> Don Juan was a bachelor—of arts,
> And parts, and hearts: he danced and sang and had
> An air as sentimental as Mozart's
> Softest of melodies; and could be sad
> Or cheerful, without any "flaws or starts"
> Just at the proper time: and though a lad,
> Had seen the world—which is a curious sight,
> And very much unlike what people write.

1. All quotations from *Le Rouge et le noir* are taken from Stendhal, *Romans,* vol. 1 (Paris: Gallimard, Bibliothèque de la Pléiade, 1952); page numbers are given immediately after the quotation.

2. This basic pattern has, of course, often been observed. See the excellent study by Gilbert Chaitin, *The Unhappy Few* (Bloomington: Indiana University Press, 1972); and more recently, Steven Sands, "The Narcissism of Stendhal and Julien Sorel," *Studies in Romanticism* 14 (1975): 337–63.

3. Victor Brombert, "Stendhal et les 'douceurs de la prison,'" *La Prison romantique* (Paris: Corti, 1975).

4. Stendhal, *Œuvres intimes* (Paris: Gallimard, Bibliothèque de la Pléiade, 1956), p. 60.

5. For the epigraphs in *Armance,* see Jeanne Cumming, "Sur les épigraphes d'Armance: Stendhal et Shakespeare," *Stendhal-Club* 58 (1973): 120–32.

6. Brombert, "Stendhal et les 'douceurs de la prison.'"

7. Denis Diderot, *Œuvres,* ed. André Billy (Paris: Gallimard, Bibliothèque de la Pléiade, 1951), p. 475.

Stendhal's *Lamiel*:
Observations on Pygmalionism

PAULINE WAHL

Lamiel has the potential to be Stendhal's most engaging heroine. Her enthusiasm, curiosity, and intelligence sweep the reader up in her adventures as she seeks an answer to the question "Qu'est-ce que l'amour?"[1] Unfortunately, she never really finds out: the novel remains unfinished, and the reader is left with the uncomfortable feeling that somewhere between Normandy and Paris Lamiel herself has become rather less intriguing.

We now know why this is so, thanks to Victor Del Litto's edition of *Lamiel*, which is the only complete one and the only one to present everything Stendhal wrote of this novel in chronological order. Exactly what Del Litto's *Lamiel* contains has been summarized very neatly by F. W. J. Hemmings,[2] who has demonstrated that the novel is actually two rather different versions of one story. The first, which he terms *Lamiel I,* is an outline of the complete plot. The second, or *Lamiel II,* is a completed manuscript of the first six chapters of the novel, ending before Lamiel's walk in the woods with Jean Berville. Hemmings has discussed the stylistic changes and descriptive additions that Stendhal brought to the second version of his story and has quite rightly concentrated on the principal difference between the two accounts; that is, the increased importance of Dr. Sansfin in *Lamiel II* over his minor role in the outline.[3] Both Del Litto and Hemmings conclude that the novel is unfinished because the independent actions of the first Lamiel cannot coexist with Sansfin's psychological domination of the second Lamiel.[4]

Yet, further questions remain to tantalize us: Why does Stendhal seem to lose interest in Lamiel? Why does Sansfin become the dominant character in the novel, and what is the importance of this change? Perhaps some possible answers can come from a study of the educational aspects of the novel.

Certain similarities between the education of Lamiel and that of Beyle himself have been perceived by G. D. Chaitin.[5] In early childhood both were repressed by the religious and aristocratic pretensions of their parents: they were under constant surveillance; they were forbidden to play with the other, supposedly lower-class, neighborhood children; and they were not allowed any amusements. At the moment of their sexual initiation both Beyle and Lamiel were about sixteen years of age and both were paying customers. Chaitin feels that "[Beyle] endows Lamiel and her parents with the same characteristics that he felt he and his relatives possessed. This picture corresponds to Beyle's psychological situation, even if it is not a completely faithful reproduction of the historical situation."[6]

One could also point out other similarities in their development. In general, the direction of their education is the same: they both began with private lessons, then took advantage of the educational opportunities available in the home town, and finally arrived in Paris, where they chose their own instructors. Both youngsters overheard a phrase that seemed to trigger in them the analytical process and turn them away from religion.[7] Their dreary childhood was brightened by their love of adventure stories; and in Paris when they were independent, they both took an enormous number of lessons, some of which were very much alike. For example, a young actress taught Lamiel to avoid using her "patois normand" (p. 139); and two retired actors, La Rive and Dugazon, trained Beyle to eliminate "les derniers restes du parler *traînard* de [son] pays."[8] One can also find a similarity of vocation and character between Lamiel's English teacher, Abbé Clément, and Beyle's English teacher, Père Jéki.

In fact, their educations have so much in common that, by telling Lamiel's story, Stendhal is, in many respects, retelling his own. If we compare the *Vie de Henry Brulard* to *Lamiel* it becomes clear that, in addition to the similarity of details, there is also a decided similarity of intention on the part of the author. Certainly, in embarking on *Lamiel*, Stendhal knew that he was writing a novel; but also by relating the *Vie de Henry Brulard*, says Victor Brombert, "he knew that he had undertaken not a simple recounting but an act of creation and that what he was creating was precisely the boy Henry Brulard, if not Beyle-Stendhal himself."[9] Because Stendhal ceased work on *Brulard* only three years before writing *Lamiel*, it is possible that he did not want to persevere with virtually the same story so soon again. This repetition might account in part for Stendhal's abandonment of his alter-ego heroine of *Lamiel I* and his subsequent interest in Sansfin. *Lamiel I* can be seen, then, as a novel of education that Stendhal did not want to rewrite.

Another possible explanation of Stendhal's increased interest in Sansfin arises from an examination of the teacher-student relationships in the novel. Lamiel's part in these relationships is always the same. She is a willing student who profits from her lessons; but, with regard to her instructors, she displays all the indifference of a statue. On the other hand, Lamiel's educators usually exhibit a much warmer attitude toward their pupil. Except for the Hautemares, who consider their instruction simply the dutiful dispatch of an obligation; for Jean Berville, who calmly but greedily accepts payment for services rendered; and for the Sansfin of *Lamiel I*, who plays too minor a role to be considered a significant teacher figure, all of the educators show great good will toward their pupil.

In fact, they are so anxious to mould Lamiel that their zeal seems unbelievable to the reader. Mme Le Grand, the hotelkeeper who guides the young woman through her first days in Paris, is typical in this respect. Stendhal explains: "L'unique passion de Lamiel était alors la curiosité; jamais il ne fut d'être plus questionneur; c'était peut-être là ce qui avait fait la source de l'amitié de Mme Le Grand qui avait le plaisir de répondre et d'expliquer toutes choses" (p. 107). It is evident here that the pedagogical function itself constitutes the source of the instructor's affection for her pupil. Mme de Miossens is no different: she instructs Lamiel, first, because she enjoys her task, and second, to relieve the boredom of long evenings in her dismal château. Ultimately, she forgets her boredom as all her feelings are made to revolve around Lamiel. At this point the teacher's affection for her pupil is developed to such an extent that a paradoxical situation arises. Instead of the teacher's sanctioning the student's excellence, it is the student who becomes the judge of her teacher's merit,[10] as we see in the episode where Mme de Miossens shows Lamiel a portrait of her son, Fédor: "Elle voulait montrer ce beau portrait à l'aimable Lamiel, et elle n'osait en quelque sorte se livrer à son ravissement avant d'avoir l'opinion de l'être aimable qui disposait de son cœur. Arrivée dans la chambre de Lamiel, la duchesse se livra aux éloges les plus exagérés, mais son œil interrogeait sa favorite qui ne répondait guère" (p. 258).

The same pattern is evident in Lamiel's relationship to her male teachers; but here, if anything, the teachers develop an even deeper affection for their pupil, again precisely because they are educating her. For example, like those of Mme de Miossens, Abbé Clément's feelings arise first from boredom and a desire to instruct; however, the young priest actually falls in love with Lamiel. Similarly, when Comte d'Aubigné Nerwinde eyes Lamiel through his drunken stupor, he boasts to all and sundry: "il y a quelque chose de singulier, d'original chez cette jeune fille. Et moi je veux la former. Avec ses grandes enjambées, elle me fera rougir quand je lui donnerai le bras; elle ne sait pas porter un châle; mais je lui plairai ou je mourrai à la peine" (p. 111).

The entire situation is reflected clearly in the relationship of Lamiel and Fédor de Miossens. The young man is enamored of explaining everything to his mistress, and his passion knows no bounds when she asks him to expound the principles of geometry to her. She, however, feels no love for her teacher: "Quant au duc, elle le regardait par curiosité et *pour son instruction*" (p. 78).

This situation seems unusual. The teachers, motivated by the ignorance and need for guidance they perceive in their pupil, give so generously of their time and effort to form her character that they develop great affection and even love for her. Furthermore, although they receive virtually nothing in return from Lamiel, they persist in their helpful, affectionate attitude. Is such behavior altruistic to the point of foolishness? Not according to Pierre Fauchery, who observed the same phenomenon in many eighteenth-century novels and termed it pygmalionism.[11] He believed that pygmalionism expresses the teacher's dream of modeling and possessing another human being, perhaps without having to confront the uncertainties that a physical possession implies.[12]

Stendhal was no stranger to the experience of pygmalionism. In his letters to his sister Pauline, he tried to form all facets of her taste and character.[13] When in Marseille he wished to turn Mélanie Guilbert into one of the outstanding actresses of her time and felt confident that he could do so,[14] especially after his success at training Adèle Rebuffel for amateur theatrics when he himself was only a part-time drama student.[15]

Obviously, pygmalionism interested Stendhal very much. Perhaps it interested him so much that he wished to explore it further than he could in *Lamiel I*. Certainly, in this preliminary version of the novel we have many examples of the phenomenon; however, the emphasis is always on the student. We constantly see Lamiel acting and reflecting, while we learn of the teacher's attitude rather as background information and only insofar as it affects Lamiel's life. By changing the emphasis of the narrative, by putting the accent on the teacher, Stendhal could explore the other half of the relationship in greater depth. This is what he does in *Lamiel II*.

Here he concentrates on Dr. Sansfin, who was simply a background figure in the first version of the novel, and on Sansfin's relationship with Lamiel, an association that was merely suggested in the earlier draft. A rather sinister portrait of the Pygmalion figure thus emerges. Unlike Ovid's Pygmalion, who was basically a nice, if overly perfectionistic, young man, Sansfin is driven above all by vanity and fear of ridicule. The hilarious "scène du lavoir" (pp. 196–206) establishes the hunchback as humorless and ill-tempered. Instead of love, Sansfin's motives are lust and power, which will enable him to compensate for his deformity

At the outset the plot of *Lamiel II* revolves not around Sansfin and Lamiel only but around Sansfin, Lamiel, and Mme de Miossens. The good doctor initially plans to garner for himself the delights of Lamiel's sexual awakening and to savor the more mature pleasure of Mme de Miossens's company somewhat later. This is quite a change from *Lamiel I*, where Stendhal simply toyed with the idea of having Sansfin mastermind a liaison between Lamiel and Fédor. The modifications in the second version are obviously due to the author's deepening interest in Sansfin's character. This new outlook has in turn changed the roles of Lamiel and Mme de Miossens. Instead of Mme de Miossens's being simply a teacher for Lamiel, in the second version we see her, as well as Lamiel, linked to Sansfin. Because of the similar purpose he has in mind for the two women, their roles tend to converge.

To begin with, both women are bored: Lamiel because she is compelled to behave decorously in a musty old château, and the duchess because she has imposed the decorous behavior and can find no one to dispel it. Because of their boredom both Lamiel and Mme de Miossens require medical care. Lamiel falls quite seriously ill from her cheerless confinement in the château. The duchess is not really ill at all, but in her boredom she has plenty of time to dally in front of her mirror. Upon noticing crow's-feet around her eyes, she hastens to summon a specialist who confirms the possibility of disease. Just as Sansfin, who attends Lamiel, decides that he will be her tonic by amusing her and cheering her up, so Mme de Miossens's Parisian specialist in a sense does the same thing. By substituting an illness for the natural process of aging and by changing her life with the suggestion that she engage a reader, he too provides a tonic. Furthermore, both women have newspapers read aloud to them: Sansfin reads the *Gazette des Tribunaux* to Lamiel, and Lamiel reads the *Quotidienne* to the duchess.

During Lamiel's illness Mme de Miossens actually does become indisposed herself out of worry for the girl. At this point Sansfin attends the duchess as well, and the roles of the two women become increasingly similar. The doctor's first action is to make Lamiel and the duchess even more ill, the better to manipulate them, of course. In their worsened state Sansfin controls them by the "magnétisme de son éloquence infernale" (p. 237). Finally, he arranges for them to live side by side in peasants' cabins for the duration of Lamiel's illness. After a final paroxysm of vanity in which Sansfin envisions marrying the duchess, he decides instead to concentrate on Lamiel and to settle for "les prémices de cœur de cette jeune fille" (p. 244). From this point on, because of Sansfin's conscious decision, the teacher-student relationship develops between himself and Lamiel only. Stendhal is still concentrating on the Pygmalion figure.

Sansfin spares no effort in his attempt to control Lamiel. He ensures her complicity through the use of terror and systematically destroys the power of others over her, concentrating his efforts on the formative influence of the Hautemares. This sinister aspect of Sansfin's undertaking is emphasized by his fear of losing his pupil to another male teacher figure, either Abbé Clément or Fédor. Whereas in *Lamiel I* Sansfin was to have promoted a romance between the heroine and Fédor, in *Lamiel II* he cannot bear the thought of a liaison between them; and it is he, not the prudish Mlle Anselme, who suggests that Lamiel leave the château before Fédor's arrival.

We can see, then, that the two versions of the novel constitute, in effect, an inquiry into the nature of pygmalionism, by exploring the possibility of liberty for the pupil in *Lamiel I* and the possibility of control for the teacher in *Lamiel II*. Stendhal carries his meditation on freedom and constraint one step further: it becomes the subject matter of Sansfin's lessons to Lamiel. In this way Stendhal is able to examine pygmalionism not only through the structure of the novel but also through its ideological content.

The doctor calls his first lesson the "règle du lierre" (p. 247), by which he intends to rid Lamiel of her preconceptions much as one would cut an overgrowth of ivy from an oak tree. In his desire to cleanse Lamiel's mind of all false ideas, Sansfin is employing a sort of "anticrystallization" technique:[16] instead of allowing Lamiel's thoughts to build one upon the other like crystals on a branch, he wishes to strip the trunk of its growth and to start it afresh. Although his intention here may seem honorable—he wants Lamiel to learn to think for herself in complete intellectual freedom—his method is perhaps questionable. His anticrystallization actually puts Lamiel totally at the mercy of his suggestions and does not permit her to think for herself. In this sense the "règle du lierre" becomes a meditation on pygmalionism. It demonstrates the paradoxical nature of the situation: the overbearing mentor cannot create an independent human being from a statue by chiseling away all of its ideas, even though they may be false.

Sansfin's second lesson concerns his "doctrine du plaisir," in which he urges Lamiel to find her pleasure where she will, but to preserve her reputation at all costs (pp. 261–62). This course of action seemed to work quite well in *Lamiel I*, where the heroine worked out these ideas for herself. However, in *Lamiel II*, although the principle is stated much more categorically by Sansfin, Lamiel's acceptance of it is actually more problematical. There are two explanations for this. The first arises from the relationship between Sansfin and Lamiel. While she is totally dominated by him she cannot possibly practice his ideas on pleasure and hypocrisy: he will always be able to guess at her motives, and thus she will never be able to achieve perfect, unfathomable hypocrisy. Once again Stendhal has demonstrated the overwhelming control that the mentor can assume in the Pygmalion-type situation.

The second explanation for Lamiel's inability to practice the "doctrine du plaisir" comes from a polarization of teacher-student relationships in *Lamiel II*. Sansfin's reasoning is echoed by Abbé Clément, who also speaks to Lamiel of the horrors of a reputation forever lost. However, as one would expect, Clément advises Lamiel to mistrust any man who does not follow his protestations of affection with an offer of marriage. Basically, the young priest gave the same advice in *Lamiel I*; however, in *Lamiel II* his words take on a new emphasis because they are contrasted in the heroine's mind with Sansfin's advice. The contrast between the two suggestions confuses the impressionable Lamiel and makes her unable to choose a course of action. Once again, the inevitable impasse of pygmalionism is posited.

Given these circumstances, it is not surprising that Lamiel's question "Qu'est-ce que l'amour?" is never answered. For an answer to be forthcoming there would have to be an intervention from on high, like that of Venus bringing to life the statue Galatea in Ovid's tale of Pygmalion. Stendhal was not prepared to play that part here; instead, it seems that he was more interested in a role he had often chosen for himself: he wished to be the observer and investigator of relationships, the "connaisseur du cœur humain."

1. Stendhal, *Lamiel,* ed. Victor Del Litto (Geneva: Cercle du Bibliophile, 1971), p. 52. All subsequent references to *Lamiel* will be to this edition.

2. F. W. J. Hemmings, "A propos de la nouvelle édition de *Lamiel.* Les deux *Lamiel.* Nouveaux aperçus sur les procédés de composition de Stendhal romancier," *Stendhal Club* 15 (1973): 287–315.

3. Ibid., pp. 307–12.

4. Del Litto, preface to *Lamiel,* p. iv; and see Hemmings, pp. 312–16.

5. Gilbert D. Chaitin, *The Unhappy Few: A Psychological Study of the Novels of Stendhal* (Bloomington: Indiana University Press, 1972), pp. 174–77.

6. Ibid., p. 175.

7. In *Lamiel,* p. 30, La Merlin characterizes Lamiel's adoptive parents with the exclamation: "C'est bon comme du bon pain les Hautemare, *mais c'est bête*"; cf. ibid., p. 216. Here, as in subsequent quotations from Stendhal, the italics are Stendhal's. In the *Vie de Henry Brulard* (Paris: Le Divan, 1949), 1: 49, Beyle recounts that when his mother died he overheard Abbé Rey say to his father: "Mon ami, ceci vient de Dieu."

8. Beyle, *Vie de Henry Brulard,* 1:311–12.

9. Victor Brombert, *Stendhal: Fiction and the Themes of Freedom* (New York: Random House, 1968), p. 15. For a detailed analysis of the fictional elements of the *Vie de Henry Brulard,* see pp. 15–26.

10. Georges Blin, *Stendhal et les problèmes de la personnalité* (Paris: José Corti, 1958), 1:76, explains this type of reversal in existential terms, as a kind of "'toi qui devant moi me saisis moi devant toi,' si bien que là où je semblais, comme candidat à un examen, tenir, des deux, le rôle faible, c'est moi qui, au contraire, contraignant mon expert à prendre acte de ma contingence, le requérant, au nom de la vérité 'objective,' de me compter pour tout ce que je suis et ne le comptant, lui, que pour bon à ce faire, c'est moi qui, de l'opération, dirige le procès, et en l'alignant tout sur ma loi."

11. Pierre Fauchery, *La Destinée féminine dans le roman européen du dix-huitième siècle, 1713–1807: Essai de gynécomythie romanesque* (Paris: Armand Colin, 1972), p. 528.

12. Ibid., pp. 528–29.

13. Stendhal's entire correspondence with Pauline is evidence of pygmalionism. For two among countless examples, see Stendhal, *Correspondance* (Paris: Gallimard, 1962), 1:28–30, 38–39.

14. Stendhal, *Journal,* in *Œuvres intimes* (Paris: Gallimard, 1955), p. 584. This observation lends credence to the theory of André Doyon and Yves du Parc, *De Mélanie à Lamiel, ou D'un amour d'Henri Beyle au roman de Stendhal* (Aran, Switz.: Editions du Grand Chêne, 1972), that Mélanie is the model for Lamiel.

15. Stendhal, *Journal,* p. 439.

16. For Stendhal's explanation of "cristallisation," see his *De l'amour* (Paris: Garnier, 1959), pp. 8–9.

Love, the Intoxicating Mirage: Baudelaire's Quest for Communion in "Le Vin des amants," "La Chevelure," and "Harmonie du soir"

ENID RHODES PESCHEL

A mirage: a beautiful illusion, an unrealizable hope, an oasis, a vision incorporating desire and its fulfillment; promise, purity, perfection. But a mirage also portends disappointment, insubstantiality, unreality; a vision that fades, vanishes, a dream. Still, the memory of the mirage remains, revives, reanimates the hope. Unreal, the mirage cannot be touched, reached, grasped. And yet it continues to allure, entice, and refresh, in its own particular way, the weary, thirsty desert traveler. This traveler knows, even as he doggedly continues his desperate quest, that his longed-for vision will eventually disappoint him, deceive him, desert him. Attraction to the mirage—for the quester knows that it is a mirage—implies hope and despair; prayer and damnation; fulfillment and emptiness; momentary ecstasy coupled with painful, poignant, irremediable loneliness; the blessing and the burden of consciousness of self, of others, and of time.

Love in Baudelaire's poetry often takes the form of such a mirage. It is a vision that intoxicates him. Such is the case, for example, in "Le Vin des amants."

Le Vin des amants

Aujourd'hui l'espace est splendide!
Sans mors, sans éperons, sans bride,
Partons à cheval sur le vin
Pour un ciel féerique et divin!

Comme deux anges que torture
Une implacable calenture,
Dans le bleu cristal du matin
Suivons le mirage lointain!

Mollement balancés sur l'aile
Du tourbillon intelligent,
Dans un délire parallèle,

Ma sœur, côte à côte nageant,
Nous fuirons sans repos ni trêves
Vers le paradis de mes rêves![1]

Lovers' Wine

Space today is exquisite!
Without spurs, or bridle, or a bit,
Let's gallop now away on wine
For a sky fairylike and divine!

Like two angels in the throes of torture
Of an implacable calenture,
Let's follow into the crystal blue
Of morning the mirage in distant view!

Softly balanced upon the wing of some
Intelligent whirlwind for a ride,
In a parallel delirium,

My sister, swimming side by side,
We'll flee without rest unceasingly
Towards the paradise of my reveries![2]

The lovers here are intoxicated with love, with wine, with intoxication itself. Their frantic flight toward the "mirage lointain" is at once full of hope and full of despair.

Space for these lovers is exquisite: it expands, opens into the heavens. But even in the first stanza the intoxications envisioned offer not a reality, but a mirage, an image that simultaneously creates and negates itself. For while the sky promises something religious, "divin," some kind of exalted experience, nevertheless it also contains something that is merely from the realm of make-believe, of fantasy, since it is "féerique." Transcendence, however, is actively sought in this poem through a quasi-religious communion involving wine, a communion that will enable the intoxicated lovers to "gallop" toward their cherished goal.   ·

What is their goal, if not the tantalizing "mirage lointain" of love depicted in the second stanza? By means of this image the poet reveals his lucid consciousness of the lovers' flight toward escape in unreality and his consciousness, as well, of their inevitable failure. Here surfaces the poet's ironic vision of lovers, of the intoxication of wine, and even, perhaps, of intoxication itself. "Angels," he calls these intoxicated lovers, a word that in this context evokes both purity and its opposite; for how often, one may ask, do heaven's angels become drunk on wine? And the angelic-demonic lovers here are propelled not by love, but rather by disease, those fevers called calentures, caused by exposure to great heat. These lovers are not merely propelled: they are "tortured." Does the torturing heat arise from the passion of their love, or from the wine they have imbibed, or from their frantic desire to escape from reality? All of these are possible. The wine has been transformed not into the blood of Christ, the divine transubstantiation, offering the ultimate experience of communion with love, but rather into fevers, disease, in the lovers' blood. In contrast with their fever looms the coolness, the "crystal blue" of the morning, with its gleaming far-off mirage. Following that "fairylike and divine" mirage, then, is for these intoxicated lovers an experience that combines ecstatic vision with torture. And so there is despair, and there is hope. For Baudelaire, after all, degradation and torture may open the path to purity and redemption: blessing and spiritual truth.

The tercets highlight the dizziness, the delirium, the constant motion ("tourbillon," "délire," "nageant," "Nous fuirons sans repos ni trêves") that must be experienced by the intoxicated lovers in their flight toward the mirage. The poet here balances opposites in his description of this quest, which, by its nature, embodies contraries: gentleness with passion, reason with delirium, delicate balance with a whirlwind. The reader here is caught up in the poet's words, swirling along with the lovers in their dizzying flight. Their voyage is desperate, driven, "sans repos ni trêves." The words recall Baudelaire's splendid prose poem "Enivrez-vous" in which the reader is told about the desperate, determined nature of his undertaking: "il faut vous enivrer sans trêve."

Is each lover in "Le Vin des amants" intoxicated with the other? This question is not answered in the poem. Certainly communion—through wine, through love, through action in common—is sought. The woman is called tenderly (as she is at times in other places in Baudelaire's poetry) "ma sœur," which at once distances her from her lover (by insinuating an idea of incest) and yet brings her closer to him spiritually, as a sister-spirit. But the mirage toward which they flee, he says ecstatically, is "le paradis de mes rêves!" Are they *her* dreams as well? Perhaps, since she may be his spiritual sister, but one can hardly forget Baudelaire's numerous ironic descriptions of the fundamental lack of communion, even of communication, between two lovers.

The metaphor for the lovers' motion changes in the final stanza from the figure of galloping in the opening quatrain. Now the figure used describes swimming ("côte à côte nageant"), suggesting an immersion in their intoxication, in the intoxication that will allow them to flee toward the experience of divinity, toward the "paradise" of the lover's dreams. Communion in this poem, then, is frantically sought through love, through wine, through intoxication, through a goal that will necessarily delight and deceive: a wonderful and terrible mirage.

The lover's quest in this poem helps explain two of Baudelaire's most beautiful lyrics about love: the gloriously erotic but strangely rational "La Chevelure," written for Jeanne Duval; and the dizzying, dazzling, supremely spiritual but nevertheless compellingly sensuous "Harmonie du soir," inspired by Mme Sabatier. Instead of enchanting the poet in the future, however, the mirage of love looms in these two poems as an intoxicating image from his past, or rather from his memory, which recreates the past.

La Chevelure

O toison, moutonnant jusque sur l'encolure!
O boucles! O parfum chargé de nonchaloir!

Extase! Pour peupler ce soir l'alcôve obscure
Des souvenirs dormant dans cette chevelure,
Je la veux agiter dans l'air comme un mouchoir!

La langoureuse Asie et la brûlante Afrique,
Tout un monde lointain, absent, presque défunt,
Vit dans tes profondeurs, forêt aromatique!
Comme d'autres esprits voguent sur la musique,
Le mien, ô mon amour! nage sur ton parfum.

J'irai là-bas où l'arbre et l'homme, pleins de sève,
Se pâment longuement sous l'ardeur des climats;
Fortes tresses, soyez la houle qui m'enlève!
Tu contiens, mer d'ébène, un éblouissant rêve
De voiles, de rameurs, de flammes et de mâts:

Un port retentissant où mon âme peut boire
A grands flots le parfum, le son et la couleur;
Où les vaisseaux, glissant dans l'or et dans la moire,
Ouvrent leurs vastes bras pour embrasser la gloire
D'un ciel pur où frémit l'éternelle chaleur.

Je plongerai ma tête amoureuse d'ivresse
Dans ce noir océan où l'autre est enfermé;
Et mon esprit subtil que le roulis caresse
Saura vous retrouver, ô féconde paresse!
Infinis bercements du loisir embaumé!

Cheveux bleus, pavillon de ténèbres tendues,
Vous me rendez l'azur du ciel immense et rond;
Sur les bords duvetés de vos mèches tordues
Je m'enivre ardemment des senteurs confondues
De l'huile de coco, du musc et du goudron.

Longtemps! toujours! ma main dans ta crinière lourde
Sèmera le rubis, la perle et le saphir,
Afin qu'à mon désir tu ne sois jamais sourde!
N'es-tu pas l'oasis où je rêve, et la gourde
Où je hume à longs traits le vin du souvenir?

Head of Hair

O fleece, foaming down upon the neck! O curly
Locks! O scent filled with nonchalance! Ecstasy!
To people tonight the alcove's obscurity
With memories sleeping in this hair I wish
To wave it in the air like a handkerchief!

Asia languorous and Africa ardent,
A whole world distant, absent, almost dead,
Lives, aromatic forest, blent
In your depths! Just as other spirits sail ahead
On music, mine, O my love! swims on your scent.

I'll go over there where, full of sap, man and tree,
Slowly swoon beneath the climates' ardor; be,

Strong tresses, the surge that carries me. You contain
A dazzling dream, O sea of ebony,
Of sails, and rowers, pennants, masts and flames:

A resounding port where my soul may drink odors sweet,
Sound and color in great streams; a port where the
Large ships, gliding into the gold and the moire of the sea
And the air, open their vast arms to embrace the glory
Of a pure sky where quivers eternal heat.

I'll plunge my head in love with drunkenness
Into this black ocean where the other is enclosed;
And my subtle spirit which the rollings caress
Will know how to find you again, ô fecund laziness!
Infinite cradlings of perfumed leisure composed!

Blue hair, pavilion of outstretched night, you unbar
Once more the azure of the vast, round sky for me;
On the downy shores of your hair coiled twistingly
I become intoxicated ardently
With mixed scents of musk, and coconut oil and tar.

Long! forever! my hand in your heavy mane will sow ruby,
Pearl and sapphire, so that never to my
Desire may you be deaf! Are you not the
Oasis where I dream, and the gourd where I
Suck in long, slow drafts the wine of memory?[3]

The poet's quest in "La Chevelure" is impassioned, intoxicated, spiritual: he craves communion with his vision, with his inebriation, his exaltation. He seeks immersion in his mirage.

In the first stanza he evokes a sea voyage upon his mistress's "foaming" hair. He exults in the ecstasy her hair holds for him and in the memories it contains. As in "Le Vin des amants," Baudelaire balances opposites here. The first two lines portray the fleecelike hair foaming down upon Jeanne's neck. They create a vision of billowing, curling waves. The exclamatory words are sensual, animal, primitive, barbarous—and suddenly: detached, indifferent, cool, removed, since the "parfum" of her hair is "chargé de nonchaloir!" This is a state the poet revels in ("Extase!"). But it also symbolizes the lovers' detachment from each other. The exclamation "Extase!", which comes right after its contrast, "nonchaloir!", highlights the poet's transport, or desire for transport, outside of himself. In order to awaken the memories sleeping in Jeanne's hair he now wishes to wave it in the air "comme un mouchoir!" But what a change in imagery from the first two lines where Jeanne's hair evoked an ocean! From the grandiose, the sublime, to something so delicate, almost pathetic—from a curling, coiling ocean to a fluttering handkerchief. The poet seems rather pitiable, weak here. Still, his desperate desire is to achieve a fertile state, to "people" the evening with the "memories" that Jeanne's head of hair holds for him, and to try to create thereby the "Ecstasy!" for which he longs.

The sensuous and richly suggestive lines opening the second stanza create a whole world out of the poet's image of his mulatto mistress. She combines for him erotic languor and ardor, physical and spiritual passion, the Orient and Africa, a world almost dead that miraculously springs to life in her hair—"Vit . . . !" in the exclamation beginning the third line. Her hair, with its "profondeurs," a "forêt aromatique," now suggests the rich correspondences of Baudelaire's famous sonnet. And now the poet-traveler plunges into the depths of this ocean-"forest of symbols": "Comme d'autres esprits voguent sur la musique, / Le mien, ô mon amour! nage sur ton parfum." The verb "nager" recalls the intoxicated lovers' flight toward the mirage in "Le Vin des amants," but here the flight seems ecstatic rather than frantic. Immersed in her scent, which will transport him, the poet is at once supremely sensuous and supremely spiritual. His "esprit," his spirit-mind, he says (not his body), swims on her scent. The comparison with other "esprits" that sail along on music seems to highlight the intended spirituality, or sublimated sensuality. The woman is addressed as "his love!"—or is she? Is he in love with his mistress or with love itself, "ô mon amour!"? In stanza five, after all, the poet will reveal that his head is "in love with drunkenness."

Stanzas three and four climax as the dreaming poet becomes a boat and Jeanne's hair, an ocean that transports him to an ideal country, the image of his love. A voluptuous, spiritual harmony characterizes this land where man and tree, "pleins de sève," resemble each other both internally and externally as they swoon beneath the "climates' ardor." Sap suggests the life force, the blood of life. This is a harmonious state during which the same liquid flows in both man and nature. The swooning recalls the poet's "esprit" in "Elévation" "qui se pâme dans l'onde / . . . / Avec une indicible et mâle volupté." After the images uniting man and nature in "La Chevelure," the poet suddenly apostrophizes Jeanne's hair, calling it "Fortes tresses." Her hair is portrayed as powerful; there is even perhaps wordplay suggesting "forteresses." And he begs her "Fortes tresses" to carry him, to uplift him, toward the sky, toward his dream. Darkness and light contrast in her black hair, that "sea of ebony," which contains for the lover "a dazzling dream" of ships, and parts of ships, and rowers and flames, "flammes" evoking both pennants and flames: the voyage, passion, and destruction. And then, with stanza four, we enter further into the lover's dream.

Here, as in several other privileged places in Baudelaire's poetry, we penetrate the temple of nature where "de longs échos . . . de loin se confondent / Dans une ténébreuse et profonde unité"; here, sublimely, divinely: "Les parfums, les couleurs et les sons se répondent." Sensuousness is intensified, made sacred in this "port retentissant" as the poet's soul drinks in great streams "le parfum, le son et la couleur." The ships gliding into the gold and the moire of the surrounding sea and atmosphere are personified as they "ouvrent leurs vastes bras." The poet, after all, had become a ship in the preceding stanza where he begged Jeanne's "fortes tresses" to carry him. The personified ships are also spiritualized as they embrace "la gloire / D'un ciel pur où frémit l'éternelle chaleur." The last two lines of this stanza flow together, carrying the reader along in this experience of glory suggesting purity, the quivering of intense light and intense love, divine love and transcendence. Eros is simultaneously evoked, kept present, and surpassed in this dazzling display of embracing, in a passionate but also ethereal gesture, pure illumination.

The next stanza, the fifth, is pivotal in this poem, and pivotal, I believe, in an understanding of Baudelaire's quest for love.[4] His search is a "plunge" into the depths ("Plonger au fond du gouffre . . . !" he will exclaim later in "Le Voyage"). Here he will plunge into the "noir océan" of Jeanne's hair, which, he reveals, contains within it the ocean of his dreams, the sea that will carry him to that "resounding port." His plunge is at once a physical and a cerebral act: "Je plongerai ma tête amoureuse d'ivresse / Dans ce noir océan où l'autre est enfermé." His quest is not for communion or communication with the beloved, but rather for the ecstasy of intoxication itself. It is the poet's voyage into the depths within himself. The ocean is "enfermé" within his own mind, spirit, and soul. He yearns to commune with himself, not with another human being: his vision is internal. He will clearly depict it as such in "Harmonie du soir," but his quest in "La Chevelure," a poem ostensibly occasioned by his mistress's head of hair, is an internal one as well.

As the poet continues in stanza five of "La Chevelure," the voluptuous, the spiritual, and the intellectual are combined. The poet's spirit-mind that the rolling waves "caress" will "know how to find . . . again" what he seeks: "ô féconde paresse!", a fertile and yet inactive state that recalls the poet's contrasting "nonchaloir" and volition ("Je . . . veux . . . !") to people "l'alcôve obscure" with memories in the first stanza. It is important, too, that the poet uses the verb "retrouver" ("mon esprit . . . / Saura vous retrouver . . ."): he yearns to find something, or recreate something, from his past. In the last line of stanza five, sexual, sensuous images, as well as an image suggesting the innocence of a child's cradle, combine to create the erotic and spiritual pleasures of the poet's sought-for transcendence through intoxication. The senses commingle dizzyingly as mind and body are transported: "Infinis bercements du loisir embaumé!"

The last two stanzas of the poem continue the study of the poet's intoxication. Jeanne's hair, "blue" or black, evokes in its elaborate array a "pavillon de ténèbres tendues." In the present her hair, which he once compared to an ocean, opens once more for him the sky, an expansion into immensity: "Cheveux bleus, . . . / Vous me rendez l'azur du ciel immense et rond." Once again the past is the poet's present preoccupation. Now her hair evokes water, as the poet becomes inebriated on the "shores" of her "mèches tordues." The words "tordues" and "tendues" suggest tension, artificiality, perhaps even intoxication in a "paradis artificiel." The poet labors "ardemment" at his intoxication—passionately, burningly. He is driven, and he drives himself. His is a desire, a desperation. The scents with which he becomes "intoxicated ardently" ("des senteurs confondues / De l'huile de coco, du musc et du goudron") suggest the tropics, heat, and blackness, as well as evil, the infinite, and the rapture of mind-spirit and body. Significantly, musk is in "Correspondances" one of the "parfums" that are "corrompus, riches et triomphants, / Ayant l'expansion des choses infinies, / . . . / Qui chantent le transport de l'esprit et des sens."

Uniting past, present, and future in the final stanza ("Longtemps! toujours!"), the poet pathetically says that he will try to bribe his mistress, buy her, with jewels that he will "sow" in her hair so that she may never be deaf to his "désir." Her hair now evokes a horse's mane ("ta crinière"), echoing the suggestion of animality that appeared in the first stanza. The word "desire" is at once erotic and intellectual. Does the poet desire to love the woman, or does he desire instead to pursue his own state of intoxication? The last two lines are beautiful and frightening as they simultaneously open and close the world of the poet's love: "N'es-tu pas l'oasis où je rêve, et la gourde / Où je hume à longs traits le vin du souvenir?" They ask a rhetorical question. But is the woman satisfied with being not a companion, not a person to commune with or even to talk to, but merely an occasion for the poet's fertile dreaming? She is the poet's "oasis," the verdant place in the desert of his life, a fecund place for his dreams, for his communion with the intoxicating vision. The sublimely erotic final words create a vision of sensuality and transform it into an intoxicating spirituality. The ambiance, the oasis in the desert where he sucks in "long, slow drafts the wine of memory," recalls the atmosphere in stanza three, where "l'arbre et l'homme, pleins de sève, / Se pâment longuement sous l'ardeur des climats." The wine of the final stanza echoes the sap-blood of stanza three, suggesting here, too, the possibility of transubstantiation, a holy vision, perfect harmony between man and nature. With his head "in love with drunkenness," the poet in "La Chevelure" celebrates what P. M. Pasinetti calls in Baudelaire's poems to Jeanne a "ritual of recollection."[5] The poet savors ultimately the intoxicating dream, the intoxicating memory, the intoxicating oasis-mirage of love. With all these, created out of his own mind and emotions, he craves to commune.

"Harmonie du soir" is a very different type of love lyric. Still, in some ways, it sheds light on "La Chevelure." In addition, it helps deepen an understanding of the poet's quest for communion with his image of love. In both "La Chevelure" and "Harmonie du soir," dizziness, dream-memory, an idealized vision of the beloved, sensuousness and spirituality, and images of communion—or longed-for communion—permeate the atmosphere.

Harmonie du soir

Voici venir les temps où vibrant sur sa tige
Chaque fleur s'évapore ainsi qu'un encensoir;
Les sons et les parfums tournent dans l'air du soir;
Valse mélancolique et langoureux vertige!

Chaque fleur s'évapore ainsi qu'un encensoir;
Le violon frémit comme un cœur qu'on afflige;
Valse mélancolique et langoureux vertige!
Le ciel est triste et beau comme un grand reposoir.

Le violon frémit comme un cœur qu'on afflige,
Un cœur tendre, qui hait le néant vaste et noir!
Le ciel est triste et beau comme un grand reposoir;
Le soleil s'est noyé dans son sang qui se fige.

Un cœur tendre, qui hait le néant vaste et noir,
Du passé lumineux recueille tout vestige!
Le soleil s'est noyé dans son sang qui se fige . . .
Ton souvenir en moi luit comme un ostensoir!

Evening Harmony

Here come the times when swaying on its stem's crest
Each flower like a censer exhales its fragrancy;
Sounds and scents revolve in the evening's obscurity;
Melancholy waltz and languid dizziness!

Each flower like a censer exhales its fragrancy;
The violin quivers like a heart in distress;
Melancholy waltz and languid dizziness!
The sky like a lofty altar is sad and lovely.

The violin quivers like a heart in distress,
A tender heart, which hates vast black nihility!
The sky like a lofty altar is sad and lovely;
The sun has drowned in its blood that is clotting yet.

A tender heart, which hates vast black nihility,
Is gathering every trace of past luminousness!
The sun has drowned in its blood that is clotting yet . . .
Your memory, like a monstrance, shines in me!

Here, through his portrayal of nature as a temple, the poet creates his vision, at once sensuous and spiritual, beautiful and sad, of the woman loved. Because of the poem's structure, based on the Malayan pantoum form (the second and fourth lines of each stanza become the first and third of the following stanza), the poem has only two rhymes, which are repeated in the "rimes embrassées" of each quatrain. This construction, along with the limited echoing rhymes, contributes to the poem's dizzy, intoxicating effect. When the lines are repeated, they modify and intensify their meanings.

The vibrating *v* sounds of the first stanza place the reader directly in the vertiginous atmosphere that evokes and recreates the poet's feelings about his love. Nature is a vast church in which each flower seems a censer, and the censer-flower seems to become spiritualized as it "s'évapore." The vibrating motions of the first two lines become swirling movements in the following two lines, where sounds and scents revolve in the darkening air of evening, creating sensations of elegant dancing, delicious dizziness, pleasurable sadness, and sought-for languor: "Valse mélancolique et langoureux vertige!" The exclamation seems a cry of ecstasy. The sensuous and spiritual evening is ever so appealing to this poet who loves sadness,[6] languor, and the dizziness of intoxication.

The second stanza intensifies and elaborates upon the feelings of sadness mentioned only once in the first stanza, for now three lines vividly portray sadness or suffering. Each flower's exhalation in the new context evokes an idea of death, and the last line of the quatrain bears the image of death itself. The sky now seems to depict the sadness and beauty of the "reposoir," the altar upon which the Host is carried in procession: it is at once the image of death and divinity. And so, in this temple of nature, the sky suddenly becomes the altar itself. The violin that might accompany the "valse mélancolique" is personified and compared to a heart being tortured. The sounds ("comme un cœur qu'on afflige") seem to echo the disruption, the torture, the anguish. Here is the first suggestion of the poet's heart, the lover's heart: the lover's quivering, tormented heart. The melancholy dance, the dizziness and the languor of the first stanza are now more frightening as the third line of the second stanza. Through its imagery and echoing sounds this stanza suggests the torments of love; its sensuous pleasures and pains; and its deathlike, but also exalting, qualities.

Whereas evening was evoked in the opening stanza, darkness descends upon the physical, emotional, and spiritual ambiance of the third stanza. The lover's tortured, sensitive, "tender" heart is now described more fully: "Un cœur tendre, qui hait le néant vaste et noir!" The "néant" implies night, death, loneliness, emptiness, a "néant" that seems all-encompassing, blinding in its blackness "vaste et noir." It is noteworthy that nowhere in this poem about love (or at least occasioned by the poet's memory of love) does the narrator use the word *love*. But he does use the word *hate* here, summoning by its opposite what he loves, craves: light, love, transcendence, all of which he will call upon in the final stanza. The altar-sky shocks, becomes vibrant, blood-tinged in lines three and four of stanza three: "Le soleil s'est noyé dans son sang qui se fige." The altar, the sky, blood, death, drowning, congealing blood: these figures, while portraying the sunset, also intimate sacrifice, the crucifixion, the blood-wine of communion—blood sacrifice that will reveal spiritual truth, darkness that prepares the way for dazzling light.

The suffering lover, the "cœur tendre," at last becomes an active agent in the final stanza, where the darkness suddenly gives way to a spiritual illumination.

The light the lover gathers for himself, surrounded as he is by the vast, black nothingness of night, which he hates—a night both real and symbolic, dark and devoid of love—is from the "passé lumineux." Contrasted and combined with the image of the sun that has "drowned in its blood that is clotting," a figure suggesting the wine of communion, is the poet's final line, addressed to the beloved: "Ton souvenir en moi luit comme un ostensoir!" Janine N. Wickers has perceptively written about this poem: "The 'ostensoir' contains the consecrated Host, the body which corresponds to the blood of the sun, so that both elements of the Communion are present. Thus, in a sense, the poem becomes a musical celebration of the Mass in memory of the beloved."[7] The Host was already introduced in stanzas two and three of the poem with the word "reposoir": there it appeared exterior to the poet, in the image of the sky. But now the "monstrance," the receptacle in which the consecrated Host is exposed for adoration, appears within the poet as the image of his love. From the intoxicating, swirling sensuousness of the first stanza, the poet has moved through torture, blood, and darkness to images of Holy Communion, a mass, and light. The figures of sacrifice in the poem ("chaque fleur s'évapore," "reposoir," "Le soleil s'est noyé dans son sang," "ostensoir") all lead finally toward the poet-lover's vision of spiritual truth: love that is enshrined in his memory. The evening "harmony" is sensuous on the outside and spiritualized within as the poet retreats from reality into his own vision, or memory, or recreation of love, or love.

In all three poems—"Le Vin des amants," "La Chevelure," and "Harmonie du soir"—the poet-lover seeks transcendence, the exalting vision. Marvelous images of intoxication and craved-for communion permeate these poems. But the communion imagery is ironic in a way because Baudelaire never really communed with, or even communicated well with, his mistresses, or, for that matter, anyone.[8] The last lines of these three poems about craved-for communion actually highlight the lover's isolation, his loneliness. He will flee "towards the paradise" of his own "reveries" in "Le Vin des amants." He will "dream" at the woman-"oasis" where, voluptuously, he will suck in "the wine of memory" in "La Chevelure." And in "Harmonie du soir" he will be comforted, in the face of darkness and death, by the divine "memory" of the woman, who is present only in this way in the poem. In Baudelaire's love poetry the "delight most often sung is that of solitariness," notes Henri Peyre in his excellent essay "Baudelaire as a Love Poet."[9] And so Baudelaire seeks, in the future of reverie or in the past of dreams and memory, communion not with the woman but rather with his own dream, with his own vision of love. It is a lonely vision full of longing.

While these lyrics occasioned by love explore Baudelaire's quest for communion on a personal level, revealing thereby the poet's isolation, they also approach communion in a religious sense. The images of wine, blood, agony, and ecstasy all point to love as a kind of sacrifice that may reveal spiritual truth. At certain points in the poems, in fact, a kind of transubstantiation seems to be suggested, opening the door to divine light. Spiritual truth here is revealed in terms of the flesh as the poet transcends erotic love through sensuality itself. In this state of transcendent ecstasy, the poet loses sight of terrestrial things and is joined with the infinite: "Cheveux bleus . . . / Vous me rendez l'azur du ciel immense et rond," he tells Jeanne's hair. The poet cherishes these moments of transcendence, even though he knows that they do not, cannot, last.[10] They belong, after all, to the realm of the mirage. But they make life more agreeable, tolerable, and so he accepts—even begs for—the lie. This he implies in the last stanza of "La Chevelure," where he says he will sow gems in Jeanne's hair so that she may never be deaf to his desire. And this he says directly in "Semper eadem," the first poem in *Les Fleurs du mal* inspired by Mme Sabatier:

> Laissez, laissez mon cœur s'enivrer d'un *mensonge*,
> Plonger dans vos beaux yeux comme dans un beau songe,
> Et sommeiller longtemps à l'ombre de vos cils!

Baudelaire's quest for communion—physical, emotional, spiritual, at times quasi-religious—in these lyrics occasioned by love reveals his desperate, driven, and yet lucid desire to commune with what he knows is actually the intoxicating mirage of love: an image rising out of his own dreams and desires. That vision is at once exalting and evanescent, divine and diabolical. It promises truth and is sure to deceive. But it is gloriously redeeming in the moments of transcendence it affords the poet's mind, imagination, and memory.

1. Charles Baudelaire, *Œuvres complètes* (Paris: Gallimard, Bibliothèque de la Pléiade, 1961), p. 104. Future quotations are from this edition.

2. The three translations that appear in this chapter by Enid Rhodes Peschel also appear in *Four French Symbolist Poets: Baudelaire, Rimbaud, Verlaine, Mallarmé*, trans. Enid Rhodes Peschel (Athens: Ohio University Press).

3. This translation was first published in the special issue of *Sou'wester*, 6 (1978) devoted to French symbolist poetry.

4. For a discussion of the importance of this stanza, see Victor Brombert, "The Will to Ecstasy: The Example of Baudelaire's 'La Chevelure,'" *Yale French Studies* 50 (1974): 55–63.

5. P. M. Pasinetti, "The 'Jeanne Duval' Poems in *Les Fleurs du mal*," in *Baudelaire: A Collection of Critical Essays*, ed. Henri Peyre (Englewood Cliffs, N.J.: Prentice-Hall, 1962), p. 90.

6. One cannot forget Baudelaire's "définition du Beau,—de mon Beau. C'est quelque chose d'ardent et de triste, quelque chose d'un peu vague . . . qui fait rêver à la fois,—mais d'une manière confuse,—de volupté et de tristesse" (*Fusées*, p. 1255).

7. Janine N. Wickers, *Explicator* 33 (September 1974), item 8.

8. For example, these frightening words from *Mon Cœur mis à nu*: "Dans l'amour comme dans presque toutes les affaires humaines, l'entente cordiale est le résultat d'un malentendu. Ce malentendu, c'est le plaisir. L'homme crie: 'Oh! mon ange!' La femme roucoule: 'Maman! maman!' Et ces deux imbéciles sont persuadés qu'ils pensent de concert. —Le gouffre infranchissable, qui fait l'incommunicabilité, reste infranchi" (pp. 1289–90).

9. Henri Peyre, "Baudelaire as a Love Poet," in *Baudelaire as a Love Poet and Other Essays,* ed. Lois Boe Hyslop (University Park: Pennsylvania State University Press, 1969), p. 36.

10. Baudelaire "a aimé seul, adoré et chanté ce qu'il savait être *masque ou décor,*" writes Jean Prévost in *Baudelaire* (Paris: Mercure de France, 1964), p. 229.

The Danaïdes' Vessel:
On Reading Baudelaire's Allegories

NATHANIEL WING

An inquiry that proposes to reexamine the functions of allegory in *Les Fleurs du mal* risks, at the outset, recalling with particular insistence that most famous of Baudelaire's allegorical personifications, the delicate monster in "Au lecteur," L'Ennui, who threatens to engulf the world in a vast yawn. Conventional poetic devices, at least since the mid nineteenth century, are not held in good repute, insofar as they have been associated with normative rhetoric and with the use of figurative language as an "ornament of discourse." Yet there is a profusion of allegory in *Les Fleurs du mal* that cannot be written off simply, as Valéry and others would have it, as lapses into an outmoded eloquence, or as sententious and moralistic posturing.[1] Furthermore, Baudelaire praises the figure un- equivocally as "ce genre si spirituel, que les peintres maladroits nous ont accoutumés à mépriser, ... est vraiment l'une des formes primitives et les plus naturelles de la poésie."[2]

In the familiar late-eighteenth-century and romantic schema, allegory as a figural transfer of meaning is eclipsed in importance by symbol, which comes to stand for processes of analogy functioning within a radical monism. The problem of allegorical constructs in *Les Fleurs du mal* is considerably more complex than this opposition between symbol and allegory would lead us to believe. Our reading cannot place itself outside of the debate, however; that controversy, which inextricably mixes considerations about language with metaphysics and aesthetics, necessarily informs a reading of the poems; for its delimiting concepts are to be found in those texts, in the art and literary criticism, and in the *Journaux intimes,* and it is for that reason that I review it briefly here.[3] The aesthetic devaluation of allegory, furthermore, is the source of irony in many of *Les Fleurs du mal,* in which the texts play with and against a shopworn rhetorical figure. Within a certain aesthetic and metaphysical enclo- sure, however, concepts are frequently turned against themselves and their presuppositions undermined by processes of meaning that cannot be accounted for by the traditional rhetorical/aesthetic definitions. My inquiry will consider the interplay between these configurations of meaning.

For Baudelaire the term *symbol* frequently stands for figurative language in general; it is assumed to be capable of transforming all individual experience into general truth, since, as De Man summarizes, "The subjectivity of experience is preserved when it is translated into language; the world is then no longer seen as a configuration of entities that designate a plurality of distinct and isolated meaning, but as a configuration of symbols ultimately leading to a total, single, and universal meaning."[4] The numerous passages that Baudelaire devotes to symbol give a privileged status to the symbolic mode as the poetic language of concrete intuition, designated by various interchangeable expressions, such as "symbole," "correspondance," "analogie universelle," "surnaturalisme." Allegory, on the other hand, as the morpheme *allos*—other—indicates, differs from the process of universal analogy in both its function and its finality. It relays meaning from one semantic level to another, within a limited polyvalence. The suggestiveness of allegory in art is criticized as too rational, exhausted as soon as the meaning (signified) is attained.

The short essay "L'Art philosophique" (1859) formulates this contrast succinctly and in terms sufficiently general to apply equally well to the signifying systems of painting or literary language. Baudelaire reproaches philosophical art for meddling in concerns that are properly those of didactic prose by seeking to replace the book and to teach history, morality, and philosophy:

> Toute bonne sculpture, toute bonne peinture, toute bonne musique, suggère les sentiments et les rêveries qu'elle veut suggérer.
> Mais le raisonnement, la déduction, appartiennent au livre.
> Ainsi l'art philosophique est un retour vers l'imagerie nécessaire à l'enfance des peuples, et s'il était rigoureusement fidèle à lui-même, il s'astreindrait à juxtaposer autant d'images successives qu'il en est contenu dans une phrase quelconque qu'il voudrait exprimer. . . .
> Plus l'art voudra être philosophiquement clair, plus il se dégradera et remontera vers l'hiéroglyphe enfantin. [Pp. 1099–100]

As an example of the aberration, Baudelaire describes in detail a representation of "une bonne mort," a virtuous man surprised in his sleep by death; each figural element in the painting is correlated to an extrinsic meaning: "Il faut, dans la traduction des œuvres d'art philosophiques, apporter une grande minutie et une grande attention; là les lieux, le décor, les meubles, les ustensiles (voir Hogarth), tout est allégorie, allusion, hiéroglyphes, rébus" ("L'Art philosophique," p. 1101).[5] Both the separation of levels of meaning and the rational link between them provoke Baudelaire's criticism, for in this mode the signifier is cut off from a (mythical) consubstantial relationship between the sensible and the nonsensible, which would obtain in the symbolic mode of "pure," "modern" art. The conventionalized relay between levels of meaning in allegory both maintains a separation of the levels and claims to link them conceptually through a translation. In terms of contemporary semiotics, the first level of meaning is constituted by the link between a signifier and a signified and subsequently becomes a signifier for a secondary signified.

Allegory thus functions through its parallel systems as both a deferral and an attainment of meaning; in positing and incorporating a second semantic level, it can be recognized as a figure of containment. As such, it is inimical to that expansion of meaning in the symbolic mode through universal analogy, which, for Baudelaire, is a virtually limitless multiplicity and concentration of being produced by the associative potential of language. The opening paragraph of "L'Art philosophique" briefly states that ideal: "Qu'est-ce que l'art pur suivant la conception moderne? C'est créer une magie suggestive contenant à la fois l'objet et le sujet, le monde extérieur à l'artiste et l'artiste lui-même" (p. 1099). In this passage characteristic elements of the symbolic mode are a fusion between the semantic and representative functions of language, in analogy, an abolition of the distinctions between the particular and the general, and a synthesis between subject and object in a relation of simultaneity.[6]

I return to these distinctions because, as I have noted, they function according to the schema outlined in many of Baudelaire's poems and because they are undercut in others by certain textual processes. Furthermore, the terms in which a discussion of the figures is necessarily formulated—binary relationships (semantic or intersubjective), separation between levels of meaning, a temporal dialectic between interconnected sign systems—lead to a reconsideration of the problems of duality in Baudelaire, to a reexamination of meaning, not as a system of containment, but as an irreducible and genetic multiplicity.[7] Finally, these questions invite us to look again at the still taunting problem of ironies in Baudelaire.

This reading will not propose an all-inclusive typology of allegory in Baudelaire's verse. A comprehensive system as a totalizing discourse, whether that of the poetic or critical text, is subject to suspicion, as Baudelaire notes in a passage written in 1855: "un système est une espèce de damnation qui nous pousse à une abjuration perpétuelle; il en faut toujours inventer un autre, et cette fatigue est un cruel châtiment. Et toujours mon système était beau, vaste, spacieux, commode, propre et lisse surtout" ("L'Exposition universelle de 1855," p. 955). In various ways, however, the question of control is central to the inquiry, as each text manipulates and undermines allegory as a figure that delimits and masters meaning. In "Le Masque" the opacity or transparency of an allegorical enigma is unveiled with ironic astonishment as the allegorical signified is revealed, yet that ironic control of meaning is itself subjected to irony by the text. In a second group of poems—"Le Cygne," "Les Sept Vieillards," "Le Tonneau de la haine"—allegory momentarily effects a recuperation of meaning, hidden and controlled by the figural system, only to be caught in a vertiginous and virtually limitless multiplication of meaning in a process of production and open displacement. Irony in this second group of texts is far more unsettling than in the first; it is a delirium verging on madness.

"Le Masque," in "Spleen et idéal," is dedicated to the sculptor Ernest

Christophe and subtitled "Statue allégorique dans le goût de la Renaissance."
The poem describes a statue of a woman in a profusion of visual detail
commensurate with the physical abundance of the model:

> Contemplons ce trésor de grâces florentines;
> Dans l'ondulation de ce corps musculeux
> L'Elégance et la Force abondent, sœurs divines.
> Cette femme, morceau vraiment miraculeux,
> Divinement robuste, adorablement mince,
> Est faite pour trôner sur des lits somptueux,
> Et charmer les loisirs d'un pontife ou d'un prince.

Her gaze is a combination of fatuousness, languor, and mockery:

> —Aussi, vois ce souris fin et voluptueux
> Où la Fatuité promène son extase;
> Ce long regard sournois, langoureux et moqueur;
> Ce visage mignard, tout encadré de gaze,
> Dont chaque trait nous dit avec un air vainqueur:
> "La Volupté m'appelle et l'Amour me couronne!"

Both narrator and reader are set in the text as spectators; and, as the poet
invites the reader to approach the statue, the narrator, in a series of hyperboles,
proclaims astonishment at the deception of art ("O blasphème de l'art! ô
surprise fatale!"). The voluptuous face is only a mask, the statue a two-headed
monster: "La femme au corps divin, promettant le bonheur, / Par le haut se
termine en monstre bicéphale!" A parallel series of terms designating unequivocally the artistic travesty of truth ("masque," "décor," "suborneur," "la face
qui ment") and those that identify the "true representation" ("La véritable tête,
et la sincère face") point unmistakably to the dual structure of meaning in
allegory:

> —Mais non! ce n'est qu'un masque, un décor suborneur,
> Ce visage éclairé d'une exquise grimace,
> Et, regarde, voici, crispée atrocement,
> La véritable tête, et la sincère face
> Renversée à l'abri de la face qui ment.

The enigma is articulated explicitly: "Mais pourquoi pleure-t-elle? Elle, beauté
parfaite . . ." and answered three lines below, as the key to the allegory is
provided:

> —Elle pleure, insensé, parce qu'elle a vécu!
> Et parce qu'elle vit! Mais ce qu'elle déplore
> Surtout, ce qui la fait frémir jusqu'aux genoux,
> C'est que demain, hélas! il faudra vivre encore!
> Demain, après-demain et toujours!—comme nous!

The poem contains elements of surprise and mystery, which in Baudelaire's
aesthetic are necessary to artistic effect, and which are inscribed throughout *Les*

Fleurs du mal. These effects are ironized here, however, by their very explicitness, by the mock exaggeration of surprise, and by the singularly direct question and answer format in which the moral of the fable is presented. In this way the text plays ironically with the dual (perhaps one could say two-faced) structure of allegory, with both the initially enigmatic distance between levels of meaning and the necessarily rational correlation between those levels. A reading of the poem that would delimit the ironic effects to this implicit devaluation of a didactic rhetorical figure could be substantiated by reference to Baudelaire's comments on sculpture in the Salons of 1846 and 1859. In the section "Pourquoi la sculpture est ennuyeuse" of the Salon of 1846, sculpture is criticized as either too primitive ("un art de Caraïbes") or too naïvely mimetic. In the "Salon de 1859" Baudelaire discusses the statue by Christophe that was the model for this text, noting: "Le caractère vigoureux du corps fait un contraste pittoresque avec l'expression mystique d'une idée toute mondaine, et la surprise n'y joue pas un rôle plus important qu'il n'est permis" (p. 1095).

In both the poem and the prose analysis, effects of surprise, allegory or irony, are strictly controlled. To delimit allegory and irony in "Le Masque" in this manner is to read them as vehicles of containment. This is true in part, of course, but one may question whether the moral is that simple and explore the possibility that a critique of the irony of containment is already inscribed in the text. A reexamination of the final stanza suggests that the ironic distance between the poet/reader/spectator of the allegory and the allegorical signified is itself the subject of irony. The accumulation of logical connectors and the periodic syntax of the conclusions ("Mais ce qu'elle déplore / Surtout, ce qui la fait frémir . . . C'est que . . .") seem to posit the truth of the text very much in the manner of those literal translations of philosophical art that Baudelaire criticizes elsewhere. The final words of the poem, however ("comme nous!"), unexpectedly narrow the distance between the message figured by the allegorical statue and the reader/spectator as judge by including both the reader and the poet as protagonists in the same metaphysical conflict as that conveyed by the allegory. The clear conscience of ironic containment is itself the subject of irony through the revelation that it is a mystified consciousness. There is thus a far more complex and indeterminate interplay of irony here than our initial reading anticipated, and one that links the metaphysical dilemma allegorized by the text to the structure of the allegory. The meaning constituted by the allegorical system can consist, as De Man has shown, only "in repetition of a previous sign with which it can never coincide, since it is of the essence of this previous sign to be pure anteriority."[8] Meaning is structured here as a process of deferral. An indefinite temporal displacement of sense is oriented simultaneously in two directions: the meaning of the allegory depends upon a previous sign, the first face of the statue derives its meaning from the second, the face of suffering. Yet the discovery of that second face does not delimit meaning in a stable manner but projects it as irony in a displacement toward an indefinite future ("encore").

The initial interplay between allegory and aesthetic conventions is less marked in several other texts of *Les Fleurs du mal* in which meaning subverts the traditional mode of allegory as a figure of containment and concurrently undermines the status of the textual first person as a stable subject. I shall outline this problematic in readings of "Le Cygne," "Les Sept Vieillards," and "Le Tonneau de la haine."

The allegorical signified in "Le Cygne" is introduced in the opening line of the poem and thereby reinforces the traditionally rational connection between the two levels of meaning:

> Andromaque, je pense à vous! Ce petit fleuve,
> Pauvre et triste miroir où jadis resplendit
> L'immense majesté de vos douleurs de veuve,
> Ce Simoïs menteur qui par vos pleurs grandit,
>
> A fécondé soudain ma mémoire fertile,
> Comme je traversais le nouveau Carrousel.

A link between the decor and, by extension, the forthcoming narrative anecdote is established as a correlation between signifieds, in which an immediate experience is read by the poet as the relay of an anterior meaning. The first section of the poem describes a construction site at the Nouveau Carrousel, which figures in its rapid change and disorder the instability of the heart. An analeptic narrative then recalls an earlier scene in which a swan had escaped from its cage in a menagerie since destroyed. This allegory of exile is too well known to require elucidation here; my main interest is in the interrelation between allegories in the two sections of the poem. In the first, the figure clearly functions as a circumscribed polyvalence, in the traditional manner, whereas the second part of the text puts in'question the possibility of that very containment of meaning. The opening stanza of the second section repeats the descriptive framework and returns explicitly to the poet/observer as interpreter of the allegorical landscape, in an apparent reassertion of his mastery over meanings:

> Paris change! mais rien dans ma mélancolie
> N'a bougé! palais neufs, échafaudages, blocs,
> Vieux faubourgs, tout pour moi devient allégorie,
> Et mes chers souvenirs sont plus lourds que des rocs.

The exclamation "tout pour moi devient allégorie" may be read initially as a rather conventional hyperbole exalting the poet's inventiveness, yet read "dans tous les sens," as Baudelaire counsels elsewhere;[9] and in context it is hardly a reassuring statement, as it precedes an enumeration of no fewer than nine allegorical figures in a series that remains open.

An anaphoric sequence, structured as a repetition of the verbal unit "je pense à," presents the series of synonymous figures: a negress, nostalgic for "la superbe Afrique"; an indefinite "quiconque a perdu ce qui ne se retrouve / Jamais, jamais!"; those who nurse suffering like a she-wolf; orphans; the poet's own memory, which sounds like a horn in the forest; sailors forgotten on an island; captives; the vanquished; and, finally, an indefinite "à bien d'autres encore," which leaves the series perpetually open. The supposedly rational monosemic or polysemic figure functions, then, in a curious and unsettling manner, to inscribe the predicament of a thought caught in an open and endless displacement. Poetic thought is no longer delimited by the semantic horizon of the allegorical signified; it breaks that horizon by the repetition of an endless discontinuity. Each allegorical figure reiterates the impossibility of retrieving a lost origin; the loss that is allegorized here is that which is always already absent. The "object" ("ce qui ne se retrouve jamais"), moreover, is not easily compensated for by the language that figures its displacement, for language is here powerless to restore the plenitude of an original presence.

The following poem in "Les Tableaux parisiens," "Les Sept Vieillards," to which I shall allude only briefly, carries one step further the process of displacing meaning in an allegorical system, and that is the step into madness. To think the reiteration of an allegorical figure as a repetition cut from any link to a signified, as origin of its own replication "Sosie inexorable . . . Dégoûtant Phénix, fils et père de lui-même," is to think the production of sense as non-sense. There is no nostalgia here for a lost plenitude, an absence that is the deluded form of presence, but its ultimate guarantor. In the pure interplay of allegorical signifiers, the poem provokes the terror of non-sense, as an attack on the formation of meaning. As the poet encounters

> . . . un vieillard dont les guenilles jaunes
> Imitaient la couleur de ce ciel pluvieux,
> Et dont l'aspect aurait fait pleuvoir les aumônes,
> Sans la méchanceté qui luisait dans ses yeux

he is assaulted by a series of baroque spectres; the old man appears seven times: "Car je comptai sept fois, de minute en minute, / Ce sinistre vieillard qui se multipliait!" The enigma here is not formulated as a sense veiled by the allegory; the mystery is the meaning of repetition. Again the poet is the reader of the allegory, but what he seeks to interpret is the process of its proliferation.

An extension of the completed cycle of seven would represent the leap into infinity:

> Aurais-je, sans mourir, contemplé le huitième,
> Sosie inexorable, ironique et fatal,
> Dégoûtant Phénix, fils et père de lui-même?
> —Mais je tournai le dos au cortège infernal.

Death menaces the poet at the moment that the proliferation threatens to become engaged in an infinite spiral. Exasperated, he turns away from the allegorical scene to take refuge in his room, hoping to recover his reason; the solace that he finds there, however, is the delirium of madness:

> Vainement ma raison voulait prendre la barre;
> La tempête en jouant déroutait ses efforts,
> Et mon âme dansait, dansait, vieille gabarre
> Sans mâts, sur une mer monstrueuse et sans bords!

Repetition is both the insistence of meaning and its impossibility within the enclosure of a system that requires that meaning circulate as the sense *of* something. That need is figured here by the allegorical decor, by the poet as reader, by the room, even by the anticipated, but absent, limits of the sea. Madness begins where reason contemplates pure gratuitousness, and, in this text, that is the undoing of the first person as a subject. That gratuitousness, however, is an uncanny repetition; as the allegory escapes the control of the subject/reader there is a terrifying shift in the functional value of the allegory from a figure of containment to a figure of the uncontrollable return of the fearful. The rhetoric of mastery is violently displaced by the rhetoric of the uncontrollable.[10]

"Le Tonneau de la haine," the last text I shall consider, takes the myth of the Danaïdes' vessel as its literal level. The vat that the Danaïdes were condemned to fill as punishment for having slaughtered their husbands is allegorized here as Hate. The role of the Danaïdes is taken by Vengence, who "A beau précipiter dans ses ténèbres vides / De grands seaux pleins du sang et des larmes des morts," and it is the devil who pokes holes in the vat through which flow the blood and tears:

> Le Démon fait des trous secrets à ces abîmes,
> Par où fuiraient mille ans de sueurs et d'efforts,
> Quand même elle saurait ranimer ses victimes,
> Et pour les pressurer resusciter leurs corps.

This overfilling, which is both an excess (there is too much to be contained) and a deficiency (the container cannot fully enclose), repeats a process figured in "Le Cygne" and "Les Sept Vieillards." Once again, this endless proliferation is a very threatening indeterminacy, for what is figured here is the loss of the illusion of meaning. Containment, fullness, completion are necessary, since the buckets are themselves being filled and continually being emptied into the vat, but the process is inadequate to the task. Allegory thus inscribes the impossibility of figurative language to contain what it would hold.

This allegory of indeterminacy is doubled in the tercets by a second allegory, this time presenting Hate as a drunkard whose thirst multiplies with its satisfaction. An unhappy boozer, Hate can never know oblivion by passing out under the table:

La Haine est un ivrogne au fond d'une taverne,
Qui sent toujours la soif naître de la liqueur
Et se multiplier comme l'hydre de Lerne.

—Mais les buveurs heureux connaissent leur vainqueur,
Et la Haine est vouée à ce sort lamentable
De ne pouvoir jamais s'endormir sous la table.

The tragically grotesque image of Hate in the final tercet not only reiterates the characterization of desire (Hate) as seeking an object endlessly displaced, but it ironizes in a most deprecatory manner the ironic consciousness. The self-multiplication that forms the ironic interruption of being is written elsewhere as a process of demystification asserted, as in "L'Héautontimorouménos," as a lucid sadomasochistic doubling of the self, both victim and torturer, wound and knife:

Je suis la plaie et le couteau!
Je suis le soufflet et la joue!
Je suis les membres et la roue,
Et la victime et le bourreau!

In "L'Irrémédiable" irony is consciousness contemplating its own fragmentation: "Tête-à-tête sombre et limpide / Qu'un cœur devenu son miroir!"

In "Le Tonneau de la haine," however, desire's victim cannot turn awareness of the predicament into an investigation of inauthenticity. In an interplay between irony and allegory, meaning as a process of positing and circumscribing effects of sense is interrupted and indefinitely deferred. In the quatrains the poem inscribes a figure of the figure of allegory as a system that both calls for and denies the possibility of sense. The text also inscribes irony as a turning away of meaning by figuring a poetic language discontinuous with its own telos. Where he anticipates rhetorical constructs that deflect, yet ultimately reappropriate, meanings, the reader is engaged by, and in, the writing of a limitless deferral, which demystifies some of Baudelaire's most persistent myths.

1. See my "Stylistic Functions of Rhetoric in Baudelaire's 'Au Lecteur,'" *Kentucky Romance Quarterly* 19, no. 4 (1972): 447–60.

2. Charles Baudelaire, "Le Poëme du haschisch," in *Œuvres complètes,* ed. Y.-G. Le Dantec and Claude Pichois (Paris: Gallimard, Bibliothèque de la Pléiade, 1961), p. 376. All quotations from Baudelaire are taken from this edition.

3. For discussion of this opposition between allegorical and symbolic modes that merged in the literature of England, Germany, and France in the late eighteenth century and early nineteenth century, see Meyer Abrams, "Structure and Style in the Greater Romantic Lyric," in *From Sensibility to Romanticism: Essays Presented to F. A. Pottle,* ed. F. W. Hillis and H. Bloom (New York: Oxford, 1965); Paul De Man, "The Rhetoric of Temporality," in *Interpretation: Theory and Practice,* ed. C. S. Singleton (Baltimore: Johns Hopkins University Press, 1969); H.-G. Gadamer,

Truth and Method, trans. and ed. G. Barden and J. Cumming (New York: Seabury Press, 1975); T. Todorov, *Théories du symbole* (Paris: Seuil, 1977); and W. K. Wimsatt, "The Structure of Romantic Nature Imagery," in *The Verbal Icon* (Lexington: University of Kentucky Press, 1967).

4. De Man, p. 174; see Gadamer, pp. 67–73.

5. Baudelaire groups different semiotic processes in the four terms *allégorie, allusion, hiéro-glyphe,* and *rébus;* what is of interest to me here is the common link provided by the term *translation,* which supposes a separation between levels of meaning and a correlation to be established rationally between them.

6. See De Man on Coleridge, pp. 177–79, and Todorov, "Symbole et allégorie," in *Théories du symbole,* Goethe and Schelling, pp. 235–59.

7. See J. Derrida, *Positions* (Paris: Editions de minuit, 1972), pp. 57–64, for a summary of distinctions between meaning considered as accessible to thematic (polysemic) readings and meaning as *dissémination,* a nonfinite number of semantic effects. See also "La Double Séance" in his *La Dissémination* (Paris: Seuil, 1972).

8. De Man, p. 190.

9. The expression appears in the opening pages of "Du vin et du hachish," p. 323, in which Baudelaire crticizes Brillat-Savarin's *Physiologie du goût* for its blindness to the poetic properties of wine: "Vous aurez beau feuilleter le volume, le retourner dans tous les sens, le lire à rebours, à l'envers, de droite à gauche et de gauche à droite." The passage is an invitation to disrupt the traditionally linear, metonymic process of reading and anticipates better-known statements by Mallarmé and Rimbaud.

10. See Freud's discussions of involuntary repetition as the return of material repressed by consciousness: "The Uncanny," in *On Creativity and the Unconscious,* ed. B. Nelson (New York: Harper & Row, 1958), pp. 122–61; *Beyond the Pleasure Principle,* ed. J. Strachey (New York: Norton, 1961).

Seeing and Saying in Baudelaire's "Les Aveugles"

Les Aveugles

Contemple-les, mon âme; ils sont vraiment affreux!
Pareils aux mannequins; vaguement ridicules;
Terribles, singuliers comme les somnambules;
Dardant on ne sait où leurs globes ténébreux.

Leurs yeux, d'où la divine étincelle est partie,
Comme s'ils regardaient au loin, restent levés
Au ciel; on ne les voit jamais vers les pavés
Pencher rêveusement leur tête appesantie.

Ils traversent ainsi le noir illimité,
Ce frère du silence éternel. O cité!
Pendant qu'autour de nous tu chantes, ris et beugles,

Éprise du plaisir jusqu'à l'atrocité,
Vois! je me traîne aussi! mais, plus qu'eux hébété,
Je dis: Que cherchent-ils au Ciel, tous ces aveugles?[1]

This text has attracted little interpretative commentary. Apart from speculation on the sources, pictorial and literary,[2] the most notable contribution has been Peter Nurse's fine explication de texte,[3] which contains some remarkable metric analysis and offers a reading that is the point of departure for the present study. Nurse concentrates on the relationship between "je" and "les aveugles" in the sonnet; I wish to draw attention more specifically to the presence of two other actors, "mon âme" and the "cité." These are of most immediate interest in that they are the subjects of an act of seeing, which is called for in the imperative mood by "je" ("Contemple-les, mon âme," "O cité! . . . Vois!"), the objects of the act being respectively "les aveugles" and "je." Since "les aveugles" are by definition unseeing, whereas "je" explicitly delegates the function of contemplation to his soul while no less explicitly conferring on himself that of speaking (speaking the poem, speaking the imperatives, and also speaking the embedded question in line 14), it may be worth examining not only the bond between "je" and "les aveugles" but also the relationship between "les aveugles" and the seeing instances, "mon âme" and the "cité," which are also the two objects of "je"'s address; and, finally, the specificity of the speaking "I."

This investigation is part of ongoing research into the structure and unity of the "Tableaux parisiens" sequence in *Les Fleurs du mal,* the hypothesis of which is that since Paris is not omnipresent in these poems and since the pictorial element is itself always presented in a subjective framework through the intervention of poetic functions like dreaming, remembering, and interpreting, the unity of the poems is more likely to reside in the problematics of the omnipresent subject, "je," as he reveals himself not only through his seeing but in the content and mode of his saying.

THE BLIND

The blind, though they cannot see, have traditionally been regarded as seers, endowed with inner vision. As Victor Hugo puts it, in "A un poète aveugle," "L'aveugle voit dans l'ombre un monde de clarté. / Quand l'œil du corps s'éteint, l'œil de l'esprit s'allume." Mediating the sacred, they occupy a central position in the profane world, standing, according to a Rilke poem, as "ein Markstein namenloser Reiche," "der Gestirne stiller Mittelpunkt" ("Pont du Carrousel"). Baudelaire's blind men retain something of this numinous quality, being "terribles, singuliers comme des somnambules"; but they are deprived of the inner and spiritual virtù that provides mythical justification for the aura that surrounds the blind and the awe in which they are held. Like tailors' models they have no inner reality; and their outer-directed eyes turn to a sky whose dubious noological status is indicated by the orthographical alternation between upper- and lowercase c in the word "ciel." Objectless in this sense, their look becomes directionless as well, "dardant on ne sait où leurs globes ténébreux." Hence, if the phrase "vraiment affreux," which describes them, is an ambivalent one (since it may be taken as a colloquial expression of repugnance, or else held to direct attention to the etymological sense of *affreux,* derived from *les affres*), they are "vaguement"—but unequivocally—"ridicules."

Furthermore, the term *aveugles* is plural; and the centrality of the single blind figure of the archetype has dissolved into a type of collective anonymity that has led commentators to think of Breughel and to invoke popular wisdom about the blind leading the blind. From being sacred figures, and hence unique, the blind have acquired representative status: "tous ces aveugles" are an allegorical figure of humanity in the mass, of the crowd—or they would be if the poem did not distinguish them from the noisy, pleasure-seeking "cité" all around them. The suggestion is that we are all in torment in this poem: the human collectivity at its most general, "éprise du plaisir jusqu'à l'atrocité," is self-tormenting in its mindless unconcern for the transcendent dimension; more aware, the blind in their "affres" traverse the immensity of darkness while seeking a transcendence where they are unlikely to find it, in the external world of the sky; only "I" is in communication with a transcendent entity, but it is a purely inner and personal one, "mon âme," and he too drags himself like the blind through the world of the city, which "autour de nous" sings and laughs and bellows.

One might think of Hölderlin, "Aber weh! es wandelt in Nacht, es wohnt, wie im Orkus, / Ohne Göttliches unser Geschlecht" ("Der Archipelagus"), were it not that Baudelaire's underworld is less a place of explicit negation of the divine ("Ohne Göttliches") than it is one of anxiety and interrogation: "Que cherchent-ils au Ciel, tous ces aveugles?" This questioning is the characteristic response, in the "Tableaux parisiens," to the perception of the allegorical, which poses the problem of meaning in a world from which the divine—the meaning-giving dimension of existence—is to all intents and purposes absent. Thus, the emblematic "squelette laboureur," a more explicit figure of the living dead than the blind themselves, provokes equally anguished metaphysical questioning; whereas in the poem in which the key phrase "tout pour moi devient allégorie" occurs, the exiled swan—

> Vers le ciel quelquefois, comme l'homme d'Ovide
> Vers le Ciel ironique et cruellement bleu,
> Sur son cou convulsif tendant sa tête avide,
> Comme s'il adressait des reproches à Dieu!

—adopts exactly the same heaven-scrutinizing posture as the blind.

"JE"

Unlike the blind, however, who seek the unknown in the heavens, the "I" of the poem seeks understanding of a spectacle in the here below; and to that end he has recourse to a seeing instance that is both internal and endowed with a specifically named faculty, that of contemplation. The nature of contemplation and its implications for "je" will be examined later; but it should be noted that "je" relates also to an external instance, the "cité," in a way that directly parallels the relationship of the blind to the sky. The blind look to a sky they cannot see, and "je" asks to be seen by a community that (it is clear) cannot hear him: each seeks a response that cannot be forthcoming. Hence the imperative "Vois!" has an illocutionary force very different from that of "Contemple-les, mon âme," the exclamation point (present in line 13, absent in line 1) distinguishing the urgency of an impassioned appeal, presupposing failure, from the calmer mode of address that assumes it will be heeded.

"Je" relates to the city because he is a speaking entity ("je dis") in a world of sound; for the city is distinguished from the blind as the hell of sound is distinguished from the hell of silence. The blind traverse the darkness, "frère du silence éternel," whereas the city's "atrocité" (etymologically blackness) derives from a pleasure-seeking that is directly equated with noise: "tu chantes, ris et beugles." Just so does the speech of "je" set him apart from the silent contemplation of the soul. But speech also disjoins "je" from the "cité" as much as it conjoins him. The function *dire* contrasts with the functions of the city partly in terms of articulateness versus inarticulate expression (*dire* and *chanter* versus *rire* and *beugler*), partly in terms of pedestrian versus lyric modes of articulation (*dire* versus *chanter*), and entirely in terms of volume and control, the unemotional mildness of *dire* contrasting with the spontaneity and loudness of *chanter, rire,* and *beugler.* The implied inaudibility of "je"'s questioning speech in the sound-world of the city, and hence the similarity of his vain questioning with the vain seeking of the blind, is what makes him of a piece with the latter, silently looking in a city too noisily addicted to pleasure to pay them heed. And this community of "je" with the blind is recorded in the phrase "autour de nous."

This unity is quickly modified, however, by the assertion that "je" is "plus qu'eux hébété." In this way the contextual meaning of *hébétude,* as the common quality of "je" and the blind, becomes clear: it is that which distinguishes them from the uncaring city, the awareness implied by their joint questioning and seeking. But if "je" is "plus qu'eux hébété," it seems that it is because to their seeking, obstinate and dogged as it is, he adds the questioning that inquires after the meaning of the seeking itself. This adds a further degree of consciousness that is a direct result of contemplating the blind; hence it is through his mastery of the function of contemplation, through his possession of a soul, that "je" stands out as an isolated individual, distinct even from those whose paradigmatic loneliness in the city he shares. Contemplation—which opposes him to the blind—is one of the keys to the specificity of "je"; speech—which distinguishes him from the contemplating soul—will prove to be the other.

CONTEMPLATION

Contemplation versus Seeking

One needs to distinguish not only the function of contemplation from the function of seeking but also the different relationships between "je" and the soul's contemplation, on the one hand, and between "je" and the blind men's seeking, on the other. A comparison between the opening and closing phrases of the poem enables us to do both. The calm initial imperative is perlocutionary and presupposes unproblematic relationships both between "je" and the soul and between the soul and the object of its contemplation, the blind. But the final question implies dubiousness and uncertainty—on the one hand in the relationship between the questioner, "je," and the object of his question, the blind (whom he does not understand), and on the other between the blind and the object of their search, which is and remains an enigma. The difference in relationship between "je" and the contemplating soul and "je" and the seeking blind is further reflected in the contrast between the possessive "mon âme" and the deictic "tous ces aveugles," with implications of control and intimacy in one case, and of exteriority, bafflement, and lack of control on the other. (There is some resemblance between the unindividuated blind men and the menacing multiplication of identical figures that occurs in "Les Sept Vieillards.") Contemplation mediates relationships between "je" and the soul, and between the soul and the blind, that are continuous (in the sense that no difficulty is assumed); whereas questioning and seeking produce relationships of discontinuity between "je" and "les aveugles" and between "les aveugles" and "le ciel," respectively. It thus becomes clear that contemplation is to be distinguished not only from the seeking of the blind but also from the speech activity of "je." Let us first examine in more detail how it differs from the activity of the blind.

It is evident that the major distinction between the soul's *contempler* and the blind men's *chercher* derives from the differing axes, horizontal versus vertical, that define the direction of the two functions. The locative "au Ciel" implies the type of answer expected by the question "que cherchent-ils?" by exploiting the traditional connotations of verticality (as well as of capitalization); but the question arises precisely because of the vertical direction of the search. The implication is one of incredulity that the blind can indeed be seeking what they appear to be seeking—the noological—where they are seeking it, "au Ciel." The zero locative in "contemple-les" has the opposite implications: the locative is unexpressed because it is understood that the appropriate axis of contemplation is the horizontal; it takes place in the world of *ici-bas*. But a further significant difference between contemplation and seeking—and one not unrelated to the difference of axes—derives from the comparison of the metaphysical status of the respective subjects and objects of the two functions: *chercher* involves a cosmological subject ("ils") in search of a noological (or transcendent) object; but, conversely, *contempler* involves a noological subject ("mon âme") addressing itself to a cosmological object ("contemple-les"), the blind. The coincidence of the object of contemplation (the blind) with the subject of the search (the blind), and that of the object of the search (the noological) with the subject of contemplation (the soul), effectively define the basic *donnée* of the poem and relate it in historical terms to the sensibility of the "disappearance of God." The blind are seeking the spirit of the universe where it is not, in the sky, and as the object of vision—whereas it is in fact the subject of vision, and situated within man.

Contemplation versus Dreaming

That spiritual power lies within man and controls his relationship, not with the heavens, but with the world, is a fundamental assertion of the second quatrain. In a hasty reading these lines appear to be saying the same thing twice: the blind look upward, they do not look downward. Closer analysis points up the difference in value attached to the two statements: the relationship of "leurs yeux" and "au ciel" couples significantly with that of "vers les pavés" and "leur tête" so as to produce a contrast between two types of illusion—the false illusion ("comme s'ils regardaient au loin") in which the blind obstinately persist ("restent levés"), and the compensatory mental faculty that would be available to them, were they to accept the implications of the departure of the "divine étincelle" from their eyes and allow their head to bend, heavily but "rêveusement," toward the pavement. Dreaming thus appears as the function common to humanity that most resembles the individual privilege awarded to those who, being in possession of a soul, have at their command the function of contemplation: in each case the spiritual faculty is inner, and internal to man.

But a head is not a soul, and the two are significantly contrasted, not only by the difference between first person and third person possessives, "mon âme" and "leur tête," but also through their respective positions in the initial and closing hemistichs of the quatrains. There is a clear hierarchization of the two functions—that of the soul and that of the head—that is implicit in the poem: "rêveusement," as an adverb of manner, tells nothing about the outcome of the function of dreaming, but only how it may modify the action of bowing one's head toward the city environment; and the further adverbial "vers les pavés" also emphasizes the intransitivity of the action described here. But in "contemple-les" the verb is transitive and its relationship with the object is direct; we have posited that the function of contemplation is to understand the sights of the world as meaningful—it is *allegoresis*. As such it has both direction and an object; whereas dreaming has direction ("vers les pavés") but, as an intransitive activity, has no object. Both contrast with seeking, which is a transitive activity but—taking an erroneous object and a false direction—results in a sense both of directionlessness ("dardant on ne sait où leurs globes ténébreux") and of objectlessness ("que cherchent-ils au Ciel, tous ces aveugles?").

SPEECH

The poem opens with a voice eliciting from the soul the function of contemplation and closes by attributing to "je" a locutionary act: "je dis." Speech thus characterizes "je" as contemplation characterizes the soul; and if the two are at first closely akin, so that the content of speech appears equivalent to the soul's contemplation, the implication of serenity in the act of contemplation contrasts strongly with the questioning that, in the final self-quotation, is the form taken by "je" 's speech, a questioning that has already been seen to be akin to the seeking of the blind. The pronoun "je," we know, is a shifter: its content changes with its context; and the "je" who addresses his own soul in line 1 is in a different illocutionary context from the "je" who draws explicit attention to himself as a self-conscious speaking subject in line 14. This shift in the content of the word "je," as defined by the relationships in which the act of speech involves the entity "je," not only defines the narrative movement of the poem; it also delineates a profound division in the functioning of "je" as the subject of the act of speech.

Speech implies a referent, which for most of this poem is equivalent to the object of the soul's contemplation, the blind. But, as Benveniste would put it, in addition to this *je/il(s)* relationship, speech also requires a complex set of agreements between an emitter and a receiver of speech, in short a *je-tu* relationship.[4] Among these agreements is agreement about the contextual referent, so the complete model is therefore *je-tu/il(s)*. It is by reference to this model that "je" may most conveniently be described as the locus of a shifting set of relationships in the poem.

Speech and the Soul

With "mon âme," the *je-tu* relationship is truly an intimate one, and it is based on "je"'s assumption that the description he gives of the blind men is equivalent to their contemplation by the soul. As a corollary of this *je-tu* intimacy and agreement, the *je/ils* relationship in the quatrains is one of distance: the description focuses on the terribleness and ridiculousness of the blind men, on the emptiness and the disorientation that contrast with "je"'s possession of a soul and the steadiness of gaze implied by contemplation. Yet, as the speaking instance, or *destinateur*, "je" is not fully identified with the soul, as *destinataire*; and the assumed equivalence between his description and the inner understanding that is posited on the soul's part has in fact no benefit of an absolute guarantee. It is "je" who assumes full responsibility for what is said, and the externality of situation and vision implied by speech is inscribed in the poem by means of the contrast between "Contemple-les, mon âme" of line 1 and "on ne les voit jamais" in line 7. Here the distance between "je" and "les aveugles" continues to be stressed in the semantic content (their failure to lower their eyes and to dream), but there has been a subtle shift in the alignment of "je" as a speaking agent: the point of view with which he identifies is no longer that of the individual soul but has become that of a community, with which the use of the pronoun "on" identifies the speaker. The adverbial phrase "on ne sait où" of line 4 mediates this important change of perspective.

Speech and the City

"Je"'s exteriority as a speaker with respect to the inner soul has two consequences in the tercets. We find him turning now to the "cité" and attempting to set up a new *je-tu* relationship with the community addressed in the vocative "O cité!" and the imperative "Vois!": men, not the personal soul, are now taken to be the appropriate partners in the speech act. In other words, "je" is no longer a simple observer of humanity, relaying the soul's contemplation; he is a member, or more accurately a would-be member, of the human community. For the externalization of "je" through speech has also been accompanied by a transformation of his own role: he is no longer simply the emitter of speech, but also the object of reference. As such he has joined "les aveugles" as object of the city's vision and referent of his own speech. "Contemple-les, mon âme" translates a *je-tu/ils* relationship; whereas "Vois! je me traîne aussi!", by grouping "je" and "ils" in a common "nous" of referentiality, now situates "je" on both sides of the slash, as speaker and spoken about: *je-tu/nous*.

This is a model of "je"'s double integration into the community, through identification with the blind and through communication with the city. However, the final model proposed by the poem disintegrates both the "nous" of identification, which becomes again a *je-ils* relationship, and the *je-tu* of communication with the city, since communication is not established; so that one is tempted to rewrite the situation in the tercets as *tu/je + ils*. There is no *je-tu* communication relationship, be it with the soul or the city; and the referent of speech is itself divided, as between "je" and "les aveugles." Thus "je" speaks alone.

Consequently, the third-person verbs characteristic of the description of the blind in the quatrains spill over into the opening lines of the tercets, describing them, from a distanced point of view, in terms of their movement and their affinity with the "silence éternel." And if, in the penultimate line, "je"'s sense of affinity with them extends to his movement ("je me traîne aussi"), the connotations of this movement are very different. There is none of the solemn majesty of: "Ils traversent ainsi le noir illimité / Ce frère du silence éternel." For him there is only the dragging motion of the social outcast, and—explicitly distinctive of "je"—there is, instead of the eternal silence that makes the blind akin to the silent soul, speech. Thus, the third-person reference returns, significantly, in "plus qu'eux hébété" and in the final question, which restores the original distance between "je" and "les aveugles." But now it is the blind who appear as closer to the soul, as silent seekers of the transcendent; whereas "je," explicitly attributing to himself the locutionary act—"je dis"—aligns himself with the noisy world of the city.

Yet here, too, his position is one of solitude: we have seen that his speech is drowned in the singing, laughing, and bellowing of the multitude; but in illocutionary terms it can be seen also, unlike the imperative "Vois!", to be not even specifically addressed to a hearer. It is formally a question, but there are two reasons why it does not expect an answer: one is that it is posited (ironically, of course) by the speaker as unanswerable, but the other is that there is no illocutionary partner to answer it. It is not, then, an interrogation but a simple statement ("je dis") in question form.

It is only as speaker of the poem (and not as an actor in the poem) that "je" may expect his utterance to find a hearer, in the person of that hypothetical construct, the implied reader.[5] Within the poem, the power of speech appears as an isolating force, detaching "je" from his silent soul without bringing him into communication with his fellow men. And if it puts him in the category of other marginals, such as the blind, as the rejects of the social world, his solitude with respect to them also derives from speech, since his easy communication with the soul contrasts with their vain seeking of the transcendent; whereas on the other hand their single-minded commitment to the dark heavens contrasts in turn with his would-be involvement, as a speaker, in the life of the city.

So the ego of this poem is a very modern figure, in spite of the apparently transitional stance he takes as the possessor of a soul in a world from which the divine has otherwise disappeared. He is modern, first and foremost, because of his identification with language: he is not soul, but "je," the producer of speech. And this language describes him in turn as the locus of a series of conflicts that we may identify with a historical problematic of the modern. The possessor of a soul and master of the power of contemplation, he comes into sharp contrast with the mindless pleasure-seeking of the city. It is meaningfulness and understanding he seeks, and this sets him apart, not only from the city but also from those more traditional seekers, the blind. Their residual numinousness makes them relatively prestigious figures, traversing the limitless darkness, in spite of their ludicrous appearance; whereas the poet—"Vois! je me traîne aussi!"—is at best a pathetic figure, but the poet who seeks the meaning of their own search is by definition also a more troubled figure than they, "plus qu'eux hébété." Thus poetic seeing, or contemplation, is a source of loneliness.

But so too does poetic speech set the poet apart, and this is so not simply in the failure of his attempted communication with the contemporary world of the city, but also in his relationship to the poetic tradition. For in this poem lyrical speech—singing—has become part of the mindless activity of the city. The poet speaks, and his speech is not the speech of beauty and certainty; he speaks to ask a question, and his utterance has the flatness and almost the vulgarity of a near-colloquial mode, with its familiar phraseology: "vraiment affreux," "vaguement ridicules," "que cherchent-ils au Ciel, tous ces aveugles?" The words "Je dis" here announce the arrival of a new poetic diction, something that might be called the speech of *hébétude*.

"Je," however, has no other existence than that conferred by such speech. This poem gives strong support to the hypothesis that the true subject of the "Tableaux parisiens" will prove to be not the city, not even the function of seeing, but the *sujet de l'énonciation,* a subject defining himself, then, as "je," that grammatical entity which, as a shifter, has no content in itself but acquires meaning exclusively from the circumstances and content of its own discourse. The function of saying is no longer the act by which the poet makes manifest his self, his soul, his inner existence; it is the act that constitutes him as the locus of a network of problematical relationships without which he would have no being.

1. Charles Baudelaire, *Œuvres complètes* (Paris: Gallimard, Bibliothèque de la Pléiade, 1975), p. 92.

2. The sources, notably in Breughel and Champfleury, are discussed in the major editions of Baudelaire's works: Crépet-Blin (Corti), Adam (Garnier), Pichois (Pléiade). See also G. A. Brunelli, "I pittori-teologi dei secoli XV e XVI e Baudelaire," *Studi Francesi* 20 (May–August 1963).

3. Peter Nurse, "Les Aveugles de Baudelaire," *L'Information littéraire* 8 (November–December 1966).

4. See E. Benveniste, *Problèmes de linguistique générale* (Paris: Gallimard, vol. 1, 1966, vol. 2, 1974), "L'Homme dans la langue."

5. For an extended discussion of the illocutionary relationships implied in and by Baudelaire's poetry, see Klaus Dirscherl, *Zur Typologie der poetischen Sprechweisen bei Baudelaire* (Munich: Wilhem Fink Verlag, 1975). A question not touched on in this paper is that of the tension between the voice *in* the poem, with its illocutionary aloneness and its flat discourse ("Que cherchent-ils au Ciel, tous ces aveugles?"), and the voice *of* the poem, which chooses the traditional sonnet as a medium of communication with a reader who is assumed not only to heed but also to understand the problem of loneliness.

L'œil était dans la tombe,
et regardait Caïn.

I am grateful to Professors Ross Chambers and
Robert Greer Cohn for their incisive reactions
to an earlier version of this study. Without the
initial stimulus of Professor Cohn's book, this
essay could not have been written.

Artistic Self-Consciousness in Rimbaud's Poetry

LAURENCE M. PORTER

Modern criticism has become increasingly aware of its own methods, like the centipede that started to watch its feet. "Je suis étant, et me voyant me voir" might be its byword. Depending on whether it is projected toward artist, work, or audience, this newly self-conscious critical vision projects an ever self-conscious artist, one wrestling with the angel of influence, or weaving his signifiers into a Penelopean tissue; a hermetically self-referential work, like the worm ouroboros; or a search for meaning governed by the personal myth of the reader (e.g., Norman Holland's "transactive criticism"). These versions of the current fashion all give short shrift to the artist's development over time, as a meaning for him and a model for us. So critics reading Rimbaud's poetry as the chronicle of a psychic or spiritual itinerary have come to appear old-fashioned, if not merely self-indulgent. Where Rimbaud is concerned, the uncertain dating of the texts makes diachronic studies all the more problematical. Synchronic views seem to have won the day. I shall nevertheless attempt to mediate between them and the older diachronic ones, for I believe that the Rimbaldian self-consciousness itself evolves and has a history.

Self-consciousness, as distinct from self-awareness, implies a generalized sense of inhibition experienced in the presence of a mocking, disapproving, or enslaving other, real or imagined (as in Rimbaud's poems "Roman," "Le Cœur volé," "Le Bateau ivre," "Mauvais Sang" of *Une Saison en enfer,* and others). To say "artistic" self-consciousness limits such inhibition to the communicative axis of sender/message/receiver.[1] The lyric self experiences either himself as poet, or his language, or both as inadequate; he may also imagine his potential public as hostile or uncomprehending, so that the poetic message is sent at the risk of rejection. All of the many forms that artistic self-consciousness assumes foreground the act of writing and communicating poetry. (1) Dramatized or implied social disapproval of the role of poet, as opposed to the warrior or producer ("Le Bateau ivre," last stanza and passim; the "soupirail" as metaphorical intrusion of the outside world at the conclusion of "Enfance"). (2) Rivalry with other intellectuals ("Les Assis") and poets ("Ce qu'on dit au poète à propos de fleurs," *Album zutique,* and so on). The desire to surpass the

achievements of one's literary forebears—Bloom's "anxiety of influence"—
may lead to self-defeating satire; even when successful, the effort to subdue and
to expel one's rivals fills poems with their corpses' reek—the stranded, rotting
monster in "Le Bateau ivre," for one. (3) Inadequacy of the verbal vehicle,
expressed by overt discrepancies between signifier and signified (the dead
soldier boy in the idyllic pastoral setting of "Le Dormeur du val"; "Clara
Vénus" engraved on repulsive buttocks in "Vénus Anadyomène"; the love of
poor, preliterate orphan children communicated in the form of an ornate
medallion inscribed "A Notre Mère" in "Les Etrennes des orphelins"). (4)
Inadequacy of the verbal vehicle, expressed by self-negating or self-cancelling
formulas such as the refrain "(elles n'existent pas)" in "Barbare." Frequently
the conclusions of Rimbaud's poems say or imply "This was an imaginative
construct." Thus he simultaneously calls into question his fantasies, by exposing them as a mere semblance of reality, and reaffirms them by asserting their
willed and autonomous origin. Yet from birth they are bound by the systems of
language that embody them. The paradigmatic explosion of metaphor falls
promptly back toward the syntagmatic axis of convention. I speculate that
Rimbaud attempts to transcend the inadequacy of the verbal medium through
exuberant self-referential punning ("le lit"—"lire"; "corbeaux"—"corps beau"
[with a buried metonymy: the body is muse, inspiring the song of the raven-
poets]; and perhaps "pis"—"udder" in "je pisse . . . 'Accroupissements' . . .
'tant pis pour le bois qui se trouve violon'"). Finally, Rimbaud may make the
insubstantial materials and products of writing (letters, paper, pen, and ink)
autonomous by transmuting them into the external décor that they ostensibly
represent (as in "Voyelles") and by personifying them (the sentence becomes
muse in "Phrases"). (5) Rejection of the message through a retort by its receiver
("Les Reparties de Nina"); evasion of such rejection through prosopopoeia,
actual or implied ("Le Buffet," "Les Corbeaux").

   The limitations of the linguistic vehicle of poetry, of which Rimbaud and his
critics are keenly aware, pose no greater threat than the binding syntagm of the
act of communication itself—sender/messenger/receiver—which is called into
being each time one writes. Ineluctably, the poetic voice summons its hearer.
And then the eye of the other, turning toward the clamor of the poem, imprisons
the lyric self within the categories of that other's own alien perception. To
shield his vulnerability and evade disapproval, "dans certains des premiers
poèmes de Rimbaud, on voit le poète-spectateur tenter de s'intégrer directe-
ment à son poème, se donnant tantôt comme un observateur commentant le
spectacle ('Et le Poète dit . . . ' fin d'*Ophélie*), tantôt comme spectateur et
élément du spectacle à la fois."[2] More subtly in later poems like "Mémoire,"
insistent metaphors of the eye transform an element of the décor into a "pur
regard" of the poetic consciousness.[3] By contemplating his own message, the
poet transforms himself into its receiver. This short circuit obviates the

threatening other and protects the message itself from a hostile or insensitive reception.

The device appears at the end of Rimbaud's first published French poem, "Les Etrennes des orphelins." Two four-year-olds, their mother dead, their father absent, huddle in an icy house where they are cared for by an old servant woman. They recall their former happiness in exchanging gifts at Christmastide. And at last they sleep, to dream of their *foyer* restored:

> On dirait qu'une fée a passé dans cela! . . .
> —Les enfants, tout joyeux, ont jeté deux cris . . . Là,
> Près du lit maternel, sous un beau rayon rose,
> Là, sur le grand tapis, resplendit quelque chose.
> Ce sont des médaillons argentés, noirs et blancs,
> De la nacre et du jais aux reflets scintillants,
> Des petits cadres noirs, des couronnes de verre,
> Ayant trois mots gravés en or: "A NOTRE MERE!"[4]

Cohn, one of few to pay attention to "Les Etrennes des orphelins," reacted harshly: "Rimbaud clearly had trouble finishing this poem; the emotion is exhausted and the infinite mystery is not. How familiar this is: all our adolescent poems came a cropper in this way! The medallions engraved with A NOTRE MERE offer an air of monumental (or tomb-like) finality, but, even leaving room for the possible irony, how pathetically clumsy and juvenile!"[5] That the solemn, elaborate final *ecphrasis* is quite incongruous with the helpless, inexperienced dramatis personae makes the poem all the more revealing. And (pace Cohn) few juvenilia end in so subtle and rich a way.

To be more precise, the yearning appeal conveyed by the last three words, A NOTRE MERE, is appropriate for the small children of the poem. The vehicle, letters of gold, is not. The children could neither have written nor have read those words. Their feelings have mingled with the poet's craft. Their joyous cries transmute into the poet's words, completing the depersonalized frame that was introduced in the first line with the listening "on" ("on entend vaguement" the children's whispering). Or to put it another way, an adolescent poet offers to his mother a pathetic message of love. Having implied that he feels helpless and bereft as a small orphan child, in the icy climate of maternal indifference, he sends her poetry—not mere raw sentiment, but love refined into a verbal artifact that the precocious Rimbaud knew to be of great beauty and value. A fear of rejection, combined with the guilt of nascent sexuality, has sublimated the feelings lying "près du lit maternel" into chaste words. This entire process of transformation is represented by means of a structure of three nesting layers through which sentiment-as-light ("un beau rayon rose") becomes mediated through metaphorical representation of words upon the page (black and white), which then become transparent, both sheltering the sentiment and allowing it to shine through, in a now acceptable form. Layering here mimics the movement of an impression into and out of the unconscious, from which a reaction emerges only after ego defense mechanisms have reshaped it to be socially acceptable:

(1) *light/feelings*: "resplendit . . . argentés."
  (2) *words (black)*: "noirs."
    (3) *on the white page*: "et blancs."
    (3) "De la nacre."
  (2) "Et du jais."
(1) "aux reflets scintillants."
  (2) *words framing thoughts*: "Des petits cadres noirs."
    (3) *the page integrated with feelings, forming a transparent but protective barrier*: "des couronnes de verre."
(1) plus (2) *feelings effectively sublimated as words*: "Ayant trois mots gravés en or: 'A NOTRE MERE!'"

Rimbaud's artistic vocation is revealed by his ability to step back from his emotions so as to exercise his craft upon them. The medallions, standing for the whole poem as a gift of, and an appeal for, love, form a *mise en abyme*,[6] the master emblem of the self-contemplating intellect. There is a certain narcissistic gratification in such self-absorption.

The attitude becomes less apparent in the ensuing early poems, but traces of it persist in the closures of many, where Rimbaud invokes a poet-persona, alludes to the raw materials of his art, or introduces a personified audience:

1. "—Les Dieux écoutent l'Homme et le Monde infini!" ("Soleil et chair," last line, p. 45).

2. "—Et le Poète dit . . . " ("Ophélie," last quatrain, p. 47).

3. "Bien que le roi ventru suât, le Forgeron, / Terrible, lui jeta le bonnet rouge au front!" ("Le Forgeron," last couplet, p. 57). The fat king of adult authority is humiliated by the phallic revolutionary message—the thrown cap in one sense symbolizes communication from poet to audience—delivered by the Promethean Worker in Fire.

4. "Les reins portent deux mots gravés: *Clara Venus*" ("Vénus Anadyomène," last tercet, p. 61). Here the glass shield of repression has been lifted, so to speak, from the medallions in "Les Etrennes des orphelins": the naked object of desire comes in view directly, without metonymic displacement ("le lit"—which, coincidentally or not, is a form of the verb *lire*—replaces the mother's body with the place where it is found), its fearsome physicality warring with the idealization of the poetic, verbal inscription.

5. "De grands arbres indiscrets" (the sublimated phallus) as audience frame ("Première Soirée," pp. 62–63).

Having thus affirmed and reaffirmed his artistic identity in the early poems ("I am a Poet, sender of messages"), Rimbaud feels confident enough to test it against the identity of others, first among whom is the primal father. "Les Effarés" recreates the situation of "Les Etrennes des orphelins." Wintered waifs wish woman's warmth. But this time stage center is held by the father-as-rival: a large baker putting loaves into and out of the oven enacts symbolically the primal scene, plus a procreation that quite fascinates the watching children ("ce trou chaud souffle la vie," p. 70). Overwhelmed, their own message becomes inarticulate ("grognant des choses," p. 70). But for the implied author, arranging this open confrontation with the powerful father effects catharsis. Oedipal guilt assuaged, the compelling horror of the flesh will ebb.

The phrase "belle hideusement d'un ulcère à l'anus" concluding "Vénus Anadyomène" suggests the angel with a flaming sword, barring the gates to an Eden of infantile regression (compare the metaphor "Chanaan féminin" of *Les Stupra,* p. 328). But now when the loved woman asserts her inaccessible presence, it shall be with words rather than with the body. The advent of those words nevertheless cuts short the poem as effectively as the raw rising rump of the Venus could do. "Les Reparties de Nina" brusquely deflate elaborate poetic dreams: "ELLE.—*Et mon bureau?*" (p. 68). And when the girl of "Roman" finally deigns a written reply to the poet's sonnets, he promptly returns to the cafés to drink with his friends. One must assume that her words did not match the dream she had inhabited (p. 72). In a rare equilibrium of happiness, however, "Rêve pour l'hiver" and "La Maline" (pp. 75, 78) do reintegrate the woman's words with the poet's dream. This masterful fusion of subject and object, combining the woman-figure with the poet's verbal role, recurs transposed into fantasy with "Le Buffet": "—O buffet du vieux temps, tu sais bien des histoires, / Et tu voudrais conter tes contes . . . " (p. 80; cf. Baudelaire's "J'ai plus de souvenirs que si j'avais mille ans"). The medallions from "Les Etrennes des orphelins" are to be found within (line 9). Indeed, when Rimbaud next invokes the traditional properties of muse and lyre, in "Ma Bohème," he knows the persona is doubly regressive—both old-fashioned and split—and excuses himself with the subtitle "Fantaisie."

Having so strongly proclaimed that he is indeed a poet, effectively communicating with others, Rimbaud can now direct his energies toward a struggle against rivals and precursors other than the biological father. "Les Corbeaux" (p. 82) seems a transitional poem, during which this shift occurs. The poet appears in the multiple, fantastic guise of the dark, loud-voiced birds. Wintry indifference still attacks them as it had the orphans, but their harsh cries resist without appeal: "Armée étrange aux cris sévères, / Les vents froids attaquent vos nids!" It is the human speaker of the first apostrophe in stanza one, addressed to the "Seigneur," who takes upon himself the onus of that appeal.

He seeks the blessing of the Father's sanction for the ravens' song, destined to supplant the sweet tyranny of His own melodies: "dans les hameaux abattus, / Les longs angélus se sont tus. . . . " A second apostrophe, in stanzas two and three, links the ravens to the poet's words, by being addressed to them. And a third, in the final stanza, assimilates them to a new holiness as "saints du ciel, en haut du chêne." The poem concludes with a ritual expulsion of the "bons poètes," the cloying weak voices of tradition:

> Laissez les fauvettes de mai
> Pour ceux qu'au fond du bois enchaîne,
> Dans l'herbe d'où l'on ne peut fuir,
> La défaite sans avenir.[7]

The false mask of the social persona ("fauvettes"—"faux-vêtes") is rejected in favor of unveiled spontaneous physical self-expression ("corbeaux"—"corps beau"). In comparison, the better-known "Ce qu'on dit au poète à propos de fleurs" is retrograde in its satirical explicitness. Its being aimed at a concrete human target of resentment fragments and vitiates its imaginative force.

"Les Assis," continuing Rimbaud's rivalry with the unworthy guardians of tradition, restores a desirable balance between fantasy and satire. The "Assis" function as *pharmakoi*. As it enumerates their bodily parts, the luxuriant, neologistic, mocking description dismembers them, casts them in shreds upon the ground as seeds for a new poetry. As Kittang's insightful reading explains, "Cette destruction de l'unité et de la linéarité syntaxiques et sémantiques se réalise, dans plusieurs des textes de jeunesse, précisément comme une destruction de l'unité anthropomorphe. . . . L'accent se déplace de proche en proche du signifié pour se poser au mouvement signifiant lui-même, c'est-à-dire au travail scriptural."[8] Here Rimbaud employs continual plurals, together with a metaphorical swelling, opening, and excrescence. The "Assis" are swept up in a fecundating creative movement that overmasters them, transforming them willy-nilly into artists and drunken boats. They must play and then dance to his tune:

> L'âme des vieux soleils s'allume . . .
>
> . . . .
> Et les Assis, genoux aux dents, verts pianistes,
>
> . . . .
> S'écoutent clapoter des barcarolles tristes,
> Et leurs caboches vont dans des roulis d'amour.

Ink flowers spit forth pollen commas to cradle them, infants in Rimbaud's new world, as the poem's ending reminds us of its purely verbal status. "Ceci ne constitue-t-il pas une espèce de reflet de la situation du scripteur lui-même, qui est aussi une sorte d'Assis, absorbé, bercé et emporté par le jeu même de son écriture?"[9] Yes. But more. By making the keepers of culture share his delirium, Rimbaud has cannibalistically absorbed them into himself.

As the maturing Rimbaud liberates himself from overt artistic self-consciousness in the poems, it is his body rather than his words that becomes the figurative vehicle of his communication: "Je pisse vers les cieux bruns" ("Oraison du soir," p. 87); "Fantasque, un nez poursuit Vénus au ciel profond" ("Accroupissements," p. 94, last line). The celebrated metaphors in Rimbaud's letters to Izambard and Demeny, written near the same time, express the same idea with more decorum: "Tant pis pour le bois qui se trouve violon"; "Si le cuivre s'éveille clairon, il n'y a rien de sa faute" (pp. 344, 345). But the anxiety of influence is very much with the epistolary poet: "Si les vieux imbéciles n'avaient pas trouvé du Moi que la signification fausse, nous n'aurions pas à balayer ces millions de squelettes qui, depuis un temps infini, ont accumulé les produits de leur intelligence borgnesse, en s'en clamant les auteurs!" (p. 345). Soon after this declaration we come in for a strong dose of literary history. Rimbaud remains quite aware of being watched here, by both the past and present. ("He is still a performer," Frohock demonstrates in shrewd detail.)[10] The musical instrument metaphors betray this limitation, for all their power: Rimbaud has described his awakening as a poet as the transformation of something inert into something that makes a noise—i.e., into a thing that uses language and believes that language to be its main function, as the essence of its identity, intended to be heard by others.

In a further movement toward artistic autonomy, a part of the now-poet's (or his muse's) now-dismembered body becomes not the instrument but rather the audience for the poet's communication, as he for a time adopts the practice of signing off with an apostrophe: "Comment agir, ô cœur volé?" ("Le Cœur volé," p. 101); "On veut vous déhâler, Mains d'ange, / En vous faisant saigner les doigts!" ("Les Mains de Jeanne-Marie," p. 107). This solipsistic short circuit frees the poet's message from the contingency of a potentially disapproving human audience. Rimbaud can then address his final apostrophes to the absolute of death or divinity, which he wishes to attain. The lyric impulse of the entire poem, reproduced in little by the apostrophe, becomes concentrated in an unmediated movement toward transcendence (see "Les Sœurs de charité," "Voyelles," and "Les Premières Communions"). Once this movement has been completed, the poet dramatizes his total merging with an oceanic absolute in the early masterpiece "Le Bateau ivre." Soon he must realize that the privileged moment cannot be maintained. "Les yeux horribles des pontons" (p. 131), the prison of social expectations, close round him again, with the promise of becoming increasingly disapproving as Rimbaud matures toward nonconformity.[11]

Only then does Rimbaud reach the height of his artistic development as he changes strategies. No longer does he identify himself with his goal, but with his desire. Caught up in the first spontaneous impulse, he nearly transcends artistic self-consciousness, becoming pure hunger, and thirst, and desire for death. In the poems editorially entitled *Derniers Vers* (pp. 149–81), as later in many of the *Illuminations,* to drink is ultimately to dissolve; or, to put it the opposite way around, Rimbaud tries to transform desire into an accurate description of the world. To forestall its coagulation, he adopts a kaleidoscopic role-changing theatricality in the *Illuminations.* Thus he seeks protection against the conceptualizing force of language and undermines the ontological basis of the coherent self. The freely desiring, evolving theatrical self changes each time it reaches for the momentary object of its attention.[12] But such independence cannot be forever sustained.

The cathartic tears of frustration common in Rimbaud fill the liminal poem of the *Illuminations.* Until he has washed away the old, he cannot leap for the new. The second of the *Illuminations,* "Enfance," then depicts the life cycle of the imagination. The drama begins on the beach, at forest's edge; that is, on the border between conscious and unconscious. The exotic idol introduced at the outset suggests a child's doll.[13] The toy, a small replica of reality, affords the child a first experience of self-definition, through the autonomous control of a world of his own. She comes to life, and then, imaginatively subjected to three hyperbolic fields—exoticism, princeliness, immensity—shatters centrifugally into many women.[14] By the end of section 1 (as at the endings of 3 and 5), imaginative imperialism has conquered too much land to hold against the intrusions of the conventional social world. This tiresome interloper must be rejected: "Quel ennui, l'heure du 'cher corps' et du 'cher cœur'" (p. 255).

In section 2 the artist's diegetic gesture reasserts its power, calling forth the absent and the dead, magic and legend. The upright posture of some dead, however, like any notation of posture in Rimbaud, suggests the continuing presence of some restraint. Section 3, while evoking the successive encounters of a journey, also employs the anaphora in "Il y a" to affirm the creator's power yet more strongly. This repetition creates a center that asserts the integrity of the self and permits imaginative dispersion. The sinking cathedral and rising lake signify culture submerged by nature, the superego drowned in desire. But the superego dies hard. Its last twitch of repression—"Il y a . . . quelqu'un qui vous chasse"—expels the poet from this adolescent stage of his adventure. He departs in a pluralized form, which maintains his independence, however, for he merges with a troupe of little (child) actors in costume, seen on the road, through the edge of the wood where the poet wanders.

In section 4 he assumes the successive roles of "saint . . . savant . . . piéton . . . enfant," winning through to a renewed childlike innocence and fully realizing his aspirations in a rising landscape, image of desire. But the triumph of the imagination causes its death. Since it is conquest, when it conquers all, it must then cease to be. Within the whitewashed tomb where he has taken refuge in the final section, convention reabsorbs the poet. He is condemned to the prison of others' sterile literature: "Je m'accoude à la table, la lampe éclaire très vivement ces journaux que je suis idiot de relire, ces livres sans intérêt" (p. 257). Houses, fog, mud, and night settle above him. He conjures up smooth, hard, and gleaming symbols of the self-sufficing personality: "Je m'imagine des boules de saphir, de métal. Je suis maître du silence. Pourquoi une apparence de soupirail blémirait-elle au coin de la voûte?" (p. 258). The implied eye of the other peers in through the skylight; the whole poetic evasion must begin anew in "Conte" (cf. pp. 264–65), which in turn concludes "La musique savante manque à notre désir" (p. 260).

"Parade," however, transforms the momentarily successful climax of "Enfance" (section 4) into an entire, self-contained poem. With a single stroke it calls the troupe of "maîtres jongleurs"—"Des drôles très solides"—into being and then enumerates their powers. Since they are Rimbaud's creation, his naming them flaunts his poetic force, imaginatively transformed into sexual and political dominion. Their theatrical multiplicity deconstructs the social self to create a new overarching self of poetic surges: "The combination of extreme attraction and extreme repulsion [that they inspire] creates a grotesque, baroque vitality."[15] A nest of oxymorons—"Le plus violent Paradis de la grimace enragée"—asserts their metaphoric power, one that the poet refuses to submit to the conventions of communication: "J'ai seul la clef de cette parade sauvage" (p. 261). By divorcing his vivid metaphors from their nonlinguistic source, Rimbaud attempts in exemplary fashion to "create the *impression* that language is no longer simply the linguistic code but a far richer system of signs."[16] These we never could understand, for the poet is now "réellement d'outre-tombe," this time without a skylight ("Vies," p. 265).

The autonomy of language is perfected when Rimbaud personifies language and makes it speak. Thus its role shifts from message to sender, from passive to active, from *adjuvant* to *destinateur*. This is what happens in "Phrases," an unlucky poem that has drawn the critical thunderbolts of "incoherent" and "at times irritatingly obscure."[17] Indeed the poem is populated by too many unnamed entities to permit a consistent interpretation. If we invoke the principle of Occam's razor, however, the only available antecedent for most of the feminine nouns and pronouns that pervade the poem, in both singular and plural, is the title word itself. A spokeswoman for all the sentences speaks first as an individual ("je . . . celle") and then as a member of a collectivity ("nous"). A dangerous mistress, she promises in the first section a fidelity that menaces fatally to restrict the poet's imagination by actualizing all its dreams within the straitjacket of language: "Que j'aie réalisé tous vos souvenirs,—que je sois celle qui sait vous garrotter,—je vous étoufferai" (p. 270).[18]

The masculine plural adjectives of the second section suggest that the poet now speaks of himself and his phrases together, acknowledging their inability, in concert, to act upon the real world: "Quand nous sommes très forts,—qui recule? très gais,—qui tombe de ridicule? Quand nous sommes très méchants,

—que ferait-on de nous." And then *he* addresses *them*: "Parez-vous, dansez, riez. [Despite all your activity] Je ne pourrai jamais envoyer l'Amour par la fenêtre." And after the dash beginning the third section, the poet replies to the phrase that first spoke alone: "—Ma camarade, mendiante, enfant monstre! comme ça t'est égal, ces malheureuses et ces manœuvres, et mes embarras. Attache-toi à nous [to me, and fellow-poets, and all of humankind] avec ta voix impossible, ta voix! unique flatteur de ce vil désespoir." And so she does. Impressionistic notations in the following section (which some say begins a separate poem) take their point of departure in the real, an overcast July morning. Soon the magic of language allows the poet to capture the universe in a net of harmony: "J'ai tendu des cordes de clocher à clocher; des guirlandes de fenêtre à fenêtre; des chaînes d'or d'étoile à étoile, et je danse." The mists of potentiality fill the air; it is holiday time; a bell of pink fire rings in the clouds. And when the feast of the imagination is completed, and odors revive in the evening damp, a gentle rainfall of black powder, the matter from which the poet's sentences have been made, gathers darkness around him: "Avivant un agréable goût d'encre de Chine, une poudre noire pleut doucement sur ma veillée.—Je baisse les feux du lustre [the intensity of poetic creation declines], je me jette sur le lit [*lire*—mentally, he rereads], et, tourné du côté de l'ombre [the pool of ink from which new sentences shall be born], je vous vois, mes filles! mes reines!" (p. 271). "Je vais voir l'ombre que tu devins." Rimbaud has just completed one of the loveliest, most convincing statements extolling the joys of writing poetry.

Where linguistic conventions do not stifle the poet, of course, he risks that the imaginative deluge may submerge him. Rimbaud faces this problem in the "Délires" of *Une Saison en enfer*. "Hell" comes from the poet's feeling out of joint with his Christian civilization, and his resulting guilt. "Délires" describes his attempted escape. "Délires I" and "II" dramatize the opposites of the creative faculty, its passive and its active modes (thanks here and elsewhere to the poet Steven Katz). The "Foolish Virgin" (meaning, in French, one foolish enough not to remain a virgin) of "Délires I" derives all her meaning from the other who dominates her. She opens her speech with a pathetic appeal to higher authority. "Délires II," in contrast, begins with the poet as *bricoleur,* enumerating the concrete raw materials of poetic production. With many broad gestures of taking possession, he proclaims the hyperexpressibility of his art: "J'écrivais des silences, des nuits, je notais l'inexprimable. Je fixais des vertiges" (p. 228). But then "la terreur venait" (p. 233). "Au milieu de cet espace désordonné le Moi poétique perd sa position fixe: lui qui au début du texte surgit comme une espèce de démiurge hyperbolique, se laisse peu à peu absorber et dérouter par la force dynamique de ses matériaux disparates . . . le schéma spatial et non-expressif d'un verbalisme autonome, qui, en passant par la double déformation des 'hallucinations,' s'éloigne définitivement du Discours et du Lisible."[19] "Je sais aujourd'hui saluer la beauté," Rimbaud concludes (p. 234)—presumably by replacing art with action, for the last section, "Adieu," declares: "Je demanderai pardon pour m'être nourri de mensonge. Et allons . . . Point de cantiques: tenir le pas gagné" (p. 241). Like Oedipus, Rimbaud has sacrificed an old vision to gain a new one, as he sets forth to live out the theatrical roles he had evoked with words.[20] Like Persephone he has emerged from the underworld of inadequate love and poetry. He has no wish to repeat the cycle.

As Friedrich neatly summed up, "Rimbaud institutes the abnormal divorce of the poetic 'I' from the empirical self."[21] As he clearly implies both in "Phrases" and in "Délires II," his muse is no longer the conventional guide through a purgatory of language: she has become language itself. Rimbaud exploits her powers by creating the simultaneous presence and absence of denial, a domain peculiar to language, transcending reality (e.g., the repeated "(elles n'existent pas)" of "Barbare"). In this he anticipates the symbolists Mallarmé and Valéry. ("Rien n'aura eu lieu que le lieu," concludes Mallarmé in *Un Coup de dés*.) But also he struggles against her, by uniting incompatible opposites and rejecting finite verbs, in a sustained attempt to exalt the purified imagination over syntax. For Rimbaud's historical situation as an adolescent of whom most disapproved made him keenly conscious of the other, one of whose forms is language. Knowing that the imagination can be realized only as language, he experiences an ultimately intolerable constraint. Rimbaud's poetic odyssey ends not as a romance, "a drama of self-identification symbolized by the hero's transcendence of the world of experience, his victory over it, and his final liberation from it," but as a tragedy, "the epiphany of the law governing human existence which the protagonist's [unsuccessful] exertions against the world have brought to pass."[22]

"Poor Arthur's" renunciation of poetry in favor of a preoccupation with profit in North Africa has been interpreted as a total undoing of his revolt, as "his conversion into a money-grubbing son of his mother" [23] after he had resisted her materialism so long. But life is not that simple. The myth of the father guided him too. For he promoted himself from something analogous to the status of the mother—housebound and limited to the use of coaxing, scolding, or admonishing words—to the status of the father-as-autonomous-doer, a status that his previous restless journeying and his domination of Verlaine had only partially achieved. "L'alchimie du verbe," the hope of transforming the world through incantation, gives way in his psyche to an imitation of the father, who as a soldier had been stationed in North Africa. Rimbaud settled on the same terrain, but sold guns rather than firing them. As a sort of director of warfare, rather than an actor, he situated himself at a symbolically higher level of control than the one that his father had occupied. To our regret as readers, he transcended the helplessness of verbal self-expression, at the cost of the loss of its glory.[24]

1. For a more elaborate and methodologically rigorous discussion of this act, see Nathaniel Wing, *Present Appearances,* pp. 11–19 and passim.

2. Ross Chambers, "To Read Rimbaud," p. 203.

3. Ibid., p. 217.

4. Jean-Arthur Rimbaud, *Œuvres,* p. 38. All subsequent references to Rimbaud's works will be to this edition.

5. Robert Greer Cohn, *The Poetry of Rimbaud,* pp. 36–37.

6. I have provided a formal definition of this concept, and a bibliography, in "Literary Structure and the Concept of Decadence: Huysmans, D'Annunzio, and Wilde," *CentR* 22 (Spring 1978).

7. Political militancy, precociously augmenting the force of Rimbaud's self-assertion, leads him to attack the inadequate message of the other in the closing line of an earlier poem, "Morts de quatre-vingt-douze et de quatre-vingt-treize": "—Messieurs de Cassagnac nous reparlent de vous!" (p. 58).

8. Atle Kittang, *Discours et jeu,* pp. 205–10.

9. Ibid., p. 210.

10. Wilbur Frohock, *Rimbaud's Poetic Practice,* pp. 70–92.

11. I do not wish to intrude an overt Jungian perspective into the main line of argument here, but Marie Luise von Franz's characterization of the *Puer Æternus,* unwilling to grow up, neatly fits the behavior of the restless Rimbaud, "l'homme aux semelles de vent" (*The Problem of the Puer Æternus,* pp. 1–7): "belief in one's hidden genius, refusal to adapt, arrogance towards others, inability to settle down . . . 'the provisional life,' that is, the strange attitude and feeling that one is *not yet* in real life." Literary works like *Peter Pan, Narcissus and Goldmund, Le Petit Prince,* and *Jonathan Livingston Seagull* reflect the lasting imaginative appeal of this psychological archetype. Cf. Jean-Pierre Richard, "Rimbaud ou la poésie du devenir," pp. 206–7.

12. This paragraph is inspired by Leo Bersani's brilliant chapter in *A Future for Astyanax,* pp. 230–58.

13. Cohn, p. 253.

14. Kittang, p. 229.

15. Cohn, p. 271 n.

16. Wing, p. 146; his pp. 143–46 offer a fine reading of "Parade." J. Marc Blanchard ("Sur le mythe poétique," pp. 82–84) makes interesting comments on "Après le déluge" from a similar viewpoint, although he is influenced by Bloom as well. In the light of these readings, one would have to nuance the conclusions of Douglas P. Collins and Herbert S. Gershman ("Romantic Irony in Rimbaud," pp. 683–86), who find romantic irony in such "highly ambiguous closing sequences" in *Illuminations.* Their essay does provide a useful background for the concept.

17. Frohock, p. 190; Cohn, p. 294.

18. Cohn translates these "que" 's as "even if," but I think it makes more sense to read "if and when."

19. Kittang, pp. 193–96.

20. Cf. Bersani's contrary reading, p. 238.

21. Hugo Friedrich, *The Structure of Modern Poetry,* p. 48.

22. Hayden White, *Metahistory: The Historical Imagination of Nineteenth-Century Europe* (Baltimore: Johns Hopkins University Press, 1973), pp. 8–11.

23. Cohn, p. 7; cf. the biography by Elizabeth Hanson.

24. Guy Michaud (*Message poétique du symbolisme,* pp. 153–54) reached a similar conclusion in 1961.

SELECT BIBLIOGRAPHY

Bersani, Leo. *A Future for Astyanax: Character and Desire in Literature.* Boston: Little, Brown, & Co., 1976.

Blanchard, J. Marc. "Sur le mythe poétique: Essai d'une sémiostylistique rimbaldienne." *Semiotica* 16 (1976): 67–86.

Bloom, Harold. *The Anxiety of Influence: A Theory of Poetry.* New York: Oxford University Press, 1973.

Bonnefoy, Yves. *Rimbaud par lui-même.* Paris: Seuil, 1961.

Chambers, Ross. "To Read Rimbaud. (a) Mimesis and Symbolisation: A Question in Rimbaud Criticism." *Australian Journal of French Studies* 11 (1974): 54–64.

Cohn, Robert Greer. *The Poetry of Rimbaud.* Princeton: Princeton University Press, 1973.

Collins, Douglas P., and Gershman, Herbert S. "Romantic Irony in Rimbaud." *Texas Studies in Literature and Language* 13 (1972): 673–90.

Friedrich, Hugo. *The Structure of Modern Poetry.* Evanston: Northwestern University Press, 1974 (in German, 1956; revised 1967).

Frohock, Wilbur M. *Rimbaud's Poetic Practice: Image and Theme in the Major Poems.* Cambridge: Harvard University Press, 1963.

Houston, John Porter. *The Design of Rimbaud's Poetry.* New Haven: Yale University Press, 1963.

Kittang, Atle. *Discours et jeu: Essai d'analyse des textes d'Arthur Rimbaud.* Bergen: Universitetsforlaget; Presses Universitaires de Grenoble, 1975.

Michaud, Guy. *Message poétique du symbolisme.* Paris: Nizet, 1961. Pp. 127–58.

Richard, Jean-Pierre. "Rimbaud ou la poésie du devenir." In *Poésie et profondeur,* pp. 189–250. Paris: Seuil, 1955.

Rimbaud, Jean-Arthur. *Œuvres.* Edited by Suzanne Bernard. Paris: Garnier, 1960.

von Franz, Marie Luise. *The Problem of the Puer Æternus.* New York: Spring Publications, 1973.

Wing, Nathaniel. *Present Appearances: Aspects of Poetic Structure in Rimbaud's "Illuminations."* University, Miss.: Romance Monographs, 1974.

Mallarmé and the Plastic Circumstances of the Text

VIRGINIA A. LA CHARITÉ

Mallarmé's quest for a pure poetry that would give expression to "les gestes de l'idée" has been the source of a vast corpus of criticism that is as divergent in its approaches as it is in its conclusions. Each view seems to be convincing on its own terms, mainly because of scholarly reliance upon Mallarmé's own remarks on the theory of writing. However, a close look at his reflections on the subject of poetry reveals so many inconsistencies that nearly any point of view and any sort of interpretation can be substantiated by lines taken from his prose commentaries and correspondence. In fact, Mallarmé's observations on the substance of poetry and its articulation are a veritable vortex of "variations" and "divagations," for he writes more about what poetry is not than about what it is and should be. Moreover, his theories are not interpretations of his own texts; rather, they are the expression of his aspirations for an absolute, what he calls Poetry. Consequently, any attempt to penetrate his poetic universe must distinguish between Mallarmé the aesthetician and Mallarmé the poet.

Turning to the Pléiade edition for a study of Mallarmé the poet at work, we find some eighty-six pages of verse and prose poetry that are familiar in critical circles. But such textual selectivity excludes nearly one thousand pages of poetry and other creative writings and brands them as "imitative," "charming," "unworthy." These writings include Mallarmé's translations, essays, articles, textbooks, and a volume of formal poems, *Vers de circonstance,* most of which were composed, edited, and published by Mallarmé in 1894 under the title *Les Loisirs de la poste.*

What I should like to propose here is that attention to Mallarmé's creative writing reveals that his conquest of the art of suggestion and mastery of the ambiguous are based on the plastic circumstances of the text. The manipulation of words as objects of a literary game coheres the structure of his work from his adolescent endeavors in *Entre quatre murs* to his masterpiece, *Un Coup de dés,* including the fragments of *Le Livre* and *Un Tombeau pour Anatole.* By setting aside the theory and focusing on the poet at work, we see his poetic practice as one that consistently depends on the familiar worlds of experience, myth, and language.

The 471 poems of *Vers de circonstance* were written between 1881 and 1896. Although this is not the only group of texts that is deliberately ignored in Mallarmé studies,[1] it does constitute the only group that seems to embarrass the faithful.[2] True, the *Vers de circonstance* are pieces of whimsy that exhibit playfulness, wit, and linguistic virtuosity. Hardly serious in either tone or subject, they are, paradoxically, serious in treatment; and in these formal quatrains and doublets of lightheartedness are indications of Mallarmé's working method during his most productive years as a "pure" poet.

In *Vers de circonstance* everything and anything are taken up by Mallarmé: addresses, fans, New Year's gifts, birthdays, Easter eggs, albums, pebbles, bottles of Calvados. Tied to people, places, and things, these verses are directly related to the world of human activity, and they are concrete in the most basic sense of the term. Mallarmé delights in the events that transform ordinary daily life; he writes on the occasion of a trip, a baptism, the founding of a journal, the publication of one of his poems, over-drinking, a WC, the return of a fishnet, an exclamation point, a lecture, the opening of a circus; there are even mocking, humorous verses about an edition of *L'Après-midi d'un faune,* as well as a text written in *-or* rhymes for a friend who did not like *-or* rhymes. The verses are populated by objects of every kind: teapot, plate, glass of water, handkerchief (and there are eight of these), music box, china dog, real dog, "fruits glacés." The sense of satire and irony that runs through these poems reveals a Mallarmé who never turned his back on actuality. On the contrary, he is acutely aware of the actual, the real world, for he not only evokes the concrete things around him, but he also writes on them: dyed Easter eggs, fans, envelopes, pebbles from Honfleur, photographs. He amuses, but at the same time he is sharpening his skills, for to conquer the realm of the ambiguous demands familiarity with the concrete.

Technically, *Vers de circonstance* is based on wordplay, punning, visual affectation. The texts must be read with the eye in order to be understood; rhyme schemata depend on divided syllables (*l'/un, becque-/té*), syntactical distortions, purposeful orthographic changes, dislocated end rhymes, double entendres. In one sense, Mallarmé is rebelling against formalism, against all rhetorical devices, even against all accepted poetic practice, something he did as a schoolboy in *Entre quatre murs.* Yet what seems to be a refutation of poetic good taste in *Vers de circonstance* is actually a verbal game in which words are the pieces to be placed in play upon the board of written expression by a masterful gamester, the poet. Objectively, detachedly, and deliberately Mallarmé scrutinizes words as objects; he continually moves them around to form new patterns with which to dazzle the spectators. The text is indeed "l'autre."

Throughout these brief poems Mallarmé is conscious of an audience,[3] the presence of others who enjoy a good game; and, as in games, the texts demand visual skill. The rhyme between "cueille" and "Eye," for example, is inane until the reader translates *eye* into the French, *œil*. There is no reason to spell *guéritte* (sentry box) with a double *t*, but visually such an orthography makes a better rhyme with the double *t* in a soldier's family name *Margueritte*. As in the fragments of *Le Livre*, *Vers de circonstance* shows that "Représentation" must precede "Interprétation."[4] Despite Mallarmé's avowed preference for oral reading of his work, his texts must be seen to be grasped because they depend primarily on the tactile sense: "dans telle"/"dentelle," "Cold"/"Hérold," "m'accommode"/"comme ode," "rêveur"/"ever," "Commentaire"/"comme en terre," "qu'on fit"/"confit." His use of irregular verse and inconsistently pronounced mute *e*'s attests to a linguistic gamesmanship at the basis of his poems.

Vers de circonstance is not atypical of Mallarmé's work. *Entre quatre murs* is replete with texts of a similar vein; though they are youthful in enthusiasm, there can be no doubt that they represent a revolt against existing literary dicta and dogma ("Racine"/"déracine") and manifest a certain verbal plasticity that only a love for words as things could bring about. In *Mallarmé lycéen* Mondor notes that Mallarmé's more serious youthful texts show him to be under the influence of others, mainly Hugo; uneasily, Mondor hopes that the satire that is so blatant in many of the texts is a form of exorcism of the past.[5] With regard to the three notebooks of *Glanes,* which represent some eight thousand lines of poems by others that Mallarmé faithfully recopied in 1859 as a means of learning and mastering poetic methodology, Mondor remarks that Mallarmé's taste in the texts copied is rather unorthodox. He is not interested in the esoteric works, but in the humoristic, ironic, satirical, and even scatological ones.

A cursory glance at *Entre quatre murs* and the choices in *Glanes* shows us a Mallarmé fascinated by language tricks. A word gains potential in meaning by its setting and in its association ("Héraclite"/"hétéroclite"); words are objects that can be arranged and rearranged; their very fixity of meaning can be altered topographically. And, in fact, these early texts show interest in the placement of words on the page (descending order, spacing) and in type size. Mondor cautiously ventures the possibility that Mallarmé is throwing off the influence of Hugo. Why then would not the texts of the 1870s—the ones ignored because Mallarmé only wrote four "pure" poems during the decade—be a way of throwing off the influence of Baudelaire that marks his writing during the 1860s? And why would not *Vers de circonstance* be a pivotal work that turns literary exorcism into a celebration of the plasticity of language?

Looking at the 1870s, we find that these so-called years of impotence are marked by a rather tremendous output of work. In 1871 Mallarmé wrote about the International Exposition in London: articles on things of the world, articles in which he observes objects and describes them for his readers. In 1874 he published the witty fashion journal *La Dernière Mode,* in which clothing, menus, and other aspects of Parisian cultural life are painstakingly, but cleverly and amusingly, described, pictured, and enumerated. In 1877 *Les Mots anglais* appeared; again, a work of objects, only this time the things painted verbally are words, English words. Although hardly a true work of philology, *Les Mots anglais* is important for what it reveals about Mallarmé's plastic sense of words. Written in a chatty, conversational tone, with numerous asides and direct addresses to his readers, *Les Mots anglais* is amusing to read; as a textbook, it enlivens language, breathes life into words, makes jokes out of linguistic inconsistencies. Unfortunately, it is becoming stylish to use this work as supportive material for the theoretical interpretation of Mallarmé's "pure" poetry. True, he makes some observations that seem to be borne out later in *Variations sur un sujet,* but close attention to the linguistic details of the work reveals that it is a naïve rendering of the English language in terms of what was known and espoused by philologists of the time.[6] In fact, *Les Mots anglais* is a highly imaginative book, which declares that language is fun, a game to be played and enjoyed.

Hence, Mallarmé's interest in language manipulation is borne out by his light verse, his textbooks and translations, and his fascination with the appearance of a printed word. He examines words in their visual setting as early as *Entre quatre murs*; his experimentation with type size is evidence of his long-standing awareness that the form of a word has a dramatic effect on the reader. His use of capital letters, italics, and punctuation, notably parentheses, underscores the plasticity that is inherent in his texts. In the proofs for *Un Coup de dés,* for example, we are struck by his careful attention to the form of the *f*'s and to linear alignment.[7] In *L'Après-midi d'un faune,* as well as in *Hérodiade* and *Igitur,* Mallarmé pays strict attention to the setting, offering the reader a scenic, tactile atmosphere. His use of objects instead of paper for many of the verses in *Vers de circonstance* presents later and further evidence of his insistence on the plastic.

In addition to the paginal appearance of the written word, however, Mallarmé was intensely preoccupied with "éditions de luxe." In fact, in *A rebours* des Esseintes is drawn to Mallarmé's poetry first by the luxuriousness of the cover and second by the aura of fantasy ("le suc concret") of the texts.[8] Certainly, Mallarmé's attraction to painting is well known; his friendships with Manet, Morisot, Whistler, Chavannes,[9] Renoir, Gauguin, and others have been well documented. His work, published in his lifetime, was illustrated by Manet, Laurent, Renoir, and Regnault; and the *Chansons bas* were originally written as the legends for sketches by Jean-François Raffaëlli under the title *Les Types de Paris*. In preparation at one time was *Le Tiroir de laque,* which was to have been quite ornate in appearance and accompanied by John Lewis Brown's illustrations, and Odilon Redon was asked by Mallarmé to illustrate *Un Coup de dés*. Mallarmé also did some sketching, as his drawings of peacocks on notes to Méry Laurent show; many of his fan poems are colorful juxtapositions of written word and decorated object, just as the Easter poems are written in gold ink on red eggs. The very title of *Quelques médaillons et portraits en pied* is taken from the world of plastic art and offers us verbal portraits of writers and painters alike, for words, the pen, and paper are to the poet what the palette, brush, and canvas are to the painter.

By his interest in combining the plastic and the written, Mallarmé demonstrates that he seeks not an absolute realm beyond our reach but one that is within our very grasp. Although man may look to the stars for his destiny, he plays out his role in the *hic et nunc*. Considering all of Mallarmé's writing, we are struck by his constant return to, and reliance upon, the familiar world of myth. In his *Mythologies* Barthes could easily have been writing about Mallarmé when he says: "Ce que le monde fournit au mythe, c'est un réel historique . . . et ce que le mythe restitue c'est une image *naturelle* de ce réel."[10] What is myth if it is not man's attempts to personify, make concrete, "plasticize" if you will, those things that he does not understand? Mallarmé's *Les Dieux antiques,* published in 1880 at the end of the decade of impotence, presents myth in terms of Barthes's definition: deformation of the meaning, but not destruction and disappearance of meaning.

Myth occurs and recurs frequently in Mallarmé's work. The nymphs and faun of *L'Après-midi d'un faune* surface in "Pan" in *Entre quatre murs*; Venus is another myth that continues from this earliest work to *Un Coup de dés*. Other mythological references include Syrinx, Phoenix, Chimera, Paphos, Styx, Prometheus, Hebe; there are allusions to biblical legends (angel, demon, Lucifer, Idumea), historical tales (Anastasius, Cecilia), literary creations (Hamlet); fairies, sirens, and heroes populate all decades of his writing. The constant reference to constellations is basically mythological: Big Dipper, Little Dipper, Berenice's Hair, Swan, Clock, Unicorn, Peacock, Phoenix. Even his fascination with the sea and the life of adventure and risk are indicators of the use of archetypal figures and themes in his poetry.

According to Barthes, "La fonction du mythe, c'est d'évacuer le réel."[11] Setting this statement alongside Cohn's observations that Mallarmé's poems are marked by a standard vocabulary, and a rather limited one at that,[12] we note that it is, indeed, the evacuation of the real that accounts for a reworking of the same objects, the same words, over and over again in his work. An object is, of course, external to the mind; it is something that can be experienced and known in an empirical sense. Moved to a different, unfamiliar setting, the object gains in its dimensions and in the possibilities of its meaning. The effect becomes an affect,[13] as simple everyday things are mutated into emblems.

Looking now at Mallarmé's "pure" poems, the texts of *Poésies,* we find the banal real world at every turn, and picture words abound: "écume," "nuage," "plume," "astre," "soleil," "fleur," "cygne," "joyau," "pli," "aile." Mallarmé's word choices are drawn heavily from the classical animal, vegetable, and mineral kingdoms;[14] ephemeral terms are rare, for even "ciel" is always used in conjunction with "soleil," "nuage," "étoile," and so forth. Every part of the human body is evoked directly, and emotional terms occur in amazing frequency ("heureux," "cruel," "triste," "las," "sourire"). These texts are also rather noisy poems ("cloche," "angélus," "sonneur," "glas," "fanfare," "voix," "rire," "chant," "appel," "cri," "tonnerre"), and musical instruments are used throughout his work ("flûte," "cymbale," "viole," "clavecin"). There are very few silences in a Mallarmé poem. It is as though the reader must first be subjected to a visual display, then to an oral enchantment.

Many of Mallarmé's earlier poems are simply verbal portraits and scenes. "Le Guignon" is a picture of bad luck, and "Le Pitre châtié" describes the poet as a clown; though the rewritten lines that evoke a prostitute at work in "Une Négresse par le démon secouée" are less graphic than the original ones, they are still descriptive. Vision is at the basis of "Les Fenêtres," the simple natural objects of "Les Fleurs" involve four of the five senses, and "Renouveau" is an anecdote on spring fever. The last seven lines of "Las de l'amer repos" actually paint a landscape on a cup: the moon sinking into the waters of a lake. In "Le Sonneur" we see the poet ringing the bell, and the famous "L'Azur" teems with the concrete and the picturesque, in both form and content. "Brise marine" paints a quayside scene, "Soupir" describes the falling of autumn leaves, "Don du poème" is an allegory. In the four versions of "Aumône," we find Mallarmé reworking the description of the coin thrown to the beggar: from twenty sous, to one hundred sous, to a piece of gold, to just some metal in the final version; but all four are concrete, and the last one, "métal," is the original plastic source for the others, the "myth" for the object thrown.

Hérodiade is spectacle, remarkable for its use of colors, jewels, ingenious but graphic end-rhyme play, and the recurrent folds, which serve as a point of reader orientation: folds of the tapestry, folds of thoughts, folds of a bad dream, folds of words. The use of light and shadow, type variations, and the universal myth of Pan contribute to the highly scenic quality of *L'Après-midi d'un faune*, which Mossop describes as "magnificently plastic."[15] "Sainte" draws its inspiration from a stained-glass window; "Quand l'ombre menaça" is dependent upon the view of the constellation in the black night; "Le Vierge, le vivace et le bel aujourd'hui" is what Carol Clark describes as an emblem poem, a poetic commonplace, borne out by Morisot's illustration of the text.[16] "Victorieusement fui le suicide beau" is based on a sunset, "Surgi de la croupe" describes a vase, "Une Dentelle s'abolit" refers to a piece of lace, "Toute l'âme résumée" is vividly related to the smoking of a cigar. "Prose (pour des Esseintes)" (and I agree with those who see the term *prose* as an ironic one as in "Prose des fous" and "Prose pour Cazalis") has two historical events at its base: Huysmans's *A rebours* and the Byzantine rulers; Fowlie even describes it as a narration with characters and some action.[17]

"Salut" is a toast, inspired by the bubbles in a glass of champagne, a description found earlier in the same context in *Entre quatre murs*; whereas "Le Tombeau d'Edgar Poe" actually describes the frieze on the tomb. The highly hermetic and mysterious "Sonnet en yx" is replete with concrete referentials that have a priori significance: "onyx," "ongles," "minuit," "Phénix," "salon," "bibelot," "Styx," "licornes," "nixe," "miroir," "septuor"; even the famous "ptyx" exists: it is a precise English botanical term for a leaf in the bud.

The plastic points of departure in these "pure" poems do not detract from the refinements of Mallarmé's treatment of them.[18] On the contrary, discovering the circumstances of each text—and Mallarmé's verse and prose are circumstantial—increases the possibilities of their interpretation. Cohn, for example, poses five different logical, concrete referentials for "dentelle,"[19] and in his study of "Don du poème," Riffaterre asserts that Mallarmé's poetry depends on the reader's determination and ability to decipher the verbal referentials.[20] Mallarmé's objects are unembellished in and of themselves; they are there to be detected by the skillful reader. Each detail in its unadorned natural state and with its underlying legend invites the reader to reestablish the adornment that identifies it. Hence, Mallarmé does not abolish matter from his work; rather, he eliminates the particular modification that identifies the object, but the object is always there. Granted, this is the art of suggestion, but it is also the gamesmanship noted in Mallarmé's "impure" poems. Why is it not permissible to see "A la nue accablante tu" as another tub poem, which Berthe Morisot believed it to be,[21] and why can "M'introduire dans ton histoire" not be about a bidet? Why do we continue to insist on an unreal Mallarmé when his writing is of the concrete, everyday world? Breton may well have put his finger on the actual Mallarmé when, in 1924, he declared: "Mallarmé est surréaliste dans la confidence"[22]—confidence in man's creative ability, confidence in man's capacity to attain the absolute, confidence in our untapped potential to throw the dice, play the game, and win.

Dice are a preferred Mallarmé referential, as is the notion of game. As his *Vers de circonstance* shows, Mallarmé plays games with words; they are his poetic dice. Keeping in mind that a good number of these light poems were reedited and published by him in 1894, and keeping in mind his demonstrated plastic sense of poetry, we see that *Un Coup de dés* emerges as an example of his "Littérature"/"rature."[23] It is visual, as Cohn and others have established. What's more, it is "clear as myth," as Williams says, although he fails to say what kind of myth or which myth.[24] Based on topographic concerns in the use of seven different type settings, it appeals to the eye first. It is highly tactile, demanding that the reader turn the pages, and we are reminded that in the fragments of *Le Livre* the role of the reader in unfolding the pages and changing their position is of great importance to Mallarmé. It is directly linked to painting in that Redon was asked to do the illustrations.

Beginning with a concrete object, a pair of dice, Mallarmé structures his entire poem around the rolling of the dice, the act of forming a pattern. His preface (and Cohn terms it "coy" in tone) calls for "un lecteur habile," a player skilled in verbal games. And this structuration is the basis of the text; every time the reader-player rolls the dice—turns the page—a new pattern turns up. Dice, as we know, always form a pattern and, being cubes, a three-dimensional one at that. The pattern may or may not be the one we would prefer, but it is there on the double page, just as the dots are on the die. Hesitation to roll the dice or turn the page ends the act or game; acceptance of the risk is commitment to continued play, hence the circularity of the text, which begins and ends on the same phrase, returning the reader-player to the initial plastic object, "dés." Can the reader-player beat the house, the poet? Can chance be conquered and the reader-poet together form the constellation of Poetry? It is not a matter of the master's failure to throw the dice; the dice have already been thrown once ("lancé"); the risk lies in what the reader sees.[25] Just as dice always form a pattern, so do constellations, and both are fixed in space. But, unlike the dice, which are pluridimensional, the constellation is one-dimensional, the "issue stellaire" of our skill: "rien n'aura eu lieu que le lieu." The constellation makes space contract into an absolute, but visual, unity.

The constellation that Mallarmé uses is Ursa Minor, the Little Dipper, and it is to be noted that this is the only constellation that contains a fixed star, Polaris, and the only constellation that never goes below the earth's horizon: it is always visible from any point on the globe. Is this not another version of the Orphic explanation of the earth? In the Orphic mysteries, the earth is the shell of an egg; chaos is surrounded by night, ether is the day or life within; the upper egg is the sky, and the lower part is earth.[26] Hence, the pattern of the multidimensional dice on earth is reflected in the singularity of the stellar constellation if the reader can roll the right combination.

The myth of Orpheus is not the only one present in *Un Coup de dés,* for the myth of the Halcyon birds also provides the poem with its basic anecdote. Ceyx is the master of the ship lost during a storm at sea; as the fury of the storm increases and the ship begins to break up, the sailors lose their skill and courage. The waves triumph, the mast and rudder are broken, the vessel is shattered. Clinging to a piece of floating debris, Ceyx thinks of his wife, Halcyon, and prays that the foam of the waves will carry his body to her for burial. Losing the struggle, Ceyx drowns, as clouds cover the face of the grieving Day Star. In the form of Ceyx, Morpheus flies to Halcyon to tell her of her husband's fate. Refusing to live without him, Halcyon goes the next morning to the seaside where the waves bring Ceyx's body to her. In grief she leaps on a jetty, and, as wings appear on her, she flies over the surface of the water, brushing the sea with her wings. The pitying gods change both of them into birds, who mate and produce young.[27]

The parallels between this fable and *Un Coup de dés* are striking. Although the fragments of *Un Tombeau pour Anatole* also bear relationship to the text, it is doubtless accurate to say that the death of his son was too personal for the detachment necessary in a text that would appeal to a skillful reader: hence, Mallarmé jettisoned the story of his son's death and substituted one of classical mythology. Be that as it may, the use of myth in *Un Coup de dés* is essential to its plastic structure. Giving form to a legend is the writing of a poem; it is rolling multidimensional words-objects until a fixed unity, an agreement between player and house, a constellation emerges simultaneously for the reader and the poet. In addition, the use of a myth in *Un Coup de dés* allows Mallarmé the freedom to play with his codes of communication: word, sound, gesture, syntax, groupings, topography, typography. The capital letters of the beginning phrase serve to make the basic act in the text an allegorical one: every thought does send forth a throw of the dice that will never abolish the chance of playing.

Hasard is generally interpreted as chance, happenstance beyond human control, but it originally meant "le jeu de dés." Moreover, when we look at all of Mallarmé's writing, we find a penchant for wordplay, which increases the meaning of the text. Usually Mallarmé writes this word with a *z*, that is, in other texts, the word appears in its English spelling, but *hazard* is not the English translation of *hasard*. Typical of Mallarmé's love of linguistic games is the distinct possibility that *hasard* is a play on the English dice game Hazard, which is described in full by Littré. Hazard is a complicated game of dice with arbitrary rules, based on odds favorable to the one who holds the dice. Hazard can be played with two or three dice, and the betting is done on a given layout. In terms of *Un Coup de dés,* such an explanation for the construct of the text is certainly tenable.

Mallarmé's subtitle for *Un Coup de dés* is "Poème" because of its invitation to the reader to participate actively in the interpretation (reading-playing) of his representation. In no way, then, can this poem, or any of his work, for that matter, be viewed as the negation of a negation that embraces the pure idea, for matter continually rejoins matter in the Mallarmé universe: dice-constellation.[28] His practice, not his theory, demonstrates that what concerns him is the visual, concrete world and the language used in it. Only words—language—can conjoin the earth and the stars, the sea and the skies by making them plastic objects. In reading Mallarmé we should look at the patterns his dice have formed, not at his thoughts about throwing them. He is not abstract, but very, very real. Not an idealist, but a humanist. Not a postromantic, a wayward Parnassian, or a presymbolist, but a modern cocreator whose sense of the literary game led him to write ideograms before Apollinaire, to be concerned with topography before Reverdy, to write of the marvelousness of the everyday before the surrealists, to combine the visual and graphic before Michaux, to pulverize the text before Char, to be on the side of things before

Ponge, to affirm acting as being before Sartre, to know that the text is plural before the structuralists, new novelists, *Tel Quel*. Before Proust, Mallarmé knows that art is "la vraie vie."

Paula Lewis has observed that Mallarmé finds all aspects of reality valid,[29] and Judy Kravis has noted that Mallarmé's prose investigates the relationship of language with reality.[30] I would like to add that only reality is valid in the Mallarmé text. Writing poetry for him is the experience of life, and the experience of life—its circumstances—is the game of words. Mallarmé consciously deletes his own personality from his texts, but he leaves the objects that permit us to reconstruct our own worlds as poems. As Barthes says: "Le vrai jeu n'est pas de masquer le sujet mais de masquer le jeu lui-même."[31]

As early as 1864 in "Le Démon de l'analogie," Mallarmé demonstrated that his poetic practice would be based on plastic circumstances and verbal challenges to the reader: "La Pénultième est morte."[32] Of course, the penult is dead; it died when it dropped in the development of the French language. But we know what the penult was because we have the remaining syllables on each side, the parentheses that indicate its form and identity. It is this very kind of ordinary, really plastic sign that Mallarmé uses in the structuring of his poetry.[33] The problem, then, is to accept the invitation to play skillfully a literary game of interpretation, to rediscover the penult, to see our dice patterns in the plastic experience of a poet's poem.

1. In *Toward the Poems of Mallarmé* (Berkeley: University of California Press, 1965), Robert Greer Cohn bases his analysis of "Tombeau (de Verlaine)" on the word play technique of *Vers de circonstance*; he is the only scholar to date to perceive any relationship between Mallarmé's "pure" and "impure" poems (pp. 170–76).

2. Charles Chassé, in *Les Clés de Mallarmé* (Aubier: Montaigne, 1954), dismisses them as Parnassian calembours that console Mallarmé "d'une renonciation forcée à son ancien idéal" (p. 57). Yet in chapter 21 of this same work, he offers the only available study of Mallarmé's scatological texts (pp. 210–18).

3. In *Structuralist Poetics* (Ithaca, N.Y.: Cornell University Press, 1975), Jonathan Culler faults Mallarmé for being too conscious of his audience, for assuming reader expectations (pp. 88–90).

4. Jacques Scherer, *"Le Livre" de Mallarmé* (Paris: Gallimard, 1957), p. 178 (A).

5. Henri Mondor, *Mallarmé lycéen* (Paris: Gallimard, 1954).

6. In fact, one is struck by Mallarmé's lack of philological knowledge, as well as by his choice of examples. From a scholarly standpoint, the work is faulty.

7. The proofs and Redon's illustrations have been reproduced by Robert Greer Cohn in his *Mallarmé's Masterwork: New Findings* (The Hague: Mouton, 1966), pp. 83–111; see especially Cohn's "Comments," pp. 77–80.

8. J. K. Huysmans, *A rebours* (Paris: Fasquelle, 1955), pp. 240–46.

9. In *Toward the Poems of Mallarmé*, Cohn shows how Mallarmé's homage to Chavannes is constructed faithfully along the lines of a Chavannes painting (pp. 186–88).

10. Roland Barthes, *Mythologies* (Paris: Seuil, 1957), p. 251.

11. Ibid.

12. Robert Greer Cohn, *L'Œuvre de Mallarmé: Un Coup de dés* (Paris: Librairie Les Lettres, 1951).

13. See Charles Mauron, *Introduction à la psychanalyse de Mallarmé* (Neuchâtel: A la Baconnière, 1968): "L'objet se divise en images . . . un réseau de métaphores affectives" (p. 162).

14. For a discussion of Mallarmé's "Matières favorites," see Jean-Pierre Richard, *L'Univers imaginaire de Mallarmé* (Paris: Seuil, 1961); also see Georges Poulet, *La Distance intérieure: Etudes sur le temps humain,* 4 vols. (Paris: Plon, 1952), 2:298–355; Gardner Davies, *Les "Tombeaux" de Mallarmé* (Paris: Corti, 1950) and *Mallarmé et le drame solaire* (Paris: Corti, 1959). For discussions of Mallarmé in empirical terms, see Jacques Derrida, *La Dissémination* (Paris: Seuil, 1972), pp. 199–317; and Julia Kristeva, *La Révolution du langage poétique* (Paris: Seuil, 1974). In "Mallarmé's 'Quelle soie . . .' and 'M'introduire dans ton histoire,'" *Modern Language Review* 71 (1976): 779–87, D. J. Mossop suggests that the earthy and trivial are essential to Mallarmé's view of the unity of things.

15. D. J. Mossop, *Pure Poetry* (Oxford: Clarendon, 1971), p. 125.

16. Carol Clark, *Colloque Mallarmé* (Paris: Nizet, 1975), pp. 86–87.

17. Wallace Fowlie, *Mallarmé* (Chicago: University of Chicago Press, 1953), p. 192.

18. See James Lawler, "Mallarmé and the 'Monstre d'or'" in his *The Language of French Symbolism* (Princeton: Princeton University Press, 1969), for a discussion of the interrelationship between Mallarmé's plastic vision and his theory (pp. 3–20); also see Ursula Franklin, *An Anatomy of Poesis: The Prose Poems of Stéphane Mallarmé* (Chapel Hill: University of North Carolina Press, 1976).

19. Cohn, *Toward the Poems of Mallarmé,* pp. 207–8.

20. Michael Riffaterre, "On Deciphering Mallarmé," *Georgia Review* 29 (1975): 75–91.

21. Robert Goffin, *Mallarmé vivant* (Paris: Nizet, 1956), p. 278.

22. André Breton, "Premier manifeste du surréalisme," *Manifestes du surréalisme* (Paris: Pauvert, 1962), p. 36.

23. Mallarmé couples "littérature" and "rature" at the end of "Toute l'âme résumée," a "pure" poem, and on two occasions in *Vers de circonstance* (*Œuvres complètes* [Paris: Gallimard, 1945], pp. 73, 109, and 119).

24. Thomas Williams, *Mallarmé and the Language of Mysticism* (Athens: University of Georgia Press, 1970), p. 89.

25. In other words, the reader's risk of interpretation is Mallarmé's constituent structuring element; it is not the risk of an *either-or* situation, but the opportunity to conjoin the reader and poet in an *and* situation.

26. Again, noting that the Orphic explanation of the universe is a graphic one, we cannot help but see a relationship between this mythological vision and Mallarmé's use of fans, Easter eggs, and pebbles in *Vers de circonstance.*

27. See *Bullfinch's Mythology* (New York: Doubleday, 1948), pp. 76–83, for a full description of the myth of the Halcyon birds. In his early texts Mallarmé often refers to "l'alcyon" (kingfisher).

28. It is interesting to note that dice are black on white, whereas a constellation is white on black; they are plastic reversals of each other.

29. Paula Gilbert Lewis, *The Aesthetics of Stéphane Mallarmé in Relation to His Public* (Cranbury, N.J.: Fairleigh Dickinson Press, 1976).

30. Judy Kravis, *The Prose of Mallarmé* (Cambridge: Cambridge University Press, 1976).

31. Roland Barthes, *Roland Barthes* (Paris: Seuil, 1975), p. 145.

32. Mallarmé, *Œuvres complètes,* p. 272.

33. In his preface to *Mallarmé* (Paris: Gallimard, Collection Poésie, 1952), Jean-Paul Sartre asserts that Mallarmé's refusal to dirty his hands in a protest against the world leads him to put it instead between parentheses (p. 5); in the introduction to Ernest Fraenkel's *Les Dessins transconscients de Stéphane Mallarmé* (Paris: Nizet, 1960), Etienne Souriau agrees that Mallarmé places meaning between parentheses (p. 8).

Lautréamont's Plagiarisms;
or, The Poetization of Prose Texts

PETER W. NESSELROTH

Since two texts that are verbally identical do not necessarily have the same sense or implications, it is useful to distinguish different types of meaning. E. D. Hirsch differentiates between *meaning* and *significance*.[1] Meaning, for him, is what a text means originally, what the author intended it to mean; significance is what a text means subsequently, to later generations of readers. This distinction, however, requires one modification: *meaning* is not what the author intended (although Hirsch makes a valiant attempt to defend the intentional fallacy), but rather the literal meaning that a statement or textual fragment has in its initial generic and cultural context. *Significance* is, then, what a text would mean in other historical periods, as a consequence of the evolution of the reader's culture, or when it is in a different verbal or situational context. A fictional account of this process can be found in the Borges story entitled "Pierre Ménard, Author of the *Quixote*" in which an imaginary nineteenth-century French symbolist decides to rewrite *Don Quixote* without actually copying Cervantes's novel, but by recreating the mental conditions of its production. Ménard does indeed reproduce a part of the work, and it is exactly the same as the original, although as Borges tells it, Ménard's text is "almost infinitely richer." Written by a contemporary of Valéry and of William James, it has a completely different import and effect.[2]

In actual literary practice, many examples of semantic shifts, far from being only expressions of Borges's playfulness, are due to diachronic changes or to contextual transpositions. The effect is all the more striking when the displacement is made from a nonliterary genre to a literary one. André Breton's poem "PSTT," for instance, seems to reproduce the page of the Paris telephone directory that lists his name. It is a verbal collage, a literary analogue of Marcel Duchamp's ready-made sculptures. But when such a segment appears in a collection of poems (*Clair de terre*), the reader is forced to seek out the features that make it an artistic composition, i.e., the name Breton as the invariant of the poem and the added signature (Breton, André) whose inversion imitates the style of the listings and, simultaneously, marks it as an original creation. A collage, however, stands out, by its very nature, as a borrowed fragment against the background of the supposedly personal compositions that make up the rest of the book of poems. It has shock value as an improper intrusion. Plagiarisms, on the other hand, are more sneaky. They tend, if they are at all well done, to go unnoticed because their source cannot be easily identified (otherwise, they would simply become quotations or parodies). They have to be integrated into an existing verbal framework so as not to be perceived, for they are not simply amusing little provocations. They are serious transgressions, a theft of other people's property, a major cultural taboo. It is therefore not surprising to find examples of this transgression in works that are representative of a type of writing that puts into question ordinary modes of composition and narration and has thus become emblematic of what the *Tel Quel* group used to call the "pratique signifiante de l'avant-garde." A case in point is Lautréamont and *Les Chants de Maldoror*.

In 1952 Maurice Viroux discovered that six bird descriptions in *Les Chants de Maldoror* were taken from *L'Encyclopédie d'histoire naturelle du Dr Chenu*.[3] Subsequently Marguerite Bonnet found that certain scientific references in *Les Chants* seemed to come from Michelet (*La Mer, L'Insecte,* and so forth), or, more precisely, from Michelet's scientific informant, Dr. E. A. Pouchet, who was an opponent of Pasteur in the controversy over spontaneous generation. When, for instance, Lautréamont writes, "Et, de même que les rotifères et les tardigrades peuvent être chauffés à une température voisine de l'ébullition,"[4] he is referring to one of Pouchet's experiments, in which the scientist demonstrated that these creatures died when the temperature reached about 90°C.[5] Similarly, Marie-François Guyard has shown that some of the more sadistic themes in *Maldoror,* such as the human body used as a slingshot, come from Lamartine.[6] But the last two cases are, at best, allusions in which the surface texts in *Les Chants* are noticeably dissimilar from the texts of origin. I shall therefore only deal with the examples uncovered by Viroux, outright plagiarism being a more unusual method of composition than the traditional allusion (see Appendix for the plagiarized texts). Lautréamont does perform a certain number of minor modifications on the encyclopedia fragments. They are minor, but essential, for they erase the marks of their provenance and thus integrate the borrowed texts into the new contexts perfectly. These are the changes:

1. The reduction of capitals to small letters: "oiseaux" in Plagiarism 1, "stercoraires" in P2, "pélicaninés" in P3, "buses" in P5.

2. Explicitations for the reader's understanding: "Ces troupes" ⟶ "Les bandes d'étourneaux" in P1, "Cette famille" ⟶ "la famille des pélicaninés" in P3, "Il a" ⟶ "Le milan royal a" in P5.

3. Suppressions such as "Labbes" in P2; "1°," "2°," and so forth, and "n'est que la reproduction de celle des Pélicans de Cuvier et Lesson" in P3.

4. Additions like "aimanté" in P1, the demonstrative adjectives and the color "jaune" in P4, the phrase "la queue ne se trompe pas" in P5.

5. The continuation, after a colon, of the last sentence in P5, with the casual address to the reader, "vous ouvririez les yeux comme la porte d'un four, que ce serait d'autant inutile."

6. Transformations such as the fusion into one sentence of "les stercoraires . . . se plaisent" in P2; the shift from "qui y comprenaient les genres" to "comprend quatre genres distincts" in P3 and from "une large membrane dilatable" to "cette large poche" in P4; the syntactic inversion, after "comme" in P6, to make "caroncule charnue" the main subject of the comparison.

Other changes could be the result of a concern to write well, in the normative sense: the transfer of the conjuction "et" from before "creusée" in P4 to the beginning of the clause, making the sequence an asyndetic, falling group; the poetic noun/adjective inversion in P5, "sa situation favorite" ⟶ "sa favorite situation"; or, in the same passage, the replacing of one "semble" by "croit" to avoid repetition.

On the semantic and stylistic levels, the integration of the borrowed descriptions into other contexts brings to the foreground meanings and effects that were dormant in their former contexts. P1 ("les étourneaux"), P2 ("les stercoraires"), P5 ("le milan royal"), and P6 ("le bec du dindon") are vehicles for similes. That is, given that shape A is like B, A would be the tenor and B the vehicle.[7] But, except for P6, Lautréamont uses the form B so A, which, in P1 and P5, make the encyclopedia articles seem like arbitrary insertions, introduced only to confuse the reader, until the postplaced tenor ("Toi, de même . . .") reveals a meaningful connection. P2 is clearer since it has the mark of a simile ("de même que . . . ainsi"), and P6 occurs as one of many vehicles in an example of the well-known *beau comme . . .* group of comparisons. P3 and P4, on the other hand, are presented as statements of factual scientific and personal knowledge ("je savais que . . ." and "Je recherchais vaguement, dans les replis de ma mémoire, dans quelle contrée torride ou glacée, j'avais déjà remarqué ce bec . . ."). As descriptive units in vehicles, or as statements of facts, these fragments are, like all vehicles, smuggled into the fiction;[8] but they also become part of the fiction, insofar as they force the reader to make them consistent with his search for literary coherence. This is how the process works: the first of the plagiarized passages is in the opening stanza of *chant* 5. The flight of the starlings illustrates the organization of the whole work. The starlings move forward as a group, but each individual bird flies in a circle toward the center of the flock, in a spirallike manner. This description is a counterpoint to the flight of the cranes, at the very beginning of the book, where the reader is warned that he ought to be very careful before adventuring into such unknown and dangerous territory as the pages he is about to read. He is told to behave like the crane who leads the group but who, sensing the storm ahead, wisely turns around. The difference between the flight of the cranes and the flight of the starlings is that the former fly in a straight line toward a specific point on the horizon. The opposition *cranes versus starlings* actualizes, in bird code, the thematic structure *linear versus circular*.[9] This opposition, as Blanchot has pointed out, goes back at least as far as Dante. In Artaud de Montor's translation of the *Inferno* (the one closest in time to *Maldoror*), we read in the fifth canto: "De même que le froid fait prendre aux étourneaux un vol *irrégulier*, de même cette tourmente emporte, heurte, repousse, ramène les âmes coupables. Sans qu'aucun espoir vienne leur rendre quelque courage // Telles les grues disposées en *files allongées* fendent l'air et le frappent de leurs cris lugubres, telles les ombres enlevées par la tempête poussent de longs gémissements."[10]

In *Les Chants* the distance between the two flight descriptions (from stanza 1, *chant* 1, to stanza 1, *chant* 5) is much greater because they represent two modes of composition, the straight line classical narration against the repetitive and elliptical type of exposition. The space between those two stanzas is taken up by a search, through constant repetitions, for the proper formal expression. The whirlwind as a motif progressively becomes the whirlwind as a form and it is precisely when Lautréamont becomes aware of how this can be done that the first plagiarism appears. (There are probably no direct transcriptions of other texts before *chant* 5.) The whirlwind catches in its own motion whatever surrounds it (here, other texts) and symbolizes therefore the instinctual manner of writing that is repressed, for the sake of clarity and communication, in culturally sanctioned literature. But Lautréamont writes the forbidden;[11] his message is obscure and is communicative only when he addresses the reader directly, as he does in the context of the copied segment. Up to this point in the text the reader probably suspects that he is reading nonsense and it has become necessary to show him that there is some master plan for all these disconnected, supernatural stories, that the description of the flight of the starlings really does have a function: "Toi de même, ne fais pas attention à la manière bizarre dont je chante chacune de ces strophes. Mais sois persuadé que les accents fondamentaux de la poésie n'en conservent pas moins leur intrinsèque droit sur mon intelligence." It now becomes clear that there is a metaphoric relationship between the stanzas and the starlings, and from here on, all the other constitutive elements fall into place: "une manière de voler qui leur est propre" corresponds to "la manière bizarre dont je chante chacune de ces strophes," "la voix d'un seul chef" to "je chante," and so on. Lautréamont even completes the description of the flight, to make certain that the analogy is inescapable: the birds never lose sight of their ultimate destination ("Malgré cette singulière manière de tourbillonner . . . "), and the reader can rest assured that the poet also knows where he is heading ("Mais sois persuadé que les accents fondamentaux de la poésie n'en conservent pas moins leur intrinsèque droit sur mon intelligence"). The same method of semantic integration governs P2: the reduction of the two kinds of birds to one, by the suppression of "Labbes," so that there is a single subject in the vehicle to correspond with the "je" of the tenor, the deletion of "plus voraces encore que les autres et" and its replacement by "oiseaux inquiets" in apposition (just in case the reader does not know that "les stercoraires" are birds); this emphasizes the adjective "inquiets," which shares with "je n'étais pas tranquille" the semantic features that make the analogy possible. And, true to the principle of a crisscross progression (one theme coming out of the form of another), the context of P5 ("le vol du milan royal") is a theory of similes that discusses the problem of distance (or lack of common features) between the two parts of a comparison. The topic is the appearance of the face of a dead child high above his coffin, and it leads to a digression on difference and similarity:

> C'est, généralement parlant, une chose singulière que la tendance attractive qui nous porte à rechercher (pour ensuite les exprimer) les ressemblances et les différences que recèlent, dans leurs naturelles propriétés, les objects les plus opposés entre eux, et quelquefois les moins aptes, en apparence, à se prêter à ce genre de combinaisons sympathiquement curieuses, et qui, ma parole d'honneur, donnent gracieusement au style de l'écrivain, qui se paie cette personnelle satisfaction, l'impossible et inoubliable aspect d'un hibou sérieux jusqu'à l'éternité. Suivons en conséquence le courant qui nous entraîne. [*Chant* 5, stanza 6, p. 208.]

This is followed by the encyclopedia fragment, then by comments on its apparent lack of motivation and its self-evident reason:

> Chacun a le bon sens de confesser sans difficulté (quoique avec un peu de mauvaise grâce) qu'il ne s'aperçoit pas, au premier abord, du rapport, si lointain qu'il soit, que je signale entre la beauté du vol du milan royal, et celle de la figure de l'enfant, s'élevant doucement, au-dessus du cercueil découvert, comme un nénuphar qui perce la surface des eaux; et voilà précisément en quoi consiste l'impardonnable faute qu'entraîne l'inamovible situation d'un manque de repentir, touchant l'ignorance volontaire dans laquelle on croupit. Ce rapport de calme majesté entre les deux termes de ma narquoise comparaison n'est déja que trop commun, et d'un symbole assez compréhensible, pour que je m'étonne davantage de ce qui ne peut avoir, comme seule excuse, que ce même caractère de vulgarité qui fait appeler, sur tout objet ou spectacle qui en est atteint, un profond sentiment d'indifférence injuste. Comme si ce qui se voit quotidiennement n'en devrait pas moins réveiller l'attention de notre admiration! [*Chant* 5, stanza 6, pp. 208–9]

The relationship between the flight of the "milan royal" and the face of the child is their majestic, and perfectly peaceful, appearance. They are both superior and immovable (as in *Le Sommeil du condor*). Although the thematic difference between this flight and the starlings' is a dynamic versus static opposition, it nonetheless repeats the same meaning (the narrator's creative technique), so that "et la queue ne se trompe pas" simply becomes a vulgar way of saying "c'est à la voix de l'instinct que les étourneaux obéissent."

A similar point is made, in anatomical code, in P3 and P4, through the metaphor of a hybrid mythical being, the man with a pelican's head. In the previous stanza Lautréamont had tried to reassure the reader that the logic of his narrative is not inconceivable, and he cited as an example one of the wonders of modern science: "Eh quoi, n'est-on pas parvenu à greffer sur le dos d'un rat vivant la queue détachée du corps d'un autre rat?" (p. 189). (The editor of the Pléiade edition tells us [p. 1132] that such an operation was described very precisely in *La Revue des deux mondes* of 1 July 1868.) This scientific procedure can be applied to literature, since the description of the transplanted pelican's head is itself a transplant from an encyclopedia. But, unlike the original context, in which the term precedes its definition, the words "tête de pélican" appear after the description, like the word to be guessed in a riddle or a crossword puzzle, the space between the formulation of the enigma and its solution (about thirty lines further down) being filled with an interior monologue that proceeds, by elimination, through a series of negative statements (*x n'était pas y*) until, out of four possible types of birds, there is only one left.

Once he has become conscious of the fact that his undertaking requires the text that is being written to include, within itself, texts that are already written elsewhere, Lautréamont simultaneously puts the theory into practice by telling the reader, through a plagiarized article, that his developments are inclusive. From then on the circular motion accelerates, and the text begins to incorporate, not just paragraphs from other books, but as many sentences as possible, and ever more closely together—which is what happens in the *beau comme* comparisons that provide the context for P6: all the vehicles, except the last one, have a recognizably nonliterary origin (the third is even given as a quotation), but they are assimilated into a literary framework (the genre *chant*) through the aesthetic judgment *beau comme,* which is the center, the "point aimanté," of the formal cyclone.

Syntactically and semantically Lautréamont's borrowed descriptions blend into his own text. Yet lexically they are marked enough to prompt scholars to go to the reference rooms of libraries in order to search for sources. And, because the conditions of reading are different, it would appear that the more similar the surface texts are, the greater is the change in their meanings. The integration of the encyclopedia articles into the poetic text makes it possible to produce an exegetical discourse about them. Thus, Marcel Jean and Arpad Mezei are able to write:

> Le cinquième Chant, scientifiquement, systématiquement, va développer les aspects de ce retour cyclique. Dans la première strophe, nous trouvons une sorte de théorie mathématique de l'obsession, exposée au moyen de la remarquable description du *vol des étourneaux.*

. . . Il s'agit d'un mouvement suivant une courbe du quatrième degré, c'est-à-dire non pas une courbe, mais un groupe de courbes, semblable, si nous le simplifions, à celui de la roue d'une voiture. Tous les petits points de la roue (excepté le centre) décrivent une cycloïde: ils reviennent à leur position première tout en étant, pendant ce temps, entraînés par le déplacement de la voiture, lequel est fonction des mouvements particuliers. Par exemple, le point de la roue qui touche terre à un moment donné, s'élève, puis s'abaisse et touche terre à nouveau, tandis que la voiture avance d'une distance égale à la longueur de la circonférence décrite.

. . . Ce mouvement possède donc la caractéristique de reproduire, après un déplacement en avant, les positions précédemment occupées par les différents points de l'ensemble. C'est l'image même du mécanisme de l'obsession cyclique.[12]

Unlike Maurice Viroux, I am quoting this interpretation not to ridicule it (I tend to agree with it) but to suggest that this type of explication could not, or at least would not, have been generated by the same description in its encyclopedia context.

In a broader perspective, we may consider the question of the validity of plagiarism as a creative technique for the global meaning of *Maldoror*'s message. It seems to me that the criterion of originality, even if it were not illusory to begin with, can apply only to an author who presents a work as his own product. But as far as Lautréamont is concerned, it is not really relevant to speak of plagiarism, since there is no plagiarizer. "Le Comte de Lautréamont" was not a human being of flesh and blood. The name's reference is not Isidore Ducasse but Eugène Sue's *Latréaumont* and the historical character who is the subject of Sue's novel. It is a name used simply to fill the slot for an author's name on the title page of a book. The knowledge that Lautréamont was Isidore Ducasse's pseudonym did not reach the general public until the 1890 edition of *Les Chants,* when the fact was revealed in Léon Genonceaux's preface. The first *chant* had even been published twice anonymously before the first complete edition. Ducasse, the author of *Poésies I* and *II,* had done his best to erase his biography when he wrote Lautréamont's *Chants de Maldoror.* In other words, that text is rather like Dr. Chenu's *Encyclopédie d'histoire naturelle,* containing the knowledge of our culture, circular in composition and consisting of other people's contributions (the bird articles were written by Guéneau de Montbeillard, who used the material of his collaborator Buffon), so that the question of literary property is, in any case, very nebulous. Written *from* an *Encyclopédie d'histoire naturelle, Les Chants de Maldoror* is actually an *Encyclopédie d'histoires surnaturelles.* Its signature is a name that has no substance, a mask, a persona. Lautréamont is literally a self-made man of (purloined) letters. His text, through the incorporation of texts around it, is a self-centered, narcissistic artifact. And, like all personae, or personalities, it is made up of fragments stolen from others.

But beyond the question of the logic of plagiarism within the global meaning of Lautréamont's work, the transposition of these articles helps to explain the process of the poetization of nonliterary texts. The literariness of a message, i.e., the specific quality by which it imposes itself as an artistic text on the reader's perception, is not limited to a particular formal arrangement of its internal features. The contextual framing of a statement contributes as much to its poeticalness as does Jakobson's syntagmatic projection of linguistic equivalences. The Jakobsonian poetic function is obviously an important element of aesthetic verbal sequences, especially in cases of phonological repetitions of the "I like Ike" type.[13] When we come to less noticeable features, however, similarities and parallelisms can be found in just about any text.[14] The principle of equivalence cannot really be restricted to intrinsic phonological, morphological, or grammatical components. The paradigm from which the equivalences are selected is one of sentences and paragraphs, and these combine with the existing sentences and paragraphs to make up the whole discourse. Any text can indeed become literary, but only if it is placed in a context where its literal meaning is so blurred that the reader has to find a significance that can be justified in terms of literary coherence.

1. See E. D. Hirsch, *Validity in Interpretation* (New Haven: Yale University Press, 1967), pp. 6–10.

2. Jorge Luis Borges, "Pierre Ménard, Author of the *Quixote*," in *Labyrinths: Selected Stories and Other Writings,* trans. James E. Irby (New York: New Directions, 1964), pp. 42–43. Maurice Saillet, in "Défense du plagiat," *Les Lettres nouvelles* 1 (April 1953): 205–14, was the first to allude to this fiction in connection with Lautréamont's plagiarism. I repeat it here because my readers may not be familiar with Saillet's article and because it is pertinent to any discussion of changes in the meaning of verbal messages.

3. See Maurice Viroux, "Lautréamont et le Dr Chenu," *Mercure de France* 1070 (December 1952): 632–42. For the texts of both Lautréamont's plagiarisms and the "original" passages in *L'Encyclopédie d'histoire naturelle du Dr Chenu,* consult the appendix at the end of this study.

4. Lautréamont, *Œuvres complètes,* ed. P.-O. Walzer (Paris: Gallimard, Bibliothèque de la Pléiade, 1970), p. 189. All the references for Lautréamont are to this edition.

5. See Marguerite Bonnet, "Lautréamont et Michelet," *Revue d'histoire littéraire de la France* 64 (1964): 605–22.

6. See M.-F. Guyard, "Lautréamont et Lamartine," *Travaux de linguistique et de littérature* 3, no.2 (Paris: Klincksieck, 1965), pp. 77–82.

7. I adopt I. A. Richards's terminology. See his *Philosophy of Rhetoric* (New York: Oxford, 1965), pp. 96–100; see also my "The Stylistic Analysis of the Literary Image," in Pierre Léon, et al., *Problems of Textual Analysis* (Montreal, Paris, Brussels: Didier, 1971), pp. 123–31.

8. See I.A. Richards, *Principles of Literary Criticism* (New York: Harcourt, Brace, 1961), p. 240.

9. On thematic structure, see Michael Riffaterre, "Le Poème comme représentation," *Poétique* 4 (1970): 401–18, especially p. 402 n. 3.

10. See Maurice Blanchot, *Lautréamont et Sade* (Paris: Editions de Minuit, 1963), p. 292 n. 2.

11. See my article "Lautréamont: Le sens de la forme," *Littérature* 17 (February 1975): 73–84.

12. Marcel Jean and Arpad Mezei, *Maldoror* (Paris: Editions du Pavois, 1947), pp. 79–80.

13. See Roman Jakobson, "Closing Statement: Linguistics and Poetics," *Style in Language* (Cambridge, Mass.: MIT Press, 1960), pp. 350–77.

14. See, for example, Jonathan Culler's Jakobsonian analysis of a page from Jakobson's *Questions de poétique*, in *Structuralist Poetics* (London: RKP, 1975), pp. 63–64.

APPENDIX

Les Chants de Maldoror	*L'Encyclopédie d'histoire naturelle du Dr Chenu* (Paris: Marescq and Cie Editeurs, 1850–1861)

Chant 5, stanza 1

P1 *Les bandes d'étourneaux* ont une manière de voler qui leur est propre, et semble soumise à une tactique uniforme et régulière, telle que serait celle d'une troupe disciplinée, obéissant avec précision à la voix d'un seul chef. C'est à la voix de l'instinct que les étourneaux obéissent, et leur instinct les porte à se rapprocher toujours du centre du peloton, tandis que la rapidité de leur vol les emporte sans cesse au-delà; en sorte que cette multitude d'*o*iseaux, ainsi réunis par une tendance commune vers le même point *aimanté,* allant et venant sans cesse, circulant et se croisant en tous sens, forme une espèce de tourbillon fort agité, dont la masse entière, sans suivre de direction bien certaine, paraît avoir un mouvement général d'évolution sur elle-même, résultant des mouvements, particuliers de circulation propres à chacune de ses parties, et dans lequel le centre, tendant perpétuellement à se développer, mais sans cesse pressé, repoussé par l'effort contraire des lignes environnantes qui pèsent sur lui, est constamment plus serré qu'aucune de ces lignes, lesquelles le sont elles-mêmes d'autant plus, qu'elles sont plus voisines du centre.

Ces troupes ont une manière de voler qui leur est propre, et semble soumise à une tactique uniforme et régulière, telle que serait celle d'une troupe disciplinée, obéissant avec précision à la voix d'un seul chef. C'est à la voix de l'instinct que les étourneaux obéissent, et leur instinct les porte à se rapprocher toujours du centre du peloton, tandis que la rapidité de leur vol les emporte sans cesse au-delà; en sorte que cette multitude d'Oiseaux, ainsi réunis par une tendance commune vers le même point, allant et venant sans cesse, circulant et se croisant en tous sens, forme une espèce de tourbillon fort agité, dont la masse entière, sans suivre de direction bien certaine, paraît avoir un mouvement général d'évolution sur elle-même, résultant des mouvements particuliers de circulation propres à chacune de ses parties, et dans lequel le centre, tendant perpétuellement à se développer, mais sans cesse pressé, repoussé par l'effort contraire des lignes environnantes qui pèsent sur lui, est constamment plus serré qu'aucune de ces lignes, lesquelles le sont elles-mêmes d'autant plus, qu'elles sont plus voisines du centre. (Gueneau de Montebeillard.) [Oiseaux, Cinquième partie (1853), p. 179]

Chant 5, stanza 2

P2 [*car, de même que* les *s*tercoraires, *oiseaux inquiets* comme s'ils étaient toujours affamés, se plaisent dans les mers qui baignent les deux pôles, et n'avancent qu'accidentellement dans les zones tempérées,] ainsi je n'étais pas tranquille, et je

Les uns, tels que les *Labbes ou* Stercoraires, *plus voraces encore que les autres et* inquiets comme s'ils étaient toujours affamés. . . . *Ils* se plaisent dans les mers qui baignent les deux pôles, et n'avancent qu'accidentellement dans les zones tem-

portais mes jambes en avant avec beaucoup de lenteur. Mais qu'était-ce donc que la substance corporelle vers laquelle

P3 j'avançais? Je savais que [*la famille des pélicaninés* comprend *quatre* genres *distincts*: *le* fou, *le* pélican, *le* cormoran, *la* frégate.] La forme grisâtre qui m'apparaissait n'était pas un fou. Le bloc plastique que j'apercevais n'était pas une frégate. La chair cristallisée que j'observais n'était pas un cormoran. Je le voyais maintenant, l'homme à l'encéphale dépourvu de protubérance annulaire. Je recherchais vaguement, dans les replis de ma mémoire, dans quelle contrée torride ou glacée

pérées. [Oiseaux, Sixième partie (1854), p. 271]

Cette famille [des Pélicaninés] *n'est que la reproduction de celle des Pélicans de Cuvier et Lesson, qui y* comprenaient les genres: *1° Fou* . . . *2° Pélican* . . . *3°Cormoran* . . . *4° Frégate.* [Oiseaux, Sixième partie (1854), p. 261]

P4 j'avais déjà remarqué [ce bec très-long, large, convexe, en voûte, à arête marquée, onguiculée, renflée et très crochue à son extrémité; *ces* bords dentelés, droits; *cette* mandibule inférieure, à branches séparées jusqu'auprès de la pointe; *cet* inervalle rempli par *une peau membraneuse*; *cette* large *poche, jaune* et sacciforme, occupant toute la gorge et pouvant se distendre considérablement; *et ces narines* très étroites, longitudinales, presque imperceptibles, creusées dans un sillon basal!] [P. 191]

[Le Pélican]
Bec très long, large, convexe, en voûte, à arête marquée, onguiculée, renflée et très-crochue à son extrémité; bords dentelés, droits; mandibule inférieure à branches séparées jusqu'auprès de la pointe, *et l'*intervalle rempli par une membrane . . . (cet) intervalle des branches de la mandibule inférieure rempli par une peau membraneuse. . . . Une large membrane *dilatable,* sacciforme, occupant toute la gorge et pouvant se distendre considérablement. . . . Narines très étroites, longitudinales, presque imperceptibles, et creusées dans un sillon basal. [Oiseaux, Sixième partie (1854), pp. 262–63]

Chant 5, stanza 6

P5 *Le milan royal* a les ailes proportionnellement plus longues que les *b*uses, et le vol bien plus aisé: aussi passe-t-il sa vie dans l'air. Il ne se repose presque jamais et parcourt chaque jour des espaces immenses; et ce grand mouvement n'est point un exercice de chasse, ni poursuite de proie, ni même de découverte; car, il ne chasse pas; mais, il semble que le vol soit son état naturel, sa *favorite situation.* L'on ne peut s'empêcher d'admirer la manière dont il l'exécute. Ses ailes longues et étroites paraissent immobiles; c'est la queue qui *croit* diriger toutes *les* évolutions, et *la*

Il a [*dit Buffon du Milan royal*] les ailes proportionnellement plus longues, que les Buses, et le vol bien plus aisé: aussi passe-t-il sa vie dans l'air. Il ne se repose presque jamais et parcourt chaque jour des espaces immenses; et ce grand mouvement n'est point un exercice de chasse ni *de* poursuite de proie, ni même de découverte, car il ne chasse pas; mais il semble que le vol soit son état naturel, sa situation favorite. L'on ne peut s'empêcher d'admirer la manière dont il l'exécute. Ses ailes longues et étroites paraissent immobiles; c'est la queue qui semble diriger toutes ses évolu-

queue ne se trompe pas: elle agit sans cesse. *Il* s'élève sans effort; il s'abaisse comme s'il glissait sur un plan incliné; il semble plutôt nager que voler; il précipite sa course, il la ralentit, s'arrête, et reste comme suspendu ou fixé à la même place, pendant *des* heures entières. *L'on ne peut* s'apercevoir d'aucun mouvement dans ses ailes: [P. 208]

tions, et elle agit sans cesse; il s'élève sans effort, il s'abaisse comme s'il glissait sur un plan incliné; il semble plutôt nager que voler; il précipite sa course, il la ralentit, s'arrête et reste comme suspendu ou fixé à la même place pendant des heures entières, sans qu'on puisse s'apercevoir d'aucun mouvement dans ses ailes. [Oiseaux, Première partie (1851), p. 87]

Chant 6, stanza 6

P6   ou encore, *comme* la caroncule charnue, de forme conique, sillonnée par des rides transversales assez profondes, qui s'élève sur la base du bec supérieur du dindon; [P. 235]

Sur la base du bec supérieur s'élève une caroncule charnue, de forme conique, et sillonnée par des rides transversales assez profondes. [Oiseaux, Sixième partie (1854), p. 100]

PART THREE : CONTEXT

The Myth of the *Poètes Maudits*

DIANA FESTA-McCORMICK

Verlaine's formula for the *poètes maudits,* if such we may call it, was not accompanied by any cogent definition. Yet when the work was first published in 1883, its striking title aroused a far-reaching resonance. The unfortunate poets who appeared in that original selection have had a long lineage of descendants in several countries, down to this very day, almost one hundred years after the phrase was coined. The concept was not new, however, even if only then it claimed a halo of respectability and an assertive power in the world of letters. There have at all times been poets who were, or thought themselves, unhappy—in their passions, in their ambition and their desire for affluence or power, in their isolation from the society in which they lived. Happiness seems in fact to have been a rare blessing for the "genus irritabile vatum," as Horace called it,[1] and was probably spurned by most of them. The poet is supposedly ill-adapted to his environment. His vocation, it is often assumed, only comes to the fore through a feeling of alienation and, possibly, little interest in happiness. Sorrow, at least in the romantic tradition, lurks at the fountainhead of creative impulse. An anthology of Epicurean poetry in the ancient and modern languages would very probably pall on modern readers. We tolerate only a moderate amount of drinking songs, of odes or hymns to blissfully rewarded love. Horace's praises of wine, Propertius's celebration of a quiet country retreat fulfilling all of the poet's wishes, Ronsard's admonitions to his ladies to surrender to beauty's fleeting instants—even Goethe's felicitous renderings of Hafiz—are likely to strike most of us, heirs to romantic pessimism, as limited in their strained oblivion of the Johnsonian "vanity of human wishes."

The idea that a curse weighs upon the poet appeared immediately plausible with Verlaine's manifesto. Artists have always been considered a group apart from all mortals, in pursuit of their own creative demons, removed from life's more pedestrian endeavors. The concept went through various evolutions, with a few variations, seeming in turn less pessimistic or utterly dispirited. But doom appears, on the whole, as the faithful companion of the artist, the shadow thrust upon him by a chastising bourgeois force and a greedy society, or the scourge born from within the poet himself. Artists are prey to their own fears, to the menace of sterility, or to mysterious, hostile, satanic forces, to inner torments that push them to drink, drugs, suicide. The myth thus took shape. It was given impetus by Baudelaire's presentation of Poe as the unhappy American poet only grudgingly recognized by his compatriots—and it was accorded full life by Verlaine's *Les Poètes maudits*.

The early nineteenth century in France had rediscovered François Villon, the first authentic "accursed poet" in French. The romantics of Italy, England, and Germany made much in their verse of the unfortunate Tasso (1544–95) who, a precocious genius, idolized at first, had turned into the lamentable victim of his own mental delusions and insane fears. Byron sang the "Lament" (in 1817) of the incarcerated poet:

> I have been patient, let me be so yet;
> I had forgotten half I would forget,
> But it revives—Oh! would it were my lot
> To be forgetful as I am forgot!
> Feel I not wroth with those who bade me dwell
> In this vast lazar-house of many woes?
> Where laughter is not mirth, nor thought the mind,
> Nor words a language, or ev'n men mankind;
> Where cries reply to curses, shrieks to blows,
> And each is tortured in his separate hell—
> For we are crowded in our solitudes—
> Many, but each divided by the wall,
> Which echoes Madness in her babbling moods.[2]

"To sleep, perchance to dream," was Hamlet's anguished cry. "To be forgetful," echoes Tasso in Byron's verse, "as I am forgot." The haunting presence of deceived hopes, of loves forfeited in neglect, pursues the wretched poet. Lost in his own labyrinthine hell, he heeds the vast echo of man's madness, of its helpless "shrieks" and forlorn hopes. The "wall" that casts a shadow upon his life is the same that stands implacable between man and all cherished dreams.

In an exhibition of 1844, Delacroix had shown a powerful portrait of "Le Tasse en prison." The painting inspired one of Baudelaire's less successful sonnets, perhaps, but one that is nevertheless suggestive of the poet's plight in an insensitive world:

> Le poète au cachot, débraillé, maladif,
> Roulant un manuscrit sous son pied convulsif,
> Mesure d'un regard que la terreur enflamme
> L'escalier de vertige où s'abîme son âme.[3]

The "cachot" of the verses evokes the poet's double prison, that which arises from his inner tumult and the one imposed by society's indifference to beauty. Tasso, we know, had been confined for seven years to St. Anna, an asylum closely resembling a criminal prison. There he struggled against his intimate horrors, the ridicule and neglect of the world of men, and the nightmarish oscillations of his poetic imagination. His numerous flights on foot across Italy's countryside made him the true precursor of that other famous *maudit,* the Rimbaud "with the soles of wind," as Verlaine was to call him. Goethe's drama *Torquato Tasso,* composed as early as 1788–89, was published later and pictured the Italian poet as a Wertherian character tortured by a wretched and impossible love.

A compatriot of Tasso, Giacomo Leopardi, composed, a little earlier in the nineteenth century, a dialogue between Tasso and his familiar genie. The poet appears in his hospital prison, rationally arguing with his muse to prove the ubiquity of "la noia" and the radical impossibility of happiness in love: "Know that between the real and the dreamt, there is no other difference, if not that the latter can be much more beautiful and sweeter, than ever the other can be."[4] Dream is the only valid truth in life. The poet cherishes an impossible vision, and beauty lives over the horrors of reality. "Between dream and imagination, you will wear out your life," the genie admonishes. Exhausted, reviled, alone—but with an image of candor to sustain him—the poet will sing his verses. From the darkest of nights, "without moon nor stars," a crepuscular shadow will emerge, with a hint of light. "Tell me," implores the poet to his genie, "when despair overtakes me, where can I find you?" "In qualche liquore generoso" is the answer—in some generous liquor—in drunkenness and oblivion, we must conclude, in madness and the denial of man's wisdom.

A precocious scholar and voracious reader, Leopardi had been afflicted with poor health and physical deformity. He was in love with a dream of love and was condemned forever to be thwarted. He felt certain that he was doomed by fate to live a short existence, steeped in "infelicità." In March 1818 he wrote to another writer, Pietro Giordani, "Fate meted out to me the condition of poor health . . . with the intellectual and sentimental ability to acknowledge that joy is not for me and that, dressed as it were in mourning garb, I welcome melancholy as my eternal and inseparable companion. . . . It is prudent to leave me to my melancholy and to myself, who am my own pitiless execution-er."[5] For nearly twenty years Leopardi was to sing in austere verse the same anthem to the ubiquitousness of "infelicità," persuaded that the curse that doomed him to pain was preordained and unavoidable. In 1835, two years before his brief life was to come to an end, he wrote his own desolate and concise testament in a sixteen-line poem, "A se stesso" ("To himself"):

> Posa per sempre. Assai
> Palpitasti. Non val cosa nessuna
> I moti tuoi, né di sospiri è degna
> La terra. Amaro e noia
> La vita, altro mai nulla . . .
>
> [Rest forever. Enough
> You have palpitated. Nothing deserves

> The beats of your heart, nor of your sighs is
> The earth worthy. Bitterness and boredom
> Is life, nothing ever else . . .]

Doom hangs heavy upon the young poet's life, his faithful companion, accomplice of the waiting grave. His verses are the epitaph to the bleakness that filled his days, to his anguish and desperate cries. "Dans ta tombe précoce à peine refroidi," was to write Musset, "Sombre amant de la Mort, pauvre Léopardi."[7]

The middle of the nineteenth century was a period that gave rise to the phenomenon of the *poètes maudits,* driven to Bohemia and to starvation by the creed of a materialistic society. It constituted the disillusioned answer of authors to the boastful or prophetic claims of romantic poets to be "the unacknowledged legislators of the world."[8] Many of those poets who had asked for the privilege of leading mankind to higher and better destinies, in France at any rate, attempted to enter the political arena: Lamartine, Vigny, Hugo. Their hopes were blighted with the reaction that, in Western Europe, followed upon the revolutions of 1848. Poets then took refuge in their solitude, martyrs of an industrial civilization that ignored and scorned them, or in the creed of "art for art's sake." They would fondly imagine that the fate of their predecessors had been more fortunate, in the Athens or Rome of old, where a cultured elite had been capable of understanding them.

The mythical Sisyphus, bent under the weight of a malediction from the gods, has many spiritual heirs among the romantics. Alfred de Musset saw in his life the presence of an obstinate curse that dragged him into an oppressive vacuum. He meant to write on his own decline as a poet—we are told by his brother—on *le poète déchu* that he had become, a prey to drunkenness, debauchery, and weariness. Vigny was the recognized spokesman for all oppressed poets. His *Stello* (1832) is a semifictional essay on the theme of poets reduced to misery and starvation by a complacent and inimical society. The poet's life, wrought in sorrow and solitude, will find a lasting echo only in the grace of his verse: "le poète a une malédiction sur sa vie et une bénédiction sur son nom." Vigny calls upon those martyrs of beauty whose very names hold a lasting resonance by the altar of poetry: "Avoir toujours présentes à la pensée les images, choisies entre mille, de Gilbert, de Chatterton et d'André Chénier."[9]

Nicolas Gilbert (1751–80), mentioned among those exemplifying the creed of the poet's evil fate, is by now practically forgotten. Yet he wrote some touching poems, lamenting the anathema of a life and all desultory hopes:

> Malheur à ceux dont je suis né!
> Père aveugle et barbare, impitoyable mère!
> Pauvres, vous fallait-il mettre au monde un enfant
> Qui n'héritât de vous qu'une affreuse indigence?[10]

Poverty, the social curse for those who vow their breath to poetry's ethereal appeal, has thrust him amidst the shadows of the forgotten ones:

> Au banquet de la vie infortuné convive
> J'apparus un jour, et je meurs.
> Je meurs, et sur la tombe où lentement j'arrive,
> Nul ne viendra verser des pleurs.[11]

Life is a brief parenthesis for the miserable poet, straddling fear over the abyss of death.

André Chénier, also included in Vigny's work, died on the scaffold during the Terror. He appears, however, as the victim of society rather than of a political revolution. Chatterton himself was treated by Vigny and his French audiences with far more respect than he is today by historians. Vigny portrays him as the woeful prey to materialism and British society, jostled by antagonistic currents and only half consoled by the tender Kitty Bell. The lively interest aroused by that drama (*Chatterton,* 1835) turned Vigny into the arch defender for all poets threatened or maligned by a society of greedy philistines.

Madness, we now recognize, is the last refuge against anguish and the feeling of oppression. There was no dearth of poets threatened or afflicted by insanity among the French romantics. Victor Hugo himself was at the brink of utter mental derangement when he passionately consulted the "turning tables" at Jersey in 1853. Only with great effort and the hypertrophy of his self-confined ego was he able to keep the demons of madness at bay. His answer to society's threat was to proclaim the superiority of the poet as Magus and to indulge his own proclivity as a prophet in verse: "Allez, prêtres! Allez, génies! / Cherchez la note humaine, allez."[12] Under the Third Republic Hugo was indeed to assume the part of a venerated oracle. But his eloquent cries could not dispel the fate that others felt as a crushing weight. Charles Lassailly, one of the most promising talents among the romantics, died insane in 1843. Antoni Deschamps, a theorist of the young romantic school and translator of Dante's *Inferno,* spent most of his life at a mental clinic—the same in which Gérard de Nerval repeatedly crossed "the Acheron" of madness. Antoine Fontaney, also a member of the romantic "cénacles," author of ballads and elegies in the sentimental vein, died of gloom and consumption in 1837, at thirty-four.

The fate that dooms so many poets to a life of dejection, to an early death, or to flight into the illusory refuge of insanity was particularly harsh on the romantics of Germany and of Britain. Kleist, Lenau, Hölderlin—the first a suicide, the others surviving for years in a deranged state—are, along with Novalis (dead at twenty-eight), among the most pathetic and most genial poets of their country. In England the tragic and visionary force of the Elizabethan dramatists seemed to live again with Thomas Lowell Beddoes—a poet pursued by an unbalanced temperament and in love with the macabre: he eventually committed suicide. Thomas Hood, whose famous line was to be rescued by Poe and then by Baudelaire ("anywhere out of the world"), lived on until the age of fifty-five, in destitution and pain. Shelley, who influenced both of them, depicted Keats, dying in Rome at twenty-five, as the victim of "envy and calumny and hate and pain." His long *Adonais* (1821) is not only an apotheosis of the dead poet, but an indictment against the callousness of a society unattuned to gentleness and beauty. "It may be well said that these wretched men know not what they do. They scatter their insults and their slanders without heed as to whether the poisoned shaft lights on a heart made callous by many blows or one like Keats's composed of more penetrable stuff," he explains in his introduction to the elegy mourning Keats.[13] His lyrical tribute to that young poet is replete with bitterness against society:

> The Priest, the slave and the liberticide,
> Trampled and mocked with many a loathed rite
> Of lust and blood; he went, unterrified,
> Into the gulf of death.[14]

Earlier, in 1818, Shelley had movingly related his visit with Byron to a madhouse in Venice. *Julian and Maddalo* lets a madman speak, a poet "cradled into poetry by wrong." The disconnected lines lent to that deranged man upon the island stand as one of the most touching treatments of insanity in the poetry of the last century. "I refrain / From that sweet sleep which medicines all pain," cries the man to the phantoms he yearns to embrace. "Let oblivion hide this grief. . . . Let death upon despair!" he begs.[15]

> Then, when thou speakest of me, never say
> "He could forgive not." Here I cast away
> All human passions, all revenge, all pride;
> I think, speak, act no ill; I do but hide.[16]

Shadows envelop the poet, victim of unassuaged love and the pitiless vengeance of man's baser instincts. He stands forlorn under the curse that rejects him from society. The hero of Tennyson's *Maud* is yet another victim of love and life and the ravings of madness. The Victorian Tennyson recoiled from dwelling too long on despair; his dejected lover is cured at the end, but only after he has pitifully mourned the wretchedness of fate:

> Dead, long dead,
> Long dead!
> And my heart is a handful of dust,
> And the wheels go over my head,
> And my bones are shaken with pain.[17]

The gloom that enveloped those English romantics—and from which they sought escape into opium, like Coleridge, or in praying, like De Quincey, who addressed his fervent poetical prayers to the Ladies of Sorrow and of Death—was not dispelled with the advent of the Victorian era. The complacency and the prosperity that characterized the upper strata of society after the middle of the nineteenth century did not extend to the working classes. There existed a number of outcasts among the artists. Their lot was poverty, solitude, silent and vain revolt. The melancholy tone of their romantic predecessors, who found at times a kind of bitter comfort in the lyrical strains of their dirges, now became less personal. It was not only the conspiracy of materialism and of cant that they indicted. Their grief was broadened into a condemnation of life itself: they denounced the Creator for his work. Swinburne, in one of the sonorous choruses of *Atalanta,* spurned the fallacious solace of religious faith and of conventional optimism:

> Before the beginning of years,
>   There came to the making of man
> Time, with a gift of tears;
>   Grief, with a glass that ran;
> Pleasure, with pain for leaven;
>   Summer, with flowers that fell;
> Remembrance fallen from heaven,
>   And madness risen from hell.[18]

All hope seemingly granted to man with his first breath of life is a cruel mockery. Chaos alone issued from nothingness. Man remains caught in a "madness risen from hell," and his cup brimful of grief and tears.

The most implacably accursed of those poets was the admirer and translator of Leopardi, James Thomson, author of a Dantesque epic of despair, *The City of Dreadful Night* (1874). That Scot, who had rejected his Calvinistic upbringing, destroys, one by one, all delusions through which man consents to life: love, nature, friendship, the fallacious reasoning of philosophers, and the empty words of preachers. More tragic yet than desultory hope is the despairing knowledge of those who perceive the world's void:

> The sense that every struggle brings defeat
>   Because Fate holds no prize to crown success;
> That all the oracles are dumb or cheat
>   Because they have no secret to express;
> That none can pierce the vast black veil uncertain
> Because there is no light beyond the curtain;
>   That all is vanity and nothingness.[19]

All romantic struggle has vanished. Even tears have been dried by the futile wait. Man is caught within the paradox of life and "the city of dreadful night." The long poem closes on the word "despair"—"And confirmation of the old despair"—a symbol of the inescapable reality that condemns all quest for hope. James Thomson grants no room to vituperation against society in his verses.

But the "nothingness" that emerges assumes the magnitude of a curse—indefinite, ubiquitous, sodden with bleakness and despair. More personal but equally pervasive, the same sense of loss appears in "Insomnia," one of the rare poems by Thomson written in the first person singular. The stark verses graphically relate the endless hours of sleepless nights:

> When hideous agonies, unheard, unseen,
> In overwhelming floods of torture roll,
> And horrors of great darkness drown the soul,
>   To be is not to be
> In memory save as ghastliest impression,
> And chaos of demoniacal possession.[20]

No Hamletian doubt keeps hope alive. Nothing but the hallucinating presence of an intimate hell fills the interminable hours of suspense. Life is not a dream but merely the awesome certainty of naught and emptiness, "to be is not to be." Sternly and implacably Thomson argues his philosophy of utter and universal pessimism. Man is a desolate wanderer in the city of death. His only imploration can be for oblivion "To our Ladies of Death," to be forever "lulled into perfect sleep," while the years go on murmuring, "A dim vast monotone, that shall enhance / The restful rapture of the inviolate grave."[21]

Among the French "accursed" poets, one name is surprisingly missing from Verlaine's quite arbitrary choice of six poets to exemplify the *poètes maudits* (three more poets—Villiers de l'Isle-Adam, Marceline Desbordes-Valmore, and Verlaine himself—were added to the Vanier edition of 1884). Baudelaire, the very predecessor to whom he was most heavily indebted, is not mentioned. Yet the overwhelming sense of despondency that emerges from his poetry is at the core of all that is "maudit," or crushed under the weight of inevitable doom. Baudelaire had published, in the *Revue de Paris* in 1852, a highly influential article entitled "Edgar Poe, sa vie, ses œuvres." Alluding to Vigny's campaign for the rescue of poets exiled or reviled by modern society, he announced that he was adding a name to that list of martyrs. He pursued, "There are in the history of literatures . . . cases of genuine damnation, men who bear the word 'ill-luck' [the French *guignon* is much more suggestive] written in mysterious types on the sinuous folds of their brows. The blind Angel of expiation has taken hold of them and lashes them madly so as to teach others a lesson. . . . Society launches a special anathema upon them; it indicts in them the very weaknesses that its persecution gave them."[22] The "sacred souls" are, by a diabolical providence, doomed to act the part of martyrs in the Roman circus, to march, through their wreckage, toward their death. Society, especially that of America, bore the brunt of Baudelaire's accusation. Industry, progress even more, and the most preposterous of modern heresies, the childishness of a young nation, are held accountable for persecuting those who hold an ephemeral dream in their hearts, the poets in their midst. But are they to blame?

Baudelaire, never in awe of contradiction, remarks that the tragic plight of the poet is due to the machinations of the devil. The crime of modern society, he intimates, lies in the refusal of the notion of hell. Man's "natural wickedness," as Poe had put it, is called by him "natural perverseness," for, he asserts peremptorily, "nature makes nothing but monsters."[23]

Divine providence was absent from Vigny's or James Thomson's universe. The metaphysical and social conditions imposed upon man were thus weighted with especial harshness upon the chosen few—the martyrs of beauty. But Baudelaire is more Manichean. He prefers to detect and indict, but also pay tribute to, the adversary who challenges God and often appears more powerful than the Creator. In the opening poem of the first section of *Les Fleurs du mal*, derisively entitled "Bénédiction," the mother who brought the future poet into the world revolts against the Creator. She swears to wreak her revenge upon the wretched child. Still, the plight of the poet is past pointing an accusing finger against society. He is his own victim, prisoner of the haunting visions conjured by his febrile imagination, oppressed not so much by man as by the futility of man's world: "Le poète apparaît en ce monde ennuyé," bored and detached, more than ostracized, a loose link in the chain of the universe, contemplating an impossible dream of light and beauty. Pain is his lot, as well as solitude and despair:

> —O douleur! ô douleur! Le Temps mange la vie
> Et l'obscur Ennemi qui nous ronge le cœur
> Du sang que nous perdons croît et se fortifie![24]

A dichotomy lives here, a scission between man and his genius, tyrannized one by the other, unreconciled both to the pangs of humanity and to art's exacting solitude. Baudelaire pictured himself as reaching "the autumn of ideas," with scant hope of nurturing new flowers endowed with mystical vigor in his garden of decrepitude. Ridiculed, paralyzed, frozen in his captivity amidst men, the poet is, in effect, immobilized: "Exilé sur le sol au milieu des huées / Ses ailes de géant l'empêchent de marcher."[25] The poet's nightmare is his obsession with sterility or, as Mallarmé was to lament, the inability to bridge the gulf between too pure and lofty an ideal and the language and rhythm of the poem written "sur le vide papier que la blancheur défend."[26] Revolt itself is delusive. If, still in the romantic tradition, Baudelaire sees the poet as a noble "Prince des nuées," he recognizes that he is caught in a vise that is neither social nor political, but metaphysical. Gradually, he became convinced that "from all eternity" he himself had been chosen to be one of the damned.

In 1846, at a time when Baudelaire still felt confident that willpower was not a mirage for him, that it was indeed within reach, he denied—in "Conseils aux jeunes littérateurs"—the poet's inescapable fatality. Only six years later, however, he was to compose "Le Guignon," one of the least original sonnets in

Les Fleurs du mal but indicative nevertheless of the poet's tragic acceptance of his fate. The tercets were literally translated from the famous churchyard elegy of Thomas Gray, and the quatrains are indiscreetly close to a stanza from Longfellow's "Psalm of Life." Yet the unabashed borrowing seems to emphasize, rather than diminish, the artist's age-old plight—the madness, the futile rebellion and feverish pursuit of the unattainable that were, from time immemorial, his only inheritance in life. The "accursed poet" is, after all, a far-removed progeny of Sisyphus, even where he may have lost, through the ages, some of the vigor, of the unquenchable and desperate thirst for the absolute of his great ancestor:

> Pour soulever un poids si lourd,
> Sisyphe, il faudrait ton courage!
> Bien qu'on ait du cœur à l'ouvrage,
> L'Art est long et le Temps est court.[27]

The very act of creating is here imbued with despair, with the apprehension that the task is beyond the frailty of man. The measure of art is infinite, and the poet's allotted time is limited to a mere life's span. The name "guignon" of the title stems from the verb *guigner,* which suggests casting an envious eye— thereby bringing ill-luck—on the person envied. With Baudelaire that ill-luck turns into a destructive force, relentlessly bent upon undermining and deriding all velleities for beauty.

The forces that overwhelm the accursed poet are often incarnated in the demon. "Sans cesse à mes côtés s'agite le Démon" is Baudelaire's first verse ("La Destruction") in his section devoted to evil. The devil may at times be alluring and assume the shape of "la plus séduisante des femmes," only to wage greater injury to the defenseless lover of beauty and thrust him within a destructive vortex. Cherished fancies, enchanting visions of love and grace, the enticing smile of an ideal woman—all vanish in cruel mockery within a landscape of horror and desolation. A swarm of wicked demons pounces upon the poet (in "La Béatrice") and derides, in grotesque gestures and sneers, "cette ombre d'Hamlet imitant sa posture." The pride of creative inspiration, it is intimated, could be far greater than the hurt elicited by taunting words. The poet could dismiss the insults that plunge him among historians and fools. He could avert his gaze and seek the shape of his dream beyond the horizon of both men and devils. Such was indeed the protective mechanism of Hugo and Lamartine, of all the romantics oppressed by a reviling social order: to cherish their own visions, in spite of and beyond all scorn of man. But the dream has itself become a mockery, and the poet's muse and venerated idol now stands among the jeering devils. I could have looked elsewhere, he admits,

> Si je n'eusse pas vu parmi leur troupe obscène,
> Crime qui n'a pas fait chanceler le soleil!
> La reine de mon cœur au regard nonpareil,

Qui riait avec eux de ma sombre détresse
Et leur versait parfois quelque sale caresse.[28]

Woman is no longer the vampire of decadent romanticism nor the Messalina of old. Her image is here hauntingly overcome by the poet's own barrenness, by his despair and insufficiency in the universe of creation. Later, in "Epigraphe pour un livre condamné," Baudelaire bids his readers desist from trying to understand his book, unless they have been schooled by Satan himself. For Satan, we now surmise, is none other than the poet's own malediction.

The concept of the *poètes maudits* —certainly not a new one by the time Verlaine's essays were published initially in 1883—was immediately recognized as one that had long existed. The notion of accursed poets was now applied retrospectively to artists of earlier times. Verlaine thus happens to have originated one of the most widespread critical myths of the nineteenth and twentieth centuries. Outside France, across the Channel, this myth aroused the most lasting, and often the most heartrending, echoes. Verlaine and Villon were long the favorite French poets of the British (the two names were often put together), perhaps because they seemed free from the eloquence associated with French poetry. Articles and poems by Verlaine appeared in England. In 1899 Arthur Symons devoted to Verlaine the fourth chapter of his volume *The Symbolist Movement*. This proved influential as a disseminator of the creed of the French symbolists. It also introduced the concept of the *poètes maudits*. The first *maudit* to be recognized as such was perhaps Ernest Dowson. Only two years younger than Symons, he died at thirty-three. A drug addict, an insatiable drinker, a poor and sick man, perhaps a homosexual, fascinated by sordidness and prostitutes, he lived a life of malediction. Thoroughly familiar with the poetry of Baudelaire and Verlaine (he translated the latter's verses into English), he survives mostly through one poem of his own, "Non sum qualis eram bonae sub regno Cynarae," with the haunting refrain, "I have been faithful to thee, Cynara! in my fashion." Reminiscent of Baudelaire's "Une nuit que j'étais près d'une affreuse Juive," his verse is even closer to Verlaine's in imagery and rhythm. A victim of his own weakness, Dowson did not parade his malediction but bowed to it, without cynicism or remorse, knowing that there was no place for him in the world.

If Verlaine's felicitous phrase of the "poètes maudits" was able to claim so many past and present poets among the disciples of gloom and neglect, that is because the phenomenon had been for some time a widespread one. He himself was neither a theoretician nor the "prosateur étonnant" he recognized in Rimbaud. His essays offer only superficial analyses of the six poets he chose to exemplify as those victimized by a curse: Corbière, Rimbaud, Mallarmé, Villiers de l'Isle-Adam, Desbordes-Valmore, and "Pauvre Lélian" (the anagram for Paul Verlaine himself). The most important element to emerge from the volume is the emphasis given to the poet no longer as an Olympian force among men but as a discordant note within a scornful society. Three years after the publication of *Les Poètes maudits,* Verlaine wrote *Mémoires d'un veuf,* a collection of sketches that echo the poet's alienation from the world about him. Clearly inspired by the great Baudelairean "Spleens," he evokes, in "Corbillard au galop," the vision of a hearse and an increasing sense of doom: "Dans ce corbillard, il y avait un cercueil recouvert d'un drap noir, sans broderies, ni croix, ni couronnes, ni rien; un cercueil avec un drap noir dessus et derrière, personne. Personne derrière."[29] The swift passage of the hearse galloping toward its destination elicits a moment of pause. Who is there in that coffin, poor and already forgotten, with not a tear to accompany him to his last abode? All answers seem uncertain, until a name, more like a sob, surges from within and rings true: "Un poète!" he exclaims. He sees himself in the place of the other, rigid and silent at last, his fists tight and powerless and his mouth gaping in a soundless cry: "moi, vieilli, poings crispés,—crispés?—entortillé à la diable d'un linceul trop étroit." Where the Baudelairean anguish had appeared as a private domain, the helplessness of the individual caught in his own hell, Verlaine stresses the plight of the artist rejected by society, misunderstood and languishing in solitude. The physical and spiritual agony of Baudelaire's "de long corbillards, sans tambours ni musique, / Défilent lentement dans mon âme" becomes exteriorized in the vision of the actual coffin speeding by in "Corbillard au galop." The mood is less forceful and suggestive than that of the older master. Baudelaire's tormented vision is replaced by meditative considerations on those despotic forces that crush and humiliate all hope in the poet.

Replete with an overwhelming sense of despair are some of the poems from *Sagesse,* written at the time of Verlaine's imprisonment in Brussels, when his own tragic perplexity made him measure all ephemeral reality against metaphysical needs. Muted cries of anguish now emerge from his verses:

> Un grand sommeil noir
> Pèse sur ma vie:
> Dormez tout espoir,
> Dormez toute envie.[30]

The very first line evokes an abyss of nothingness: one thinks of Hugo's hell ("Une chute sans fin, dans une nuit sans fond"). The bottomless fall is divested of all intimation of a distant paradise shrouded behind dark clouds. Not a flicker of hope relieves this endless present. The bleak days ahead resemble heavy, dreamless sleep. The short five-syllable verses with alternate rhymes are halting, terse, lulling:

> Je ne vois plus rien
> Je perds la mémoire
> Du mal et du bien. . . .
> Ô la triste histoire.[31]

The syncopated rhythm of the first three lines, each falling heavily on the last word, becomes distended in the fourth. The initial "Ô" is arresting here and balanced at the end by the lengthening sound of "histoire." The association dictated by the rhyme "mémoire"-"histoire" is one of almost cynical gloom, which plunges all recollection into an impersonal and lifeless chronicle of time past. The concluding stanza conveys to despair the shape of a crib suspended upon a chasm:

> Je suis un berceau
> Qu'une main balance
> Au creux d'un caveau:
> Silence, silence![32]

Ageless, in this image of infancy rocked by the hand of fate, the poet stares at the immense squalor around him. Half-imploringly he reaches toward the implacable stillness and bids that the wordless void be echoed only by "silence."

With that half-naïve, half-malicious cunning that was his, Verlaine pictured himself as "that accursed one who will have had the most melancholy fate . . . due to his innate candor and to his incurable indolence."[33] He delighted in displaying his own contradictions, which served him as a pretext for addressing himself "parallèlement," to both pious readers and salacious ones. Several of his most moving, and most artistically successful, poems are those in which he carefully cultivates his naïveté and appeals to his readers as a victim of fate. Character itself becomes part of the poet's inescapable fatality, just as it had been with the Greeks of classical time. Flesh is the symbol of his own tragic dimension, the temptation that drives him away from celestial visions: "la tristesse, la langueur du corps humain."[34] It is, indeed, inescapable fatality that holds him prisoner of its yearnings and reduces him to a doubting, languorous prey of the demons of desire. Unashamed of tears, lamenting a curse that condemns him from within, Verlaine was able to give grief the dimensions of beauty and fallibility the mournful echo of man's condition:

> —Qu'as-tu fait, ô toi que voilà
> Pleurant sans cesse,
> Dis, qu'as-tu fait, toi que voilà,
> De ta jeunesse?[35]

One of the poets whom Verlaine attempted to vindicate was a woman, Marceline Desbordes-Valmore.[36] Baudelaire had presented her, not without a few reservations, in an article of *La Revue fantaisiste* of 1 July 1861. He, who had been so harsh on George Sand, praised Marceline for having been a woman poet, and a touchingly sentimental one at that. Her merit was to be found, according to Baudelaire, in her having elicited "hysterical tears" from her admirers without resorting to feminine or social poses. Marceline, we know, never took pity on herself, nor did she lay her heart bare with complaints of society's indifference, in the way that Musset, Baudelaire, and Verlaine indulged. She evoked sorrow as a lover might a lost mistress, nostalgically, in doleful and unrecriminating verses:

> Que mon nom ne soit rien qu'une ombre douce et vaine,
> Qu'il ne cause jamais ni l'effroi ni la peine,
> Qu'un indigent l'emporte après m'avoir parlé
> Et le garde longtemps dans son cœur consolé![37]

Feminine indeed, in the tradition of sacrificial candor and "renouncement." Yet Verlaine's sketch of this sad poet, and of the lyrical desolation of her verses, did not quite succeed in spreading her fame. Corbière fared somewhat better; we know him, in fact, in great part thanks to Verlaine.[38] But the one poet with whom Verlaine was able to score a critical success remains Mallarmé.

Mallarmé was only twenty when, under the sway of Baudelaire, he published his own "Le Guignon." Here too, ill-luck appears as a powerful and venomous tyrant, "un Ange très puissant / Qui rougit l'horizon des éclairs de son glaive."[39] The diabolical angel whips and mocks the helpless poet who "nurses upon pain as he had on his dream."[40] Fourteen years later, when Mallarmé composed his "Tombeau d'Edgar Poe," the sword ("le glaive") no longer appeared as a threatening weapon brandished by the tormenting angel. In a less pessimistic view, it now became the attribute of the poet himself, emerging victorious and almost sanctified after the common man's vain attempts at persecuting him.

To what degree Mallarmé can truly be considered a *maudit* remains open to question. His life was not desperate or oppressed, either by dire poverty or by total neglect. Verlaine's choice of names for his volume—and the inclusion of Mallarmé's—was, possibly, more an effort at bringing recognition to a few poets than at pointing to them as singular victims of an ineluctable fatality. Verlaine never gave us a clear definition of what constitutes a *poète maudit,* and his lack of precision may result from both the fluidity of the concept and its longevity. We are free to classify among them not only those poets who lived in torment and at the mercy of fiendish forces, but also the artist who struggled in the effort of giving life to his creation—as in the case of Mallarmé—or the restless youth pursuing his own chimera, with pride more than with anguish— as did Rimbaud. We should perhaps distinguish between the poet and the poem of the accursed. But such restrictive canons might deprive the concept of its suggestiveness and mysterious beauty. They might also remove, from the opaque periphery of the *poètes maudits,* the artist's vaguely delineated anguish that reaches above and beyond personal interest, wisdom, or glory and craves for an absolute.

Not many poets in this second half of the twentieth century read Verlaine's articles on the *poètes maudits*. A growing number of them, and of scholars and students, have been increasingly appreciative of his best verse. But, above all, the myth that he bequeathed to us when he coined the phrase has not perished. Poetry was intermittently honored and rewarded in the Soviet Union, for instance. Alexander Block and Maiakovsky hailed the 1917 revolution as the coming of a new era. We then heard of the suicides of several Russian poets, of the martyrdom of the greatest woman poet among them, Anna Akhmatova. Poets in America have been assisted by foundations, welcomed as bards-in-residence at many universities, published in a number of magazines, and granted prizes. Still, some of them, from Hart Crane to Sylvia Plath, chose exile from society and from life. The post–World War II years in France were a period of renascent optimism, of economic growth, and of generalized social and financial help to the underprivileged and to the struggling youth. Yet no poetical anthology makes gloomier reading than the *Poètes maudits d' aujour-d' hui,* compiled and published in 1972 by an editor-poet, Pierre Seghers. Of twelve poets represented, seven committed suicide, three at the age of twenty-nine (Jean-Pierre Duprey, Gerald Neveu, Roger Rivière), one at thirty (J. P. Salabreuil), one at forty-one, jumping from a bridge into the Seine (Roger Milliot), and two in their early forties, fleeing "the scandal of being," as Seghers put it (André Frédérique and Ilarie Voronca). They were all desperate seekers of the absolute. The wretched existence of one of their elders, Antonin Artaud, dead in 1948 at fifty-two after wrestling with drugs and derangement, is well known. Haunted by other *maudits,* he had written of Poe, Nerval, Rimbaud: "I want their poems to become true, and life to be freed from the books and the theater and the religious mass which hold it captive and crucify it."[41]

Between Verlaine's *maudits* and their unfortunate descendants of 1946–70 there had been the surrealists. They too had their martyrs, unconverted to the creed of love and faith in the "lendemains qui chantent." Michel Leiris attempted suicide twice. René Crevel succeeded, in 1935, as had Jacques Vaché in 1919 and Jacques Rigaut in 1929. Paul Eluard, who survived them, declared in his "Poetic Evidence": "Sombre are the truths which appear in the work of true poets; but truths they are and almost everything else is lies."[42] The creed, repeatedly asserted by André Breton, implied refusal of the social, political, and even metaphysical conditions stringently imposed upon man's life. They glorified themselves on the malediction that struck all poets.

A tradition has by now been established. The poet's self-pitying attitude is accepted as standard and even unavoidable. Few are the poets who proudly disclaim any right to compassion for their sublime sorrows. Most recently one of them, the Nobel prize laureate of 1977, Vicente Aleixandre, spurned all commiseration that might be lavished on him with the warning, "above all do not consider me a 'poète maudit.' "[43] The curse of the poet, whether accepted as a patrimony or haughtily rejected, remains a form of identification and a springboard for all artists.

1. Horace *Epistles* 2. 2. To Julius Florus, line 103.

2. George Gordon Noel Byron, *The Lament of Tasso* (1817), section 4, lines 1–13.

3. Charles Baudelaire, "Sur le Tasse en prison, d'Eugène Delacroix," lines 1–4, composed in 1844, *Les Fleurs du mal* (1864).

4. Giacomo Leopardi, *Operette Morali*, vol. 9: "Dialogo di Torquato Tasso e del suo Genio familiare" (1824).

5. Giacomo Leopardi, *Lettere* (A Pietro Girodani, March 1818).

6. Giacomo Leopardi, "A se stesso," lines 5–10, *Canti*, no. 28.

7. Alfred de Musset, from the collection *Poésies nouvelles*, dated 1850. The poem itself, "Après une lecture," dates from 1842 (stanza 19, line 3).

8. The oft-quoted phrase is from Shelley's *Defense of Poetry*, published in 1822.

9. Alfred de Vigny, *Stello*, chap. 40 ("Ordonnance du Docteur-Noir"), section 3.

10. Nicolas Gilbert, as quoted in *Stello*, chap. 12; in Gilbert, *Œuvres complètes* (Paris: Dalibon, 1823), p. 211.

11. Ibid., p. 243.

12. Victor Hugo, "Les Mages," *Les Contemplations* (1856), book 6, no. 22, lines 1–2.

13. Percy B. Shelley, preface to *Adonais* (1821).

14. *Adonais*, stanza 4, lines 5–8.

15. Percy B. Shelley, *Julian and Maddalo* (1818), lines 508–9.

16. Ibid., lines 500–504.

17. Alfred Tennyson, *Maud* (1855), section 27, lines 1–5.

18. Algernon C. Swinburne, *Atalanta in Calydon* (1865), chorus, lines 1–8.

19. James Thomson, *The City of Dreadful Night* (1874), section 21, lines 64–70 (included in *Poetical Works* [London: Reeves & Twiner, 1895], 1:172).

20. Ibid., 2:38, lines 154–59.

21. Ibid., 1:119, lines 174–75.

22. Charles Baudelaire, "Edgar Poe, sa vie, ses œuvres," *Revue de Paris*, section 1, March 1852.

23. Ibid.

24. Baudelaire, "L'Ennemi," lines 11–14, from the section "Spleen et idéal" of *Les Fleurs du mal*.

25. "L'Albatros," line 14, ibid.

26. Stéphane Mallarmé, "Brise marine." First published in the *Parnasse contemporain* on 12 May 1866, the poem was most likely written a year earlier, as a letter from Eugène Lefèbre dated May 1865 seems to attest. See the 1945 Pléiade edition of Mallarmé's *Œuvres complètes*, p. 1430.

27. Baudelaire, "Le Guignon," lines 1–3, from the section "Spleen et idéal" of *Les Fleurs du mal*.

28. Baudelaire, "La Béatrice," lines 26–30, from the section "Fleurs du mal," ibid.

29. Paul Verlaine, "Corbillard au galop," *Mémoires d'un veuf* (1886) (*Œuvres complètes* [Paris: Club du meilleur livre, 1959]).

30. This poem, number 5 in the third section of *Sagesse*, was dated 8 August 1873. The quotation given is lines 1–4.

31. Ibid., lines 5–8.

32. Ibid., lines 9–12.

33. Paul Verlaine, "Pauvre Lélian," p. 1, *Les Poètes maudits,* second series (*Œuvres complètes,* 1:884).

34. *Sagesse,* part 3, poem 5, line 1.

35. Ibid., poem 6, last strophe.

36. I shall not discuss here the merits of Desbordes-Valmore as a poet. Undoubtedly she belongs to the group of the *maudits.* Yet Verlaine was not sufficiently discriminating, perhaps, and made too much of her by placing her in context with the other poets included in his study.

37. Marceline Desbordes-Valmore, "Renoncement," lines 21–24, *Œuvres complètes* (Grenoble: Presses Universitaires, 1973), 2:547.

38. See Robert L. Mitchell's *Tristan Corbière* (Boston: Twayne, 1979), which places that poet in the proper light. (An entire chapter is devoted to "Malediction and Poetry" in nineteenth-century France.) My essay deals only with the general concept of the *maudits,* both in France and abroad. Only a few poets have been given significant attention, chosen mostly from among those less recognized in the framework of the accursed. I shall not discuss Villiers, whose originality resides mostly in prose works—plays, novels, and tales. Verlaine's treatment of Mallarmé and Rimbaud was, moreover, wholly inadequate, but that was probably unavoidable at the time, when no one could yet evaluate the true nature of those poets. Discussing them further might crush them under the weight of our present view and appraisal.

39. Stéphane Mallarmé, "Le Guignon," version given by Paul Verlaine in *Les Poètes maudits,* p. 498.

40. Ibid., line 16 (my translation).

41. Pierre Seghers, *Poètes maudits d'aujourd'hui* (Paris: Seghers, 1972), p. 19.

42. Paul Eluard, "Poetic Evidence," in *Surrealism,* ed. Herbert Read (New York: Harcourt, Brace, 1936), pp. 171–83 (text of a lecture delivered in London in 1936).

43. Vicente Aleixandre, interview reported in *Le Monde,* 10 December 1977 (my translation).

Mallarmé's Living Metaphor:
Valéry's Athikté and Rilke's "Spanish Dancer"

URSULA FRANKLIN

The motif of dance and dancer was a preoccupation shared by Mallarmé, Valéry, and Rilke, three major poets who—despite their obvious and radical differences—are linked by deep-seated affinities, and especially by the influence that Mallarmé, *maître* of French symbolism, transmitted to his select progeny. In this study I intend to explore briefly that motif as it was developed by all three poets. Valéry inherited his master's profound reflections on that art, reflections expressed in Mallarmé's unique poetic prose. Valéry's meditations on the subject come to us in the form of several literary essays and one of his Socratic dialogues. In Rilke dance and dancer had become *matière* for lyric expression long before he met Valéry. After the encounter with Valéry, whose dialogue "L'Ame et la danse" he especially loved, Rilke summoned the dancer of the *Sonette an Orpheus* to share and participate in the poet's Orphic mission, bequeathed by Mallarmé.

Dance, we know, was one of Mallarmé's favorite forms of art.[1] Like music, it rivaled poetry; yet toward the dance the poet never appeared to feel that jealousy and distrust that he repeatedly expressed toward music. Mallarmé enthusiastically admired, and most discretely celebrated, some of the dancers of his day: "La Cornalba me ravit . . . "[2]

The dancer per se is absent from the *Poésies*. There are "des loqueteux dansant" (p. 29) in the still Baudelairean "Le Guignon"; the gestures of the "Pitre" (p. 31) are those of the acrobat-"histrion" rather than of a dancer; and there is an early "Hérodiade en fleur" in the symbolist "Les Fleurs" (p. 34). In "Aumône" (p. 39) the beggar sees through the window separating the rich from the poor "les plafonds enrichis de nymphes et de voiles," which already foreshadow the "sylphe de ce froid plafond" of the much later "Surgi de la croupe et du bond" (p. 74). But the first great—and doubly solitary—dancer in Mallarmé's lyric poetry is Hérodiade, and her dance is characteristically evoked by its very absence: " . . . et pour qui, dévorée / D'angoisses, gardez-vous la splendeur ignorée / Et le mystère vain de votre être? Pour moi" (p. 46).

In the *Chansons bas* ballet is evoked in the little "Billet à Whistler" with

" . . .   une danseuse apparue / Tourbillon de mousseline ou / Fureur éparses en écumes" (p. 65), and the ballet dancer is again, if most fleetingly, summoned up in the prose poem "Un Spectacle interrompu."[3] We must turn to Mallarmé's prose—his theater articles—for the poet's notions on dance, while recalling that even these articles are poetic, "poëmes critiques" as he himself calls them.[4] In these essays, later grouped under *Crayonné au théâtre*, he writes about dance and the dancer not merely in "Ballets" (pp. 303–7) and "Autre étude de danse: Les fonds dans le ballet" (pp. 307–9), but in some of the other "divagations" as well. For dance was, indeed, one of Mallarmé's obsessive themes.

In almost all his utterances on dance, he insists on the dancer's impersonality ("l'impersonnalité de la danseuse, entre sa féminine apparence et un objet mimé, pour quel hymen," p. 296), an impersonality that brings to mind that of the poet himself ("la disparition élocutoire du poëte, qui cède l'initiative aux mots," p. 366), of which he speaks in *Crise de vers*. Mallarmé was fully aware of the structuralist implications of this language, which speaks itself through the poet and which, by extension, is the rhythm manifesting itself through the dancer's body: "le rythme même du livre, alors impersonnel et vivant, jusque dans sa pagination" (p. 663). Mallarmé's fascination with dance, then, lies in the analogy between dancer and poet, dance and poetry, an analogy that Valéry was to inherit and elaborate in his most significant statements about *poesis*. Mallarmé compares the dancer's legs, "les jambes—sous quelque signification autre que personnelle, comme un instrument direct d'idée," to the poet's pen, which traces the idea, at once visual and veiled, that is a sign: "à proprement parler, pourrait-on ne reconnaître au Ballet le nom de Danse; lequel est, si l'on veut, hiéroglyphe" (p. 312). The poet states this analogy most explicitly in the "Rêverie d'un poëte français," his Wagner article: "la Danse seule capable, par son écriture sommaire, de traduire le fugace et le soudain jusqu'à l'Idée" (p. 541). For Mallarmé the dancer *is* a metaphor, and in becoming this living metaphor she ceases to be a woman who dances, ceases to be woman: "A savoir que la danseuse *n'est pas une femme qui danse,* pour ces motifs juxtaposés qu'elle *n'est pas une femme,* mais une métaphore résumant un des aspects élémentaires de notre forme, glaive, coupe, fleur, etc., et *qu'elle ne danse pas,* suggérant par le prodige de raccourcis ou d'élans, avec une écriture corporelle ce qu'il faudrait des paragraphes en prose dialoguée autant que descriptive, pour exprimer, dans la rédaction; poëme dégagé de tout appareil du scribe" (p. 304). Mallarmé's great dancer, we have said, is Hérodiade; and her essence is not realization, but anticipation—of the solitary dance that would annihilate her.

Valéry appreciated dance much less than his master: "Ego. La danse me plaît à penser, m'ennuie généralement à voir."[5] His favorite art form—dare one say *after* poetry?—was architecture. Innumerable are the statements in its praise in

the *Cahiers*—"ma première amour fut l'architecture" (*C,* 1:81)—and in Valéry's poetry architecture and poetry fuse in the mythic Amphion-Orphée, the
archetypal singer-builder who transforms and structures chaos into order and
harmony.[6] Yet Valéry not merely inherited but, as we have said, elaborated the
Mallarméan analogy of poetry and dance.[7] He restates it frequently in the
Cahiers—"le passage de la prose au vers; de la parole au chant; de la marche à
la danse" (*C,* 2:932)—and develops it most systematically in "Calepin d'un
poète": "Le passage de la prose au vers; de la parole au chant, de la marche à la
danse . . . moment à la fois actes et rêve. La danse n'a pas pour objet de me
transporter d'ici là; ni le vers, ni le chant purs. . . . faire parler la musique et
chanter ou danser le langage" (p. 1449).

Valéry, however, not only reflected and wrote about dance; he made dance,
as he had made architecture, part of his poetic universe. This he achieved in one
of his most accomplished dialogues, "L'Ame et la danse." As is frequent with
Valéry, we owe this masterpiece to a "commande." The poet himself tells us
that he had never seriously thought about dance, that he felt, moreover, that
Mallarmé had exhausted the subject from a literary point of view, and that he
had therefore at first refused the proposal to write the piece for the *Revue
musicale.*[8] Nevertheless, "L'Ame et la danse" becomes Valéry's poetic
summation on dance and dancer; it generates both a fictitious (and therefore
ideal) dancer, Athikté, and a striking metaphor for dance and dancer, the flame.
The very form of Valéry's Socratic dialogue reminds us that according to
Aristotle's *Poetics,* "the greatest thing by far is to be a master of metaphor. It is
the one thing that cannot be learnt from others; and it is also a sign of genius."[9]

Before approaching "L'Ame et la danse," we must recall two essays that
Valéry published almost fifteen years after the dialogue: "Dégas danse dessin"
of 1934 and the "Philosophie de la danse" of 1936. In the former, principally
devoted to his favorite painter, Valéry interpolates a chapter "De la Danse,"
for "pourquoi ne pas parler un peu de la Danse, à propos du peintre des
Danseuses?" He proceeds to discuss dance in terms of "ornement de la durée"
and "ornement de l'étendue" (2:1172). The discussion culminates in an equation of dance with an idealized erotic fantasy—thus indirectly evoking Hérodiade's unrealized fulfillment: "Jamais danseuse humaine, femme échauffée,
ivre de mouvement, du poison de ses forces excédées, de la présence ardente de
regards chargés de désir, n'exprima l'offrande impérieuse du sexe . . . comme cette grande Méduse . . . se transforme en songe d'Eros; et tout à coup,
rejetant tous ses falbalas vibratiles, ses robes de lèvres découpées, se renverse
et s'expose, furieusement ouverte" (2:1173).

The "Philosophie de la danse" is a lecture the poet gave at the Université des
Annales, which he published later that year, and whose specific muse was Mme
Argentina: "Avant que Mme Argentina vous saisisse, . . . il faut vous ré-
signer à entendre quelques propositions que va, devant vous, risquer sur la

Danse un homme qui ne danse pas" (1:1390–91). The lecture could almost serve as an introduction to "L'Ame et la danse," had it not been written much later: "cependant, un philosophe peut bien regarder l'action de quelque danseuse, et, remarquant qu'il y trouve du plaisir, il peut aussi bien essayer de tirer de son plaisir le plaisir second d'exprimer ses impressions dans son langage" (1:1394). The stage appears to be set for Athikté's dance before Socrates. But Valéry speaks, even here, not as a philosopher, but as a poet; and as he sets out to find the answer to "qu'est-ce donc que la Danse?" he finds the poet's response: the analogy of dance and poetry, and the great metaphor of the dialogue. The dancer creates and exists in a universe analogous to the poetic one: "C'est donc bien que la danseuse est dans un autre monde, qui n'est plus celui qui se peint de nos regards, mais celui qu'elle tisse de ses pas et construit de ses gestes. Mais, dans ce monde-là, il n'y a point de but extérieur aux actes" (1:1398). The familiar analogy of dance and poetry becomes most explicit as a simile: "Un *poème,* par exemple, est action, parce qu'un poème n'existe qu'au moment de sa diction: il est alors *en acte.* Cet acte, comme la danse, n'a pour fin que de créer un état: . . . il crée, lui aussi, un temps et une mesure du temps qui lui conviennent et lui sont essentiels: on ne peut le distinguer de sa forme de durée. Commencer de dire des vers, c'est entrer dans une danse verbale" (1:1400). And Socrates' metaphor, the flame of the dialogue, is restated here as a simile by our poet-philosopher: "Notre philosophe peut aussi bien comparer la danseuse à une flamme, et, en somme, à tout phénomène visiblement entretenu par la consommation intense d'une énergie de qualité supérieure" (1:1396).

Valéry "un homme qui ne danse pas"? No; on the contrary, the very essay constitutes an ideal dance about dance: "mais il est grand temps de clore cette danse d'idées autour de la danse vivante" (1:1402). And the spiritual ideal dance of the poet around the real dancer finally culminates in a celebration, once more, of the Mallarméan analogy: "Qu'est-ce qu'une métaphore, si ce n'est une sorte de pirouette de l'idée . . . toutes ces figures dont nous usons . . . toutes les possibilités du langage, qui nous détachent du monde pratique pour nous former, nous aussi, notre univers particulier, lieu privilégié de la danse spirituelle?" (1:1403).

In "L'Ame et la danse" (2:148–76), Valéry explores dance from both the physiological and the psychological points of view, for this art, more than any other, links the two; here body work, the physical, transports us into that other realm, the metaphysical, and these two related opposites are the two poles of Valéry's title itself. In the letter to Séchan from which we have already quoted, Valéry says: "la pensée constante du *Dialogue* est physiologique,—depuis les troubles digestifs du début prélude, jusqu'à la syncope finale." Athikté, the star, is dancing, moreover, before Eryximaque, her physician, and Socrates, the great doctor of the mind, with Phèdre serving as sort of a choral figure commenting on the scene. In the opening it is Eryximaque, ironically, who calls upon Socrates for a remedy: "O Socrate, je meurs! . . . Donne-moi de l'esprit! Verse l'idée! . . . Porte à mon nez tes énigmes aiguës!" And Socrates' first words concern the physical, the reasonableness of the most basic body function: "l'homme qui mange est le plus juste des hommes."

Only later, as he observes the dancers preceding Athikté, does Socrates begin to liken dance to *poesis:* "Les claires danseuses! . . . Quelle vive et gracieuse introduction des plus parfaites pensées! . . . Leurs mains parlent, et leurs pieds semblent écrire; . . . on dirait que la connaissance a trouvé son acte." Finally, "l'extrême danseuse, Athikté! Athikté! . . . O dieux! . . . l'Athikté la palpitante!" And as Socrates now calls her "chose sans corps!" it is Eryximaque, the physician, who recalls that marvelous body: "la belle fibre tout entière de son corps net et musculeux, de la nuque jusqu'au talon, se prononce et se tord progressivement; et tout frémit." Socrates now begins his "midwifery," asking himself, his companions, and us: "ô mes amis, qu'est-ce véritablement que la danse? . . . Mais qu'est-ce donc que la danse, et que peuvent dire des pas? . . . O mes amis, je ne fais que vous demander ce que c'est que la danse?" Eryximaque again, now seconded by Phèdre, calls on Socrates for his own analysis: "Parle, ô Maître . . . Auteur toujours heureux des conséquences merveilleuses d'un accident dialecti- que![10] . . . Parle! Tire le fil doré. . . . Amène de tes absences profondes quelque vivante vérité!" The philosopher turns poet, for his answer is a metaphor: "cette créature qui vibre là-bas . . . a l'air de vivre . . . dans un élément comparable au feu . . . cette exaltation et cette vibration de la vie . . . ont les vertus et les puissances de la flamme." Phèdre responds: "Admirable Socrate, regarde vite à quel point tu dis vrai!" And Socrates then elaborates his metaphor: "O Flamme! . . . O Flamme! . . . O Flamme, toutefois! Chose vive et divine! . . . Mais qu'est-ce qu'une flamme, ô mes amis, si ce n'est *le moment même*— . . . Flamme est l'acte de ce moment qui est entre la terre et le ciel. O mes amis, tout ce qui passe de l'état lourd à l'état subtil, passe par le moment de feu et de lumière."Dance is of body and spirit: "la flamme follement chante entre la matière et l'éther"; dance is a fiction, like poetry—Mallarmé's "sublime lie"—and thus also itself "mensonge": "la grande Danse, ô mes amis, n'est-elle point cette délivrance de notre corps tout entier possédé de l'esprit du mensonge, et de la musique qui bondit comme la flamme remplace la flamme, voyez comme il foule et piétine ce qui est vrai!" And Athikté, the woman, is "devoured" in the process, "ce corps . . . sort incessamment de soi! Le voici enfin dans cet état comparable à la flamme. . . . Cette femme qui était là est dévorée de figures innombrables." Like Mallarmé's dancer, Athikté is consumed in and by her art, annihilated in her final "tourbillon": "Elle tourne, elle tourne. . . . Elle tombe! Elle est tombée! Elle est morte." When Athikté "comes back to life," she says: "Je ne suis pas morte. Et pourtant, je ne suis pas vivante! . . . ô tourbillon!—j'étais en toi, ô mouvement, en dehors de toutes les choses."

Thus concludes Valéry's poetic text on dance. It is, however, not merely about dance, for its very form—not only its *matière*—reflects precisely that rhythm which it traces. In the letter about this dialogue, Valéry tells us what he had intended to do: "quant à la forme d'ensemble, j'ai tenté de faire du *Dialogue* lui-même une manière de ballet dont l'Image et l'Idée sont tour à tour les Coryphées. L'abstrait et le sensible mènent tour à tour et s'unissent enfin dans le vertige." Many years after the composition of "L'Ame et la danse," he confesses: "j'ai écrit sur la danse sans l'aimer" (*C,* 1:276), but he knows now that he has, indeed, realized and fulfilled his own artistic "commande" to himself: "Mon dialogue sur danse est une danse dans laquelle tantôt le brillant des images, tantôt le profond des idées sont coryphées, pour s'achever en union" (*C,* 1:268).

Rilke's veneration of Valéry is a commonplace of the history of comparative literature.[11] It was in February of 1921 that Rilke discovered "Le Cimetière marin" in an issue of the *Nouvelle revue française,* and this reading, Renée Lang tells us, "wirkte schlagartig."[12] After a long gestation, from 1912—the beginning of the *Duineser Elegien*—until 1922, exactly one year after the decisive encounter with Valéry's poetry, the crowning achievements of Rilke's *Werk,* the *Duineser Elegien* and the *Sonette an Orpheus,* literally burst forth.[13] The *Sonette* were, incidentally, dedicated to the memory of a young dancer—"geschrieben als ein Grabamal für Wera Ouckama Knoop"—and thus constitute one of the most magnificent of literary *tombeaux.* Any discussion of the obvious and radical differences between Rilke and Valéry, or their more hidden and profound affinities, lies beyond the scope of this study. But we must recall that the late Rilke, the poet of the *Elegien,* the *Sonette,* and some French verse (*Vergers, Les Quatrains valaisans, Les Roses, Les Fenêtres,* and *Tendres Impôts à la France*), was certainly influenced by Valéry. Not only did Rilke admire Valéry, but he translated most of the "Charmes," and he was particularly enthusiastic about this *Nachdichtung*—for when one great poet "translates" another it is never mere *Übertragung*—"Der Friedhof am Meer."[14]

The poets met twice, the latter time in the late summer of 1926, and these hours counted among the happiest of Rilke's last year; later the same year, already seriously ill, he nevertheless translated two Valéryan dialogues, "Eupalinos ou l'architecte" and "L'Ame et la danse."[15]

Unlike Valéry, Rilke shared Mallarmé's fascination with dance. Except in his correspondence, however, the absolute poet[16] did not write about, but rather poeticized, the subject.[17] In his letters Rilke, for example, mentions Nijinskij, the great dancer of the Diaghilev company, whose 1912 performance of "Prélude à l'après-midi d'un faune" had inspired some of Rodin's most dynamic sculptural sketches;[18] but he immediately projects a poem for the dancer, a poem that would be danced.[19] The dance-dancer motif permeates Rilke's poetry to culminate finally in the *Sonette an Orpheus,* the most accomplished poetic expression of those elements that dance and poetry share: rhythm, repetition and variation, dynamics, and finally the metaphorical transposition of the world, a metaphor that is danced by the dancer and sung by the Orphic lyre.

One might expect that the "middle Rilke" of the *Neue Gedichte,* [20] where the *Ding-Gedicht*—after the assimilation of the Rodin encounter—reached its masterful perfection (for example, "Der Panther," "Die Gazelle" [pp. 505–61]), would be characterized by, and would emphasize, the static rather than the dynamic. Yet it is precisely from these poems that we learn most about the tremendous driving and swinging force, the kinetic energy—emotion transformed into motion—of Rilke's poetry. Poems like "Römisch Fontäne" (p. 529) and the sculptural "Archaïscher Torso Appolos" (p. 557) are motion poeticized and thus already foreshadow the very heart of Rilke's late work, the "Fifth Elegy." Rilke himself knew that he had accomplished that near-impossible "unsagbare," namely, pure motion put into words with the *Neue Gedichte* poem "Der Ball" (p. 639).[21]

The poem I have chosen to discuss, "Spanische Tänzerin" (pp. 531–32), is from the same collection; it was written in 1906 and was occasioned by the performance of a Spanish folk-dancer at the Montmartre christening party of the painter Zuloaga's daughter, which the poet had attended.[22] Thus the poem precedes "L'Ame et la danse" by many years; yet it, too, celebrates dance and the dancer by means of the flame metaphor. The Rilke poem, in fact, constitutes an accomplished metaphorical and lyric expression and is a "pure" poem in Valéry's sense of the term. It has realized, moreover, Valéry's "passage de la prose au vers—de la marche à la danse."

The first stanza introduces dancer and her dance with the simile of the glowing match, just before it bursts into flame:

> Wie in der Hand ein Schwefelzündholz, weiss,
> eh es zur Flamme kommt, nach allen Seiten
> zuckende Zungen streckt—; beginnt im Kreis
> naher Beschauer hastig, hell und heiss
> ihr runder Tanz sich zuckend auszubreiten.[23]

The dancer's beginning rhythmic movements are the match's "zuckende Zungen," translated but poorly by "quivering tongues." The round-dance is suggested by "Kreis," the circle of spectators surrounding the dancer, and later spelled out by "ihr runder Tanz." The "zuckend auszubreiten" of the last line echoes "zuckende Zungen" of the third; in "hell und heiss," "bright and hot," woman and fire fuse to prepare for the poem's major metaphor—dance/flame—set off from the rest of the piece in a separate line:

> Und plötzlich ist er Flamme, ganz und gar.

Woman has become dance, and dance has become flame; then in the following stanza we see the progressive consumption of the dancer by fire, "par la consommation intense d'une énergie de qualité supérieure," as Valéry had put it. But hers is a *self*-annihilation, *Vernichtung* by her own fire:

> Mit einem Blick entzündet sie ihr Haar
> und dreht auf einmal mit gewagter Kunst
> ihr ganzes Kleid in diese Feuersbrunst,
> aus welcher sich, wie Schlangen die erschrecken,
> die nackten Arme wach und klappernd strecken.

She is not passively consumed by the fire; rather the dancer-artist herself ignites her hair with her burning glance, and then, "mit gewagter Kunst," "with daring art," twirls her skirts into the "Feuersbrunst," the passionate fire of her dance. The Spanish dancer's arms, which beat the rhythm with their castanets, are likened to the clattering of frightened rattlesnakes. This dancer, like Mallarmé's, is no longer "une femme qui danse," but has transformed herself, has become her dance. Yet, as artist, she masters her art; at the moment of ecstatic climax—like Athikté in her final *tourbillon*—Rilke's dancer clutches her own fire and "throws it haughtily to the ground":

> Und dann: als würde ihr das Feuer knapp,
> nimmt sie es ganz zusamm und wirft es ab
> sehr herrisch, mit hochmütiger Gebärde

—and there it lies before her, before the spectators, before us, defeated but still alive in its burning:

> und schaut: da liegt es rasend auf der Erde
> und flammt noch immer und ergiebt sich nicht—

Rilke's dancer does not succumb to her esctatic *tourbillon* in a swoon like Valéry's Athikté but with a victorious smile tramples her dance's fire to death, "with small, firm feet":

> Doch sieghaft, sicher und mit einem süssen
> grüssenden Lächeln hebt sie ihr Gesicht
> und stampft es aus mit kleinen festen Füssen.

The onomatopoeic last line renders the accelerated rhythm of the culminating, whirling tap dance.

The poem's circular structure, from the "hand" of the first line to the "feet" of the last, traces the round-dance—"ihr runder Tanz"—which terminates in a final *tourbillon*, like Athikté's. Its fast beat is scanned by the dancer's feet and the poet's line, and the circularity, which was also spatially imagined by the circle of onlookers surrounding the dancer—"im Kreis / naher Beschauer"—is further temporally suggested by the igniting match, which then bursts into flame and is finally extinguished. Dance is a spatiotemporal art—"ornement de

la durée—ornement de l'étendue"—and both dimensions are fixed in "Spanische Tänzerin," which accomplishes that perfect fusion of *forme* and *fond* that,
according to both Mallarmé and Valéry, constitutes "pure poetry."

Rilke wrote the *Sonette an Orpheus* after, and unquestionably under the
influence of, the crucial encounter with Valéry. They and the *Duineser Elegien*
are his "explication orphique de la Terre," in which Mallarmé saw "le seul
devoir du poëte et le jeu littéraire par excellence" (p. 630). In the sonnets both
poet and dancer participate in *das Orphische Sagen,* rendering the invisible
visible, the visible invisible—"Erde, ist es nicht dies, was du willst: *unsicht-
bar* / in uns zu erstehn?" ("Ninth Elegy")—in that ideal rhythmic transposition
of the world, the taming of nature by art. Only two of the fifty-five sonnets are
directly addressed to the young dancer to whose memory the cycle was
dedicated. Sonnet 25 of "Erster Teil" evokes the dancer's dance arrested by
death; sonnet 28 of "Zweiter Teil" links her "dance-figure'" to the cosmic:

> O komm und geh. Du, fast noch Kind, ergänze
> für einen Augenblick die Tanzfigur
> zum reinen Sternbild einer jener Tänze
> darin wir die dumpf ordnende Natur
>
> vergänglich übertreffen. Denn sie regte
> sich völlig hörend nur, da Orpheus sang.[24]

The "dance-figure" here becomes a "pure constellation" in a cosmos created out
of chaos by art.[25] For nature "first stirred fully only when listening to Orpheus'
song," and when the dancer's "beautiful steps" danced to his lyre:

> Du wusstest noch die Stelle, wo die Leier
> sich tönend hob—; die unerhörte Mitte.
>
> Für sie versuchtest du die schönen Schritte.
>
> [P. 770]

In sonnet 15, "Erster Teil," the poet transforms nature's nourishment into art
and dance: "Mädchen, ihr warmen, Mädchen ihr stummen, / tanzt den
Geschmack der erfahrenen Frucht! / Tanzt die Orange" (p. 740). And in sonnet
18, "Zweiter Teil," the dancer becomes a transformer of the transient into
action: "Tänzerin; o du Verlegung / alles Vergehens in Gang" (p. 763); for this
dancer's final *tourbillon* the poet creates the original metaphor of the pitcher
and the vase twirled on the potter's wheel, beautiful images both of motion and
of motion arrested and fixed in pure form:

> Und der Wirbel am Schluss, . . .
>
> . . . .
> Sind sie nicht seine ruhigen Früchte: der Krug,
> reifend gestreift, und die gereiftere Vase?

Another of the *Sonette an Orpheus* (12, "Zweiter Teil") again celebrates the flame. It is now not merely a metaphor for dance, but rather the very symbol of Orphic transformation:

> Wolle die Wandlung. O sei für die Flamme begeistert,
> drin sich ein Ding dir entzieht, das mit Verwandlung prunkt;
> jener entwerfende Geist, welcher das Irdische meistert,
> liebt in dem Schwung der Figur nichts wie den wendenden Punkt.[26]

[P. 758]

The "devising Spirit which masters earthly laws" is not God but Orpheus, and in the "soaring figure," the dance-figure, he loves nothing as much as the "turning point," "den wendenden Punkt," the flaming *tourbillon* of Athikté and the Spanish dancer.

The Mallarméan analogy of poetry and dance, which underlines Valéry's reflections on dance and his great dialogue, has in the last Rilke sonnet cycle grown into the poet's and dancer's shared participation in "l'explication orphique de la Terre." The dancer has become as impersonal as the poet, for the *Sonnets' Tänzerin* is a mythical archetype like Orpheus.

1.See Haskell M. Block, *Mallarmé and the Symbolist Drama* (Detroit: Wayne State University Press, 1963), pp. 93–96. For more recent discussions of dancer and dance in Mallarmé, see Julia Kristeva's chapter "L'Auteur ou la danseuse" in her *La Révolution du langage poétique* (Paris: Seuil, 1974), pp. 599–607; Paula Gilbert Lewis, *The Aesthetics of Stéphane Mallarmé in Relation to His Public* (Cranbury, N. J.: Fairleigh Dickinson University Press, 1976), pp. 47, 92, 101–2, 124–25, 182–83; and Judy Kravis, *The Prose of Mallarmé* (Cambridge: At the University Press, 1976), pp. 35, 119, 145–57, 154–62, 172, 173.

2. Stéphane Mallarmé, *Œuvres complètes* (Paris: Gallimard, 1945), p. 303. All quotations from Mallarmé will be from this edition and identified in the text by page number.

3. Cf. my *An Anatomy of Poesis: The Prose Poems of Stéphane Mallarmé* (Chapel Hill: University of North Carolina Press, 1976), pp. 100–01.

4. Ibid., pp. 9–10. See also Block, p. 94: "Mallarmé's criticism is at its most poetic in both style and subject in his reflections on the dance."

5. Paul Valéry, *Cahiers,* 2 vols. (Paris: Gallimard, 1973–74), 2:977. All quotations from Valéry's *Cahiers* will be from this edition and identified by the letter *C* and the volume and page number.

6. Cf. Paul Valéry, *Œuvres,* 2 vols. (Paris: Gallimard, 1957–60), 2:1277: "L'architecture a tenu une grande place dans les premières amours de mon esprit . . . l'idée même de la *construction,* qui est le passage du désordre à l'ordre . . . se fixait en moi comme le type de l'action la plus belle et la plus complète que l'homme se pût proposer" ("Histoire d'Amphion"). All quotations from Valéry, other than the *Cahiers,* are from this edition and indicated by volume and page number.

7. Valéry knew that Bouhours, classicism's spokesman on poetry and rhetoric, first made the analogy: "la prose a un autre nombre que la poésie et il y a pour le moins autant de différence entre elles qu'il y en a entre deux personnes dont l'une marche et l'autre danse parfaitement bien." Cf. Paul Valery, *Œuvres,* 1:1370; and Jean Hytier, *Questions de littérature* (New York: Columbia University Press, 1967), p. 149.

8. Cf. Valéry's letter about "L'Ame et la danse" to Louis Séchan, some ten years after the dialogue's composition, in *Lettres à quelques-uns* (Paris: Gallimard, 1952), pp. 189–91.

9. *Princeton Encyclopedia of Poetry and Poetics,* rev. ed. (Princeton: Princeton University Press, 1974), p. 481.

10. The "conséquences merveilleuses d'un accident dialectique" recall what Valéry has frequently expressed in the *Cahiers:* "il ne faut jamais oublier que nos pensées sont uniquement portées et développées par les *occasions.* L'accident est ce qu'il y a de plus constant," and "toute puissance spirituelle est fondée sur les innombrables hasards de la pensée" (*C,* 1:251, 924).

11. See, for example, Charles Dédéyan, *Rilke et la France,* 4 vols. (Paris: Sedes, 1961), 1:358–83; Maurice Betz, *Rilke in Paris* (Zürich: Verlag der Arche, 1948), pp. 179 ff.; and J. F. Angelloz, *Rainer Maria Rilke Leben und Werk* (Zürich: Verlag der Arche, 1955), pp. 303 ff.

12. Renée Lang, "Ein Fruchtbringendes Missverständnis: Rilke und Valéry," *Symposium* 13 (Spring 1959): 51–62.

13. Monique St. Hélier, *A Rilke pour Noël* (Bern: Edition du Chandelier, 1927), p. 21, quotes Rilke: "Ich war alleine, ich wartete, mein ganzes Werk wartete . . . eines Tages habe ich Valéry gelesen: ich wusste, dass mein Warten zu Ende war."

14. Cf. Renée Lang, "Rainer Maria Rilke et 'Le Cimetière marin,'" *France Illustration* (July 1955).

15. Cf. Karin Wais, *Studien zu Rilkes Valéry-Übertragungen* (Tübingen: Max Niemeyer Verlag, 1967), pp. 107 ff., for an analysis of Rilke's "Die Seele und der Tanz."

16. I mean by "absolute poet" a man whose sole and unique preoccupation was poetry; Rilke constructed his whole existence around his art, sacrificing his entire destiny to it: "mein Schicksal ist dass ich kein Schicksal habe." In this respect Rilke is, of course, much closer to Mallarmé than to Valéry.

17. Dietgard Kramer-Lauff has devoted an entire book to *Tanz und das Tänzerische in Rilkes Lyrik* (Munich: Fink Verlag, 1969).

18. For five beautiful photographs of Rodin's Nijinskij plaster "sketches," see Robert Descharnes and Jean-François Chabrun, *Auguste Rodin* (Lausanne: Edita Lausanne, 1967), pp. 256–57, and the chapter "Rodin and the Dance." A discussion of Rodin's overpowering and highly formative influence on Rilke lies beyond the range of this study.

19. In 1911, Rilke writes to the Fürstin von Thurn und Taxis, "Ich glaube, ich muss etwas für Nijinskij machen, den russischen Tänzer. . . . Ein Gedicht, das sich sozusagen verschlucken lässt und dann tanzen." See Kramer-Lauff, pp. 26–27.

20. Rainer Maria Rilke, *Sämtliche Werke,* (Frankfurt: Insel Verlag, Werkausgabe, 1976), 2:481–642. All quotations from Rilke will be from the second volume of this edition and will be identified in the text by page number.

21. Kramer-Lauff quotes Rilke about this poem of the *Neue Gedichte* as follows: "Da habe ich gar nichts als das fast Unaussprechbare einer reinen Bewegung ausgesprochen."

22. Brigitte L. Bradley, *R. M. Rilkes Neue Gedichte: Ihr Zyklisches Gefüge* (Bern and Munich: Francke Verlag, 1967), pp. 131–32, quotes from a letter Rilke wrote to his wife about the event: "eine Gitane, mit dem gewissen schwarz-bunten Tuch, tanzte spanische Tänze."

23. For an English translation of "Spanische Tänzerin," see C. F. MacIntyre, *Rilke: Selected Poems* (Berkeley: University of California Press, 1974), p. 89.

24. For an English translation of this and the other sonnets, see C. F. MacIntyre, *Rilke: Sonnets to Orpheus* (Berkeley: University of California Press, 1960), p. 111.

25. For a full exegesis of this and all of the *Sonette an Orpheus,* see Hermann Mörchen, *Rilkes Sonette an Orpheus* (Stuttgart: Kohlhammer Verlag, 1958).

26. For an English translation of this sonnet, see MacIntyre, *Sonnets,* p. 29.

Emile Nelligan, *Poète Maudit* of Quebec:
The Pervasion of Black and White Coldness

PAULA GILBERT LEWIS

The son of a French-Canadian mother and an Irish father, Emile Nelligan was born in 1879, lived most of his life in Montreal, died intellectually in 1899 when he was interned for mental disorders, and died in 1941. Almost all of his poetry was composed between 1896, when he was still a student at the Collège Sainte-Marie, and 1899, when he was sent to the Retraite Saint-Benoît, leaving it in 1925 for St.-Jean-de-Dieu where he later died. Nelligan never visited France—other than one short trip to England, he never even left Quebec—but his entire poetic career was imbued with French literary influences.

In 1905 there appeared in Paris an article in *La Revue d'Europe et des colonies* entitled "Un Poète maudit: Emile Nelligan."[1] The author of the article placed the Quebecois poet in a direct line of French symbolist poets and named as his clearest influences Heredia and Verlaine. The major contemporary critic of Nelligan's poetry, Paul Wyczynski, in his massive work *Emile Nelligan: Sources et originalité de son œuvre,* goes far beyond the 1905 assessment and exactingly describes, chronologically, thematically, and in reference to individual poems, the influences of, especially, Baudelaire, Verlaine, Rimbaud, Mallarmé, Rodenbach, Poe, and Rollinat.[2]

But whichever influence was the profoundest on any particular poem, it remains evident that Nelligan was essentially a French symbolist poet and, specifically, a *poète maudit.* True to Verlaine's original meaning of *malédiction,* Nelligan saw himself as a poor misunderstood genius scorned by the majority of his fellow "vulgar" Quebecois, isolated in an aesthetic world of his own and dreaming of an absolute purity by means of poetry. His poems express an inner revolt and pathetic cry, more musical than intellectual, against his obsessions with the cruel world, *la nostalgie du berceau,* the passing of time, sensations of *le spleen* and *le gouffre,* and inevitable death. They complain of the impossibility of attaining absolute perfection in art but attest to the poet's wishes to continue the struggle. And, above all, Nelligan's poetry chronicles his macabre voyage toward insanity.

He has always been considered more French than French-Canadian. Living at a time in Canada when almost all artistic endeavors were modeled on those of the French, Nelligan was representative of the vast period of time before the growth of Quebecois national consciousness that began in the mid twentieth century. Although for this reason alone he is important to the history of Quebecois literature, it is equally interesting to analyze his poetry in order to discover if any elements reveal his Canadian origins. A pervasion of black and white coldness appears to be the sole link.

The predominance of poetic themes such as winter, snow, ice, frost, night, a distant past and future, pure unattainable or sterile ideals, *le gouffre, la névrose,* insanity, and death—all painted either in black or in white in an absence of color and of warmth—can be viewed as exterior or interior psychological décors. They are to be treated, especially when used as interior descriptions of the poet's heart and mind, as *maudit* obsessions. But, in their frequency as exterior décors for his poems, they stress primarily the Canadian landscape, permeating the inner self through a dual window overlooking both wintery scenes and the shuddering soul.

Of 177 known poems by Nelligan, a large percentage are concerned with the presence of an exterior coldness, specifically mentioning winter, the white snow, ice, and frost. The opening verse of "Soir d'hiver" offers the reader an idea of the constant décor of Nelligan's poetry: "Ah! comme la neige a neigé!"[3] Similarly, in "Frisson d'hiver," the poet sees "le givre qui s'éternise / Hivernalement" (p. 96). In many of Nelligan's poems, this white coldness, associated with purity, possesses positive characteristics; it is good and desired and, perhaps, the only possible warmth available to the poet. "Que le froid des hivers nous réchauffe les cœurs!" cries Nelligan in "Hiver sentimental" (p. 93); and in another poem dedicated to *la froideur blanche* he speaks of "l'immaculé / De ce décor en blanc," a cold décor filled with ice and snow ("Caprice blanc," p. 66).

If the poet is referring to Canada in most of these poems, he sees his homeland as related to other northern countries in a fraternal bond. He mentions Belgium, Flanders, and Norway, in particular, all viewed as snowy, white, and cold, as well as melancholy under gray skies. And he identifies himself almost as a Canadian Norwegian when he writes "Je suis la nouvelle Norvège / D'où les blonds ciels s'en sont allés" (p. 82).[4]

There is only one poem in which Nelligan truly localizes his wintery landscape. In "Notre-Dame-des-Neiges," Ville-Marie, that is, Montreal, is described as "Ma ville d'argent au collier de neige," protected by Sainte-Marie, whereas Canada is seen as a "pays de givre." But, true to his love for France, Nelligan ends his poem with a wish that the Virgin Mary soon see "refleurir en même jardin / Sa France et sa Ville-Marie," when she chases out the Protestant, English-speaking conqueror (pp. 148–49).[5]

If Emile Nelligan is the poet of the cold, white winter, he is equally the poet of the cold, black night. At least one quarter of his poems are specifically described as nocturnal. In a few instances that night serves a calm and soothing function for the poet, a form of preferred consolation and inspiration (pp. 134, 210, 215, 218, 219, 234, 247). But generally night is feared. It is a hallucinatory night whose progressive invasion engenders the sensation of a black void, of eternity.[6] It is always a winter night, described as "vos soirs affreux, ô Décembres!" ("Soirs hypocondriaques," p. 277) in which "Des sons / Gémissent sous le noir des nocturnes frissons" ("La Cloche dans la brume," p. 188). It is often seen as evening at the time of vespers just before the death of day when all possible light disappears.

Despite his terror of the encroaching black coldness, this nocturnal poet is obsessed with the absolute blackness of the winter night. Like Mallarmé, haunted by his vision of the frightening sky of his ideals, Nelligan utters the same desperate cry in "Confession nocturne": "je suis hanté." And like the French symbolist poet who immediately clarifies his haunting vision ("L'Azur! l'Azur! l'Azur! l'Azur!"),[7] the Quebecois symbolist poet immediately explains: "c'est la nuit dans la ville," a silent night punctuated by the sounds of Lucifer, prowling "En le parc hivernal" (p. 126).

Just as twilight serves as a transition between daytime and its death into night, October, or autumn, is often used by Nelligan to symbolize the season immediately preceding the death of nature into winter. If the white snowy coldness of Canadian winters represents at times purity and warmth, more often it can be seen as precipitating the cold blackness of nature's death. Nature herself shudders "avec des frissons noirs" ("Prière du soir," p. 151) or a "sinistre frisson" ("Soir d'hiver," p. 82), since all of her living organisms will soon be frozen under "l'immobilité glaciale des jets d'eau" ("Five o'clock," p. 85).[8]

Winter can be dangerous both to nature and to man; Nelligan paints a typically stark scene in "Paysage fauve": "La bise hurle; il grêle; il fait noir, tout est sombre." He had turned to the cold white snow as toward some form of purity, but now, overcome by the cold, he falls "sur les neiges arctiques" in the middle of "Un farouche troupeau de grands loups affamés"; for "C'est l'Hiver; c'est la Mort" (p. 158).[9] The Quebecois Nelligan had hoped that his snowy white or nocturnal exterior cold décor would inspire him in his poetic dreams, but he was bitterly deceived. All he discovered was cold black death lying beneath the cold white snow:

> Sûrs vous pourrez y vivre
> Sans peur des soirs de givre,
>   Morne flambeau!
> Souventes fois, cortège
> Qu'un vent trop dur assiège,
> Vous trouvez sous la neige
>   Votre tombeau.
>
> ["Les Petits Oiseaux," p. 111]

One additional type of exterior coldness surrounding the poet should be mentioned, especially since it appears in Nelligan's best-known poem, "La Romance du vin." Here the poet haughtily complains of the coldness of the Canadian public toward him and his art. As a *poète maudit,* it is his destiny "De se savoir poète et l'objet du mépris, / De se savoir un cœur et de n'être compris." But cynically he addresses the mediocre crowd: "Je bois à vous surtout, hommes aux fronts moroses / Qui dédaignez ma vie et repoussez ma main!" (pp. 198–99). Such a situation was, of course, typically *maudit,* although also Canadian in that the average Quebecois of the late nineteenth century neither understood nor accepted such French intellectual literary thoughts. Nelligan's reaction to this exterior coldness was also typical: he withdrew into himself, into his own world of artistic dreams and, eventually, into insanity, only to discover, once again, a permeating white and black cold.

Paul Wyczynski states in several of his critical works on Nelligan that the color (or absence of color) white symbolized for the poet his nostalgically remembered childhood, his mother, and, therefore, his former happiness and secure warmth.[10] Despite the truth of this observation, substantiated in several poems, it is also evident that this past life is now dead and, therefore, although still white, cold and silent. The poet recognizes this state when he wanders to a cemetery "où gît ma belle enfance au glacial tombeau" ("Ténèbres," p. 197). Similarly, religion, and especially his beloved Sainte Cécile, are described by Nelligan as being pure and white, but in a form of "cold warmth," distant from the poet and offering him little consolation.[11]

This distant white but cold purity is associated not only with past happiness and memories but also, and predominantly, with the future. Like so many poets before and contemporary to him, Nelligan constantly viewed ideal beauty, both female and artistic, as white, pure, and virginal. For Nelligan in particular, all female beauty, be it real or absolute, was cold and unapproachable. All of his women remained at a distance.

His aesthetic ideals, dreams, and goals of reaching an absolute world were similarly sterile or unattainable. Many of his poems speak of his desires to flee "vers le château de nos Idéals blancs" but are immediately recognized as a flight "Aux plages de Thulé, vers l'île des Mensonges" ("Tristesse blanche," p. 191).[12] Although Nelligan is often the poet of escape, of the voyage toward the infinite and the absolute, his art soon becomes, as he himself interpreted that of Baudelaire, "un violon polaire," a frigid musical poetry that, according to popular tradition, made dance the Aurora Borealis, the Northern Lights seen in northern latitudes ("Le Tombeau de Charles Baudelaire," p. 241).[13] If nature dies, frozen under the glacial immobility of water, so do the poet's hopes, frozen and fallen like leaves from a tree in winter. And if "Tous les étangs gisent gelés," Nelligan, "la nouvelle Norvège" from whom all sunny skies have departed, sees that "Tous ses espoirs gisent gelés" ("Soir d'hiver," p. 82).[14]

Not only are the poet's artistic ideals described as pure and white (though cold and frozen), but Nelligan sees himself, at times, in an identical manner. In the midst of a perverted world, it is difficult "D'avoir une âme ainsi qu'une neige aux hivers" ("Mon Ame," p. 42). And again, identifying himself as a northern poet in a fraternity with others of similar origins, Nelligan portrays Georges Rodenbach as a pure white swan flying toward the azure of the north, but living under the melancholy gray skies of Belgium ("A Georges Rodenbach," p. 233).

It is noteworthy that Nelligan, himself living in a cold, wintery country, creates his inner artistic ideals as pure, white, and cold. He seldom expresses a desire to escape to a land of warmth and sunshine. His absolutes are not the exotic realms of inner light, but the cold, feared, but desired obsessions of art and the artist, expressed, ironically, in moving, personal tones. If there is any light present in his poetry, it is, although examples are rare, that of gold, itself a distant, harsh light, seen almost as white and viewed, in effect, as another "cold warmth."[15]

But if, as Wyczynski states, "le ciel serein trouve momentanément sa place dans le cœur du poète, il y doit changer et de résonance et de couleur. Nelligan est un artiste inquiet. Souvenir d'enfance [and future ideals], le rêve ensoleillé n'est qu'une évasion passagère. D'abord blanche et dorée, la tristesse devient vite grise et noire," as one sees "le noir sentiment qui envahit son être."[16] As Nelligan looks around and sees the cold, white, wintery, nocturnal landscape, while dreaming of pure white aesthetic ideals, he examines his own inner being: his life, his thoughts, and his soul. He writes a poem to "La Vierge noire" and says, "Certes tu la connais, on l'appelle la Vie!" He composes the poem "Musique funèbres" in which the cold, black motif is pervasive in words such as "absent," "noir," "deuil," "silence," "clos," "sanglots," "plongeant," "mort," "me noyer," "bière," "croquemorts," "fantômes," "nuits," "ombre," "engouffrez," "Enfer," "descend," "cercueil," and, finally, "Ah! que je hais la vie et son noir Carillon!" (pp 276, 171–72). He experiences the occupational hazard of *l'étouffement* and of an inner, cold void. And he is, especially, obsessed with the sensation of depth, with falling into a deep, black, cold *gouffre*. "Mon âme est le donjon des mortels péchés noirs," laments Nelligan ("Confession nocturne," p. 126). As "un grand cygne noir," the poet is haunted by hollow objects and sensations: "Dans le puits noir que tu vois là / Gît la source de tout ce drame" ("Le Cercueil," p. 129; "Le Puits hanté," p. 175).

Emile Nelligan's obsession with falling into a cold, black abyss is dual, with both fates envisioned as inevitable and terrifying. Passing through stages of macabre hallucinations, he fell into *la névrose*, becoming insane, and, therefore, mentally dying well before his actual death. The poet predicted his own "mental shipwreck" in "Le Vaisseau d'or," where the golden-white vessel, about to reach "l'azur, sur des mers inconnues," was coldly struck by the night:

"Et le naufrage horrible inclina sa carène / Aux profondeurs du Gouffre, immuable cercueil." The treasured cargo of this vessel was revealed to be "Dégoût, Haine et Névrose," and, finally:

> Que reste-t-il de lui dans la tempête brève?
> Qu'est devenu mon cœur, navire déserté?
> Hélas! Il a sombré dans l'abîme du Rêve!

[P. 44]

Beyond his immediate mental death, Nelligan was constantly haunted by his actual death. The cold, black night can only precipitate an identical catastrophe for the poet. Images of coffins, tombstones, hearses, mourning crapes, cemeteries, and skeletons abound in his poems. Death and the ensuing funeral procession always arrive on a cold, winter evening when "les noirs des musiques" can be heard. And since the cold rigidity of death is inevitable, Nelligan, already experiencing the black coldness of life and of encroaching insanity, may as well hasten the process:

> Et de grands froids glacent mes membres:
> Je cherche à me suicider
> Par vos soirs affreux, ô Décembres!

["Soirs hypocondriaques," p. 277]

Using this stanza as an example, as well as considering all that has been discussed thus far, we may conclude that there exist many interdependences and fluctuations between exterior and interior coldness, both black and white, in the poetry of Nelligan. In anticipation of his cold, black insanity and eventual death, the poet often experiences a shudder (*le frisson*) of his soul, fearful of the future in a cold *néant*.[17] This inner shuddering corresponds to the cold, white shudder of wintery nature in the black night. Similarly, in accord with the exterior landscape, Nelligan sees "Mon cœur cristallisé de givre!" ("Rêves enclos," p. 81). The pure white heart of the poet, melancholy and black with visions of macabre death, becomes immobile, sterile, frozen into the Canadian snow.

In order to effect the passage of this black and white coldness between both exterior and interior décors, the poet views these pervading relationships through a window, the Nelliganian counterpart of the Mallarméan *vitre*:

> La nuit s'appropriait peu à peu les rideaux
> Avec des frissons noirs à toutes les croisées,
> Par ces soirs, et malgré les bûches embrasées,
> Comme nous nous sentions soudain du froid au dos!

["Prière du soir," p. 151][18]

Like Mallarmé, Nelligan uses *la vitre* in order to contemplate both the landscape and the distant ideal azure skies. Through the window pass these exterior images into the claustrophobic room and into his closed heart. The movement is, of course, reversible. But the windowpane serves also as a transparent obstacle, for the poet cannot reach his goals, either in the absolute realm of art or in the purity of snow. Everything he sees, touches, and dreams is frozen and imprisoned, "un soupir emprisonné dans la glace."[19]

His passing life is also trapped in *la vitre* or in a cold mirror, dating from his past. Like the Canadian landscape, it has become eternally frozen. Mallarmé, in "Frisson d'hiver," speaks of the "vitres usées," as well as of "ta glace de Venise, profonde comme une froide fontaine."[20] Nelligan, in his poem of the same title, cries:

> Quand le givre qui s'éternise
> Hivernalement s'harmonise
> Aux vieilles glaces de Venise.
>
> [P. 96]

Both poets, although fearful of this cold reflection ("Loin des vitres!" warns Nelligan in "Hiver sentimental" [p. 93]), can never turn away from its haunting presence: "Mallarmé et Nelligan parlent tous les deux le langage des rêveurs emprisonnés dans leur propre moi,"[21] or rather, for Nelligan, frozen within himself.

It remains accurate to state the Emile Nelligan was essentially a French symbolist *poète maudit* who loved France and her literary traditions. But despite his overt disregard of his Quebecois milieu, his poetry does betray the influence of his Canadian homeland. The poem "Soir d'hiver" could only have been written by a northern poet:

> Ah! comme la neige a neigé!
> Ma vitre est un jardin de givre.
> Ah! comme la neige a neigé!
> Qu'est-ce que le spasme de vivre
> A la douleur que j'ai, que j'ai!
>
> Tous les étangs gisent gelés,
> Mon âme est noire: Où vis-je? où vais-je?
> Tous ses espoirs gisent gelés:
> Je suis la nouvelle Norvège
> D'où les blonds ciels s'en sont allés.
>
> Pleurez, oiseaux de février,
> Au sinistre frisson des choses,
> Pleurez, oiseaux de février,
> Pleurez mes pleurs, pleurez mes roses,
> Aux branches du genévrier.
>
> Ah! comme la neige a neigé!
> Ma vitre est un jardin de givre.
> Ah! comme la neige a neigé!
> Qu'est-ce que le spasme de vivre
> A tout l'ennui que j'ai, que j'ai!
>
> [Pp. 82–83]

1. Charles ab der Halden, "Un Poète maudit: Emile Nelligan," *La Revue d'Europe et des colonies* 13 (January 1905): 49–62.

2. Paul Wyczynski, *Emile Nelligan: Sources et originalité de son œuvre* (Ottawa: Editions de l'Université d'Ottawa, 1960). (Cited hereafter as *Sources et originalité.*)

3. Emile Nelligan, *Poésies complètes 1896–1899,* edited and annotated by Luc Lacourcière (Montreal: Editions Fides, 1974), p. 82. All quotations from Nelligan, taken from this edition and identified in the text by page number, are reprinted by permission.

4. His love of Belgium is, of course, also related to his admiration of Belgian symbolist poets.

5. See also Wyczynski, *Sources et originalité,* pp. 139–41, where the critic offers examples of newspaper articles, contemporary to Nelligan's poem, in which tributes to a beautiful Canada under the weight of ice and snow are given, as well as 1898 photographs in which the Virgin Mary is described as being covered with snow.

6. Paul Wyczynski, *Emile Nelligan* (Montreal: Editions Fides, 1967), p. 59.

7. Stéphane Mallarmé, "L'Azur," *Œuvres complètes* (Paris: Gallimard, Bibliothèque de la Pléiade, 1945), p. 38.

8. One is reminded, once again, of Mallarmé's "Le Vierge, le vivace et le bel aujourd'hui" (Mallarmé, pp. 67–68). The similarities in reference to the poet's frozen hopes and dreams will also soon be seen.

9. See also Wyczynski, *Sources et originalité,* pp. 201–2; and idem, *Emile Nelligan,* pp. 57–59.

10. See Wyczynski, *Sources et originalité,* pp. 255–56, 285; idem, *Emile Nelligan,* p. 39; idem, *Nelligan et la musique* (Ottawa: Editions de l'Université d'Ottawa, 1971), p. 60; and idem, *Poésie et symbole: Perspectives du symbolisme* (Montreal: Librairie Déom, 1965), pp. 102–3.

11. In Nelligan's poetry, the purity, distance, and, above all, silence of this religion and, in particular, of Sainte Cécile, the leader of the angelic orchestra, can be likened to Mallarmé's Sainte Cécile, the "Musicienne du silence." See Mallarmé, "Sainte," pp. 53–54; Nelligan, pp. 74, 75, 133–34, 135, 136, 137.

12. Thulé is the name given by the Romans to an island that marked the extreme northern limit of the known world.

13. See also p. 317. Such a result caused by his polar art can   also be seen as a positive characteristic.

14. See also "Five o'clock," p. 85; and Wyczynski, *Nelligan et la musique,* pp. 54, 56–57, 59–60.

15. Wyczynski, *Nelligan et la musique,* p. 109.

16. Wyczynski, *Emile Nelligan,* p. 39; idem, *Sources et originalité, p. 215.*

17. See "Prière du soir," pp. 150–51; "Eventail," p. 159; "Marches funèbres," p. 174; "La Cloche dans la brume," p. 188. See also Wyczynski, *Emile Nelligan, pp. 57–59.*

18. See also "Five o'clock," pp. 84–85. For a psychological interpretation of this stanza and of "Hiver sentimental" in reference to Nelligan's hatred and fear of his father and almost unnatural love of his mother, see Gérard Bessette, *Une Littérature en ébullition* (Montreal: Editions du Jour, 1968), pp. 72–77.

19. Wyczynski, *Emile Nelligan,* p. 58.

20. Mallarmé, p. 271.

21. Wyczynski, *Emile Nelligan,* p. 58.

Molière est moins un homme que
la conscience vivante d'une nation.

R. Fernandez, *Itinéraire français*

This essay was translated by Patricia Pecoy

The Molière Myth in Nineteenth-Century France

RALPH ALBANESE, JR.

Upon examining the literary and cultural fortunes of the great classical authors—Corneille, Racine, and Molière, to mention only this universally recognized triumvirate—we see clearly that a particular myth has developed around each one. Whereas Corneille evokes a moral myth appropriate to an aristocracy enamored with heroism, and Racine is the very incarnation of the myth of classical perfection, a symbol of purity, the case of Molière takes on even greater dimensions, attaining a mythological stature that far exceeds that of the tragic authors. In fact, "Moliérism" represents a veritable French institution, one created by the nineteenth-century bourgeoisie but still pervasive even today. To write the history of the various interpretations of Molière in the nineteenth century is to expose a profoundly laudatory critical position that contributes to the national canonization of the Molière phenomenon. Thus, the pious affirmation of Jean Anouilh, according to which those who are indifferent to the great comic author lack any "contact charnel vrai avec la France,"[1] is revealing: the process of institutionalizing Molière stems from a unanimous desire to integrate him into the national patrimony. Thus, Lanson, like many other critics, saw Molière as the seventeenth-century author who was "le plus complètement français."[2] The models for Molière's theater being of a clearly national stock—authors of *fabliaux* and farces, Rabelais, Régnier, and so forth—with respect to those of Corneille and Racine, this theater, by raising problems that were more immediately recognizable to the French, addresses itself directly to the everyday awareness of the country. This desire to place the author of the *Misanthrope* on a purely French pedestal assumes, as we shall see, numerous meanings.

Within the scope of this essay, it is hardly possible to give a complete list of the multiple interpretations occasioned by the Molière myth in France in the nineteenth century. Rather, our purpose is to draw upon a certain number of examples taken from the abundant critical corpus: spread throughout the century, the successive visions of Molière—romantic, academic, and positivistic in turn—manifest an incontestable historical and ideological significance. To differing degrees, these various interpretations reveal the extent to which the secular bourgeoisie honored Molière in order to appropriate him better, at the same time conferring particular value on the constitutive elements of his value system. And, from the point of view of nineteenth-century pedagogical practices, this bourgeoisie managed to transform the great comic author into both a subject for scholarly investigation and an object of privileged knowledge.

The lukewarm reception accorded to the Molière repertory by the general public in the first half of the century is well known, and Musset bemoans this general negligence:

> J'étais seul, l'autre soir, au Théâtre français,
> Ou presque seul; l'auteur n'avait pas grand succès:
> Ce n'était que Molière . . .

[_"Une Soirée perdue"_]

How paradoxical that Musset, Stendhal, Balzac, and Flaubert, whose anti-bourgeois biases are evident, took it upon themselves to communicate to the public of their era their admiration for Molière, who, himself, would eventually become the spokesman for the bourgeois values of this very public. The romantic interpretation of the comic poet, which, in fact, persisted throughout the century, presented a somber image of the poet, fallen prey to a sublime melancholy. Musset saw in the _Misanthrope_ a " . . . mâle gaieté, si triste et si profond / Que, lorsqu'on vient d'en rire, on devrait en pleurer!" The same was true of Goethe, who considered the comedies to be a projection of Molière's own personal suffering, an expression of his own unconscious desires. As such, Arnolphe, Alceste, and Harpagon become eminently tragic figures; and numerous actors (Perlet, Guitry) portrayed these roles by insisting on their pathetic nature. Hugo and Michelet, whose interpretations also belong in part to this strongly subjective school, admired in Molière the libertarian spirit, which castigates all forms of imposture. They saw in him a progressive who contested the alliance of church and state, in short, the apostle of oppressed humanity. They were particularly aware of the political implications of _Tartuffe_, for example, a play that became the object of a veritable infatuation under the Restoration.[3] This play, whose performances provoked uprisings in the provinces, constituted a focal point of opposition under the reign of Louis XVIII, rallying the romantic, anticlerical youth of the _Globe_ and the _Constitutionnel_, for example, around their hostility toward the Jesuits and the Congregation. In the case of Stendhal and Balzac, we notice a certain posthumous rivalry that operated between the comic poet and those who tried to be the "nouveaux Molières" of the nineteenth century.[4] Both authors exhibited a conscious desire to imitate the playwright; this mimesis was a challenge that was both tempting and discouraging. Stendhal tried unsuccessfully to write a sequel to _Tartuffe_, and Balzac dreamed of undertaking the same endeavor. Although Molière's portrayal of hypocrisy and *arrivisme* must surely have tantalized Stendhal, the massive enterprise of *La Comédie humaine* betrays Balzac's concern for transposing into his novelistic universe a breadth of vision and a typology of characters that are very much a part of Molière's comedies.

However, it is undoubtedly the scholarly criticism of Nisard and Saint-Marc Girardin, as well as that of Sainte-Beuve, that, between 1830 and 1848, provided the greatest impetus to the development of Moliérism. It is important to go back to this criticism in order to appreciate the extent to which the scholarly myth of Molière became codified. On the whole, this myth, which has been transmitted from one generation of students to the next, can be defined on the basis of these principles: carefully avoid originality, respect prudence as a cardinal virtue, and do not go beyond the bounds of the cherished golden mean. All these elements of the famous shopkeeper's morality—which we are tempted to call "petty bourgeois"—were endowed with a clearly didactic value by numerous nineteenth-century critics. Wishing to reduce the moral and philosophical ideas found in Molière's theater to simple academic and moralizing pronouncements, these critics were able to impose a fundamental image of the comic poet that persists even today. Thus, in the tradition of Villemain, Nisard attributed an essentially literary and moral obligation to criticism, making the seventeenth century an object of absolute, dogmatic veneration. One could hardly exaggerate the importance of his role as "intellectual regent" in the domain of criticism under the July Monarchy.[5] Emphasizing the relationship between genius and moral goodness, Nisard advanced the notion of Molière's generosity, placing him at the same time in moral revolt against Tartuffe. Having a taste for "universal truths,"[6] he praised the profound morality of the *Misanthrope,* which, according to him, placed a sort of distributive justice in the balance. Finally, Nisard took pains to establish the connection between the preoccupations of the seventeenth-century bourgeoisie and that of the nineteenth century, a connection that was firmly cemented by Molière's comedy: "De toutes les conventions elle [i.e., comedy] est le plus près de la réalité: ce sont nos mœurs, nos scènes de famille, nos travers; c'est nous. . . . Ces mœurs ont été celles de nos ancêtres; leurs travers nous appartiennent. Nous revendiquons nos marquis d'autrefois, si peu différents d'ailleurs des marquis d'aujourd'hui dont les parchemins sont à la caisse du sceau."[7]

Along these same lines, Saint-Marc Girardin stated that the task of criticism is to communicate good taste, which is indissolubly linked to the moral order. Assigning a privileged status to Molière, he was the first to draw attention to the moral exactitude characteristic of *Psyché.* Attentive to the interests of the bourgeoisie, he also undertook a certain moral rehabilitation of M. Dimanche: "[Men] sont plus sages dans leurs affaires que dans leurs idées. . . . M. Dimanche se moquera de vous [i.e., of Dom Juan], aujourd'hui surtout que M. Dimanche est électeur, député ou ministre, et que vous, de notre côté, vous n'êtes plus gentilhomme, puisqu'il n'y en a plus."[8] Sainte-Beuve demonstrated an acute critical understanding of Molière.[9] Throughout his praise of the playwright runs a strain of Moliérophilia: each repetition of his refrain "Aimer Molière" introduces yet another justification—dramatic, moral, political, and humanitarian—for his adulation. This famous triumphal hymn—the *nec plus ultra* of the laudatory epithets applied to Molière in the nineteenth century—constitutes, as we shall see, a vast source of inspiration for other admirers of the comic poet.

As Sainte-Beuve's criticism became more and more "une critique bourgeoise de jugement,"[10] a classical criticism on the whole, based on restraint and common sense, it extended the critical lineage of Villemain, Nisard, and Saint-Marc Girardin, who systematically denounced contemporary works then viewed as decadent. The resurgence of classical criticism went hand in hand with the bourgeois recovery of political power by means of a kind of literary police force. Stated differently, we may call this a transposition of the conservative ideology of de Maistre and Bonald in the domain of literary criticism to a collective desire to use the critical function in the service of political restoration.

To the extent that literary positivism represents the official scientific doctrine of the university system of the second half of the nineteenth century, we can see the early outlines of this positivistic interpretation in the extraordinary outpouring of works on Molière dating from the 1860s. Committed to a method of thorough documentation, scholars such as Bazin, Soulié, and Compardon set out in search of the "vrai Molière."[11] These relentless researchers succeeded in establishing a "scientific" critical position based on the patient analysis of provincial archives, in short, a biographical approach to the comic poet that was especially concerned with correcting the numerous errors that had been transmitted by his legend. This desire to establish a sort of *corpus moliericum* is best expressed by the creation of the *Moliériste,* a journal whose monthly publication extended from 1879 to 1889. Directed by G. Monval, a librarian and *archiviste* at the Comédie-Française, this journal became an instrument of official propaganda devoted to the cult of Molière. In his preface to the first issue, Monval pointed out that the *Moliériste* was directed not only to the "grands prêtres et adorateurs du Dieu," but also to the "chercheurs obscurs, moliérisants, moliérophiles, moliéromanes mêmes."[12] To establish with meticulous precision the various peregrinations of the of the Molière troupe in France and abroad; to verify, with the help of civil status documents, the identity of those who were related to the comic poet; to propose a new, unpublished source for a given play; and, finally, to present a purely dramatic criticism: these were some of the numerous aspects of the research undertaken by the team of Tascherau, Truffier, Mesnard, Souday, Lacroix, Lapommeraye, and others. A clearly hagiographic inspiration characterized a good number of these essays. One by one, the "pèlerinages" undertaken in the name of Molière, "le Maître," for many long years, were evoked; the Moliéristes considered themselves to be the *dévots* of their idol, invoking at the same time their "violente amour pour celui qui [leur] paraît être la plus complète incarnation du génie français."[13] Occasionally they took exception to a critic who disparaged their spirit of fanatic coterie and staunchly upheld their claim to the title of "Moliériste." Confronted with the virulent criticism of E. Scherer, the editors of the journal came to the rescue of their hero by alluding to Sainte-Beuve's famous passage, which, in fact, they designated as their "Credo."[14] Other articles scrutinize various objects that attain the status of relics and thereby reinforce the purely legendary dimension that crystallized around the comic poet. It is thus that Molière's famous armchair, the house in which he died, his tomb, his signature, and even his jawbone were all transformed into objects of erudite piety. There were also highly laudatory speeches delivered at commemorative banquets, to say nothing of the sonnets that were written to glorify the poet. Finally, an analysis of the *Moliériste* reveals a tendency to emphasize the anecdotal. The following story of "un cocher moliérophile" is one example: "Je passais, le lundi 28 novembre dernier, rue de Richelieu, et j'étais occupé à regarder la fontaine Molière, lorsqu'un cocher de fiacre, qui se dirigeait vers la place du Palais Royal, me cria du haut de son siège: 'Inclinez-vous devant le *Monsieur*!' Puis il fouetta ses chevaux et s'éloigna, après avoir tiré un grand coup de chapeau à l'auteur du *Tartuffe*."[15]

In spite of the uneven quality of certain pages of the *Moliériste,* the reader is forced to recognize the demonstrative rigor that characterizes several of these articles. Due to the growing number of public lectures—Sarcey, Faguet, and Lemaître delivered their lectures before publishing them as articles—the role of journalists, and especially the impetus provided by this partisan journal, the "Moliériste" movement managed to become organized, and it acquired an exceptional amplitude during the last thirty years of the nineteenth century. The Despois-Mesnard publication of 1882 can be considered justifiably the crowning glory of this prodigious scholarly activity on Molière.

To grasp the Molière phenomenon in its totality is to take into account a certain politicizing of this phenomenon in the course of the century. Although it was exploited for ideological purposes under the July Monarchy, this practice was resumed with particular vigor from the advent of the Third Republic on. A satisfactory understanding of this practice could hardly exclude an overview of the sociohistoric facts in question.

A turning point in the intellectual and moral history of France, 1870 inaugurated an era of national urgency: the crushing defeat of the Franco-Prussian War and the anguish of the Commune came as a highly emotional shock to the French, a profound moral jolt that forced upon them an attitude of meditative introspection. The shame and humiliation of an entire generation of young Frenchmen—represented by such diverse authors as Faguet, Lemaître, Sarcey, Lavisse, France, Bourget, Barrès—who experienced the defeat of 1870 as a stinging moral wound has not been sufficiently analyzed. The fruit of their collective meditation is what C. Digeon calls "a new intellectual structure,"[16] coinciding with the advent of the Third Republic. Republican ideology postulated the ideal of national regeneration as the supreme value. In this perspective the cult of the "unhappy homeland" and the reestablishment of institutions such as the family and the university dominated the thought of many intellectuals of the period. Thus, in its probe of the origins of the catastrophe of 1870, Taine's analysis of contemporary France was an essentially moral one.[17] The philosophical writings of A. Fouillée proposed the moral and intellectual reunification of the country as the necessary remedy.[18] Renan, describing the defeat as a "frightening moral collapse,"[19] attempted to console the national consciousness with his historical analyses. In short, it was a time of powerful patriotic resurgence characterized by the forging of a nationalistic ideology whose avowed purpose was the moral recovery of the country.

In this general crisis of conscience, the radical insufficiency of the national educational system came under particularly heavy fire. While Fouillée exhorted the French not to submit to an "intellectual Sedan,"[20] Renan, like many others, deplored the defects of the educational institution, to the point where he held it responsible for the defeat of 1870. In fact, there existed an abundant corpus of philosophical and pedagogical literature that dealt not only with numerous reform proposals but also with the moral function that the university should fulfill, a function that was seriously questioned after 1870. Seeing themselves, from that time on, invested with a moral obligation, teachers sought to mobilize the vitality of the nation's youth by inculcating in it the principles of a strongly developed sense of republican civicism. To the extent that moral and civic instruction formed an integral part of the academic curriculum—the teaching of of history, geography, and literature were especially affected by such preoccupations—the system of national education became the privileged domain of a profound patriotism, a patriotism that "fut ainsi élevé à la dignité d'une véritable religion laïque."[21]

Within this network of sociological and historical factors, the function of the Molière myth appears more clearly to us. In the first place, everything points to the fact that the development of a cultural nationalism nourished the Molière fervor. This strong, albeit paradoxical, confusion between nationalism and Moliérism is manifest in the writings of D. Saurat, for example, who exalted, with a dash of chauvinism, the Moliéresque notion of common sense.[22] In a pastiche of Sainte-Beuve's well-known eulogy, F. Flutre glorified the patriotic mission fulfilled by the author of the *Misanthrope*: "Aimer Molière enfin, qui possède à un si haut degré toutes les qualités de notre génie national, c'est comme nous le disions en commençant, c'est aimer, c'est servir la France."[23]

In still another domain Rageot summarized a speech delivered by E. Haraucourt on the occasion of the tricentennial of Molière. Acknowledging the therapeutic effect the latter had on France, the speaker stressed the necessity of turning to the comic poet "toutes les fois que nous avons à nous refaire. Il n'y a rien qui remette la France comme une cure de Molière."[24] Thus, according to this point of view, Molière's popularity increased in proportion to the moral concerns born out of profound social disturbances.

Such testimonials clearly demonstrated that in the last thirty years of the nineteenth century, Molière was becoming more and more the object of national glory, the epitome of France's cultural heritage. This phenomenon of hero-worshipping of Molière is firmly linked to the efforts on the part of the Catholic and secular bourgeoisie to establish an *ordre moral* (1873) that would imply "la restauration des disciplines monarchiques, religieuses, éducatives."[25] In this search for a purely national culture, the bourgeoisie was particularly reliant upon the erudite culture of the seventeenth century and drew from it the idealization of the *grand siècle,* a nostalgic return to a somewhat fantasized past; the *siècle de Louis XIV* thus became a privileged moment in French history, a period of cultural perfection characterized by clarity, restraint, and good taste. This search for past glory stems, in my opinion, from a defensive reflex typical of the bourgeoisie after 1870.[26] For this bourgeoisie that still maintained classical values, Molière was made the object of a kind of cultural authority, in truth, the object of a veritable national celebration. If at this time the myth of the comic poet acquired a profoundly bourgeois stature, it is because its function, according to A. Ubersfeld, was "installer rétrospectivement la classe bourgeoise dans l'éternité de la grandeur, de l'ordre et de la beauté classiques."[27] Being the most capable of transmitting seventeenth-century classical humanism, Molière, by his essentially human orientation, increasingly incarnated the specific cultural values of the *génie français.*

To the extent that the bourgeoisie assumed responsibility for the system of national education in order to ensure its own social mobility and class identification, it follows that the academic culture of the nineteenth century reflected these immediate preoccupations.[28] An inventory of the literary history manuals of the nineteenth century demonstrates to what point this bourgeoisie insisted upon the pedagogical usefulness of Molière's works. It endeavored to make of Molière an *instituteur national,* to extract from his works the constitutive elements of an inalterable morality capable of preserving national cohesion. Before examining specific examples it is necessary to review several basic postulates of classical humanism, a philosophy that permeated the manuals and, as a result, the various levels of education in nineteenth-century France.

As Villemain, Nisard, and Saint-Marc Girardin perceived it, the literature of the *grand siècle,* like that of Greco-Roman antiquity, offered eternal models of humanism. The classical works presupposed a transcendental metaphysics: the indissoluble alliance of truth, beauty, and goodness as well as the existence of a static, unchanging human nature. This classical vision was thus predicated on a fundamentally moral representation of the world, and it is hardly surprising that the school textbooks were devoid of historical specificity; rather, as we shall see, their purpose was to expose commonly accepted truths, to extract the timeless quality of these truths, a fact that explains their constant reliance upon selected passages, found in the vast majority of the anthologies of this period.

It is within this perspective that we find the academic clichés inspired by Molière in the nineteenth century: above all, what was sought in him was a canonical authority, implying the existence of an absolute truth; a sort of bourgeois bible was constructed from the numerous moral maxims found in his work. Apostle of the "golden mean," Molière thereby succeeded in teaching a secular philosophy based on moderation, wisdom, and common sense. He was often seen as the source of cleverly drawn proverbs; Faguet, in fact, referred to him as "the Sancho Panza of France."[29] The *prudhommesque* truths ponderously voiced by the bourgeois characters in his theater were often cited. We see here the origin of the excessive role attributed to his *raisonneurs,* those spokesmen of universal reason who faithfully translated the bourgeois moralism of their author. Sometimes perceived as enlightened philosophers, sometimes reduced to a series of normative models, the *raisonneurs* had, for some time, occupied an important position in Molière criticism.[30]

Another lesson drawn from this eminently practical morality is the utter futility of heroic virtue. Faguet, having drawn up a list of all the postulates of bourgeois common sense in Molière, gave preferential treatment to the notion that it was necessary to shun extremes systematically, to avoid risk carefully. It is true, of course, that this critic was struck by the mediocrity of these teachings, to the point that he saw in them, if not an antimorality, at least one "d'assez bas degré."[31] Other manuals insisted upon the ideal of mental hygiene, a veritable therapy contained in Molière's comedies. Des Granges and Doumic both felt that this morality was worthwhile precisely because of its healthy attitude, and Lafenestre praised the "salubrious" work effected by the comic poet.[32] Merlet and Lintillac portrayed the *Misanthrope* as a procession of characters each of whom represented a particular moral trait; their admiration for the moral perfection and truth of this play aside, they justified the filial indignity of Cléante by Harpagon's greed, believed to be a "degrading passion," invoking at the same time the implacable law of retribution: "like father, like son."[33] Although the comic poet did not dogmatize, according to Fournel, a good number of his plays illustrate "living models of dramatic morality."[34] Finally, in Lanson's famous manual we are told that in the work of Molière, the representation of the truth is always "pleasing and moral."[35]

Thus, owing to the oversimplified approach that characterized numerous nineteenth-century literary manuals, the image we are given of Molière is, of course, manifestly bourgeois: an evocation of his name immediately conjures the image of homemade soup, earthy language, and the homilies of everyday life that form an integral part of his philosophy. Moreover, the celebration of bourgeois virtues (such as marriage viewed as the natural result of love and family cohesion) being another essential component of the nineteenth-century image of the comic poet, we can agree wholeheartedly with the following comment by A. Albalet: "Il ne s'agit dans Molière que de position sociale, testaments, mariage, dot, notaire, contrat. C'est, on l'a dit, l'avènement du bourgeoisisme et du pot-au-feu au théâtre."[36]

Complementary to the role of the manuals in the formation of the Molière myth are the various critical editions of his theater in the nineteenth century. It is not difficult to understand the objection of Louis Jouvet to these editions, which, according to him, were characterized by "des soucis pédagogiques imbéciles."[37] On the whole, the editors were careful to relegate the purely entertaining aspect of the Molière repertory to a secondary position. Hence, arbitrary excisions were made in the farces, whose vulgarity was deemed as hardly edifying. With little concern for historical specificity, they preferred to deal with considerations of the psychology of the comic characters who were, in fact, nothing less than representatives of man envisioned *sub specie aeternitatis*; clearly, then, they were attempting to capture a timeless Molière. Furthermore, the moralizing intent of the editors is particularly striking. Although Despois and Mesnard praised the excellence of the lessons in the *Misanthrope*, they deplored the insufficiency of the moral study implicit in *Les Femmes savantes*.[38] In the Louandre edition we find a synthesis of nineteenth-century critical judgments that reveals, for example, that since farce is only acceptable when it does not offend morality, the moral intention of *Sganarelle* consists in correcting the sentiment of jealousy between husband and wife; in addition, one finds a justification of the treatment of ethical problems in *Les Femmes savantes*; Louandre presented Molière as "a great moralist," not only because of his depiction of vice, but more so because of his canonization of the virtues of Philinte and Chrysalde.[39] The Jouaust edition, annotated by G. Monval, begins with *L'Etourdi,* for farces were considered unworthy of the Molière repertory. Though being utterly scandalized by Angélique's wickedness, Monval ended up by sententiously justifying George Dandin's position.[40] Although his edition appeared somewhat later, Faguet also relegated the court diversions to a secondary level and focused instead on the morality of the *Mariage forcé*.[41] In all, the nineteenth-century editors of Molière's works generally discredited anything that stemmed from the purely aesthetic domain (elements of farcical gratuitousness, fantasylike dénouements, and so on) in order to heighten the ethical dimension of his work.

If the critical interpretations presented here tend to favor the development of the Molière myth, it is no less true that those who constituted the teaching establishment in the nineteenth century played an equally decisive role in this development. Thus, it would be appropriate to show the relationship between Moliérism and the nineteenth-century academic institution; that is, the articulation of the curriculum, pedagogical reforms, official directives, and the nature of examinations. Exactly what place did Molière occupy in the national educational policy of this period?

At this point we need to examine several salient features of nineteenth-century academic culture, a vast institutional complex to which Moliérism was closely linked. First, we know that this culture, throughout the century, accorded primary importance to the teaching of literature, and especially French literature. Believed to be an instrument of intellectualism and moral elevation, the study of French literature profited from the official decrees of 1821, 1863, 1872, and especially those, even more numerous, that extended from 1880 to 1902.[42] The purpose of rhetoric, a discipline replaced by literary history in 1880, was essentially to encourage students to assimilate works by the classical authors and to internalize these works by means of imitation. In theory, this mimetic practice was supposed to result in an admiration for the exemplary authors of the past. At the secondary and university levels, the curriculum was characterized by a preponderance of seventeenth-century authors; Renan emphasized the extent to which his teachers, namely Nisard and Saint-Marc Girardin, were able to present, between 1830 and 1850, the classical authors as heroic models to generations of French schoolchildren.[43] Lavisse, Brunetière, and Lanson, recalling their own experiences as students, stated that the majority of their readings were drawn from a book of classical theater and a book of texts selected from seventeenth-century moralists.[44] Furthermore, the various ministers of public education in the nineteenth century, from Villemain to Ferry, advocated the pedagogical virtues of classical French literature.[45]

The university was thus permeated with works of the past; the fact that it exalted them as models was the result of a secular bourgeoisie desirous of recapturing the heritage of the *grand siècle*. This bourgeoisie created a pedagogical apparatus that allowed for the acculturation of its own fundamental values, a type of self-integrating culture in which this class could sing its own praises. The abundance of academic legislation enacted during the last thirty years of the century can be explained, to a great extent, by the policy of cultural nationalism adopted by the bourgeoisie. Especially after 1870, with patriotism believed to be the supreme remedy for the ideological battles between public and congregationalist schools, many professors, notably those wishing to establish a new type of pedagogy, took nationalistic considerations into account. Thus, in the name of national unity, A. Fouillée recommended a return to the study of French classical culture and the simultaneous study of French and Latin, both of which were to be undertaken within the context of an essentially moralistic approach. The course in civics that he proposed to elementary school teachers first studied the duties and obligations of the seventeenth-century *honnête homme* (*classe de quatrième*) and then those of the good citizen of the time *(classe de troisième).*[46] Proclaiming the moral bankruptcy of all the aspirations that had animated his era, Brunetière maintained that classical French literature must remain the gravitational center for academic curricula. This apologist of patriotic and social duty was sensitive to the "vertus éducatrices tout à fait singulières" offered by this literature as well as its undeniable originality and universality.[47] For his part, G. Boissier proposed a new plan of study wherein French—the discipline most capable of nourishing nationalistic fervor—occupied a privileged position in the secondary curriculum.[48]

The functioning of the Molière myth at every level of French education in the nineteenth century is thus clearly perceptible. And, if one further takes into account the importance of the classroom assignments of this period, such as French composition and explication de texte, the myth assumes even greater proportions. In 1872 prizes were awarded for compositions in language and literature. By 1880 this type of exercise replaced the Latin composition required for the *baccalauréat*. Even more importantly, French composition was invested with an ideological function within the academic machinery, in the sense that it represented the ideal means of attaining high moral truths and internalizing them. A. Labuda cites an academic anthology of the period that is particularly enlightening in this respect: "Chaque morceau . . . , en offrant un exercice de lecture soignée, de mémoire, de déclamation, d'analyse, de développement, et de critique, est en même temps une leçon de vertu, d'humanité ou de justice, de religion, de dévouement au Prince, et à la Patrie, de désintéressement ou d'amour du bien public. Tout dans ce Recueil est le fruit du génie, du talent, de la vertu; tout y respire et le goût le plus exquis et la morale la plus pure."[49] It is thus not difficult to imagine the extent to which the tirades of Molière's *raisonneurs* were used as exemplary models of proper moral conduct.

As for the modus operandi of the explication de texte, a fundamental exercise at the secondary level, an analogous mechanism can be seen. In 1890 the minister of public education lauded the pedagogical virtues of the explication de texte, and C. Falcucci pointed out the originality of this reform, which ultimately rendered this exercise indispensable to nineteenth-century academic culture.[50] Teachers were encouraged to choose carefully the passages to be explicated, and preferably to choose those that would allow the students to reflect upon the moral nature of man; at the same time, these passages would transmit the values of the national patrimony. Thus conceived, the explication de texte, officially established by the reform of 1902, purported to extract the universality of the works of classical authors, thereby constituting a masterful lesson in the moral philosophy of esteemed authors.

This official process of moralization by the indirect means of the teaching of literature is especially noticeable in the area of topics concerning Molière proposed for various competitive examinations. It would be helpful, therefore, to show the rather tendentious orientation of such subjects; in this respect, the following list is revelatory:

1. "Que pensez-vous de ce vers de Molière: 'Je veux une vertu qui ne soit point diablesse' et quelle idée personnelle vous faites-vous de la vertu?" (compostion on morality, subject proposed in a lycée, third year, 1893).

2. "Que pensez-vous de ces paroles de Molière: 'Rien ne reprend mieux la plupart des hommes que la peinture de leurs défauts'?" (French composition, proposed at Sèvres, 1895).

3. "En quoi l'amitié peut-elle aider au développement de notre être moral?" (*Agrégation des lettres,* 1897).

4. "Voudriez-vous avoir un ami comme Philinte du *Misanthrope?*" (French composition, secondary level, girls' school, 1898).[51]

An inexhaustible source of examination questions (for compositions and explications de texte), Molière also figured prominently in most curricula. In 1893 Lanson, having examined the academic programs from the class of *sixième* to the class of *rhétorique,* recommended the extension of Molière's comedies to the third, fourth, fifth, and sixth years of secondary training.[52]

Many authors from Renan to Taine, including C. Bigot, attempted to ascribe to the teaching of literature of kind of therapeutic or moral function at work in the interest of national unity. This was due in part to a progressive dechristianization, which was a salient feature of nineteenth-century French institutions. As Thiers so aptly stated: "Les belles lettres seront toujours pour moi les bonnes lettres. . . . Quand la religion est affaiblie en un pays, la morale s'appuie avant tout sur les grands exemples que donne l'exemple du passé."[53] The legislative contribution of J. Ferry, minister of public education after 1871, becomes even more significant when viewed from this perspective. Partisan of the laicization of the educational system and of morality itself, Ferry proposed, in 1872, his famous law concerning secularity, legislation that aimed at inculcating a child with the constitutive elements of universal morality (obedience, duty, virtue, and so forth), that is, the morality exemplified by decent men of all times and in all countries. Thus, in order to ensure the national unity that had been imperiled by the war and the disastrous experience of the Commune, it was absolutely essential, according to Ferry, to establish the unity of a positivist morality stripped of all religious trappings, in short, a morality that meets the requirements of republican ideology:

La vraie morale, la grande morale, la morale éternelle, c'est la morale sans épithète. La morale, grâce à Dieu, dans notre société française, après tant de siècles de civilisation, n'a pas besoin d'être définie, la morale est plus grande quand on ne la définit pas, elle est plus grande sans épithète.

C'est la bonne vieille morale de nos pères, la nôtre, la vôtre, car nous n'en avons qu'une.[54]

From here we are only a step away from the secular philosophy that nineteenth-century critics tried to extract from Molière's works. And, as we have seen, the nationalistic sentiment that they evinced, especially after 1870, served only to nourish further their belief in the Molière myth.

In the course of this essay, I have tried to point out the specific nature of the Molière myth in its various manifestations in nineteenth-century France. The progressive codification of the various elements of the comic poet's moral system corresponds, both historically and sociologically, to periods of political recovery: from 1830 to 1848, and, in a more striking manner, from 1870 to the First World War. Under the July Monarchy and the Third Republic, the official bourgeois ideology sought to transmit a clearly codified image of a Molière inspired by classical reason and clarity, one intent on depicting characters motivated by the psychology of "eternal man." The reification of Molière, his transformation into a privileged academic subject, and the efficacy of peda-gogical practices at all levels tend to make of the playwright an excellent instrument of moral and civic education, while at the same time articulating at the national level the bourgeois virtues of order and authority. The ideological motivations that underlie the structure of such an educational system are thus easily discernible.

That this essentially nineteenth-century image of Molière persists into the twentieth century, and even, although in a somewhat mitigated fashion, right up to the present, can be ascertained not only by the continuation of traditional pedagogical approaches but also by the fact that many French people today, educated in the last thirty or forty years, are more than reticent about rereading the classical authors in a new light. Their disaffection stems, in my view, from the moralistic and, at times, stultifying presentation of these authors to which they were subjected during their years of intellectual training. Is it surprising? Cultural myths die hard.

---

1. Jean Anouilh, "Présence de Molière," *Cahiers de la Compagnie Madeleine Renaud–Jean-Louis Barrault* 26 (1959): 4

2. G. Lanson, *Histoire illustrée de la littérature française* (Paris: Hachette, 1923), p. 396.

3. The 1,278 performances of *Tartuffe* at the Comédie-Française give a clear indication of the enormous popularity of this play from 1815 to 1829. In addition, Hugo praised the poetic merits of Molière; he particularly admired the versification of *L'Etourdi*. In Michelet's view, however, the poet would also have suffered from being reduced to the role of a mere court entertainer for Louis XIV.

4. On this subject see the excellent article by Henri Peyre, "Stendhal and Balzac as Admirers and Followers of Molière," in *Molière and the Commonwealth of Letters: Patrimony and Posterity,* ed. R. Johnson, Jr., E. Neumann, and G. Trail (Jackson: University Press of Mississippi, 1973), pp. 133–44.

5. See Désiré Nisard, *Histoire de la littérature française,* vol. 3 (Paris: Didot, 1844). Considering Nisard, toward the end of the century, as the "maître incontesté des esprits," P. Bourgin defined the critic's doctrine in terms of traditional classical humanism (see *L'Enseignement du français* [Paris: F. Alcan, 1911] , pp. 4–5).

6. Translation mine, here, as in subsequent quoted examples.

7. Nisard, p. 248.

8. *Œuvres complètes de Molière,* ed. C. Louandre, 3 vols. (Paris: Charpentier, 1958), 2:58.

9. C. A. Sainte-Beuve, *Nouveaux lundis* (Paris: Calmann-Lévy, 1884), pp. 277–78. See also idem, *Port Royal,* 7 vols. (Paris: Hachette, 1901), 3:274–76.

10. R. Molho, *La Critique littéraire en France au XIXème siècle* (Paris: Buchet-Chastel, 1963), p. 16.

11. A. Bazin, *Notes historiques sur la vie de Molière* (Paris: Techenor, 1851); E. Soulié, *Recherches sur Molière et sur sa famille* (Paris: Hachette, 1863); E. Compardon, *Documents inédits sur J. B. Poquelin Molière . . .* (Paris, Plon, 1871).

12. G. Monval, preface, *Moliériste* 1 (1880).

13. Preface, *Moliériste* 4 (1882–83): 39.

14. Ibid. Although somewhat later, Brunetière also set forth a disparaging criticism of the excesses of the Moliéristes, in "Trois Moliéristes," *Revue des deux mondes* 54 (1884): 700.

15. E. Marnicouche, "Un Cocher moliérophile," *Moliériste* 3 (1882): 304.

16. C. Digeon, *La Crise allemande de la pensée française (1870–1914)* (Paris: PUF, 1959), p. 102.

17. H. Taine, *Les Origines de la France contemporaine,* 6 vols. (Paris: Hachette, 1888–94).

18. A. Fouillée, *La Conception morale et civique de l'enseignement* (Paris: Revue Bleue, 1902); "Les Projets d'enseignement classique français au point de vue national," *Revue des deux mondes* 60 (September 1890): 241–72; "L'Education morale et sociale de la démocratie," *Revue politique et littéraire* 36 (January–June 1899): 6–10, 447–50, 706–12; *Les Etudes classiques et la démocratie* (Paris: Colin, 1898).

19. J. E. Renan, *La Réforme intellectuelle et morale* (Paris: M. Lévy, 1872), p. 119.

20. Fouillée, "Les Projets d'enseignement classique français," p. 268.

21. Digeon, p. 366. V. Isambert-Jamati quotes several speeches that, delivered at nineteenth-century awards ceremonies, emphasized the close integration of republican civicism into the academic domain. See *Crises de la société, crises de l'enseignement* (Paris: PUF, 1970), p. 126.

22.   Je prends tout bonnement les hommes comme ils sont . . .
            La parfaite raison fuit toute extrémité
            Et veut que l'on soit sage avec sobriété.

"C'est là, en somme, ce que la France a appris au monde. Et dans la pratique, c'est ce bon sens d'apparence médiocre qui s'applique le mieux sur la réalité, qui donne le plus de résultats. Ce peuple de bon sens et de mesure compte, à cause de cela, parmi les grands soldats, les grands constructeurs, les bons fabricants, les meilleurs colonisateurs du monde. C'est donc que ce bon sens n'est pas 'superficiel,' mais correspond à quelque chose d'essentiel et mord sur le monde extérieur" (D. Saurat, *Tendances* [Paris: Editions du monde moderne, 1928], p. 9).

23. F. Flutre, *Molière* (Paris: Hachette, 1926), p. 62. Within this same perspective, F. Sarcey dealt with Molière's beneficent influence on contemporary society in an article that was written at the very time that Paris was under siege by German troops. Depicting the Germans as sadistic barbarians who, in their desire to demoralize the Parisian populace, would not hesitate to destroy the Comédie-Française, Sarcey made the comic poet a war horse that remained invulnerable to the

rapacity of the Germans, motivated by their envy of his glory ("Influence de Molière sur le monde civilisé," in *Quarante ans de théâtre* [Paris: Bibliothèque des Annales, 1900], 2: 3–14). See also V. Fournel, *Le Théâtre au XVIIème siècle: La Comédie* (Paris: Oudin, 1892), p. 227.

24. G. Rageot, "A propos du tri-centenaire de Molière," *Revue politique et littéraire* 62 (January 1922): 95.

25. C. Falcucci, *L'Humanisme dans l'enseignement secondaire en France au XIXème siècle* (Toulouse: Privat, 1939), pp. 325–26.

26. On this point see Isambert-Jamati, p. 113.

27. A. Ubersfeld and R. Monod, "Molière: Trois cent ans," *La Nouvelle Critique* 69 (December 1973): 72.

28. Especially pertinent in this respect is the article by S. Citron, "Enseignement secondaire et idéologie élitiste entre 1880 et 1914," *Le Mouvement social* 96 (July–September 1976): 81–101. See also Isambert-Jamati, pp. 125 ff., 332–33.

29. E. Faguet, *Œuvres complètes de Molière,* ed. Lutetia, 6 vols. (Paris: Nelson, 1919), 1:12.

30. Such views are proposed and discussed, for example, by E. Blondet in his "Une Erreur à propos de Molière," *Moliériste* 4 (1882–83): 274–75.

31. Faguet, p. 15.

32. C. Des Granges, *Histoire de la littérature française* (Paris: Hatier, 1909); R. Doumic, *Histoire de la littérature française* (Paris: Delaplane, 1891); G. Lafenestre, *Molière* (Paris: Hachette, 1909), p. 158.

33. G. Merlet and E. Lintillac, *Etudes littéraires sur les classiques français* (Paris: Hachette, 1894), pp. 480–81.

34. Fournel, p. 227.

35. Lanson, p. 386.

36. A. Albalet, *Comment il faut lire les auteurs classiques français* (Paris: Colin, 1913), p. 179. Gauthier, for his part, denounced this narrow "bourgeois" interpretation of Molière: "C'est un grand événement de la Bourgeoisie que Molière, une solennelle déclaration de L'âme du Tiers-Etat. J'y vois l'inauguration du bon sens et de la raison pratique, la fin de toute chevalerie et de toute haute poésie en toutes choses. La femme, l'amour, toutes les folies nobles, galantes, y sont ramenées à la mesure étroite du ménage et de la dot. Tout ce qui est élan et de premier mouvement y est averti et corrigé. . . . Molière est le premier poète des bourgeois" (*Journal des Goncourt* [Paris: Charpentier, 1891], 1:315).

37. Quoted by J. Malignon in his *Dictionnaire des écrivains classiques* (Paris: Seuil, 1971), p. 324.

38. *Œuvres de Molière,* ed. Despois and Mesnard, 13 vols (Paris: Hachette, 1873–1900), 5:375; 9:4.

39. *Œuvres complètes,* ed. Louandre, 1:lxix: "Philinthe est le maître absolu de la morale sociale, et Chrysalde, le maître souverain de la morale domestique."

40. *Théâtre complet de Molière,* ed. D. Jouaust, 8 vols. (Paris: Librairie des bibliophiles, 1882), 5:387–88.

41. Faguet, 2:357.

42. On this matter, see Falcucci. The official decrees of 1890 exalted the role of literary studies in the national education program. See *Instructions, programmes et règlements* (Ministère de l'Education nationale) (Paris: Imprimerie Nationale, 1890), pp. 32, xi.

43. Quoted by H. Peyre in *Qu'est-ce que le classicisme?* (Paris: Droz, 1933), p. 29: "Ce sera, je crois, une époque qui marquera dans l'histoire littéraire que celle où les écrivains du siècle de Louis XIV ont été définitivement reconnus comme classiques et comme tels panthéonisés parmi nous."

44. See P. Nora, "Ernest Lavisse, son rôle dans la formation du sentiment national," *Revue historique* 228 (July–September 1962): 73–106; F. Brunetière, "Sur l'organisation de l'enseignement secondaire français," *Revue des deux mondes* 61 (1891): 214–25; and G. Lanson, G. Rudler,

et al., *L'Enseignement du français* (Paris: Imprimerie Nationale, 1909), p. 12. See also Lavisse's "Souvenirs d'une éducation manquée," quoted by A. Prost in *L'Enseignement en France, 1800–1967* (Paris: Colin, 1968), p. 62.

45. F. Villemain's famous speech, quoted by Falcucci (p. 179), represents a stirring tribute to seventeenth-century French literature.

46. Fouillée, *La Conception morale et civique de l'enseignement,* p. 148.

47. Brunetière, "Sur l'organisation de l'enseignement secondaire français," pp. 218–22.

48. G. Boissier, "Le Nouveau Plan d'études," *Revue des deux mondes* 50 (September 1880): 101–23. See also G. Lanson, "L'Unité morale du pays et l'Université," *Revue politique et littéraire* 47 (January 1907): 10–11.

49. A. Labuda, "La Langue de l'empereur: La Culture littéraire dans les lycées sous le Second Empire," *Littérature* 22 (May 1976): 86.

50. Falcucci, p. 417.

51. These questions appeared in the *Revue universitaire* (1893–98). For further examples of similar composition topics dealing with Molière from the 1880s, see F. Hémon, *Cours de littérature,* vol. 5 (Paris: Delagrave, 1893).

52. G. Lanson, "L'Etude des auteurs français," *Revue universitaire* 2 (1893): 258.

53. Quoted by P. Kuentz in "L'Envers du texte," *Littérature* 7 (1972): 20. C. Bigot upheld the validity of teaching literature by relating it to the nobility of the national genius and to the civilizing mission of France, which was "par son génie, une race toute littéraire" ("Les Réformes universitaires," *Revue politique et littéraire* 21 [December 1884]: 781).

54. Sénat, 1881; quoted by Prost, p. 196.

Interpréter un texte, ce n'est pas lui donner
un sens (plus ou moins fondé, plus ou moins
libre), c'est au contraire apprécier de quel
pluriel il est fait.

Barthes

Dialogue and Intertextuality:
The Posterity of Diderot's *Neveu de Rameau*

CHRISTIE V. McDONALD

As a writer, Diderot was preoccupied with the reader as interlocutor and made explicit, for instance, that for the great *Encyclopedia* posterity would constitute finally its only valid interlocutor. Curiously, the external history of the *Neveu de Rameau,* a work unknown to the reading public of the eighteenth century, exemplifies the very problem of finding its interlocutor that Diderot had prophesied for his encyclopedia. The text was first published in Goethe's translation in 1805, only appearing in France in 1821,[1] and it raises certain questions both about strategies of authorial composition and about the history of interpretation as well. A juxtaposition of Diderot's *Neveu de Rameau* with one particular reading from the nineteenth century, E. T. A. Hoffmann's *Ritter Gluck,* reveals a displacement from the intersubjective relationship traditionally associated with dialogue into an intertextual one. Indeed, it is with respect to the twofold problem of dialogue and intertextuality that I wish to situate the following schematic reading and thereby relate the status of dialogue as writing to the problem of a literary heritage; for the explicit and unabashed relationship between these texts suggests that the themes that recur are concomitant with the premises that underlie the works themselves: the question of artistic genius, dialogue, the status of the subject in language.

How and why does one talk about the posterity of a text? To show that it was important in generating a literary movement? To show it as the source of another work? Or to show that, in some way, it prefigures the problems of modernity? All of these questions are, in some sense, valid questions; all are tricky. It is the purpose of this essay to deal with such genetic questioning only insofar as it is immanent within the texts themselves and, specifically, as it relates to one major and overriding question: that of interpretation. By interpretation one may understand, first, those performances of pantomime in which the virtuosity of the mutilated genius becomes evident in the *Neveu de Rameau.* Second, the question of interpretation will arise as it is manifest in the musical performance described in Hoffmann's tale. Finally, as an outgrowth of the more limited meanings, interpretation will come to include the ways in which one text interprets another in the process of rewriting it. The choice of texts for this topic is clearly not neutral and involves the arbitrary decision to juxtapose two fictive texts: one might well prefer to play critical readings off against one another or to trace the changes that occur, for example, when a text is translated from one language to another. What can one say, indeed, about a text that reiterates another text and that is neither a translation nor a critical commentary? At the end of his book entitled *Lectures de Diderot,* Jacques Proust not only indicates that a history of criticism might be written from the illustrious posterity of Diderot's texts—passing through the hands of such notables as Hegel, Marx, Engels, Foucault, and more—but he remarks rather wistfully: "Mais il n'est pas sûr que les meilleurs lecteurs de Diderot soient ceux qui parlent ostensiblement et surtout professionnellement de lui. Je rêve d'un livre qui serait l'antidote de celui-ci et où, à la limite, le nom même de l'auteur pourrait n'être prononcé. Ce pourrait être aussi un montage de textes et d'images—mais on y recontrerait Hoffmann, plutôt que Rosenkranz, Baudelaire plutôt que Faguet, Dostoievski plutôt que Bilbassov."[2] Although primarily concerned throughout the book with those ideological presuppositions that underlie the reading given to Diderot's texts, Proust seems not to question the radical division between criticism and literature. Such an opposition divides, roughly speaking, into those who would consider criticism as a metalanguage and, in contrast, those who would view it as merely a part of the larger system of writing (*écriture*), hence refusing any distinction that valorizes the artistic over the critical work.[3]

In examining the intertextual weave between Hoffmann's and Diderot's texts, I take as a premise that there is a critical function at work that does not allow for the simple passage of meaning in the transfer from one fictive text to another; and, further, that it is this critical function that is most difficult to grasp and that ultimately puts into question the notion of interpretation. Inevitably, then, the question of how any other text—this one, for example—tampers with such a transposition repeats, if only tacitly, many of the same questions that are raised at both a thematic and a structural level in the *Neveu de Rameau* and *Ritter Gluck.* Put briefly, what is the nature of written language, whether it be critical or fictive?

It is with respect to the status of the subject in language, particularly written language, that two modes of dialogue may be introduced: one in which language functions smoothly as communication, presupposing two subjects anterior to the discursive encounter and reverting to both meaning and truth; the other in which language no longer functions smoothly as communication, in which a disruption or dispersion takes place that prevents any totalizing process of meaning.

Regarding the first mode, no one sums up better than Emile Benveniste the tradition in which language as communication is fundamentally allocutionary, fundamentally dialogue. Benveniste asks, If language is an instrument of communication, to what does it owe this property? His response is that it is the condition of dialogue that constitutes the subject in language, for it implies the reciprocity of the "I" and the "thou" ("je"/"tu"). It is the condition of intersubjectivity (subjectivity understood here as the appropriation of language by the subject) that renders possible linguistic communication, and, further, the reciprocity between "I" and "thou" that makes possible all social bonds.[5] The second mode of dialogue has perhaps been most efficiently codified by Bakhtin's use of the term *dialogic*,[6] which involves three principal elements: writing, the receptor, and other texts. The status of the word, then, is defined first horizontally, as belonging to an emitter and receptor, and then vertically, related to the exterior corpus of literature. That is, the dialogic demands a reevaluation of both the notion of the subject and that of meaning, and this may be done through analysis of dialogue and examination of the relationship among texts. What is interesting is that Bakhtin suggests that the relationships that structure narrative are possible because the dialogic is inherent in language itself.[7] Both Bakhtin and Benveniste, though each in a radically different way, seem to be making claims about the nature of language through dialogue, whether in its limited or more diffused sense; and—what is more—Bakhtin links the dialogic to the problem of intertextuality.

The precise sense in which the eighteenth century understood the philosophical dialogue was that of a system closed upon itself in which, taking off from an initial question, the interlocutors progress from the resolution of one given difficulty to another, going through all the objections until an answer is given to the initial question—all this in order to arrive at truth.[8] Just how Diderot channels the tradition of the philosophic dialogue and plays upon it is a complex matter, for almost all of his writing is laced with dialogue at one level or another. In a work such as the *Supplément au voyage de Bougainville,* Diderot turns the dialogue against itself and maintains a constant tension between the monologic and the dialogic. In the article entitled "Encyclopédie" of the vast *Encyclopedia*—in which Diderot attempts to account for the monologic totality of the work through a fragment—dialogue seems oddly enough to have both a stochastic as well as an apocalyptic function; he states that such projects as the *Encyclopedia* are proposed through accidents and in the form of a dialogue. The explicit goal of the work is to assemble all knowledge, to set forth its general system for those "avec qui nous vivons, et de le transmettre aux hommes qui viendront après nous."[9] In this quest for knowledge as truth, in the search for the constant—that is, the search for the invariant through the multiplicity of things—posterity was to be that invariable measure, and the guarantor of truthful dialogue to remain anchored in an unknown future generation referred to time and time again as "our nephews." Such a utopian vision is tested and strained to the limit in the work that takes the word *nephew* as the key element of its title.

The *Neveu de Rameau* is the story, in dialogue form, of a nephew whose uncle was a musical genius, whose interlocutor ("Moi") is a man of reason and morality, and whose identity has been the subject of major readings and interpretations ever since it was first published. If, as Diderot suggests elsewhere, in everything one must begin at the beginning, one might describe the story of the *Neveu de Rameau* as an encounter, seemingly accidental, that becomes a fragmentary inquiry into the origins and nature of a social parasite, "Lui," whose depravation is such as to put into question the social order as a whole. A long-standing tradition of criticism, which begins with Hegel's remarkable reading of the *Neveu de Rameau* in the Phenomenology of Mind,[10] has tended to make of this conversation between the philosopher, "Moi"—a man of reason without sect or prejudice—and the parasite, "Lui," a philosophical dialogue in which two opposing positions are put into dialectical confrontation; that is, on the one hand, the nephew shows the coherence of biological determinism and morality, in effect building a case for the legitimacy of anarchy and individual immoralism, whereas on the other, the philosopher defends reason and morality above and beyond the immediate needs and desires of the individual. The purpose of this essay is not to go back over this tradition but rather to concentrate on the relationship that "Lui" entertains with music in pantomime, for it is through this relationship that a series of highly charged oppositions arises between reason and madness, truth and falsity, genius and plagiarism. Let us consider the antitheses present in the latter pairing. The nephew is constantly forced to define himself by what he is not—a genius—and the title of the work alone relegates him to the position of a poor relation, deprives him of a proper name, and seemingly dooms him to the social parasite that he clearly and most cheerfully is throughout. The inadequacy of his own identity is thus to be measured in its relation to the other, Jean Philippe Rameau, whose plenitude of being may be equated with his status as genius. When he expresses jealousy for his uncle's talent and celebrity, he points to the works as if they were transparent reflections of the inspired genius.[11] The genetic quest for the individual self is not separable, it would seem, from the origins of the work of art.

The nephew's identity is both constituted and contaminated by plagiarism. Where he excels is in role-playing, and his particular virtuosity becomes manifest through the numerous pantomimes of the text, which are doubled by the narrator's description and alternate with the dialogued conversation. The pantomimes in which he plays an instrument, sings, even becomes an entire orchestra are an impromptu spectacle in which the talent of musical performance is feigned.

Let us look at two examples of pantomime from the *Neveu de Rameau* in which the nephew simulates the interpretation of a musician. In the first example, having imitated the most privileged of all the instruments next to the voice—that is, the violin—the nephew now sets about to play the harpsichord. As elsewhere in the text, the pantomime is presented by the narrator, who addresses an unknown interlocutor and recounts the scene that he is witnessing. As the nephew plays, the narrator describes the various passions that sweep fleetingly across the nephew's face, so much so that one initiated into these matters might be able to recognize the piece from the nephew's expressions, his movements, and the isolated notes of song that escape from time to time.[12] Head up, he looks toward the ceiling as though he were reading the musical score. Unlike the previous performance, however, this one is flawed. Every now and again he gropes about and starts again as if he had made a mistake and his fingers no longer knew where to go.[13]

One can distinguish here at least two levels at which the problem of artistic interpretation and creation is posed. The first is that of written notation. In this scene the nephew seems to interpret the score of another composer. The questions implicit here, and explicit elsewhere in discussions about the problem of genius, are how the work (the musical score) comes to be and who produces it. Here there is already a certain remove, since the nephew is only interpreting the music of another, and, at that, it is not a perfect performance. If, indeed, the genetic quest for the individual self is not separable from the origins of the work, this scene shows just how far the nephew really is from the plenitude of being. The second level at which one may pose the problem of artistic creation is, then, that of the interpretation itself, the actual performance.

In the imitation of musical interpretation the nephew cannot be matched: he is supreme. Music in pantomime signals oddly enough at once the unique source of genius and its seeming disruption in madness: "je musiquais . . . je faisais le fou," says the nephew.[14] Since for Diderot, here as elsewhere, the arts stand homologously one to the other (architecture, painting, music, and writing), one may wonder whether the chaotic relationship between the mutilated genius and his absent uncle does not couch a more general statement about interpretation as the constant disruption of the creative subject.

Perplexed by the extraordinary display of pantomimes, the character "Moi" says to "Lui," "vous vous êtes donné bien de la peine, pour me montrer que vous étiez fort habile; j'étais homme à vous croire sur votre parole." Thus the pantomime, which is proper only to the nephew, is supplementary to spoken discourse, and in a passage from *De la poésie dramatique,* Diderot stresses the relationship of pantomime to language: "J'ai tâché de séparer tellement les deux scènes simultanées . . . qu'on pourrait les imprimer à deux colonnes où l'on verrait la pantomime de l'une correspondre au discours de l'autre et celle-ci correspondre alternativement à la pantomime de celle-là. Ce partage serait commode pour celui qui lit, et qui n'est pas fait au mélange du discours et du mouvement."[15]

The encyclopedic image of columns divided into, on the one hand, pantomime and, on the other, spoken discourse apparently serves the reader in making clear just how one complements the other. Indeed, if one is the substitute for the other, one the completion of the other, then one may postulate gesture in pantomime as the figurative that refers to spoken language as the proper. Such a view of language carries with it the hopeful reassurance that the function of language is to signify—crucial for the encyclopedic undertaking—and that its guarantor may be found in the notion of truth. By extension, gesture as the substitute for language will also signify, for, as Diderot says, "le geste doit s'écrire souvent à la place du discours."[16]

However, the nephew's pantomimes do not fulfill this function. Through them he blurs the lines, crosses the divide between mind and matter, reason and madness and, in so doing, puts into question the possibility for an intersubjective relationship through language. Indeed, how is the narrator adequately to explain and describe those pantomimes that constantly exceed language in their play? The nephew's positions are, it would seem, nontotalizable.

If the first example of pantomime, in the harpsichord scene, makes explicit questions relating to creation and interpretation, the second example points directly to the problem of signification. In this second example "Moi" asks "Lui" why he has not created a work of beauty, and "Lui" responds without seeming to pay any attention to the question. Instead, he recounts the story of Abbé Le Blanc, who was taken and led by the hand to the door of the academy, where he fell and broke both legs. When a man of the world suggests that he get up and break open the door, the abbé replies that he did just that and received a large bump on his forehead. At this the nephew widly thumps his own forehead in search of the meaning of this story, and as he thumps he says, "ou il n'y a personne, ou l'on ne veut pas répondre," as though in conversation with an absent inner interlocutor whose function is to make sense. Then suddenly coming to life with a burst of passion, he concludes: "seul, je prends la plume; je veux écrire. Je me ronge les ongles; je m'use le front. Serviteur. Bonsoir. Le dieu est absent; je m'étais persuadé que j'avais du génie; au bout de ma ligne, je lis que je suis un sot, un sot, un sot."[17] Writing as the search for meaning in the context of an inner dialogue thus gives way to an image of reading in which his own genius is undone. The parody of self here is the last hold of meaning and unity, for if there is no unified subject, then there can be no meaning.[18] Pantomime, as it is charged with excessive meaning in its inessentiality, thus puts into question the possibility of language as communication, the possibility of language as dialogue.

Let us now turn to *Ritter Gluck* in order to examine briefly the way in which Hoffmann rearticulates the problems of artistic creation and genius. Just as in the *Neveu de Rameau,* the story begins with an encounter between two people in a café: the narrator and a man whose presence becomes instantly compelling to him. There is a descriptive prologue, again as in the *Neveu de Rameau,* in which the narrator recounts his state of reverie and his imaginary conversations.[19] During all of this there is the sound of such harsh and unpleasant music in the background that the narrator speaks of the "cacophonic racket," "the screeching upper register of the violins and flute," "the octaves that lacerate the ear."[20] However, when the orchestra begins the overture to Gluck's *Iphigenia in Aulis,* the man suddenly begins to play and conduct in pantomime, and precisely at this moment the narrator describes how meaning transcends the initial chaos and how beautiful music comes to replace the unbearable din. As the piece ends, the curious man emerges from the pantomime as if from a dream and pronounces himself satisfied with the performance; yet the narrator is quick to remind him that "only the pale outlines of a masterpiece that has been composed with vivid colors was presented." The man confesses that he has been a composer himself, and that although music and composing, in particular, seem to be the only path to truth and the ineffable, he decided to give it all up because those pieces written in moments of inspiration "afterwards seemed to be flat and boring."[21]

Part 2, if one may arbitrarily divide the tale by the various geographical locales, takes place at the Brandenburg gate, where the strange man hears what no one else does: the sound of the EUPHON, which remains an enigma throughout. When their discussion now happens onto the performances that certain composers' works enjoy in Berlin—specifically those of Gluck's works—the man rails against transgressions of the composers' intentions, again, in the *Iphigenia.*

Although the first part of the tale is almost a line-for-line adaptation of the *Neveu de Rameau,* a shift in emphasis nevertheless develops: first, in the man's relationship to dreams and otherworldliness, and second, in the focus on, and primacy of, the ideal performance. It is this second aspect that part 3 amplifies in a most striking way.

Part 3 begins when the narrator, as he is heading home one night, passes by a theater in which Gluck's *Armida* is being performed, and he decides to go to the performance. As he is about to enter the theater, he spies the same strange man outside the window. Although unable to see what is happening within, the man delivers a soliloquy outside the theater in which he repeats through language the actions of the singers and the progressions of the musical movements. At the same time he gives a rather agonized critique of what is happening. The narrator—and, by the way, neither of their names has yet been given, seemingly by mutual agreement—wishing to take his curious interlocutor away from the theater, allows himself to be led to the man's house. As they enter, he sees a piano in the middle of an ornate living room on which are to be found pen, ink, and paper for writing music. Behind a curtain on a shelf stand all of Gluck's masterpieces in large bound copies. These are the complete works. The man picks the score of the *Armida* from the shelf, for upon leaving the theater he had promised the narrator a performance of that same work. He places the book on the piano, and as it is opened the narrator discovers that there is not a single note written in it. The man then sits down at the piano and obliges the narrator to turn pages at the right moment, something he can only glean by watching the man's glance. He commences to play and, as he performs the piece, introduces myriads of new and inspired twists. The narrator is totally overwhelmed and exclaims: "What is it? Who are you?"[22] The man disappears briefly, leaving the narrator in the dark (literally, the room is darkened), then returns richly attired, strides toward him, takes him by the hand, and, smiling strangely, says: "I am Ritter Gluck."

It would be needlessly tedious to enumerate the many similarities and differences between Diderot's and Hoffmann's texts. It will suffice to compare the ending of the tale with the pantomime mentioned earlier. Whereas in the nephew's flawed performance on the harpsichord he mimed reading the musical score, here the force of genius can be sensed in the inspired performance with its slight deviations from a score whose absence becomes manifest through its physical presence (the blank pages of the book). The score, it would seem, can only be a pale and exterior representation of truth. Thus, what begins as a pantomime in the prologue—making sense of a musical interpretation— ends with an interpretation so authentic that the ineffable seems to become intelligible. And it is only after the genius proves himself that he reveals his proper name: Gluck.

If the dialogue that takes place between the narrator and the other man becomes meaningful and clear only as the strange man's relationship to performance takes on significance, it does so only through the recapitulation in language by the narrator—who is an ideal listener since he seems to understand almost instantaneously the importance of everything that occurs.

What seems clear is that Hoffmann, in writing this text, is an interpreter interpreting a text about interpretation, and that his own story indeed reflects upon this process as both a tacit theory and a practice. That is, in rewriting Diderot's *Neveu de Rameau*, Hoffmann's tale fulfills an interpretative function as it rearticulates the terms of the narrative and seemingly totalizes the meaning left fragmentary in Diderot's text. One could presumably say, then, that the understanding of the first text (Diderot's) is reflected in the interpretation of the second, completing the hermeneutic model of reading in writing. Yet, although it seems that Hoffmann's text restores the genius to his proper place (and hence reinstates his name), and though the message appears to be that one gains access to truth through authentic interpretation by the individual genius, interpretation in the context of this tale can only be a false restoration, a false totalization, for the interpretation remains a metaphor—the recuperation of a presence through an absence—as it reflects the process of its own begetting. Music is, after all, not writing, and Hoffmann not Gluck. Once again the genius is a step removed. As a distillation of Diderot's text, Hoffmann's tale plays out the drama of its own origins in the rewriting of another text and poses the question of reading as well as that of writing in terms of a disruption of the hermeneutic model. In the end, we as readers cannot be sure whether the narrator and the other man are one and the same, whether the genius possesses some higher truth or floats in the realm of madness. Perhaps like another of Hoffmann's characters, Councillor Krespel, who desperately searches for life's secret by taking violins apart, the artist along with the critic is fated always to write interpretations that are themselves interpretations—that are themselves interpretations. Maybe, even, the artist and the critic cannot make the final distinction that Saint Augustine would allow when he says that "discussing words with words is as entangled as interlocking and rubbing the fingers with the fingers, in which case it may scarcely be distinguished, except by the one himself who does it, which fingers itch and which give aid to the itching."[23]

1. During his lifetime Diderot was primarily known as an encyclopedist and dramatist but not as a novelist; many of his most daring works—*Jacques le fataliste, Le Rêve de d'Alembert, Le Neveu de Rameau*—were only published after his death. He only really became known as a literary figure through Schiller, then through Goethe's translation of the *Neveu*, and, finally, through the Paulin edition of his works, which appeared between 1830 and 1831. The *Neveu de Rameau* appeared in French in the Brière edition of 1821–23, but it was only in the Paulin edition that such works as *Les Lettres à Sophie Volland, Le Voyage à Bourbonne et à Langres, La Correspondance avec Falconet*, and *Le Rêve de d'Alembert* appeared for the first time. For an extensive discussion of the history of Diderot's works in Germany, see Roland Mortier, *Diderot en Allemagne* (Paris: Presses Universitaires de France, 1954).

2. Jacques Proust, *Lectures de Diderot* (Paris: Armand Colin, "Collection U2," 1974), p. 227. In a recent study of the *Neveu de Rameau*, Yoichi Sumi expresses a similar need to break out of a strictly classical, dualistic discourse (*Le Neveu de Rameau: Caprices et logiques du jeu* [Tokyo: Editions France Tosho, 1975]).

3. See Leyla Perrone-Moisés, "L'Intertextualité critique," *Poétique* 27 (1976): 372–84.

4. Julia Kristeva chooses to define the term *intertextualité*, which she herself introduced, in terms of a transposition: "Le terme d'intertextualité désigne cette transposition d'un (ou de plusieurs) systèmes de signes en un autre, mais puisque ce terme a été souvent entendu dans le sens banal de 'critique des sources' d'un texte, nous lui préférons celui de transposition" (*La Révolution du langage poétique* [Paris: Seuil, 1974], p. 60).

5. "Immédiatement, la société est donnée avec le langage. La société à son tour ne tient ensemble que par l'usage commun de signes de communication" (Emile Benveniste, *Problèmes de linguistique générale*, 2 vols. [Paris: Gallimard, 1974], 2: 91).

6. For Mikhail Bakhtin the monologic reverts to reason and truth and includes the traditional notion of dialogue; the dialogic reverts to no fixed meaning or subject and is nontotalizable.

7. See Kristeva's discussion of Bakhtin, "Le Mot, le dialogue, le roman," *Sémeiotikè* (Paris: Seuil, 1969), pp. 143–74.

8. In *Eléments de littérature* Marmontel states: "Le difficile . . . c'est de démêler, de classer, de circonscrire nos idées, en leur donnant toute leur étendue, d'en saisir les justes rapports, de tirer ainsi du chaos les éléments de la science et d'y répandre la lumière. C'est à quoi le dialogue philosophique est utilement employé: parce qu'à mesure qu'il forme des nuages, il les dissipe; qu'à chaque pas il ne présente une nouvelle difficulté qu'afin de l'aplanir lui-même; et que l'ignorance,

l'habitude, l'opinion opposent à la vérité" (*Œuvres complètes,* ed. Belin, 1819, 4: 377, as cited in Maurice Roelens's introduction to *Le Neveu de Rameau* [Paris: Editions sociales, 1972], p. 22).

9. Denis Diderot, "Encyclopédie," *Œuvres complètes,* ed. Assésat (Paris: Garnier, 1876), 14: 415.

10. For a discussion of Hegel's reading see Jean Hyppolite, *Genèse et structure de la "Phénoménologie de l'esprit de Hegel"* (Paris: Aubier-Montaigne, 1946), pp. 353–64. In a more recent North American context, see Lionel Trilling's elegant discussion of Hegel and Diderot, "The Honest Soul and the Disintegrated Consciousness," in *Sincerity and Authenticity* (Cambridge: Harvard University Press, 1971), pp. 26–53.

11. See James Creech, "*Le Neveu de Rameau* and the Perversion of Difference," *Eighteenth-Century Studies* 2 (Summer 1978): 439–57.

12. Regarding the philosopher's understanding of things as separate from, or at one with, his instrument, interlocutor Diderot says in *L'Entretien entre D'Alembert et Diderot*: "L'instrument philosophe est sensible; il est en même temps le musicien et l'instrument" (*Œuvres philosophiques* [Paris: Garnier, 1961], p. 273).

13. Denis Diderot, *Le Neveu de Rameau,* ed. Jean Fabre (Geneva: Droz, 1963), pp. 27–28.

14. Ibid., p. 184.

15. Denis Diderot, *Œuvres esthétiques* (Paris: Garnier, 1965), p. 250.

16. Denis Diderot, *Paradoxe sur le comédien* (Paris: Garnier, 1965), p. 269.

17. Diderot, *Neveu,* p. 181.

18. That is where the genius outdoes himself as he undercuts his own power. In the article entitled "Génie" Diderot states: "L'imagination gaie d'un génie étendu agrandit le champ du ridicule, et tandis que le vulgaire le voit et le sent dans ce qui blesse l'ordre universel" (*Œuvres esthétiques,* p. 11).

19. For a comparison of the thematic similarities and differences between the *Neveu de Rameau* and *Ritter Gluck,* see Steven Paul Scher, *Verbal Music in German Literature* (New Haven: Yale University Press, 1968).

20. E. T. A. Hoffmann, *The Tales of E. T. A. Hoffman,* ed. and trans. Leonard J. Kent and Elisabeth C. Knight (Chicago: University of Chicago Press, 1969), pp. 3–13.

21. Ibid., p. 7.

22. Ibid., p. 12.

23. Saint Augustine, *Concerning the Teacher: Basic Writings of Saint Augustine* (New York: Random House, 1948), p. 372.

Mais plus gênants encore et plus difficilement défendables
que les alinéas, les tirets, les deux points et les guillemets,
sont les monotones et gauches: dit Jeanne, répondit Paul, qui
parsèment habituellement le dialogue.

Nathalie Sarraute, *L'Ere du soupçon*

Try to strike the golden mean between the constant repetition
of "he said" and . . . such substitutes as "he asserted,"
"he asked," "he replied." . . . The use of these labels is
often necessary, but they should not be used to the point
of calling attention to themselves.

Douglas Bement, *Weaving the Short Story*

Do not discriminate against such good expressions as "he
acquiesced, admitted, argued, asked, assented, boasted, called,
cautioned, chuckled, corrected, cried, croaked, crowed, declared,
drawled, droned, ejaculated, emended, enjoined, enumerated,
exclaimed, exploded, flashed, frowned, gasped, growled, grumbled,
grunted, hinted, inquired, insinuated, intimidated, jeered,
jested, laughed, leered, maundered, mumbled, nodded, opined,
pronounced, puffed, questioned, rejoined, retorted, returned,
simpered, snarled, sneered, snickered, stammered, stipulated,
stormed, suggested, urged, volunteered, wondered, yelled,"
and a whole dictionaryful besides, each precisely suited to
the shade of mood to be depicted.

J. Berg Esenwein, *Writing the Short Story*

On Attributive Discourse in *Madame Bovary*

GERALD J. PRINCE

The study of attributive discourse in narrative—the "he said," "she said," "he asked," "she replied" that explicitly indicate who is speaking[1] and can even tell us why, when, where, or how—has been relatively neglected. Apart from writers of how-to books, Tom Swift fans, and a few novelists like Nathalie Sarraute, students of narrative have, to my knowledge, rarely commented on these clauses or parts of clauses; and, in an age where studies of sign systems abound, no one has even begun to attempt a semiotics of attributive discourse. Yet, of all the signs that may be found in narrative, attributive ones are perhaps the easiest to isolate. Besides, they create countless problems for countless narrators (should I underline their function? should I use them sparingly? should I try to do without them?); they can help define a class of writings (the dime novel, for instance)[2] or a literary period (they are, after all, "a symbol of the *ancien régime*");[3] and they can partly characterize the style of a given author or work.[4] I should therefore like to sketch some of the paths that a study of attributive discourse might follow.

An attributive clause may or may not accompany a stretch of direct discourse:

    (1) "I am sick and tired of all this!"

    (2) He replied: "I am sick and tired of all this!"

When it does, it may precede that stretch of discourse, as in (2), or follow it, or be intercalated in it:

    (3) "I am sick and tired of all this!" he replied.

    (4) "I am," he replied, "sick and tired of all this!"

Furthermore, it may mention not only who is doing the speaking and what the latter represents (a reply, a retort, a remark, an exclamation, an objection) but also who is being addressed, for what reasons, in what circumstances, and so on:

    (5) "Abandoned friends are often old," he told her when he saw her again, visibly enchanted with his observation.

(6) John, who wanted to minimize the consequences, replied good-naturedly to Mary: "Ah, my dear, there is no harm!"

Finally, it may play one or more roles. Attributive discourse clearly functions as an aid to legibility by identifying various passages as spoken by a character, pointing out who the speaker is, and commenting on the nature of the acts of speaking performed. But it can also function as a characterization device (a character who always shouts differs from one who always whispers; a character who never asks differs from one who never answers); it can reinforce a theme (repeated indications of stammering and stuttering may, for example, call for a thematic organization around the deficiencies of oral communication); it can become a marker of point of view; it can underline ironic intentions; it can help establish a rhythm; it can (partially) describe a setting; and so forth. Studying the nature of attributive discourse in a given narrative (or set of narratives) would thus require answering such questions as: When, where, and how often does it occur? What distributional pattern(s) does it follow? What forms does it take? What information does it carry? What functions does it fulfill? More particularly, it would require examining, among other factors, the class of speakers signified by attributive discourse as well as the nature of the signifiers; the class of verbs and tenses occurring in it; the relationships among speakers, verbs, and tenses; the kind of information provided; the possible connections between attributive and direct discourse; and, obviously, the significance of these various factors within the system of the work.

Let us consider *Madame Bovary*.[5] Although the "first modern French novel" has been very much studied and very well indeed; although it is animated throughout by a reflection on language, as Naomi Schor, for one, has recently demonstrated in a brilliant essay;[6] and although its dialogue has given rise to an intelligent and patient commentary by Claudine Gothot-Mersch,[7] its attributive discourse seems to have escaped the attention of critics. Yet Flaubert himself not only expressed his dislike for writing dialogue ("Tu sais . . . la haine que j'ai du dialogue dans les romans," "Mais comment faire du dialogue trivial qui soit bien écrit?", "Que ma *Bovary* m'embête! . . . Je n'ai jamais de ma vie rien écrit de plus difficile que ce que je fais maintenant, du dialogue trivial! . . . J'en ai envie de pleurer par moments, tant je sens mon impuissance");[8] he also commented specifically on the difficulties occasioned by attributive discourse: "comme je trouve très canaille de faire du dialogue en remplaçant les 'il dit, il répondit' par des barres, tu juges que les répétitions des mêmes tournures ne sont pas commodes à éviter. Te voilà initiée au supplice que je subis depuis quinze jours."[9] Indeed, for a writer who—like *Reader's Digest* devotees!—was fascinated by word power and who spent years polishing his style and using incredible cunning for the composition of the simplest sentences, attributive discourse must have constituted an intolerable problem.[10]

I have counted 1,262 instances of direct discourse in *Madame Bovary*,[11] of which 879—around 70 percent—are accompanied by an attributive clause. Whatever distaste Flaubert may feel for the elision of such clauses, he is thus able to overcome it quite frequently. In fact, he overcomes it more and more as the novel deploys itself, dialogue grows in importance, and the characters' preoccupations become more readily identifiable: there is about 13 percent elision in the first part of the novel, 25 percent in the second part, and 28 percent in the third.[12] The seven characters who are usually considered to be the most important—Emma, Charles, Léon, Rodolphe, Homais, Bournisien, and Lheureux—account for 1,033 of the 1,262 direct discourses, of which 724 (around 70 percent again) are underlined by attributive clauses. It is the latter that I intend to concentrate on and begin to analyze.

As could be expected, Emma is the most frequent contributor of direct discourse and the subject most often designated by an attributive clause, followed—in both categories—by Homais, Charles, Rodolphe, Léon, Lheureux, and Bournisien.[13] But whereas the heroine, like her husband and her two lovers, is explicitly identified as speaker about 70 percent of the time, the pharmacist and the priest are identified about 75 percent of the time, and the merchant only 60 percent of the time. These discrepancies are perhaps not unexplainable. Attributive discourse institutes a distance between a character's utterance and the reader, since the narrator's mediation is more clearly in evidence; furthermore, it is less needed as an aid to legibility in cases of sustained dialogue. Homais and Bournisien are less frequently engaged in true dialogue than the other protagonists and are often shown to be mere talking puppets. On the other hand, Lheureux is mainly heard in the scenes where he crushes Emma, and his power over her is emphasized by the narrator's (relative) absence.

Although Emma is the one most often designated by attributive discourse, the range of designations is quite limited. There are over 35 signifiers of the heroine in the novel, but only 7 of them appear as subjects of attributive clauses. "Elle" is the overwhelming choice—198 instances out of 272—followed by "Emma." The other 5—"Mme Bovary," "la jeune femme," "la bru," "sa mère," and "celle-ci"—are used 10 times in all. The heroine never speaks directly as a bride, a wife, a mistress, or a neighbor and, in general, barely speaks as a social creature. Symptomatically, her utterances are almost always the product of a first name or a personal pronoun, whereas the title of the novel as well as her situation underline the importance of social forces. At the other extreme, Homais, Lheureux, and Bournisien are practically always designated in terms of their profession—"l'apothicaire," "le pharmacien," "le marchand," "le prêtre," "le curé," "l'ecclésiastique"—or by their last name, by such passepartout appellations as "le bonhomme," "l'un" and "l'autre," and by the pronoun "il."[14] They have no first names, and their direct discourse is a manifestation of social discourse. Homais's case is particularly clear because he is designated by "il" only 30 times out of 121: little that is personal is consistently attached to him—not even a pronoun.

But there are further questions to raise with regard to the subjects of attributive clauses. What dictates the choice of one signifier over another? Why does Flaubert sometimes write "Charles," sometimes "Bovary," and sometimes "le médecin"? Why does he use, at certain points, "Léon" as opposed to "le clerc" or "le jeune homme"? It is not merely in order to avoid a repetition, since there are many instances where none of the signifiers would entail one. Nor is it always a matter of rhythm or harmony: indeed, in certain cases, the signifier used is not necessarily the most euphonious. Rather, in *Madame Bovary* the subjects of attributive clauses often function as point-of-view indicators. The heroine and her husband meet Léon at the opera house, and the young man suggests going to a café: "'Ah! pas encore! restons!' dit Bovary. 'Elle a les cheveux dénoués: cela promet d'être tragique'" (p. 233). For whom is the husband "Bovary"? It is clearly not for his wife; nor is it (only) for the narrator. We are made to see in terms of Léon and perhaps of Charles himself. For the young man, the husband is "Bovary" and not "Charles," and the latter, in Léon's presence, views himself through a last name. Similarly, in a passage representing Emma and her daughter, Flaubert writes: "'Amenez-la-moi!' dit sa mère, se précipitant pour l'embrasser. 'Comme je t'aime, ma pauvre enfant! comme je t'aime!'" (p. 178). Playing at being a mother (and seen as one by Berthe), Emma sees herself as such. Attributive discourse in *Madame Bovary* is characteristically ambivalent: the narrator comments on the characters' verbal acts and is thus at a certain distance from them, but his remarks are partly shaped by the characters' consciousness.

Like the subjects of attributive clauses, the verbs contribute to characterization. All of the main actors say, answer, go on ("reprendre"), ejaculate ("faire"), retort ("répliquer"), and add; but "penser" and "songer" are never associated with Homais and Bournisien, though they accompany some of the utterances of the other five characters. Only the pharmacist thunders ("tonner"); Lheureux alone does not cry out ("s'écrier") or exclaim, and he does not sigh or whisper either; as for Emma and Charles, they are the only ones to stammer ("balbutier"), and she is unique in that she hesitates. Not unexpectedly, Homais's range is the widest: 22 different verbs appear in the clauses tagged on to his words. Charles is a surprising second with 21, and Emma only comes in third with 20. More significantly perhaps, in terms of number of verbs per number of attributive clauses, Emma proves to be the most limited by far, and she is followed by Homais:[15] the more one speaks, the more one's verbal limitations tend to manifest themselves.

Sometimes the verbs used underline a character's feelings in a particular situation. Charles tells Emma that a colleague humiliated him in public, and

Flaubert writes: "elle était exaspérée de honte, elle avait envie de le battre, elle alla dans le corridor ouvrir la fenêtre et huma l'air frais pour se calmer. 'Quel pauvre homme! quel pauvre homme!' disait-elle tout bas" (p. 63). The novelist chose "dire tout bas" over "se dire": Emma can no longer prevent herself from expressing her scorn.[16]

More generally, however, the verbs are not very revealing. Flaubert relies heavily on "dire": that most neutral of tags appears in 325 attributive clauses, that is, in well over a third of the total. Furthermore, he uses only 44 different main verbs,[17] which is not very many when we think of his passion for lexical diversity, when we consider that he does not always avoid repetition (e.g., pp. 95, 108, 123), and when we note that he never uses such items as "affirmer," "remarquer," "insister," "admettre," and "a whole dictionaryful besides." Finally, and repeatedly, Flaubert opts for the muted rather than the expressive. To report the last words of Charles's first wife, he merely writes: "elle dit: 'Ah! mon Dieu'" (p. 21); the three verbal exchanges that bind Emma to Charles, Léon, and Rodolphe, respectively, are accompanied by the same pair of banal clauses: "demanda-t-elle"/"répondit-il" (pp. 17, 84, 147); and when Emma gives birth, the description of her husband's verbal reaction is equally insipid: "'C'est une fille!' dit Charles" (p. 91). Language is inadequate: "la parole humaine est comme un chaudron fêlé où nous battons des mélodies à faire danser les ours quand on voudrait attendrir les étoiles" (p. 196); and the attributive clauses underline this inadequacy. The words uttered and the surface act constituted by their utterance are not important in themselves. Conversation is not meaningful; *sous-conversation* is.

Indeed, although Flaubert enjoyed a well-developed auditory imagination,[18] although references to sound are quite numerous in *Madame Bovary*, and although 362 of the attributive clauses (about 41 percent) contain more than a subject and verb—a prepositional phrase, say, or an adverbial one—fewer than 30 of them explicitly mention the characters' voices. Like the words uttered, voice recedes into the background.

Flaubert's bias becomes even clearer when we examine the tenses in attributive discourse: as many as 175 of the (main) verbs—about 20 percent—are in the imperfect and not, as would be expected, in the simple past. The imperfect is perhaps used to emphasized the length of certain utterances—one of Homais's orations, for example—or to point out that the words uttered are characteristic,[19] or to satisfy an inordinate taste for rhythmical prose. Yet, because it is a marker of process and repetition, its frequent occurrence has other consequences. When the imperfect is used duratively, part of the event reported has already happened and part of it is still to come: what a character says is presumably not given in its entirety; and when the imperfect is used iteratively, a similar conclusion can be reached. Flaubert's reliance on the imperfect thus indicates the relative lack of importance and the dispensability of what is actually said. More generally and more significantly, I think, it undermines the difference between showing and telling, dramatic and descriptive, recording of the oral and inscription of the nonoral: what we are given is often not a true scene; what we are made to witness is not the action as it occurred; what we are made to hear is not the utterance itself.

In the final analysis, and rather than the capacity to function on many levels or the art with which it punctuates the characters' speech acts, what makes attributive discourse in *Madame Bovary* most interesting is this (partial) rejection of the oral. Like free indirect discourse, ironic distancing, and constant point-of-view modulation, attributive discourse leads to the appearance of an uncertain space.

1. I will not consider as part of attributive discourse clauses or sentences that *implicitly* introduce a character's utterance, as in the following: "He smiled. 'How are you?' She put the cup on the table. 'I am fine!'" On the other hand, though I will use "speaker" or "utterance" for the sake of convenience, I shall consider such clauses as "he thought" in a sentence like: "'She is very nice,' he thought."

2. See Marc Angenot, *Le Roman populaire: Recherches en paralittérature* (Montreal: Presses de l'Université du Québec, 1975), p. 120.

3. Nathalie Sarraute, *L'Ere du soupçon* (Paris: Gallimard, 1959), p. 108.

4. For instance, to describe how a character says what he says, Arnold Bennett uses such adverbs as affectionately, angrily, blandly, briefly, calmly, carelessly, coldly, contemptuously, crossly, curtly, doubtfully, eagerly, earnestly, emphatically, enthusiastically, faintly, fiercely, foolishly, formally, gravely, grimly, gruffly, hopefully, imperturbably, jauntily, kindly, laconically, lamely, loudly, maternally, menacingly, mildly, naïvely, obsequiously, pleasantly, positively, proudly, quietly, savagely, scornfully, self-consciously, sharply, sincerely, sleepily, slowly, softly, solemnly, stiffly, timidly, wearily, wildly, and willingly.

5. Gustave Flaubert, *Madame Bovary* (Paris: Garnier, 1971). All references will be to this edition.

6. Naomi Schor, "Pour une thématique restreinte: Ecriture, parole et différence dans *Madame Bovary*," *Littérature* 22 (May 1976): 30–46.

7. Claudine Gothot-Mersch, "Le Dialogue dans l'œuvre de Flaubert," *Europe* 485–87 (September–November 1969): 112–21.

8. Gustave Flaubert, *Correspondance*, 9 vols. (Paris: Conard, 1926–33), 5: 294; 3: 20, 24. All references will be to this edition.

9. Ibid., 3: 167.

10. "La phrase la plus simple comme 'il ferma la porte', 'il sortit', etc., exige des ruses d'art incroyables!" (ibid., 4: 36).

11. Dialogue is not as sparse as has sometimes been claimed. Indeed, it becomes a dominant form in the third part of the novel.

12. There are 6 elisions per 46 utterances in the first part, 165 per 655 in the second, and 212 per 561 in the third.

13. Note that Emma is also the most frequent addressee of direct discourse. She speaks less often than she is spoken to and so does Léon. On the other hand, both Homais and Lheureux speak much more often than they are spoken to. Charles, Rodolphe, and Bournisien are addressers about as frequently as they are addressees. See Appendix.

14. Homais is designated once as "son mari" (p. 172).

15. See Appendix.

16. See Léon Bopp, *Commentaire sur Madame Bovary* (Neuchâtel: A la Baconnière, 1951), p. 109.

17. See Appendix.

18. See Antoine Naaman, *Les Débuts de Gustave Flaubert et sa technique de la description* (Paris: Nizet, 1962), p. 378.

19. "Je trouve qu'il [the dialogue] doit être caractéristique" (*Correspondance,* 5: 294).

APPENDIX

Characters	Utterances	Appearances in Attributive Clauses	Addressees of Direct Discourse	Attributive Discourse Verbs	Attributive Clauses per Verb
Emma	384	272	437	20	13.6
Homais	165	121	77	22	5.5
Charles	146	106	146	21	5
Rodolphe	126	87	118	17	5.1
Léon	98	66	142	18	3.6
Lheureux	74	42	36	11	3.8
Bournisien	40	30	40	15	2

Main Verbs in Attributive Sentences

ajouter
appeler
balbutier
bourdonner (?)
chanter (?)
chuchoter
commencer
concéder
continuer
crier
déclamer
demander
dire
s'écrier
exclamer
s'exclamer
faire
faire des exclamations
grommeler
hasarder
hésiter
interrompre

juger
laisser tomber (des mots)
lire (à haute voix) (?)
ne pas manquer une plaisanterie
marmotter
murmurer
objecter
observer
penser
poursuivre
prendre la défense de
prononcer
recommencer
répéter
répliquer
répondre
reprendre
ne pas retenir une phrase
songer
souffler
soupirer
tonner

Ubu and the Signs of the Theater

MICHAEL ISSACHAROFF

If, in an attempt to formulate the bases of a semiology of the theater, recourse can be had to the Saussurian dichotomy of signifier/signified, it is nevertheless inappropriate to assume that the theatrical sign can necessarily be made to conform to this binary system. For the Saussurian construct, if applied to the theater, fails to take account of a third element that is fundamental to the nature of the stage—the referent—in other words, the extralinguistic reality that may be visible during a performance.

Research in the semiotics of the theater is still in its infancy. Some critics, among the few who have attempted to formulate an approach, have tried to come to grips with the problem of the specificity of drama through a linear analysis of the individual sign systems that compose a dramatic performance: speech, voice, facial expression, gesture, movement, makeup, hairstyle, costume, properties, décor, lighting, sound effects, music.[1] The advantage of a classification like the latter is that it represents an endeavor to systematize analysis of the units of a theatrical performance. Its drawback, though, is equally plain: it results in a *static* analysis that in no way reflects the *dynamic* specificity of the theatrical sign, the ways in which the various sign systems work in a concrete situation and their interaction. To disregard the simultaneity of, and the interplay between, the verbal and visual codes operating in unison during a performance is tantamount to overlooking the mainspring of the theatrical medium.

That there are, in a stage production, diverse visual and auditory sign systems in simultaneous operation is self-evident, at least to the semiologist. But it is no less evident that these sign systems do not, and indeed could not, function autonomously, like a kind of semiotic Tower of Babel, unless the aim of the dramatist is to convey or represent anarchy, disorder, madness, or absurdity. There has to be some general system of focus, at any given point, to channel perception, or else the spectator's attention would be inclined to wander. Clearly, the producer's constant purpose must be to get across to his audience. If he does not succeed in this respect, the audience will be liable to get bored, drop off to sleep, or walk out. In all art forms the artist focuses our attention in some way or other. In painting this is achieved through techniques of perspective, color, light, proportion; in photography and in film, through the use of close-ups and differential focusing; in fiction, through point of view. In the theater the same effect is brought about by varying the balance between the different sign systems as well as through the amplifying or temporary muting of a particular sign system. Thus, for example, during a lyrical passage (purple or otherwise), distracting movements or changes of lighting are likely to be avoided by the producer, to enable the audience to concentrate on the auditory rather than on the visual.[2] It is clear that an element in a production such as movement on stage can never be spontaneous or arbitrary—an actor can never be permitted to move according to whim. All movement on stage is necessarily organized and rigorously rehearsed. When an actor moves, the area of the stage to which he moves must be lit. Thus lighting and movement are very closely linked. Similar interdependence is manifest in other elements of stage production. Consequently, if there is a hierarchy of codes as they are perceived by the playgoer, a similar hierarchy is to be found on the other side of the proscenium (if there is one).

The system of focus that is apparent in the case of the codes of the theater can be compared to a similar system that is to be observed in a totally different domain—that of the advertising poster. Roland Barthes has shown, in a very stimulating essay on this subject, how the essentially ambiguous element—the picture—is anchored ("ancré") by the verbal caption.[3] It would not do, of course, in a utilitarian sphere such as advertising, for there to be too great a degree of ambiguity, a feature that belongs more appropriately to the realm of aesthetics and nonutilitarian communication. The visual is probably intrinsically far more polysemous than the verbal, hence the necessity of the unambiguous focus provided by the verbal caption. In the theater, then, a system of focus is indispensable, given the simultaneous presence of the numerous sign systems that are in operation.

It follows, therefore, that sign systems in the theater are placed in a hierarchy and are subject to some mode of focus. The latter can take various forms. The most apparent is a series of signals in the text itself. The text, though, may not provide this information in an explicit way, and even where such a system is provided, the producer is always at liberty to modify, complement, undermine, or even supplant it totally, should he so wish. Within the text itself, however, signals can appear in the following ways: (1) *verbal* codes—nonauditory (stage directions) and auditory (spoken text); and (2) *visual* codes, such as costume, décor, properties, and so forth (can refer to any other code, verbal or visual). The most explicit systems are the two verbal codes that may contain reference to any other codes, including themselves. Thus, for example, the stage directions or even the dialogue may refer to décor, costume, or properties.[4] But a visual code may also act as a system of focus or may itself be predominant.

There are many examples of this in contemporary French theater that immediately come to mind—space in Sartre's *Huis clos*; movement in Ionesco's *Les Chaises*; properties in Beckett's *Oh les beaux jours,* and so on.[5]

Having noted the existence of a hierarchy and a system of focus that govern the various sign systems, I should now like to explore further the nature of the theatrical sign. I referred earlier to the Saussurian dichotomy, signans/signatum. This binary system does not at all fit the case of the theater, since in a given performance three elements can be simultaneously present, namely, a signifier (e.g., "chair"),[6] the signified (the concept or idea of chair), and the referent (the object itself, which in the case of my example would be the specific furniture item). This tripartite system has the advantage of avoiding the confusion in Saussure between concept and object.[7] The theater is one of the very few (if not the only) art forms in which one finds simultaneously present, in time and in space, these three elements. Clearly, the distinction between signified and referent is of the utmost importance in the theater, where things or persons referred to verbally can be visible on stage.

It follows that the referent can take one of at least three possible forms. It can be visible onstage (in the case of characters, costumes, décor, or properties); it can exist solely offstage (i.e., verbally); it can also be synecdochical, in the case, for example, where an item of the set is used to represent elements of the décor that are not made visible on stage. In producing Ionesco's *Jacques,* I have used a doorframe (with a door) and a windowframe to suggest the whole of an interior. This is what is normally referred to as nonmimetic or stylized stage production. The same mode of visual synecdoche is to be observed in stage costume in which a single item of clothing can be used to evoke the whole—a bowler hat to suggest British dress, a beret to suggest French dress, and so on. It might be noted in passing that Jarry's own idea of stage décor and of what should be visible was close to this concept of visual synecdoche. In an article published at the time of the first production of *Ubu roi,* he wrote: "toute partie du décor dont on aura un besoin spécial, fenêtre qu'on ouvre, porte qu'on enfonce, est un accessoire et peut être apportée comme une table ou un flambeau."[8]

Furthermore, it is important to remember that any theatrical sign can represent another sign. It is in the nature of the theatrical sign to be infinitely versatile and unpredictable, often nonconventional. Hence, for example, a sound effect can depict space or décor. This is especially the case in radio plays where, for instance, the sidewalk can be represented by the sound of footsteps, an office by the sound of typewriters, and so on.[9] It can also occur that in the same play a given sign has multiple functions. Hence, in the impressive *création collective* directed by Jacques Nichet at the Cartoucherie de Vincennes in Paris in the spring of 1977 entitled *La Jeune Lune,* the same object (i.e., referent)—a chair—changed its function many times, becoming alternately the iron bars of a railing in front of a factory, a human character, a wall, and only occasionally resuming its normal existence as a chair.

We have just touched on the specific nature of the theatrical sign: it is essentially arbitrary (unmotivated), and the tripartite relationship of signifier/ signified/referent is in no way contingent on some preestablished convention. The dramatist is a creator of signs; he may set up a network of semiotic relations that has been hitherto nonexistent. The theatrical sign is not necessarily fixed or constant at the beginning of a performance; it can have a varying function during a given play. Therein lies its specifically theatrical nature and its characteristically dynamic essence.

To illustrate these theoretical concepts, I have chosen for close analysis a play in which semiotic experimentation is especially significant—Jarry's subversive text *Ubu roi*. This play is of particular interest for our purposes, since the dramatist systematically subverts the normal triad, signifier/signified/referent. The hierarchy of codes in this play is immediately apparent: the visual is subordinate to the verbal. The action supposedly takes play in Poland, that is, Nowhere, according to the author's whimsical comments;[10] and consequently the stage setting itself is straightaway relegated to a status of secondary importance. Furthermore, Jarry rejected realistic (mimetic) décor, which he considered aesthetically absurd: "L'écriteau apporté selon les changements de lieu évite le rappel périodique au non-esprit par le changement des décors matériels, que l'on perçoit surtout à l'instant de leur différence" (p. 407). In accordance with this conception, therefore, a verbal (written) sign replaces the visual code (the décor). The attenuating or omission of the visual thus automatically enhances the verbal. It will become clear that the emphasis in *Ubu roi* on distorted signifiers and the peculiar status accorded to the referent will together produce a fundamental transformation of the nature of the action expressed in such a verbal code.

Let us first consider the use of the signifiers in the play. The text begins with a most famous term whose signifier is distorted through the addition of a supplementary consonant—I refer, of course, to the ubiquitous word unleased by Ubu, "MERDRE!" The latter, probably one of the best-known cues in the whole of French theater, has been the subject of a great deal of commentary and glosses, ranging from those who have emphasized the slang component of the ending, the playful tampering with lexis, or even Jarry's alleged concern for propriety.[11] However, it seems evident that a distorted signifier has the effect of drawing more attention to a word whose resulting phonetic and semantic importance is, in some way at least, enhanced. Lexical distortion is, of course, a device frequently used, for the same purpose, in advertising. Hence, in the present instance, the particular signifier, enlarged through the addition of a phoneme and consequently containing an extra syllable, extends beyond the span of its usual signified concept and acquires links with the semantic field of "phynance." In this respect, the lexical variants "sabre à merdre," "sabre à phynance" become especially significant. Is the added [r] also, perhaps, the antisign of His *R*oyal Highness, Ubu *r*oi?

At any rate, if one proceeds to chart the occurrences in the text of "Merdre"—thirty-three in all—it becomes possible to establish a threefold link: "Merdre"/"Phynance"/"Physique," in other words, feces/finance/penis. Furthermore, it rapidly becomes apparent from such a list that "Merdre," antisign extraordinary, is the hub of the central semiotic system of the play. I shall return to this later.

Passing on now to a more complex aspect of the signifier, one finds that the text contains a large number of neologisms. Apart from a few terms relating to parts of the body, such as "gidouille" and "oneille," the neologisms are virtually restricted to the idiolect of the protagonist and are liable to be used in reference to some form of concrete action. Thus "MERDRE" is the signal that triggers the assassination of King Venceslas; similarly, it is with a neologism, the "crochet à nobles," that Ubu massacres the nobles. Accordingly, an implicit link is established between neology and violent action, the former in a sense subverting the status of the latter. This hypothesis is confirmed in the protagonist's idiolect, in the case where a neological term is explicitly associated with the semantic context of "violent death," "tuder" in this instance replacing the normal "tuer": "Décervelez, *tudez,* coupez les oneilles, arrachez la finance et buvez jusqu'à la mort, c'est la vie des Salopins, c'est le bonheur du Maître des Finances." (p. 389). Particularly significant in this respect is a complete list of all the terms in the protagonist's idiolect that refer to weapons: "crochet à nobles," "couteau à nobles," "ciseau à oneilles," "ciseau à merdre," "croc à finances," "croc à merdre," "sabre à merdre," "pistolet à phynances," "bâton à physique." These lexemes have two things in common: they are all neologisms, and they all follow an identical pattern—two substantives connected with the preposition *à*. These terms are also referents, that is, properties explicitly referred to in the verbal code (the spoken text) and visible on stage. That the series constitutes a semiotic system becomes clear when one realizes that the neologisms are contrasted with words in the same semantic category used by characters other than the protagonist. The other characters use the following terms: "épée" (Bougrelas's), "épée" (given to Bougrelas by his Ancestor), "épée," (Bordure's), "fusil," "pierre," "revolver," "couteau." The contrast between the two series becomes even more apparent in a speech by Ubu to his soldiers: "J'ai à vous recommander de mettre dans les fusils autant de balles qu'ils en pourront tenir. . . . Quant à nous, nous nous tiendrons dans le moulin à vent et tirerons avec le pistolet à phynances par la fenêtre, en travers de la porte nous placerons le bâton à physique, et si quelqu'un essaie d'entrer, gare au croc à merdre!" (pp. 381–82). The protagonist thus distinguishes explicitly between the weapons he intends to use himself and those to be used by his men.

This contrastive lexical system merits further consideration. First, it is obvious that each of the neologisms is a combination of a sign and an antisign. In other words, the second unit in a compound noun of the type *sabre à merdre* undermines semantically the whole of the neological expression. In regular usage in French, in the case of compound lexemes such as *verre à vin*, the second noun normally modifies the first, specifying its sense and function. Hence, *verre à vin* means the kind of glass used for wine, and the second noun follows the pattern that can be observed in such compound expressions as: *brosse à chaussures, brosse à dents, brosse à cheveux*; *boîte à bijoux, boîte aux lettres, boîte aux gants*; and so on. That is normal usage. In the idiolect of the protagonist of *Ubu,* on the other hand, neological compound substantives are used to subvert the normal transmission of sense and reference. The extra noun added by Ubu undermines meaning in the same way as the extra [r] in "MERDRE" lends that term a totally novel semantic dimension. In more complex cases, the compound lexical item has a variant. Hence, the following pairs: "ciseau à oneilles"/"ciseau à merdre"; "croc à finances"/"croc à merdre." Lexical items such as these thus become signs of signs, reflecting one another ad infinitum, since in each case of this type, the second unit contains a reference to another sign, which, in turn, contains a signified concept, a referent, and a connotation peculiar to the play. If one takes the analysis a step further, one finds that Jarry's text embodies a system of focus, a system of lexical hierarchy, insofar as several lexemes refer to a network governed by two key lexemes: *finance* and *merdre*. One could possibly interpret the implicit linkage of the two terms like Michel Arrivé and postulate a new connotation of *finance* produced by the juxtaposition "une substance liquide analogue à la merdre."[12] Though that explanation makes some sense in the context, it is nevertheless important to remember that *finance* as used by Jarry embraces signified meanings that are normally distinct and incompatible. Thus the result of all this is a situation in which the regular signified and its referent are subverted and overshadowed by a connoted signified. In *Ubu roi,* accordingly, denotation yields to the realm of connotation and, in many instances, to peculiar connotations. Thus the sign often becomes the sign of another sign instead of a triad in accordance with the pattern of normal communication.

The process that is apparent in the case of lexis can also be observed in the action of Jarry's play. It, too, is subverted insofar as it is contingent on a referential universe that is both irregular and unpredictable. In this strange universe it is the signifier that is the kingpin of the linguistic system. It is the signifier *MERDRE* that is the first word of the text; it is the same signifier that triggers the first concrete action of the play, the assassination of the king. Neological signifiers govern the realm of violence of the protagonist who is himself named with a comic reiteration of an identical vowel (y): *Ubu.*[13] In many instances the signified (not to mention the referent) is subordinate if not altogether eliminated, as in this example of the protagonist's invective: "Tiens!

Polognard, soûlard, bâtard, hussard, tartare, calard, cafard, mouchard, savoyard, communard!" (p. 395).

In the lexical hall of mirrors that is *Ubu,* one consequently finds a dualist network consisting of the predominant pair, *merdre/finance,* the one being the variant of the other. If *merdre* in Jarry's text seems to be semiotically or semantically ubiquitous, it is also the principal source of violence in the play. For if philology leads to crime, as Ionesco had it, Jarry's *merdre* leads to massacre, since it can cause death, or as Ubu would put it, it can *tuder. Merdre* is the signal that cues the assassination of the king; it is also the substance ferried by the unmentionable brush. The reader will remember that in the banquet scene, Ubu brings the brush on stage, with the following result:

> [Père Ubu tient un balai innommable à la main et le lance sur le festin.]
> Mère Ubu: Misérable, que fais-tu?
> Père Ubu: Goûtez un peu. [Plusieurs goûtent et tombent empoisonnés.]
> [Pp. 356–57]

The brush, of course, is the sceptre of the Maître des Finances, the sceptre of King Turd, the sign (or even, in a sense, the referent) of his royal status. If the brush is the referential emblem of King Ubu, his *chandelle verte* is no doubt its variant signifier. Moreover, the trapdoor through which Ubu dispatches the nobles might be intended to connote a convenience, since he flushes them away in his capacity as Maître des Finances.

In Ionesco's *Jacques ou la soumission,* all is *chat,* in other words, the communication process reaches total collapse. Reality for Jacques and Roberte becomes utterly shapeless, since every object, every character has lost its individuality and thus its identity. In Jarry's *Ubu roi,* in a similar way, "MERDRE" constitutes the sign of the assassination and the assassination of the sign.

---

1. See, for example, Tadeusz Kowzan, "Le Signe au théâtre: Introduction à la sémiologie de l'art du spectacle," *Diogène* 61 (January–March 1968): 59–90. This article was reprinted in idem, *Littérature et spectacle* (Paris and The Hague: Mouton, 1975), pp. 160–221. A more promising approach, however, has been that of Anne Ubersfeld in her recent volume *Lire le théâtre* (Paris: Editions Sociales, 1977). See also Patrice Pavis, *Problèmes de sémiologie théâtrale* (Quebec: Presses de l'Université du Québec, 1976).

2. Giraudoux, among others, was well aware of the difficulty of multichannel perception for theatrical audiences and felt that it was perhaps too much to expect. Hence his comments to that effect, in "Le Metteur en scène," *Littérature* (Paris: Gallimard-Idées, 1967), pp. 220–21: "[The Frenchman] vient à la comédie pour écouter, et s'y fatigue si on l'oblige à voir. En fait, il croit à la parole et il ne croit pas au décor. Ou plutôt, il croit que les grands débats du cœur ne se règlent pas à coups de lumière et d'ombre, d'effondrements et de catastrophes, mais par la conversation. Le vrai coup de théâtre n'est pas pour lui la clameur de deux cents figurants, mais la nuance ironique, le subjonctif imparfait ou la litote qu'assume une phrase du héros ou de l'héroïne. Le combat, assassinat ou viol, que prétend représenter le théâtre russe sur la scène, est remplacé chez nous par une plaidoirie, dont les spectateurs ne sont pas les témoins passifs, mais les jurés. Pour le Français,

l'âme peut s'ouvrir de la façon la plus logique, comme un coffre-fort, par un mot: par le mot, et il réprouve la méthode du chalumeau et de l'effraction. . . . La compréhension du théâtre comme d'un gala humain, et non démoniaque, ne permet donc pas que l'attention passionnée portée par lui au texte soit troublée par des interventions trop distrayantes de la régie."

3. See Roland Barthes, "Rhétorique de l'image," *Communications* 4 (1964): 40–51. On the problem of the interaction between the verbal and the visual, see also Michel Butor, *Les Mots dans la peinture* (Geneva: Skira, 1969); and Roman Jakobson, "De la relation entre signes visuels et auditifs," in *Essais de linguistique générale* (Paris: Minuit, 1973), 2:104–12.

4. Cf. M. Issacharoff, "L'Espace et le regard dans *Huis clos*," *Magazine littéraire* 103–4 (September 1975): 22–27; and idem, "Sartre et les signes: La dynamique spatiale de *Huis clos*," *Travaux de linguistique et de littérature* 15 (1977): 293–303.

5. I have given fuller treatment to this problem in my forthcoming volume on the semiotics of drama, *Théâtre et signification*.

6. Even the signifier, in a theatrical performance, differs in fact from Saussure's concept of the "signifiant," which is defined as an "image acoustique." See F. de Saussure, *Cours de linguistique générale* (Paris: Payot, 1962), pp. 98–99.

7. See Emile Benveniste, *Problèmes de linguistique générale* (Paris: Gallimard, 1966), 1: 49–55 ("Nature du signe linguistique").

8. "De l'inutilité du théâtre au théâtre," in Alfred Jarry, *Œuvres complètes* (Paris: Gallimard, Bibliothèque de la Pléiade, 1972), 1:407 (all subsequent pages references to Jarry's works are to volume 1 of this edition). In a letter to Lugné-Poe dated 8 January 1896, Jarry gives further indications as to how he wished *Ubu* to be staged, and another of his comments corresponds to a synecdochical conception of stage presentation: "Suppression des foules, lesquelles sont souvent mauvaises à la scène et gênent l'intelligence. Ainsi,un seul soldat dans la scène de la revue, un seul dans la bousculade où Ubu dit: 'Quel tas de gens, quelle fuite, etc.'" (p. 1043).

9. In this connection see Juri Honzl's suggestive comments in his article "The Dynamics of the Sign in the Theatre," reprinted in L. Matejka and I. Titunik, *Semiotics of Art* (Cambridge: MIT Press, 1976), pp. 74–93. Here is an example from Beckett's radio play *All That Fall* ([London: Faber & Faber, 1965], p. 7): "(Stage directions): Rural sounds. Sheep, bird, cow, cock, severally, then together. Silence. Mrs Rooney advances along country road toward railway-station. Sound of her dragging feet. . . . Sound of approaching cartwheels." I have attempted to explore this problem in my study "Space and Reference in Drama," *Poetics Today* 2 (1980).

10. "Quant à l'action qui va commencer, elle se passe en Pologne, c'est-à-dire Nulle Part" (p. 401). See also the editor's comments in this edition, p. 1166.

11. See, for example, A. Carey Taylor, "Le Vocabulaire d'Alfred Jarry," *Cahiers de l'Association Internationale des Etudes Françaises* 10 (1959): 307–22; Michel Arrivé, *Les Langages de Jarry* (Paris: Klincksieck, 1972); and Arrivé's comments in his edition of Jarry's *Œuvres complètes*, p. 1155.

12. Arrivé, *Les Langages de Jarry*, p. 252.

13. On the phonetic and phonological implications of the protagonist's name, see John M. Lipski, "Jarry's Ubu: A Study in Multiple Association," *Zeitschrift für französische Sprache und Literatur* 85, no. 1 (1975): 39–51.

Notes on the Contributors

RALPH ALBANESE, JR., University of Nebraska, has specialized in sociocriticism, particularly of the theater of Molière. He has written a book on Molière, and his *Invitation aux problèmes socio-culturels de la France au XVIIème siècle* appeared in 1977. He is currently working on a full-length study on criminality in seventeenth-century France.

ROSS CHAMBERS, University of Michigan, has written books on Nerval, the poetics of the theater, *le mythe de l'actrice,* and Gautier. He has published widely on nineteenth- and twentieth-century French literature and is now working on studies of theory of interpretation and Baudelaire's "Tableaux parisiens."

DIANA FESTA-McCORMICK, Brooklyn College, is author of *Balzac, Les Nouvelles de Balzac,* and *The City as Catalyst: A Study of Ten Novels.* She has written widely on nineteenth- and twentieth-century French literature.

URSULA FRANKLIN, Grand Valley State Colleges, is author of *An Anatomy of Poesis: The Prose Poems of Stéphane Mallarmé* and *The Rhetoric of Valéry's Prose Aubades.* She has written articles on nineteenth-century French poetry and prose poetry and is now doing research on the Angel and Orpheus in Valéry and Rilke.

MICHAEL ISSACHAROFF, University of Western Ontario, has written books on Huysmans, *L'Espace et la nouvelle,* Flaubert, and, most recently, the semiotics of drama. His critical interests include the semiology of the theater and literary theory.

BETTINA L. KNAPP, Hunter College and the Graduate Center, CUNY, has published books on Genet, Artaud, Racine, Duhamel, Céline, and Maeterlinck. She has recently completed a book on the Prometheus syndrome.

VIRGINIA A. LA CHARITE, University of Kentucky, is the author of *The Poetics and the Poetry of René Char, Henri Michaux,* and articles on nineteenth- and twentieth-century French poetry. Her major research area is French experimental poetry from the mid nineteenth century to the present.

PAULA GILBERT LEWIS, Howard University, is currently preparing a full-length study on the French-Canadian novelist Gabrielle Roy. Her *The Aesthetics of Stéphane Mallarmé in Relation to His Public* appeared in 1976.

CATHERINE LOWE has written on Flaubert and is currently working on Nervalian discourse and irony.

CHRISTIE V. McDONALD, Université de Montréal, has written on Rousseau and Diderot and is the author of *The Extravagant Shepherd: A Study of the Pastoral Vision in Rousseau's "Nouvelle Héloïse."* Her work in progress includes a book on the problem of dialogue and utopia in Rousseau and Diderot.

ANDREW J. McKENNA, Loyola University of Chicago, has specialized in twentieth-century critical theory and written articles on Flaubert and "poetic deconstruction." He is presently writing on Baudelaire, religion, and madness.

WILL L. McLENDON, University of Houston, has published a book on Courchamps, as well as articles on writers such as Giraudoux, Proust, and Mallarmé. He is currently studying the works of Jean Lorrain and Jean Potocki.

GODELIEVE MERCKEN-SPAAS, Rutgers College, is the author of *Alienation in Constant's "Adolphe": An Exercise in Structural Thematics* and articles on Rousseau and Constant. She is now working on a full-length study of Sade and a monograph on the Swiss filmmaker Alain Tanner.

NANCY K. MILLER, Columbia University, has published articles on women in eighteenth-century fiction and narrative structure. Her current research is on the "feminine text."

ROBERT L. MITCHELL, Ohio State University, is the author of books on Charles Cros and Tristan Corbière. He has recently completed a volume of annotated translations of Corbière, Mallarmé, and Valéry and is managing editor of the *French Review*.

MARTHA N. MOSS has published several articles on Balzac and is presently writing on Don Juan and romanticism.

SUZANNE NASH, Princeton University, is the author of *"Les Contemplations" of Victor Hugo: An Allegory of the Creative Process.* She has written on Rutebeuf and Balzac and has just completed a book on Paul Valéry.

PETER W. NESSELROTH, University of Toronto, is author of *Lautréamont's Imagery: A Stylistic Approach* and articles on Lautréamont, Baudelaire, and Jacob. His major critical interests include stylistics, literary theory, and modern French poetry.

ENID RHODES PESCHEL is a poet, translator of French poetry, and author of *Flux and Reflux: Ambivalence in the Poems of Arthur Rimbaud.* She is currently preparing a volume of essays about, and translations of, symbolist poetry and a book on the American surgeon-poet-writer Richard Selzer.

LAURENCE M. PORTER, Michigan State University, has specialized in literature and psychology as well as French romanticism. The author of books on the lyric and dream literature of French romanticism and of numerous articles on subjects ranging from La Fontaine to Gide, he is preparing a book on the devil in modern literature.

GERALD J. PRINCE, University of Pennsylvania, is author of *Métaphysique et technique dans l' œuvre romanesque de Sartre* and *A Grammar of Stories: An Introduction*. He has written extensively on semiotics and narratology in modern fiction and is currently doing research on the text as reader.

ALBERT SONNENFELD, Princeton University, is the author of *L'Œuvre poétique de Tristan Corbière* and has contributed chapters to nine books, including *The Shapeless God* and *French Poetry from Dada to Tel Quel*. He has written mumerous articles on German, French, and English literature.

PAULINE WAHL, University of Calgary, has written on Stendhal and is studying the relationship between education and fiction.

NATHANIEL WING, Miami University, has published articles on Baudelaire and Rimbaud and is presently preparing a book on the problematics of the subject in Baudelaire, Rimbaud, and Mallarmé. His *Present Appearances: Aspects of Poetic Structure in Rimbaud's "Illuminations"* appeared in 1974.

Index